PACIFIC ECONOMIC RELAT
COOPERATION OR C

G000149509

For Glenn:

Here is to
missionary work
in the UK!!

Richard

PACIFIC ECONOMIC RELATIONS IN THE 1990s: COOPERATION OR CONFLICT?

**edited by
Richard Higgott, Richard Leaver,
and John Ravenhill**

ALLEN & UNWIN

© Australian Fulbright Commission, 1993

This book is copyright under the Berne Covention.
No reproduction without permission.

First published in 1993
Allen & Unwin Pty Ltd
9 Atchison Street, St Leonards, NSW 2065 Australia

National Library of Australia
Cataloguing-in-Publication entry:

Pacific economic relations in the 1990s.

Bibliography
ISBN 186373 385 X

1. Pacific Area—Economic conditions. 2. Pacific Area—Commerce.
I. Higgott, Richard A. II. Leaver, Richard.
II. Ravenhill, John.

330.91823

Printed by Kin Keong Printing, Singapore

Contents

List of Tables and Figures

Tables

Figures

Abbreviations

ACEPT	Agreement on Common Effective Preferential Tariffs
AFTA	ASEAN Free-Trade Area
ANZCERTA	Australia-New Zealand Closer Economic Relations Trade Agreement
APEC	Asia Pacific Economic Co-operation
ASA	Association of Southeast Asia
ASEAN	Association of Southeast Asian Nations
BIC	PT Batamindo Investment Corporation
BIS	Bank for International Settlements
CAP	[European Community] Common Agriculture Policy
CBO	Congressional Budget Office
CER	Australia-New Zealand Closer Economic Relations Agreement
DAC	[OECD] Development Assistance Committee
DBS	Development Bank of Singapore
DOC	[United States] Department of Commerce
EAEC	East Asian Economic Caucus
EAEG	East Asian Economic Group
EC	European Community
EDB	[Singapore] Economic Development Board
EEC	European Economic Community
EFTA	European Free Trade Agreement
EMS	European Monetary System
EMU	[European Community] Economic and Monetary Union
EOI	export-oriented industrialisation
EPZ	export processing zones
ESCAP	United Nations Economic and Social Commission for Asia and the Pacific
FDI	foreign direct investment
FTA	[Canada-US] Free Trade Agreement
GATT	General Agreement on Tariffs and Trade
GLC	government-linked company
GSP	generalised system of preferences
IMF	International Monetary Fund
ISI	import substitution industrialisation
ITC	[United States] International Trade Commission
ITO	International Trade Organisation
IIT	intra-industry trade
JIT	just-in-time
LDC	less developed country
MIT	Massachusetts Institute of Technology
MITI	[Japan] Ministry of International Trade and Industry
MMPA	[United States] Marine Mammal Protection Act
MNE	multinational enterprise
MOSS	Market-Oriented Sector-Selective negotiations

MTE	machinery and transport equipment
NAFTA	North American Free Trade Agreement
NATO	North Atlantic Treaty Organisation
NIC	newly industrialising country
NIDL	new international division of labour
NIEO	New International Economic Order
OECD	Organisation for Economic Cooperation and Development
OEEC	Organisation of European Economic Cooperation
OPEC	Organisation of Petroleum Exporting Countries
OPTAD	Organisation for Pacific Trade, Aid and Development
PAFTA	Pacific Free Trade Area
PAFTAD	Pacific Trade and Development
PAP	People's Action Party [Singapore]
PBEC	Pacific Basin Economic Council
PECC	Pacific Economic Cooperation Conference
R&D	research and development
RCA	revealed comparative advantage
SDR	Special Drawing Right
SII	Structural Impediments Initiative
SOE	state-owned enterprise
TNC	transnational corporation
TRIP	trade-related intellectual property
UMNO	United Malay National Organization
UNCTAD	United Nations Conference on Trade and Development
VERs	voluntary export restraint arrangements

Notes on Contributors

Benjamin J. Cohen, Louis G. Lancaster Professsor of International Political Economy, University of California, Santa Barbara, United States.

Lorraine Eden, Professor, The Norman Paterson School of International Relations, Carleton University, Ottawa, Canada.

Stuart Harris, Professor and Head of the Northeast Asia Research Program, Australian National University, Canberra, Australia.

Richard Higgott, Reader in International Relations and Director of Studies in Foreign Affairs and Trade, Australian National University, Canberra, Australia.

Chalmers Johnson, Rohr Professor of Pacific International Relations, Graduate School of International Relations and Pacific Studies, University of California, San Diego, United States.

Richard Leaver, Research Fellow, International Relations, Australian National University, Canberra, Australia.

Andrew MacIntyre, Senior Lecturer, Asian and International Studies, Griffith University, Brisbane, Australia.

Maureen Appel Molot, Professor, The Norman Paterson School of International Relations, Carleton University, Ottawa, Canada.

John Ravenhill, Senior Fellow, International Relations, Australian National University, Canberra, Australia.

J. David Richardson, Professor of Economics, Syracuse University, Syracuse, United States; Visiting Fellow, Institute for International Economics, Washington DC, United States.

Alan Rix, Professor of Japanese Studies, University of Queensland, Brisbane, Australia.

Garry Rodan, Lecturer, Murdoch University, Perth, Australia.

John Gerard Ruggie, Dean, School of International and Public Affairs, Columbia University, New York, United States.

Gilbert R. Winham, Professor of Political Science, Dalhousie University, Halifax, Canada.

Preface

This volume contains a series of original essays by prominent scholars in the field of international political economy (IPE). The chapters are therefore representative of that small but growing genre of scholarship that accepts the inappropriateness of studying the operations of markets and the behaviour of states in isolation from one another. But the book is relatively novel in another respect. One of our central objectives was to bring that IPE literature into juxtaposition with the mounting practical interest in the question of international economic cooperation within the Asia–Pacific region. Our hope was that these exercises in dual transgression would satisfy a demand that has, to date, gone largely unmet.

The chapters are based upon papers delivered in Canberra in mid-December 1991 at the inaugural Australian American Education Foundation Fulbright Symposium on 'Managing International Economic Relations in the Pacific in the 1990s'. To some, the symposium title bore pretensions of grandeur insofar as it brought that epitome of the modern pro-active verb, 'to manage', into juxtaposition with a geographic region where both regulatory institutions and the conventions born from convergent behaviour have historically been absent. Our intention, however, was to accent subtly the ample space for ambiguity which existed across the range between the extremes of 'managing as administering' and 'managing as subsisting', and to let our rather different contributors make what they chose of that creative space. Since the title of this volume omits that evocative verb, we leave it to our readers to judge the worthiness of our effort at scholarly hedging.

The hedging process was financial as well as intellectual, and numerous debts were incurred in preparing this collection. We are particularly thankful to the Fulbright Foundation: their decision to conduct a competition for proposals for staging the symposium opened the way to the seed money out of which this volume grew. In particular, we thank Charles Beltz, the Executive Director of the Australian American Educational Foundation, and Jim McWilliam, the President of the Australian Capital Territory Chapter of the Fulbright Alumni Association, for their support and cooperation. We are also indebted to our colleagues at the Australian National University, Andrew Mack of the Department of International Relations, Stuart Harris of the Northeast Asia Program, Trevor Findlay of the Peace Research Centre, Cliff Walsh of the Federalism Research Centre, and Gerry Ward, Director of the Research School of Pacific Studies; all committed some portion of their discretionary budgets to the costs associated with the symposium.

Not all of the symposium proceedings are published here. Dr Neal Blewett, then the Minister for Trade and Overseas Development, opened proceedings; Professors Nancy Viviani and Ross Garnaut closed them by leading a lively discussion on the implications of the papers for the Australian Government's Asia–Pacific policy. The Secretary of the Treasury, Tony Cole, gave a rousing after-dinner speech that will long live in the memory of those present.

Several of the contributors have asked us to acknowledge the help they received in preparing their chapters. Jerry Cohen wishes to thank Joanne Gowa, Steven Reti, Stephen Weatherford and an anonymous member of the faculty of the University of Sydney for their comments on the draft chapter. Lorraine Eden and Maureen Molot thank Bruce Wilkinson for helpful comments on an earlier draft; John Ravenhill is grateful to Pru Phillips of the International Economic Data Bank, ANU, for data analysis, and to Hal Hill and Dave Richardson for providing copies of unpublished papers, to David Sullivan for tracking down many obscure references, and to Ross Garnaut and Jim Richardson for comments on an earlier draft.

Finally, this dispatch contains three mentions for service beyond the call of duty. Lynne Payne prepared the revised chapters for publication with a combination of speed and poise that should not go unmentioned simply because it is now so routine. And though a large number of people assisted with administration of the December symposium, our personal thanks go to David Sullivan and Robin Ward, Research Assistants in our department. Without their dedication, cool professionalism and attention to detail, the symposium would not have run as smoothly as it did, and the final product would have appeared without an index and composite bibliography.

Richard Higgott, Richard Leaver, John Ravenhill
Department of International Relations
Research School of Pacific Studies
Australian National University

1 Introduction: Political Economy and the Pacific

RICHARD HIGGOTT, RICHARD LEAVER,
AND JOHN RAVENHILL

As the rate of growth of the global economy has gradually slowed through the last two decades, opportunities for employing the adjective 'dynamic' have become increasingly scarce. When set against this backdrop of these relatively hard times, the concurrent emergence of 'dynamic' as the most common and most overworked description of the Pacific economy is all the more notable. In the vernacular of regional diplomacy, the phrase 'Pacific economic dynamism' commonly refers to at least two attributes: the striking sequence of 'economic miracles', where the number of countries that have sustained rates of growth above 10 per cent per annum for more than a decade continues to expand; and the even more phenomenal expansion of the region's aggregate trade induced by the outward-oriented nature of much of this hyper-growth (see USNCPECC 1991).

Not surprisingly, therefore, many efforts to divine the future of the Pacific economy start from the implicit assumption that further 'dynamic growth' along these lines and in these proportions will continue to shift the centre of gravity of the global economy towards the Pacific, while simultaneously making the agenda of distributional issues which usually attends the development process a largely residual concern. By such accounts (exemplified in Hughes (ed.) 1988), the western Pacific-designed engine of outward-oriented economic growth has a proven record which will continue to deliver results of expanded and free trade so long as an effective political coalition willing to give it free rein can be put in place.

Within this rosy future, some of the more problematic attributes of Pacific economic dynamism are either not seen or are not regarded as serious obstacles. But over the past three decades, there has been a propensity for 'dynamic economic problems' to spring up and multiply in the midst of this regional sea of hyper-growth. Some therefore argue that the political product with which the emerging Pacific economy should be associated is not free trade, but rather its no less export-obsessed historical antithesis—mercantilism (see, for example, Kurth 1989).

These economic symptoms of discord have a specific evolutionary trajectory which is itself worthy of description. They made their first public appearance in the late 1960s along the very backbone of the Pacific economy—the Japanese–US commercial relationship—when two century-old features of the global economy inverted at more or less the same point in time: Japan began to register a trade surplus, and the United States a trade deficit. At first, analysts in both countries were inclined to believe that both of these trade inversions were temporary affairs, and that the dominant pattern would naturally reassert itself over time. But the passage of time now shows that, in spite of successively greater efforts to manage and stunt it, the Japanese–US commercial imbalance has become a feature of the global economy seemingly every bit as genetically given as the configuration of deficits and surpluses which preceded it.

More importantly, the mystery which this bilateral commercial imbalance expressed has tended to spread both laterally and vertically. As other East Asian 'economic miracles' have followed (albeit with considerable variation) in the outward-oriented footsteps of the Japanese prototype, and as still more Asian economies have explicitly 'looked East' to Japan for policies worthy of emulation, so the problem of commercial imbalance has tended to spread laterally. To this extent, commercial imbalance has tended to become less of a specifically Japanese–US problem, and more of a general feature of the economic relationship between the facing rims of the Pacific.

The vertical spread of this riddle seems to have been promoted by the successive application of more powerful techniques for managing the commercial imbalance. The Pacific economy has become the design shop not only for the latest and most sophisticated instruments of managed trade, but the site where the most pronounced movements of relative prices were first conceived and then executed through currency realignments. In reaction against the overvalued dollar induced by the first Reagan administration, the Plaza Agreement of 1985 engineered a massive revaluation of the yen to nearly three times its level of two decades earlier. Taken in conjunction with the gradual process of financial liberalisation and the continuing high rate of domestic savings, this increase in the yen's value substantially accelerated Japan's transition to a capital-surplus economy of the first order. 'The virus of imbalance' seemed to have spread from the trade to the capital account. Analysts therefore began to talk of a more general 'economic conflict' between the US and Japan that had developed out of the trade conflict (see Komiya & Itoh 1988, p. 212), while some began a search for the taproot of these hydra-headed economic tensions in culture and the politics of identity.

By the mid-1980s, 'Pacific economic problems' had demonstrated the right to be considered every bit as dynamic as the regional growth matrix from which they had arisen. In recognition of this, the first awakenings of a literature concerning 'the systemic implications of continued Japanese growth' were evident well in advance of the beginning of the end of the Cold War (see Buzan 1988; Gilpin 1989a; Cox 1989; Leaver 1989; Rapkin 1990 and 1991; and Wallerstein 1991). Most of this literature was provoked by the unique conjunction of both capital and trade surpluses which marked out Japan not only as the world's second largest economy, but as a historically unique 'immature creditor', and by the intensified and reformulated interdependence of the East Asian economies that followed upon the heels of the high yen.

That was already the state of play when the progressive implosion of the Eastern bloc and the Soviet Union swept away the basic bipolar configuration of four decades of post-war international relations. The central constitutive principle of the *ancien régime*—the US–Soviet central balance—collapsed to yield, in a purely negative sense, a 'lower case' new world order. In spite of a resounding military victory in the Gulf War, whether there are sufficient connotations of affirmation and stability for the phrase 'new world order' to be inscribed in upper case over the portals of a new era remains to be seen. So far as the future of the Pacific is concerned, what is clear is that the complete list of 'systemic questions' placed on notice before 1989 have been carried forward, without political resolution, to a radically different and uncertain international environment.

At first blush, this post-Cold War environment appears to offer unprecedented opportunities for formalised inter-state economic cooperation in the Pacific. The waning of ideological disputes has broadened the acceptance of a diffuse sense of community within the region, and rekindled—for example, in the Asia Pacific Economic Co-operation (APEC) process—the hitherto episodic search for an institutional form capable of articulating Pacific interests and expressing them in multilateral forums. At the same time, however, the elevation of economic issues within the Pacific agenda highlights—and perhaps sharpens—the 'dynamic economic problems' outlined above. If the western alliance system was indeed, as Cohen (1974) long ago argued for Europe, constructed around 'an implicit bargain' whereby the United States' allies gave up the search for security in exchange for conditions favourable to growth, then the end of the Cold War may well see diminished US willingness to bear the costs of adjustment to East Asian industrialisation. And if the Cold War did indeed function as a 'security blanket' by dampening the intensity of intra-allied economic disputes, then solutions to existing economic problems could now be harder to come by. New ideas, new institutional forums, new leadership and, indeed, new definitions of cooperation may all be necessary if conflict is not to emerge as the dominant characteristic of Pacific economic relations in the 1990s. Yet the provision of each of these necessities is itself liable to be more problematic.

The horns of this dilemma frame the principal questions which the essays in this volume seek to address. What are the prospects for successfully exploiting the new environment for cooperation in the Pacific? Which countries will be willing and able to provide leadership in the drive for increased cooperation—will the United States still have to bear a disproportionate share of the burden, will Japan overcome its institutional inertia to seize the initiative, or will the more relaxed security environment provide new opportunities for smaller countries, the developed 'middle powers' such as Australia and Canada, to play a contributory leadership role? In a region characterised by a long history of inter-state hostilities, by cultural diversity, and by economic inequalities, how might the potential for economic cooperation best be realised? What forms of cooperation are most likely to be successful? Which institutional forums and configurations are most appropriate for pursuing the 'open regionalism' to which many of the political and intellectual élites of the region have committed themselves? How might the inevitable tensions that are the outcome of increased economic interdependence best be managed? How should the burden of adjustment be shared?

Lively debate about the future of the Pacific has never been difficult to produce from questions such as these; indeed, the problem has been how to modulate the loud shouting down to the level of intelligent conversation. There are essentially two reasons for this sorry state of affairs. The first—documented more than a decade ago in the microcosm of the Japanese–US trade relationship by Hadley (1982)—is that the range of opinions about the Pacific's future has traditionally tracked the fault line between the customarily hostile professions of economics and political science. The second reason is that there are all too few scholars who claim to have interests that span the region as a whole. Most of the authors published here profess no such competence, and the frequency with which they renounced the very suggestion at the symposium speaks loudly about the absence of a strong sense of Pacific identity.

To think that these old rifts have been completely eroded over recent times would be excessively wishful, but there is at least one important reason to believe that these obstacles have lost some of their ability to discourage. Trends associated with the rise of the sub-field of international political economy (IPE) have dulled the sharp edge of disciplinary competition between political science and economics in Pacific (and other regional) studies. Crane and Amawi, for example, have recently argued that the rise of IPE has established sites where a degree of cross-disciplinary convergence in international studies has become manifest. The nodal points which they identify centre upon concerns with the rationality of state action, the question of leadership, and the 'patterned behaviour' associated with international regimes (see Crane & Amawi (eds) 1991, pp. 21–7). The majority of the essays presented here share at least some of these core concerns of the evolving IPE sub-field; that the line of demarcation between optimists and pessimists about the future of the Pacific economy no longer follows strict professional categories is therefore not surprising.

Within these broad parameters and concerns, the chapters that follow conform to a rough division of labour. Those by Ruggie, Cohen, Richardson, Leaver and Higgott primarily examine or exemplify some of the newer theoretical approaches and their relationship to the principal economic trends in the Asia–Pacific region. The chapters by Winham, Harris, and Eden and Molot consider the kinds of policy frameworks that are likely to emerge after the Uruguay Round as regional states attempt to come to grips with their growing international economic interdependence. Ravenhill, Johnson, Rix, Rodan and MacIntyre focus more directly on the politics of international trade and investment issues that are specific to the Asia–Pacific region, with Johnson and Ravenhill centring upon the pivotal US–Japan relationship, and Rodan and MacIntyre upon selected newly industrialising economies.

Some assumptions about the context of current problems of international economic management are central to all essays in the volume, but are most explicitly addressed as a package by John Ruggie. They concern the context in which we must understand current problems of international economic management. Economic interdependence appears to have increased, the economic pre-eminence of the United States has diminished, and the widespread commitment to multilateralism, at other than the rhetorical level, is problematic. If these are indeed the characteristics of our time, then they generate a series of supplementary questions about the prospects for cooperation. Some have asked whether and how 'cooperation after hegemony' might be promoted; others begin a search for a new hegemon. For Ruggie, however, the first task is to separate out the elements of continuity from the elements of change, and to measure the extent of contemporary change against a meaningful historical baseline.

Ruggie has argued extensively in other places that what he calls 'the compromise of embedded liberalism'—a practical reconciliation between the principles of multilateralism and domestic interventionism—underpins the post-war era, and that questions about the extent to which current economic policies normatively deviate from past practice should be measured against the firm ground set by this compromise (for his original formulation, see Ruggie 1982). His chapter in this volume argues that this basic compromise—notwithstanding that it is somewhat battered—is still holding. Yet, as he notes, one of the problems that the global economy now faces is that its institutions have to combat a polarised 'free trade versus protection' discourse which misrepresents the task that the embedded liberalism compromise was meant to address. The original post-war institutions—notably the General Agreement on Tariffs and Trade (GATT)—were not intended to provide a framework in which national economies might restructure in the face of globalisation and interdependence. Ironically, Ruggie suggests—and in contrast to much orthodox economic theory—excessive liberalisation, especially the aggressive rhetoric of free trade, might exacerbate the very economic nationalism that the 'embedded liberalism' compromise was intended to deter.

This rhetoric has two other effects. First, it hides the degree to which certain forms of 'the new mercantilism' are capable of being incorporated under the structure of embedded liberalism. Second, it encourages premature predictions about the demise of the GATT in particular and the liberal international economic order in general. Consequently, the bulk of Ruggie's chapter examines the extent to which the particular Pacific manifestations of 'the new protectionism' can be considered an extension of the embedded liberalism compromise, with non-tariff barriers fulfilling the role in domestic economic management that tariffs previously fulfilled. He finds that many of the policies said to be pushing the Pacific economy towards economic brinkmanship—including Washington's 'Super 301'— are, in theory and intent, market-opening policies the effects of which are manageable within the embedded liberalism compromise, provided that the rhetoric of cheating can be contained. This relatively benign view of US 'crowbar diplomacy' is by no means axiomatic (for some critical discussion, see Niskanen 1989; Bhagwati 1991a; and Bhagwati and Patrick (eds) 1990), and several subsequent contributors to this volume— especially Winham, Harris and Higgott—later challenge it on various grounds.

Chalmers Johnson shares with Ruggie a particularly robust argument about the dangers of confusing economic doctrine with economic analysis: '[i]t is more than likely', he maintains, 'that history will come to judge English-language academic economics as having the same relationship to Asian capitalism that academic Marxism–Leninism taught in the USSR until August 1991 had to the Soviet economy'. Since he has long argued that the Japanese 'developmental state' represents a genetically distinct variety of capitalism (see Johnson 1988a), he is in an ideal position to examine an issue that Ruggie, while noting, did not address in detail—the higher profile which domestic economic structures now have in global economic issues.

Johnson's analysis, set against the background of the asymmetrical delusions which the Cold War induced in the Japanese–US relationship, closely examines the likely implications of various forms of 'structural difference' and historical change upon an alliance which, as he sees it, currently survives on little more than inertia. He notes that quite different interpretations of the end of the Cold War had come to prevail in the mainstream of Japanese and United States political life well before the Gulf War muddied those already murky waters of expectations. He also stresses that the theme of 'emotional friction', which in one form or another characterises much post-Gulf War Japanese writings on the alliance, should not be forgotten simply because it is difficult to evaluate. His overall assessment is that the alliance requires fundamental domestic reform on both sides if it is to survive this century, but he finds little evidence of the domestic leadership necessary to that task.

On the specific issue of the future vitality—indeed, viability—of an open Pacific trading system, Johnson holds relatively pessimistic views. While he does not rule out a continuation of GATT-style multilateralism, he sees it as less probable than either G-3 or G-2 arrangements, both of which presume *de facto* generalisation of the principles of managed trade. In reaching this conclusion, he emphasises the primary importance of the Plaza devaluation, which gave rise to a genuine East Asian division of labour and a hyper-competitive Japanese industrial sector. Popular arguments that the Japanese are incapable of strategic thinking may, he suggests, be guilty of confusing incapacity with a conscious decision to defer. What is important is that the structures through which Japanese leadership could be exercised are currently being created.

Of all the chapters in this volume, the one by Alan Rix most directly addresses the rancorous question of 'Japanese leadership'. Much of the recent interest in this question has been provoked by the apparently divergent commercial and financial trajectories of the Japanese and US economies noted above, and much of the venom in that interest comes from the quick conclusion that the fundamental cause of the United States' decline is Japan's rise.

Rix's chapter breaks free from these vindictive mirror image problems by looking for the first signs of a more general Japanese 'leadership' in the pattern of economic interactions which already link Japan to the East and Southeast Asian regions. Giving particular attention to the commercial and aid relationships, he finds that much of the infrastructure necessary for a regional leadership role is already in place, and that Japanese governments have been particularly careful to move towards that role through the mobilisation of regional consent. This conclusion confirms the suggestion of Johnson and others in this volume, notably Harris, that regionalist solutions are more probable, though Rix's relatively benign interpretation of regional economic interdependence would probably lead him to say that regional leadership can be made compatible with multilateralism.

J. David Richardson's chapter comprehensively assesses the contribution of the 'new' trade theory (the analysis of trade in strategic environments) to our understanding of international trade in general, and trade policy in the Pacific region in particular. He argues that the new theory has frequently been misunderstood and misleadingly portrayed by those who seek to use it to boost their own policy prescriptions. On the one hand, ideologues of free trade have asserted that its arguments are merely reformulations of old mercantilist thinking about issues such as optimal tariffs and infant industries, and that the conclusions to be drawn from the new theory only serve to strengthen the argument for *laissez-faire*. At the other end of the spectrum, advocates of industrial policy ignore the nuances and complexities of the theory and seize on it as a blanket justification for their prescription of greater governmental intervention.

Richardson shows that both of these interpretations are seriously flawed. The growing literature—with its emphasis on the importance of power, of threats, and of pre-emptive investments—adds a new dimension to our understanding of trade strategy in imperfectly competitive markets dominated by intra-industry trade. In a global economy increasingly characterised by significant first-mover advantages, and by rising costs of research and development, the literature suggests that market power arising from such factors as monopoly ownership of patents can be translated into excess profits, even into the long run. As Richardson's survey indicates, there is now a substantial body of empirical work that applies and tests the ideas of the new trade theory, and consequently the case for free trade can no longer be defended on the basis of ideology alone. Yet the conclusions reached by the empirical studies may not be those which the industrial policy activist hoped for. As Richardson asserts, if the new view concludes anything, it is that the case for industrial targeting is complex and necessarily pragmatic.

The widespread perception however, is that East Asian countries have been active and successful practitioners of those policy prescriptions which can be derived from the new trade theory. Richardson is sceptical of this, pointing to studies which assert the importance of sound macroeconomic management in promoting East Asia's rapid growth. He concludes his chapter by considering measures that might be adopted to ensure that 'fair' industrial competition becomes the norm in Pacific economic relations, focusing in particular on the Structural Impediments Initiative (SII), and the possibility for extending sub-regional economic cooperation arrangements such as the Australia–New Zealand Closer Economic Relations agreement, and the North American free Trade Agreement (NAFTA).

The central concerns of Ravenhill's chapter—the issue of 'unfair' practices in Japanese–US trade, and how best to respond to them—are, like the 'new' trade theory, the subject of a burgeoning literature. Ravenhill suggests that much of it is disingenuous insofar as it focuses on largely irrelevant or inappropriate indicators, or is derived from models that have unrealistic assumptions. The key question is whether Japan's trade pattern is significantly different from those of other industrialised countries once account is taken of its geographical position and economic structure. Here a new generation of empirical work is emerging that focuses specifically on the impeding effects of informal barriers to trade, and provides evidence of factors that have contributed to Japan's low ratio of intra-industry trade even after geographical position is taken into account.

The core of Ravenhill's chapter examines the extent to which Japan's position as an outlier has changed since the Plaza Agreement dramatically revalued the yen and made Japan the world's largest foreign direct investor. He concludes that although there has been a substantial increase in Japan's manufactured imports from other APEC countries in recent years, and Japan's index of intra-industry trade has risen beyond the previous peak of the early 1970s, Japan still lags considerably behind the United States in its absorption of manufactured imports from the region.

This holds not only for exports from the East Asian newly industrialising countries (NICs), but also for the rapidly expanding exports of manufactures from Southeast Asia, particularly Thailand and Malaysia.

The data analysed by Ravenhill suggest that the United States is continuing to bear a disproportionate share of the costs of adjustment to East Asian industrialisation. Unless Japan undertakes a further substantial increase in its manufactured imports from the region, trade tensions are inevitable. Ravenhill concludes by arguing that while the solution to the US bilateral trade deficit with Japan lies primarily in improved US domestic economic policies, Japan's continuing low levels of absorption of manufactured imports provide a good case for continuing foreign pressure to overcome Japanese political immobilism on the issue of effective market liberalisation.

The chapters by Benjamin Cohen and Richard Leaver address notable voids in the agendas of both Pacific cooperation and IPE by focusing on the conditions previously favourable to, and future prospects for, monetary cooperation in the Pacific region. Of all the features which have shaped the regional context through recent years, none has been more fundamental or far reaching than the progressive liberalisation of Japanese capital markets. Previously a highly regulated and inward-directed market, a series of reforms that began in the 1970s has gradually brought the still extraordinarily high rate of Japanese domestic savings into juxtaposition with an increasingly capital-hungry world. Yet paradoxically, as Strange has repeatedly pointed out through this period, very little in the agenda of IPE is capable of taking account of this central feature of our times (see Strange 1986).

Cohen and Leaver both take their point of departure from the Plaza Agreement of September 1985, where the Reagan administration broke with its previous policy of 'monetary unilateralism' to embrace a cooperative strategy—in which public and private Japanese capital balked large— that drove the dollar down from levels which were clearly unsustainable. Cohen observes that Plaza represented less the beginning of a monotonic trend towards coordination than of a cyclical process subject to occasional bouts of recidivism. Consequently, his primary concerns are to map out the phases in the process of monetary cooperation, and to develop an endogenous explanation of the stop–go dynamic of cooperation by reference to the tensions between the various objectives which compete for undivided control over monetary policy.

Leaver's analysis, by contrast, is situated within a broader framework of Japanese–US 'complex interdependence'. This highlights how the primary purpose of the 1985 turn to monetary coordination lay in the restoration of a degree of balance in Japanese–US trade outcomes. He agrees with Cohen that the conditions which prevailed in 1985 were unusually favourable to monetary coordination, and that the power of precedent should not be overrated. However, his emphasis on complex interdependence leads him to argue that outcomes from exercises in monetary coordination, either in the past or in the future, have to be assessed across the full spectrum of macro-policy issue-areas. In this regard, he argues that the distribution of vulnerabilities that collectively comprise Japanese–US 'complex interdependence' has, through the last decade, changed in ways which are basically unfavourable to future US governments. While these shifts do not preclude future exercises in monetary coordination, they would seem to imply a higher US entry price than was evident during the lifespan of the Plaza Agreement.

Recent years have also seen important political declarations that, taken at face value, suggest increasing acceptance of principles of 'open regionalism' within the broader Pacific area. Historically, the immense expansion of Pacific trade has owed more to the combined effects of colonial residues and the Cold War than GATT principles. It therefore needs to be asked whether the high level of verbal support for the Uruguay Round recently mustered through successive APEC meetings portends the end of the pattern of 'informal bilateralism' that has previously guided the expansion of Pacific trade, and the policy ascension of more pristine multilateral principles.

The chapter by Gilbert Winham looks generally at the future of the GATT after the Uruguay Round, and especially at issues of particular relevance to the Pacific. Of all the chapters published here, this is the one which bears a disproportionate share of the risks that inhere in any forward-looking venture. When he agreed to write on this, the Uruguay Round appeared primed for a December 1990 conclusion, and an investigation of the implications of the Round's achievements for the burgeoning trade of the Pacific region seemed apposite.

Since then, Winham has been forced to adapt his text to a negotiating deadline that continues to retreat like a mirage in a desert. Rather than expend his energies trying to second-guess an outcome from Geneva, he is content to point to one of the little-noticed but now inevitable consequences of delay—that any agreement may now be undone by the fickle timetables and processes of domestic US politics in electoral mode. Apart from this, he fixes his analytic gaze on some concrete issues which lie behind, around and in front of the mirage of progress.

The picture which he sees is not a happy one. In the foreground, the quick expansion of a North American bloc (albeit on open principles) suggests a mounting preference for feasible regional solutions over more ideal multilateral outcomes. In the background, the uneven groundswell of opinion for environmental standards will pose problems concerning the standards for horizontal consistency that, while not being peculiar to multilateral forums, will in all probability be more manageable in a regional framework. Furthermore, this will burst onto the GATT agenda at a time when a diffuse but slowly accumulating neo-mercantilist challenge, fuelled from a number of different quarters, continues to gather momentum.

Lorraine Eden and Maureen Appel Molot focus in depth on NAFTA and its implications for the Pacific region. The signing of the Canada–US

Free Trade Agreement in 1987 and the more recent moves towards a North American Free Trade Agreement that includes Mexico stand in sharp contrast to the more rudimentary state of deliberations within the APEC framework. Their chapter discusses how these states and their major multinational enterprises are organising for production (via what they call 'lean production') within NAFTA, and the effects that these changes may have on the locational pattern of their relationships with other major centres of the global and regional economy.

They investigate five issues raised by NAFTA that concern the Asia–Pacific region. Will it divert the current pattern of trans-Pacific trade into a bloc pattern? Will it make NAFTA members more effective competitors with the Asia–Pacific? What consequences of any subsequent expansion and deepening of NAFTA are to be expected? Will NAFTA complement or contradict multilateral efforts at trade promotion, and what effect will the regional free trade area have on Japanese–US relations? The one issue which is woven through their answers to these more specific investigations concerns the level of the domestic content requirement that will be built into NAFTA, and they conclude with the general suggestion that Pacific Rim countries have an interest in lobbying to keep that requirement low.

The next section of the volume considers the implications of the changing division of labour in East Asia. The economic transformation of the East Asian NICs has been one of the most remarkable features of the world economy in the last two decades. More recently, some Southeast Asian countries, particularly Indonesia, Malaysia and Thailand, have begun to enjoy high rates of economic growth and considerable success in exporting manufactured goods.

As noted previously, the East Asian division of labour is changing rapidly in response not only to shifts in relative costs of production but also to political pressures arising from growing trade tensions within the region. Under pressure from rising domestic costs of production, higher prices brought on by post-Plaza currency revaluations, and US protectionism, the NICs have had to rethink their strategy of reliance on low-cost labour-intensive exports directed predominantly towards the US market. One response has been significant levels of NIC investment in manufacturing for export in Southeast Asia.

Garry Rodan's chapter is a detailed case study of the Singaporean response to increasing lack of competitiveness in labour-intensive manufactures, and thus the growing irrelevance of the economic strategy that had served it so well in the 1970s and early 1980s. Of all of the NICs, Singapore was the most vulnerable to a loss of competitiveness because of its small domestic market and its greater dependence on subsidiaries of transnational corporations. Rodan argues that Singapore's development has entered a qualitatively new stage in which emphasis has turned to its potential to service the industrialisation of other Association of Southeast Asian Nations (ASEAN) countries. In particular, he focuses on the efforts of the government to promote 'growth triangles' with its regional neighbours. The development of growth triangles, Rodan argues, encourages those neighbours to follow the path that Singapore had earlier pursued, while capitalising on the new interest of transnational corporations in adopting a regional focus.

The Singaporean state, Rodan notes, actively fostered favourable investment conditions, particularly physical and social infrastructure, in neighbouring countries, and has also used government-owned companies to invest in joint ventures in Indonesia. In these respects, it has been notably more enthusiastic about the growth triangle than either Indonesia or Malaysia, which remain suspicious about the distribution of gains from this form of regional collaboration, and concerned that the triangles may strengthen the position of the local Chinese community within the region. Rodan concludes by suggesting that the extent to which the growth triangle is successful will have implications for ASEAN's recently announced move towards implementation of a regional free trade area.

Andrew MacIntyre reviews the recent experience of rapid economic growth in Indonesia and Thailand which, together with Malaysia, have been suggested by some to be at the forefront of a new generation of newly industrialising countries. Like Japan and the East Asian NICs before them, Indonesia and Thailand have experienced a large increase in the share of manufactures in their total exports coincident with this rapid growth. MacIntyre, however, provides a critical analysis of the often facile comparisons that are made between the two Southeast Asian countries and the Northeast Asian NICs.

He begins by noting that although there are different interpretations of the East Asian NICs, there were a number of common factors in their economic success, in particular the extensive and often elaborate nature of state intervention. Indonesia and Thailand differ from the Northeast Asian NIC model, MacIntyre argues, not only because of the continued importance of primary product exports to their economies, but also because of the qualitatively different degree of state intervention in markets, and the relative lack of autonomy of the state in the two Southeast Asian countries. Neither the Indonesian nor the Thai state apparatuses have developed the high-calibre bureaucracy that is often associated with the Northeast Asian NICs; neither has effectively insulated economic policy-making from the demands of particularistic groups. Another important difference between the Southeast Asian countries and the Northeast Asian NICs that MacIntyre emphasises is the former's dependence on foreign capital for the recent rapid growth in manufactured exports. He concludes by pointing out that we need to know much more about the politics of economic policy-making in Southeast Asian countries to be able to make informed estimates of their future prospects.

The volume concludes with chapters by Stuart Harris and Richard Higgott, in which issues concerning the opportunities for and constraints upon closer economic policy coordination by regional states are central.

Both pose some general questions about our contemporary theoretical understanding of cooperation and its practical utility for informing our understanding of the Asia–Pacific region.

To measure achievement in Asia–Pacific cooperation is, of course, difficult, but Harris makes the important point that much extra-regional observation has failed to grasp the rate of progress that has been made in a relatively short time. The current preference for dialogue via summitry and the absence of a formal inter-governmental organisation has to be understood in historical context. In contrast to much longer European and North American experiences of cooperation (both successful and otherwise), Asia–Pacific networks and relations are being built in a compressed post-colonial timespan. The development of economic cooperation in the Asia–Pacific therefore cannot be assessed by comparison with either European or North American historical and contemporary needs, levels of development or timetables of organisational evolution. Both Harris and Higgott suggest that the Asia–Pacific region can expect to see further progress towards the harmonisation of regional interests and the development of a regional voice to join European and North American voices in the global economic dialogue.

Harris places the recent evolution of APEC at the centre of his analysis of economic cooperation. By contrast with Higgott—for whom recent international relations theorising provides a focus—Harris pays more attention to the economic literature. He highlights the manner in which the increased globalisation of the international economy heightens the need to bridge information gaps and improve policy support capacity in the region. His conclusions about the nature of, and the continuing need for, economic cooperation in the Pacific are strongly reinforced by the arguments of Higgott.

Higgott emphasises recent significant attempts to conceptualise new trends in international economic relations and conflict management. Within the field of international relations there has been much concern about how to promote cooperation in an era of eroding US economic hegemony. This concern has centred on the realist/neo-liberal institutionalist impasse that has beset much mainstream theorising about cooperation in the international political economy (reviewed in Milner 1992).

Using APEC as his case study, Higgott suggests that the realist/neo-liberal institutionalist dichotomy has been too starkly explicated. He argues that examination of the nascent processes of economic cooperation building in the Asia–Pacific region is not well served by the relative gains arguments which inform some contemporary strands of realist scholarship. While not downplaying the importance of treating states as rational actors, he also stresses the importance of the non-structural bases of power in international economic cooperation. APEC, he argues, demonstrates that the technical, entrepreneurial and learned moral and ethical dimensions of economic cooperation offer important refinements to cruder rationalist formulations. Formal cooperation and the level of institutionalisation are still low, but this does not bear directly upon the growing importance of institutional contact for the management of economic relations in the region.

In the concluding chapter, the editors consider some of the more common focal points in the volume, and try to sharpen contrasts, identify areas of agreement, and reshape existing agendas where important questions of substance remain at stake. Among the issues discussed are the prospects for, scope of, and shape of regional institution-building; the outlook for the NICs and the newer export-oriented experiences of the ASEAN states; and the future of the trading system.

The general argument of the conclusion revolves around the overarching problem of 'economic imbalance' that has attended the expansion of the Pacific economy. While it is common for policy communities to think of the adjustment process as a problem for international relations, the editors point out that the imbalances have domestic and international manifestations—as will the adjustments that are necessary if the cause of a more cooperative future is to be in any way assured. The full complexity of the required corrective is, therefore, not fully captured when described in one dimensional terms as either a domestic or an international process. It requires a redefinition of the interaction between the domestic and international realms. The editors reflect on the norms that might guide this multi-level process, and what their implications might mean for the future of the Pacific region.

2 Unravelling Trade: Global Institutional Change and the Pacific Economy

JOHN GERARD RUGGIE

Whoever invented the old schoolyard saw that sticks and stones but not words have painful consequences must have led a very sheltered life. Much the larger number of us, I suspect, responded to the power that words wielded in our schoolyards *with* sticks and stones. An analogous situation exists in the international trade arena today, where the power of words to evoke virulent, even if not as yet violent, actions seems exceedingly high. That potential is particularly great in the Pacific, in part because it is the fastest-growing region and the one that can boast of the largest number of new entrants into the tournament of major economic players. The end of the Cold War, which had muted the intensity of trade disputes in the past, can only exacerbate this already menacing situation.

The chief verbal demons the force of which we must learn to exorcise are the terms 'free trade' and 'protectionism'. If they are allowed to continue their privileged role in framing public and to some extent even academic discourse concerning international trade, then any relevant remnant of the GATT-based (General Agreement on Tariffs and Trade) trade regime is doomed, and with it world economic stability. Contrary to what liberal economists would like us to believe, free trade in the sense of unrestricted trade has never been GATT's mandate. Commenting on the negotiations for an international trade charter in 1947, Jacob Viner wrote: 'there are few free traders in the present-day world, no one pays any attention to their views, and no person in authority anywhere advocates free trade' (Viner 1947, p. 613). Even for the relatively more liberal United States, the international edifice of the 'open door' had to accommodate the domestic interventionism of the New Deal. No country

15

anywhere was prepared then—or at any time since—to subordinate domestic stabilisation to free trade.

At the same time, the GATT-based political regime for the governance of international trade relations sought to ensure that domestic interventionism did not reproduce the mutually destructive consequences of the inter-war period. Out of those twin concerns emerged an institutional compromise that I have elsewhere described as 'embedded liberalism' (Ruggie 1982, 1991a).[1] Unlike the economic nationalism of the 1930s, the international economic order would be multilateral in character; but unlike the liberalism of the gold standard and free trade, its multilateralism would be predicated upon domestic interventionism. Domestically this was a compromise between the major societal groupings (agriculture, labour and capital), as well as between export-oriented and import-competing industries. And it was a compromise between the legislative branch, which retained the right to authorise trade negotiations and to ratify their results, and the executive branch, which was given the right to conduct trade policy. Internationally it was a compromise between the United States, where domestic stabilisation measures remained the least comprehensive and systematic and the most constrained by opposition, and the European states, where rejection of liberal orthodoxy was universal but the objects of economic protection varied widely among the left, right and centre of the political spectrum.[2]

Once negotiations on post-war commercial arrangements got under way seriously in the context of an international conference on trade *and* employment, the principles of non-discrimination and tariff reduction were affirmed, but so were safeguards, exemptions, exceptions and restrictions—all designed to protect the balance of payments and a variety of domestic social policies. The proposed charter for an all-encompassing International Trade Organisation became internally so inconsistent that it is difficult to say just what sort of regime it would have given rise to. In any case, the US Senate refused to ratify the charter, it being too intrusive

---

1 A more detailed discussion of the origins and characteristics of the embedded liberalism compromise may be found in Ruggie (1982, 1991a). See also Ikenberry (1992). I adapted the term from Polanyi (1944). In it, he developed a distinction between 'embedded' and 'disembedded' economic orders: 'normally, the economic order is merely a function of the social, in which it is contained...Nineteenth-century society, in which economic activity was isolated and imputed to a distinctive economic motive, was, indeed, a singular departure' (p. 71).

2 This was true even in Great Britain, where Labour sought to institute systematic national economic planning, which in all probability would have entailed deployment of discriminatory instruments of foreign economic policy, while the Tories remained committed to imperial preferences, which were inherently discriminatory in character (see Gardner 1980, ch. 1). In Scandinavia the overriding objective of domestic economic policy was the achievement of full employment (Paavonen 1983).

for some and not activist enough for others, as a result of which a far smaller domain of commercial relations became subject to the international regime than would have been the case otherwise. Among the most important areas excluded were the regulation of commodity markets, restrictive business practices, and international investments—the absence of which has severely plagued the international trade regime in recent years. The more traditional concerns of commercial policy—tariffs, quotas and the like—were addressed by the GATT, which the United States quickly helped to form and joined by executive order.

The GATT made obligatory the most-favoured-nation rule but a blanket exception was allowed for all existing preferential agreements (a United States concession to Britain), and countries were permitted to form customs unions and free trade areas (United States encouragement to Western Europe). Moreover, quantitative import restrictions were prohibited but were deemed suitable measures for safeguarding the balance of payments—*explicitly* including payments difficulties that resulted from domestic full employment policies. They could also be invoked in agricultural trade if they were used in conjunction with a domestic price support programme. The substantial reduction of tariffs and other barriers to trade was called for but it was *not* made obligatory, and it was coupled with appropriate emergency actions, which were allowed if a domestic producer was threatened with injury from import competition that was due to past tariff concessions. The Agreement also offered a blanket escape from any of its obligations provided that two-thirds of the contracting parties approved—the United States availed itself of the opportunity to exclude its entire agricultural trade from international scrutiny. Lastly, procedures were provided to settle disputes arising under the Agreement and for the multilateral surveillance of the invocation of most (though not all) of its escape clauses. The principle of reciprocity was enshrined as a code of conduct to guide both tariff reductions and the determination of compensation for injuries suffered.

If we use this actual historical compromise of embedded liberalism as the baseline for assessing the conduct of international trade relations today rather than the textbook models, then much of what has passed for protectionism in recent years must be sifted through rather carefully and the real stuff separated out from what may be little more than creative adaptations of the embedded-liberalism framework. That task is taken up in Part 1 of this chapter. The more problematical shift towards strategic unilateralism in trade policy on the part of the United States is addressed in Part 2.

Using this historical baseline also helps to contextualise and therefore hopefully to understand better certain new features of international economic transactions. The creators of the trade regime presupposed several key institutional parameters when they constructed the regime within which movement towards freer trade and away from protectionism had reasonably stable meanings. Three of these institutional assumptions, in particular, have become increasingly undermined over time: (i) that the major impediments to international economic transactions are point-of-entry barriers or government cheating; (ii) that the typical international economic transaction consists of the exchange of tangible products supported—or literally serviced—by the attendant invisibles sectors; and (iii) that international economic transactions are conducted at arms-length and take place between disjoint and unrelated national economic units. As discussed in Part 3, changes in these institutional parameters have eroded the efficacy of the trade regime and its most common adaptive forms, but in a manner that free-trade/protectionist rhetoric does little to elucidate.

If, however, the language of free trade and protectionism is not up to the task of expressing the resultant problems fully, how then should they be depicted? I take a stab at this question in the conclusion.

1. The new protectionism

Today, the post-war compromise is at risk in the area of international trade (see Bhagwati 1991a). But free-trade/protectionism rhetoric does little to clarify the nature of the risk. For twenty years now, liberal internationalist commentators have cried wolf. For twenty years now, they have been detecting a 'disastrous isolationist trend' in US foreign economic policy, warning of 'the first real international trade war since the 1930s', and reminding us that 'trade wars could become full economic wars, precisely as they did under similar international conditions in the 1930s' (Bergsten 1972). If imminence fails to materialise over such an extended duration, however, then it is worth exploring whether there may be something amiss, not in the world of actual state behaviour, but in the model of state behaviour that analysts are bringing to bear on it. That, at any rate, is what I intend to do.

The facts of the matter regarding the so-called *new* protectionism are straightforward and beyond dispute—the referent being various forms of administered and negotiated non-tariff restrictions on imports. For example, a recent GATT study reports on the bilateral voluntary export restraint arrangements (VERs) known to have been in effect at the end of 1987. The product categories affected include textiles and clothing (71 arrangements outside the Multifibre Arrangement); agricultural and food products (58); steel and steel products (52); electronic products (23); automobiles and transport equipment (20); footwear (15); machine tools (13); and miscellaneous (25). 'The majority of the arrangements protect the EEC market or the market of one of its member States, followed by the US market; these two account for just over three quarters of the measures listed. The arrangements mainly limit exports from Japan (38 arrangements), the Republic of Korea (35), the EEC (15) and Taiwan (13)' (GATT 1988, ch. 7). In addition, many of the countries subject to voluntary export restraints also faced anti-dumping and countervailing duty actions. Lastly, it is clear that the use of mechanisms of this sort has increased over the years.

In short, it is not the facts themselves but what they signify that is at issue. To assess what they signify, let us look first at the quantitative dimension of the issue and then at the alleged problem of coercion and discrimination that it raises.

How much? Of what?

Quantitatively there is overwhelming evidence that among the Organisation for Economic Cooperation and Development (OECD) movement towards greater international openness by an economy is statistically closely associated with governments expanding their domestic role via adjustment and distributive policies—and that openness overrides virtually all other domestic economic and political differences among them in doing so (see Cameron 1978). Thus, as trade barriers have come down governments have become more active in managing the consequences. That much is almost axiomatic. Furthermore, in managing the consequences of greater openness generally speaking 'governments merely attempt to mitigate the negative effects of trade liberalization on specific industries and not to offset them entirely' (Blais 1986, p. 210).[3] As a result, despite the recent proliferation of instruments of the 'new protectionism', the markets of the industrialised countries are more open today than they were only a decade ago (GATT 1988; United Nations Conference on Trade and Development (UNCTAD) 1989).

This apparent anomaly has led the distinguished international economist Jagdish Bhagwati to puzzle why 'the growth of protectionism appears significant but its consequences do not' (Bhagwati 1988, p. 56). Judith Goldstein, in an exhaustive study of all statutory restraints imposed by the United States since the 1950s, documents the same puzzle: while access to the institutions of administered protection has been progressively eased, and while these institutions have been increasingly pressed for protectionist measures, they 'have not become increasingly protectionist over time' (1986, p. 179; 1988).[4] In point of fact, there is every evidence to suggest that they are not intended to be protectionist in the conventional sense of the term (see also Finger 1981; Finger et al. 1982; Nelson 1987, 1989; Aggarwal et al. 1987; Morici & Megna 1983; Yoffie 1983). (The

---

3   Andre Blais (1986) examined the impact of a country's economic size, level of affluence, rate of unemployment, and the presence of left-wing parties in its electoral system—and all were outweighed by openness in determining the level of industrial subsidies, thereby confirming the findings in Cameron's study, which focused on public expenditures.

4   Goldstein examined the invocation of five statutory provisions to restrain imports into the United States: escape clause, anti-dumping, countervailing duties, adjustment assistance, and unfair practices related largely to patent claims.

corresponding situation in the European Community (EC) admittedly is more complex.)[5]

But within the embedded-liberalism framework, there is no anomaly to begin with: in terms of its overall balance of political objectives, this was how the trade regime was expected and designed to function. It is free-trade rhetoric that has produced the anomaly. From the vantage point of the embedded-liberalism compromise, the bulk of the 'new protectionism' may be seen instead as norm-governed institutional adaptation to a very different international competitive environment than existed in the past.

The embedded-liberalism baseline also suggests a critical difference between such instruments of administered protection as VERs, anti-dumping and countervailing duty investigations, and the like, and the more pernicious form of 'managed trade'. Most instruments of the so-called new protectionism do not seek to fix bilateral or overall market shares, but to slow down or limit the rate of increase in imports in the attempt to give domestic industry time to adjust to a new competitive situation. Moreover, they tend to be of limited duration: as Aggarwal and his colleagues show, the longevity of these instruments exhibits distinct patterns which largely reflect industry structure, and the majority are not permanent (Aggarwal et al. 1987).

What is euphemistically described as 'managed trade', however, does constitute a serious deviation from the norm. Under it, instead of merely limiting adjustment costs, governments in essence, and sometimes explicitly negotiate market shares. The controversial side-letter to the 1986 semiconductor agreement between the United States and Japan, which promised the United States a 20 per cent market share in Japan within a five-year period, is a case in point (Prestowitz Jr, 1988, ch. 2). The Multifibre Arrangement is another.[6] But 'managed trade' by far remains the exception to the rule.

In sum, within the embedded-liberalism framework, the puzzle posed by the new protectionism is no puzzle at all.

Coercive discrimination?

Let us turn next to the allegedly coercive and discriminatory treatment that VERs and other such 'orderly marketing arrangements' are said to embody. Exporters typically act under the threat of worse to come if they

---

5 As Martin Wolf has put it, the EC 'is not only itself a discriminatory trading arrangement, if looked at as a collection of separate countries, but is embedded in concentric circles of discrimination' (1987, pp. 56–7), consisting of a variety of preferences and restraints. *The Economist* (1991a), reports a less than flattering GATT study of Community practices.

6 The Multifibre Arrangement started on the VERs side of the ledger, but over time it has shifted to the 'managed trade' side—from embedded liberalism to illiberal protectionism (see Aggarwal 1985).

fail to reach agreement with the importing country—hence, the accusation of coercion if not outright relapse to the rules of the jungle.

Two counterarguments come to mind. First, it is well known by now that VERs and like instruments typically transfer the scarcity rents produced by government intervention in the importing country to the *exporter*, and that they are paid by consumers in the *importing* countries. Paying off exporters at the expense of one's own consumers is a very odd form of international coercion—indeed, so odd that Japanese automobile manufacturers decided unilaterally to impose such an arrangement on themselves as they shifted their efforts in the United States from selling medium-priced models to capturing the luxury market from European exporters!

Second, those who charge coercion typically ignore the fact that not only the threatened unilateral but even the existing *multilateral* alternative to VERs would leave exporters *worse off* than VERs do. As Hindley has pointed out, 'for most countries confronted with a request for a VER the alternative, should they refuse, is not unrestricted trade but an Article xix emergency action [under the GATT]. In that event, the exporting country will find itself faced with a tariff on its exports or by formal quota restrictions on them with the quota rights going to importers...rather than to exporters. In either case, the profits of the exporting industry will be reduced...' (Hindley 1980, p. 321). What is more, unlike the case of VERs, there is no effective time limit on how long Article xix safeguards may remain in force; as noted above, VERs generally do have such a limit at the end of which they either expire or must be renegotiated. Finally, no country claiming injury under Article xix has ever had its claim challenged. In any practical as opposed to a purely rhetorical sense, therefore, the charge of coercion is specious: the exporting industry typically gets a better deal under VERs than it would under the legally prescribed, multilateral alternative (Hindley 1980; see also Ono 1991).

The charge of discrimination is somewhat more complex. That these measures are discriminatory cannot be questioned; it is the very reason they are invoked. The real issue, however, is whether VERs or the legally permissible alternative, again Article xix under the GATT, do more collateral damage to the trade regime. And it is not obvious that Article xix should be preferred on those grounds. Article xix permits alteration or suspension of past tariff concessions in a non-discriminatory manner provided that interested parties are consulted. But it is clumsy. Precisely because of the necessity to apply it in a non-discriminatory manner, the invocation of Article xix is likely to affect innocent bystanders adversely—bystanders who are not causing injury to domestic producers in the initiating country. Thus, it may require widespread and lengthy renegotiation or even trigger retaliatory suspension of past concessions.

Finally, to retort that Article xix action, nevertheless, is to be preferred on principle because that is what the GATT calls for while VERs are 'GATT-illegal', simply will not do. It is a perfect example of what Robert

Aliber in another context sardonically described as 'sacrificing the state to save the constitution' (Aliber 1986, p. 120). No rational government can be expected to follow that precept when well-established and apparently acceptable alternatives are available. Moreover, the term 'illegal' is itself problematical in this context. The trade regime is at least as much a political institution as it is a set of legal prescriptions. As such, the intersubjective appraisal by states of one another's actions based on the normative understandings among them count at least as much as legally prescribed rules and procedures. And even in strictly legal terms, Hindley makes an excellent point in dismissing criticisms of VERs on the grounds that they violate the law: 'A much better analogy is the out-of-court settlement of civil legal actions, a procedure whose outcome is constrained by the law, but which both parties to the dispute expect will leave them better-off than undergoing the expenses of the full judicial process. No legal system will collapse as a result of such agreements (on the contrary, if there were no such agreements collapse would be very much more likely)' (Hindley 1980, pp. 331–2).

Let me summarise what has been said thus far. The multilateral trade regime has changed in many ways over the course of the post-war era as is only to be expected. Among those changes are the invention and deployment of mechanisms, which in a literal or formal sense may well be 'illegal' within the GATT. Nonetheless, I have resisted the notion that these mechanisms demonstrate a resurgence of protectionism. Of course countries cheat: they always have; they always will; and their propensity to cheat is likely to be higher in hard times. But there are sound reasons to reject the 'new protectionism' paradigm. First of all, it views the trade regime from a free-trade baseline. But that view is historically inaccurate and fundamentally distorts the nature of the post-war institutional compromise. Second, it has to dismiss as anomalies the most interesting and widespread innovations in the international trade regime, innovations that seem reasonably consistent with the actual shape of the post-war institutional compromise. Third, those who subscribe to the 'new protectionism' paradigm repeatedly expect governments to follow prescribed collective procedures even when those procedures cannot possibly yield collectively desired outcomes. Not surprisingly, governments rarely oblige. Fourth and finally, condemning all such practices with the single opprobrium of 'protectionism' makes it impossible to identify those specific practices, such as negotiating market shares under 'managed trade' arrangements, which do violate and corrode not only the letter but also the spirit of the post-war institutional compromise, and which should, therefore, be controlled.

2. Aggressive unilateralism

No matter what the economic inefficiencies and bureaucratic inanities of the 'new protectionism' may be, then, within the embedded-liberalism framework many of its instruments appear relatively benign and, indeed, are part and parcel of the techniques by which the multilateral trade regime functions. But can the same be claimed for the alleged 'aggressive unilateralism' (Bhagwati & Patrick (eds) 1990) in recent US trade policy? If inter-war bilateralism was the evil that energised the creation of the post-war multilateral trade regime, then unilateralism must be even more noxious.

The chief culprit here, of course, is the amended Section 301 of US trade legislation (Omnibus Trade and Competitiveness Act of 1988), especially the so-called Super 301. Under this provision the United States asserts the right to act as accuser, judge and jury in assessing unfair trading practices by others, and to impose punishment on those it finds guilty. It is clearly GATT-illegal, even under the creative and sophisticated standards of 'justified disobedience' that Robert Hudec has devised (1990). And the potential for deleterious and even destructive consequences for the international trading order is high.

It is worth examining the reasons for Super 301, however, before speculating about its adverse impact. Three stand out. One is the macroeconomic policies of the first Reagan administration, which produced record budget and trade deficits. Super 301 is no cure for that problem, as the Congress should have known if it did not. In any case, thus far the provision has not been invoked by the United States towards that end.

A second reason is precisely the fact that most instruments of the 'new protectionism' have had such a minimal impact. Super 301 imposes more severe constraints on the discretion of the executive branch than did its predecessors because in the past it was executive-branch discretion that buffered protectionist demands. Now, it has been an article of faith among students of trade policy that the executive branch is more 'enlightened' than the Congress in these matters. But keep in mind that it was Congress that mandated executive-branch discretion in the first place, thereby giving itself the opportunity to be responsive to constituency demands while at the same time avoiding serious damage to the international trade regime. By the mid-1980s Congress felt that the executive branch had become too passive.[7] Thus, it altered the strategic balance between the two branches.

---

7   According to former ITC chair Paul Stern, even during the record-breaking trade deficits under the Reagan administration, 'less than 1 percent of total U.S. imports were actually challenged as unfair under U.S. laws. The volume of U.S. imports affected by anti-dumping and countervailing duty investigations as a percentage of total imports amounted to only 0.2 percent in 1987, 0.4 percent in 1988, and 0.2 percent during the first half of 1989. Even in the cases where the

The third reason for Super 301 can be put simply: Japan. Even though the amendment is expressed in universalistic language and three 'unfair' traders were identified in its first year of operation, it would never have been adopted were it not for Japan.[8] Specifically, the provision is aimed at removing Japanese policies and practices which the United States claims have kept the Japanese domestic market relatively sheltered against foreign competition and thereby contributed to the seemingly permanent $40–$50 billion annual bilateral trade imbalance in favour of Japan.

I enter this realm with great trepidation for it is utterly treacherous terrain for the uninitiated. Experts argue vehemently about even the most basic of facts: for instance, is Japan's level of manufactured imports substantially below what would be expected of a country its size and level of industrialisation, or does it fall within the margin of error?[9] And the US Congress has never been known to exhibit great skill in economic analysis, and surely had some cause/effect relations and orders of magnitude wrong.

In these infelicitous circumstances, the safest move for me is to take refuge once again in the embedded-liberalism compromise. According to Richard Cooper, in neo-classical theory intra-industry trade is viewed as less socially profitable than inter-industry trade, all other things being equal (Cooper 1980, especially pp. 75–6). And yet governments in successive GATT rounds have encouraged the liberalisation precisely of intra-industry rather than inter-industry trade. The result has been that specialisation is achieved not by countries abandoning whole industrial sectors, but 'mainly by individual firms narrowing their product lines' (Blackhurst et al. 1977, p. 11). There are, of course, straightforward economic reasons why intra-industry trade should have grown throughout the post-war era having to do with similarity of production structures and the existence of scale economies among the major capitalist countries. But there are also strong political reasons why the governments of those countries would have wanted to encourage such trade among themselves. As I have argued at greater length elsewhere, the domestic social and political adjustment

---

U.S. International Trade Commission (ITC) and Department of Commerce (DOC) made affirmative determinations, the average dumping duty applied in 1987 on dumped or subsidized goods was 1.2 percent. In 1988, the average was 3.7 percent; in the first half of 1989, the figure was 1.4 percent' (Stern 1990, pp. 192–3).

8 Brazil and India were named in the initial US review largely because they led the Third World group in the Uruguay Round that opposed US initiatives to liberalise the services. Brazil has since been dropped from the list.

9 The 'damn right it's too low' end of the spectrum is occupied by the so-called revisionists, Chalmers Johnson, Clyde Prestowitz, Karel van Wolferen and James Fallows (see Fallows et al. 1990; Johnson 1988b). For extensive empirical evidence which concludes cautiously that 'yes, on the whole and to date, that tendency exists' see Lincoln (1990a). The margin-of-error position is taken by Saxonhouse (1983) and Leamer (1988).

costs of intra-industry trade are lower, the international vulnerabilities are fewer, and yet all the while it offers gains from trade. In a word, intra-industry trade is more compatible than inter-industry trade with the objectives of liberalising internationally while safeguarding domestic stability—the essence of the embedded-liberalism framework (Ruggie 1982).

This puts 'the Japan problem' in a somewhat clearer light. As is documented in Lincoln's recent and detailed empirical study, Japan imports least precisely in those areas in which it exports most, so that its level of intra-industry trade is at or near the bottom in virtually every industrial sector (Lincoln 1990a). Moreover, granted that Japan is resource-poor and therefore needs to import raw materials, it nevertheless exhibits a much stronger preference than any other resource-poor industrialised country for entirely unprocessed or the simplest refined forms of raw materials imports. And on the manufactured exports side, Japan exhibits a far higher level of export concentration in selected high value-added products than its competitors. Finally, while the lowering of formal trade barriers according to both theory and the historical experiences of other industrialised countries should have led to the substantial erosion of this pattern, evidence suggests that the disparities between Japan and the rest in some instances actually have widened over time (Lincoln 1990a).[10]

Leave aside for the moment the questions of *why* Japan exhibits this pattern of 'unequal trade' and *how* it is maintained. It is indisputable that, at least in *this* sense, 'Japan is a great economic power that does not play by the same rules as the other great economic powers' (Krugman 1990a, p. 44). Moreover, whatever its cause, Japan's trade posture poses fundamental *political* problems for other governments: 'The fact that intra-industry trade has become a normative pattern of behavior for other countries means that Japan's failure to conform imposes adjustment costs on the industries of other countries that they do not expect to bear' (Lincoln 1990a, p. 60). And, of course, it also imposes adjustment costs on the governments concerned as they struggle to accommodate the displaced industries—or face, in van Wolferen's words, 'a gradual loss of industrial capacity' in key sectors of their economies (1986–87, p. 288).

To call this 'protectionism' on the part of Japan, however, gives too much credit to the concept and not enough to Japan. It is not a matter of Japan 'cheating' on the formal GATT rules. Japan's tariffs are low, its quotas are few, and its outright rule violations are no more frequent than those of other industrialised countries. The structure of Japan's trade is

---

[10] Peter Drucker has described Japan's posture less generously as a form of adversarial trade. 'In adversarial trade the seller's goods displace the goods produced by the manufacturers of the buying country without any compensating purchases from that country' (1986). The structure of Japan's trade in this regard contrasts starkly with Germany's, another heavily export-dependent economy. The comparison may shed light on the argument, and thus deserves systematic study by economists.

simply, and importantly, different from the established norm around which the international trade regime revolves.

This difference, in turn, poses a fundamental dilemma for all other members of the trade regime, which the United States has sought to resolve in part by means of Super 301: how does one overcome a structural asymmetry by institutional means that require symmetrical quid pro quos? The long and desultory experience with US–Soviet conventional force reduction talks in Europe suggests that it cannot be done; those negotiations succeeded only after the Soviets unilaterally made major asymmetrical concessions (before the Soviet empire collapsed altogether). Similarly, there simply are no GATT means available to get from 'here to there' on the asymmetrical structure of Japan's foreign trade, given the GATT norm of reciprocity.[11] Super 301, then, may be seen as an attempt by the United States to evolve clumsily and, as always, inconsistently a tit-for-tat strategy intended to induce the structure of Japanese trade into greater harmonisation with its trading partners (see Axelrod 1984).

In the event, Japan was not moved to retaliate against the United States when targeted by Super 301, or even to bring action against the United States within the GATT. Though Japan refused to negotiate formally under Super 301, it sought to defuse the issue by reaching several accords with the United States under the framework of a so-called Structural Impediments Initiative. Even more strikingly, a major Japanese newspaper poll reported that 85.9 per cent of respondents in part, or fully, favoured acceptance of US demands![12]

The real danger of Super 301 is that it may prove politically difficult to contain its use to these strategic purposes, that it will become a sledgehammer rather than Carla Hills' crowbar. But surely the first steps in avoiding that possibility are to understand the strategic purposes the leg-

---

11 In opposition to Super 301, Bhagwati points out that '[o]bjectionable trade practices not in violation of GATT's rules [e.g., structural impediments] must be dealt with by negotiating what are called new 'disciplines', where acceptance of a new obligation by one country [e.g., Japan] must be paid for by an equal concession from the other' [e.g., the United States] (Bhagwati 1989a, pp. D2). But politically, that's not a solution; it is a restatement of the problem.

12 A *Nihon Keizai* poll (*Los Angeles Times* 1990) reported: '[T]he process of working out the [Structural Impediments Initiative] accord has uncovered an astonishing degree of sympathy for the United States here [in Tokyo] and support for its advocacy of a more open Japanese economic system' (p. D2). In addition to the views expressed in the public opinion poll, editorials in Japanese newspapers 'were overwhelmingly for reform' (p. D2). The reason is fairly straightforward: the same practices that have kept imports out have kept domestic prices high. A joint survey by the US and Japanese governments confirmed in 1989 that 84 of 122 products surveyed were on the average 41.7 per cent more expensive in Japan than in the United States. 'Only in the case of consumer electronic products, where U.S. manufacturers have dropped out of competition, were prices lower in Japan' (*Los Angeles Times* 1989).

islation is intended to address, and then to devise viable multilateral measures that alleviate its dangers.[13] Neither end is well served by the free-trade/protectionism rhetoric that has tended to frame criticism of Super 301 to date.[14]

3. Parametric change

Far from representing an extreme and limiting case, the resort to strategic unilateralism, on the contrary, may be a sign of things to come—*not* because countries are becoming more protectionist, but because parametric changes in the world economy increasingly are eroding the efficacy of the available multilateral arrangements. Three such changes pose particularly difficult challenges to the trade regime: the growing significance of domestic structures as an international trade issue; the growing magnitude of the services which are not easily captured by existing conceptual or institutional templates; and the process of globalisation, which makes past means of compensating for economic openness increasingly irrelevant.

Domestic structures

One of the curious and long-forgotten features of the post-war international economic regimes is that their terms of reference were drafted in such a way as to accommodate the possible membership of state-trading nations—specifically the Soviet Union. That feat was achieved, however, by simply requiring state-trading enterprises in their external purchases and sales to behave like private economic units: 'solely in accordance with commercial considerations', according to Article xvii of the GATT— which is to say, in response to factors such as price, quality, transportation costs, and other terms of purchase or sale.[15] Thus, the potential

---

[13] The ultimate compatibility between unilateral and multilateral outcomes would not be unprecedented. The original Section 301 of the Trade Act of 1974 also contained important elements of unilateralism. At the same time, it 'encouraged the United States to make greater use of the GATT dispute settlement process...[O]f the sixteen GATT complaints filed by the United States between 1975 and 1985, eleven complaints arose out of section 301 investigations' (Bliss 1987, p. 45). On the interplay between unilateral and multilateral measures during the Reagan administration, see Lincoln (1990a, ch. 6) and Prestowitz Jr (1988).

[14] A notable exception is Hudec (1990). Hudec offers the provocative and potentially productive suggestion that the United States' trading partners hold it accountable to its own (new 301) standards, in the attempt to increase the demand all around for more collectively legitimated mechanisms.

[15] The words were taken almost verbatim from the ITO Charter, which the Soviets had had a hand in drafting (see Viner 1947; Feis 1947). For the corresponding assumptions on the monetary side, see Mikesell (1947).

international incompatibility of domestic structures was assumed away. And the post-war economic regimes were designed to remove or lower point-of-entry barriers such as quotas, tariffs, and various forms of (currency) exchange restrictions, as well as deliberate acts of cheating such as dumping. Discriminatory barriers were to be removed altogether, and the obligation to move towards greater openness in the rest was broadly defined by what I have called the embedded-liberalism compromise.

What has happened as point-of-entry barriers have been progressively lowered or eliminated, however, is that the impact of domestic institutional arrangements on the volume and structure of international economic transactions has become more salient. In some measure the problem has always existed. Even the US and the West European economies have always differed in terms of their precise balance and form of state–society relations. But those institutional differences gave none of them a permanent competitive advantage *vis-à-vis* the others and thus posed no threat to the overall economic relationship among them. Besides, the differences have decreased over time. Agricultural subsidies have become more divisive in recent years. But here the United States finds itself in the odd position of having obtained a GATT waiver long ago to exempt its own extensive domestic price support programmes and now having to suffer the consequences of the EC's common agricultural policy. In any case, a quid pro quo deal that would also provide some relief to European and American consumers, as well as to commodity-exporting countries, may yet be achieved in the current GATT round.

The problem case on today's agenda is Japan. Japan's domestic structures are widely perceived to be different from those prevailing in other advanced capitalist countries: its labour markets, capital markets, production arrangements, and distribution systems, to name but a few. The experts disagree sharply and deeply on whether these differences are due to cultural, bureaucratic, or electoral factors. And there are disagreements on whether the differences are declining, as liberal economists tend to believe, or are more permanent features of Japanese society. Without waiting for expert consensus on the final truth of the matter, policy-makers in the other capitalist countries have come to hold the view that these differences give Japan unfair trade advantages. In the United States, politicians feel additionally disadvantaged by the differential structure of domestic interest aggregation, which is far more transparent in the United States and thus puts them constantly on the spot, and by the differential access to the two political systems enjoyed by foreign lobbyists and interest groups. To the extent that Japan comes to serve as a model for the newly industrialising countries in Asia–Pacific and elsewhere, for China, and even for the former East European socialist countries and the Soviet Union, this problem would multiply manifold.

But the highly charged case of Japan—with its Japan-bashers in one corner and the Chrysanthemum Club in the other—merely masks a more fundamental problem that would be with us even if Japan were not. Now that formal trade barriers have been reduced to insignificant levels, domestic policies and practices that shape the structure of foreign trade *ipso facto* are taking centre stage in the international trade regime. And if they diverge systematically and substantially among countries, an international political problem exists. As it stands, however, the GATT regime is designed 'to maintain a balance of [external] concessions and obligations, not to restructure nations' (Kalla 1986, p. 95). Yet harmonising the international effects of divergent domestic economic structures is what the international trade game increasingly is about. Once again, there are no easy multilateral means to get from here to there. Unless such means can be devised, unilateral ways of trying to resolve the problem are inevitable.

Tangible invisibles

What is called trade in services used to be the 'invisibles' appendage to merchandise trade: shipping, insurance, and the like, as well as tourism. Today the list is longer, the magnitude much higher and services are 'traded' in their own right. In addition to all of the old items, they now include information services, professional and business services, personal services, construction, consultancy and cultural services (see Kakabadse 1987, ch. 1). Their magnitude has reached somewhere between one-fifth and one-quarter of total world trade, although because of definitional and statistical anomalies the balance of world services imports and exports routinely is off by as much as $100 billion per annum (Shelp 1986–87). The growth in traded services is accounted for by a combination of factors: technological developments, especially the informatics revolution; domestic deregulation, particularly of capital markets and the telecommunications sector; and the fact that both manufactured products and primary commodities embody ever greater services inputs, ranging from data processing to bioengineering.

The institutional problem posed by this increase in traded services is not quantitative, however, but qualitative. The GATT was designed for merchandise trade: tangible manufactured products and commodities that are exported and imported across national borders. Invisibles were basically left uncovered by the GATT; the only service explicitly mentioned in its articles of agreement is trade in motion pictures—the GATT's Hollywood clause.

Traded services have been a central concern of the current GATT round. At the time of writing, agreement remains elusive; and throughout the negotiations to date, all of the major players have shifted their positions on various occasions, thus making specific predictions difficult. Preliminary indications are, however, that a services agreement will mark only the end of the beginning of a very difficult chapter in trade diplomacy. At best, it likely would bring into the conventional GATT framework *that portion* of services *which fits* the conventional trade framework (see *The Economist* 1990a; Stokes 1990a; Bhagwati 1991b; *The Economist* 1991b). But that portion is relatively small compared to a whole that cannot yet even be adequately defined. And a number of disputatious issues lurk beyond. It is these that concern me here.

First of all, because the concept of services has no well-established place in economic theory, its definition has tended to be ad hoc and arbitrary: the residual activity not included in agriculture, mining and manufacturing. Attempts to define services more theoretically have focused on the fact that they are non-storable and, therefore, require simultaneity of provision and use. But this insight has simply generated endless lists that can be endlessly argued about rather than a finite and universally agreed upon set (see Shelp 1986–87; Berg 1987; Riddle 1986; Kakabadse 1987; Giarini (ed.) 1987; Bhagwati 1987). With tongue only half in cheek, *The Economist* has proposed defining services as 'Things which can be bought and sold but which you cannot drop on your foot' (1985). But architectural plans, computer disks and magnetic tapes, not to mention Big Macs in Moscow and Budapest, in fact, can be dropped on one's foot. What this ambiguity means is that, unlike the case of merchandise trade, in traded services the very definition of the concept itself remains subject to strategic behaviour by governments. There is no reason to expect that political contesting over definitions will cease once a GATT services agreement is reached.

Second, governments regulate their domestic service industries more rigorously than most other economic activities (Shelp 1986–87; Berg 1987). Entry into many services such as law, medicine and accounting is strictly licensed; governments frequently reserve the right to approve the charges of utilities which in many places still include transportation and telecommunication; financial institutions, including banks, insurance firms and securities traders, are subject to prudential supervision; and in many countries the state still owns outright certain service industries. Most of these regulatory objectives and instruments were not designed with trade in mind, but under a GATT services agreement they potentially could become targeted as illegitimate, non-tariff barriers. The probability of such conflicts arising is even higher if the service is provided, not on the spot, but via telecommunications transmissions—which arguably represent more of cross-border transaction. The principles of national treatment, non-discrimination and transparency that a services agreement presumably would include might alleviate some of these difficulties. But the list of exceptions that governments will insist on is certain to be long and highly asymmetrical across countries, thus providing ample scope for international trade disputes.

Third, many of the providers of services themselves are undergoing profound and rapid redefinition, posing additional conceptual and regulatory puzzles for governments (*The Economist* 1990b, p. 33). Banks trade stocks; securities firms retail checking accounts; and telephone companies issue general-purpose, revolving credit cards. Thus, the classical distinctions among financial institutions, and between financial institutions and the informatics sector have become quite blurred, 'and the consequent increase in competitive inequities has given an international dimension to what has traditionally been a domestic concern' (*The Economist* 1990b, p. 12; see also *The Economist* 1990c).

Fourth and finally, it turns out, in any case, that relatively few such services are actually 'traded' in the sense we normally understand that term (Bhagwati 1987; Riddle 1986, especially ch. 9). This problem itself comes in several parts. Insofar as the defining characteristic of the provision of services is that production and consumption need to take place at the same time and in the same place, in many instances the ability to provide services depends on the establishment of local affiliates. To that extent, however, trade in services at a minimum implies a right of establishment, and at the limit it becomes indistinguishable from foreign investment. Neither constitutes trade. And both are more intrusive.

But assume for the sake of the discussion that this first part of the problem is satisfactorily resolved. A related question immediately arises: access of what or whom? In merchandise trade, the factors of production and the consumer stand still while the finished product moves. Ball-bearings and bananas cross frontiers, from producer to consumer, passing through customs along the way. In traded services, it is more likely that the factors of production do the moving while the product is fixed by location. To that extent, trade in services amounts to provider-mobility across borders (Bhagwati 1987). No economic theory explains, however, why mobile factors of production should include US banks providing services in South Korea, for example, but not South Korean construction workers offering their services in the United States.

As is obvious from the ongoing Uruguay Round, there is petty protectionism aplenty to be found in the services negotiations—not the least of which is on the part of the United States, which foisted the negotiations on its reluctant GATT partners in the first place. But even if that were not so, the underlying structural issues in traded services are so difficult that serious political conflicts will emerge no matter what. And some of these conflicts will have little enough to do with 'trade' as we traditionally understand it, let alone 'free trade' or 'protectionism'. A new and different conceptual framework is necessary, therefore, before significant progress in the institutional realm can be expected.

Moreover, once again conflict focused on the Asia–Pacific area may be higher than elsewhere in the industrialised world. Regulatory environments in general are more opaque there, thus inviting the imputation of worst-case motivations. Moreover, if past experience from direct foreign investment and patent protection is any guide, then in Japan at any rate such new institutional mechanisms as the right of establishment are likely to prove extremely elusive in practice, thereby inviting external pressure if not retaliatory measures. Using the precedent of direct foreign investment is not encouraging: 'Compared with Japan, no other industrialized country has so adamantly denied multinational corporations access to domestic markets' (Encarnation & Mason 1990). As for patent protection, the most egregious case offered up by Japan is the integrated circuit. Texas Instruments, its inventor, applied for a patent in Japan on 6 February 1960; it was granted effective 30 October 1989! By then Japanese firms accounted for 90 per cent of all sales in Japan, and 40 per cent of the market worldwide. In memory chips, Japan by 1989 accounted for 70 per cent of the one-megabit market world-wide, and over 90 per cent the the four-megabit, the most advanced memory chip in production (Hayes 1989; Sanger 1990a).

Globalisation

A third core institutional assumption of the post-war economic regimes was the notion that international economic transactions take place at arms length between distinct and disjoint national economic units. Its efficacy has been severely challenged in recent years by the phenomenon of globalisation.

Much has been written about globalisation, and nearly as much has been dismissed as 'globaloney'. Milton Friedman, as is his wont, has put the negative case most categorically: 'The world is less internationalized in any immediate, relevant, pertinent sense today than it was in 1913 or in 1929' (Friedman 1989). Friedman contends that the divergence between the price of the same good in different countries that became distinctly pronounced after the Great Depression has remained in place despite steadily decreasing transportation costs, thereby 'demonstrating vividly how powerful and effective government intervention has been in rendering the law of one price far less applicable after 1931 than it was before' (1989, p. 10).[16]

Be that as it may, a truly remarkable expansion of the 'borderless economy' (Ohmae 1990) has occurred in the increasingly extensive, diverse, and denationalised institutional links that have been forged among firms and within markets across the globe. Illustrating the poverty of conventional concepts, this phenomenon typically is described as 'offshore' production and 'offshore' markets, as if they existed in some ethereal space waiting to be reconceived by the economic equivalent of relativity.

The rapid growth in trade among the industrialised countries from the 1960s on was marked, as we noted above, by intra-industry specialisation, whereby trade took the form of simultaneous increases in exports and

---

16 Friedman also adds that immigration has slowed to a trickle compared to the nineteenth century. In a controversial paper published some years ago, Kenneth Waltz advanced an argument very similar to Friedman's, using as his measures of internationalisation (i) the size of the external sector of the major economic powers relative to their domestic economies, and (ii) the degree of inter-sectoral specialisation reflected in their trade patterns (Waltz 1970).

imports within the same industrial sector. A closely related phenomenon has been the growth of intra-firm trade, or the rise of 'the global factory' (Grunwald & Flamm 1985). Led initially by the automobile and consumer electronics sectors, components production by multinational enterprises has become fragmented across a vast array of countries, exploiting the shifting advantages of different production locales. The resultant trade in intermediate products is largely intra-firm trade or at least trade among related parties. As is the case with traded services, intra-firm trade does not exist in conventional economic theory, hence no uniform and universal statistics on it have been collected. But the available evidence on US manufactured imports suggests that somewhere around half originate with wholly owned foreign affiliates or related parties abroad; that this kind of trade is growing more rapidly than the standard stuff; and that it is less sensitive to such macroeconomic factors as exchange rates (see Little 1987; Helleiner 1981).

International financial markets are even more closely linked and their magnitude is even more impressive. Total world trade amounts to some $3 trillion a year. International capital markets turn over at least $75 trillion, and foreign exchange transactions now exceed $100 trillion. Moreover, whereas capital movements historically reflected business decisions to finance trade or to establish production facilities abroad, 'it seems apparent that the dominant proportion of the investment funds actually in movement internationally today reflects instead decisions concerning portfolio holdings...shifts among holdings of various kinds of intangible assets' (Roosa 1982, p. 4). In addition, securities firms are establishing branches in the world's major financial centres (Spero 1988–89). As a result, since 1980 foreign equity trading in the United States has increased at an annual rate of 19 per cent to reach $384 billion by 1988, and US purchases of foreign equities rose 30 per cent per annum to reach a total of some $151 billion (Wayne 1989). And numerous other financial instruments that did not exist only a decade ago are now traded internationally in rapidly expanding volumes.

The 'global office' is a more recent and still more modest phenomenon, to date consisting largely of firms moving certain routine 'back office' tasks offshore. Thus, Citibank does some of its financial data processing in Jamaica, American Airlines processes ticket stubs in Barbados and the Dominican Republic, while New York Life processes claims and McGraw Hill magazine subscription renewals in Ireland (Lohr 1988).

Finally, this globalised segment of world production, trade, and services is becoming progressively denationalised not merely by location but also institutionally. Cross-investment and other forms of inter-corporate alliances are becoming increasingly common, thereby blurring the distinction between domestic and foreign producers and products (Reich 1991a, especially Pt 2).

For the purposes of this discussion, two international political consequences of globalisation merit particular attention. The first concerns the predicament globalisation has put governments in. Government policies may have made possible the emergence of this offshore world in the first place, through favourable tariff provisions and the liberalisation of capital markets, for example. But globalisation, in turn, has created numerous policy problems for which governments have proved unable to devise effective responses.

Globalisation constrains the ability of governments to pursue independent macroeconomic policies; even Japan is reported to have become afflicted by this problem (Sterngold 1990a, 1990b). Moreover, as a result of globalisation certain aspects of trade policy have become virtually metaphysical in character—as when the US International Trade Commission finds itself confronted with anti-dumping charges brought by a Japanese firm producing typewriters in the United States against an American firm importing typewriters into the United States from its offshore facilities in Singapore and Indonesia![17] At the very least, as the multinationality of firms has increased, governments have become conflicted not simply by the traditional import/export-dependent industry preferences, but also by newer demands for 'strategic trade policy'— demands for government action to secure access to foreign markets and to vindicate other norms of fairness in international trade under threat of home-country retaliation for failure to comply.[18] On the finance side, the global offshore world exists largely in a regulatory void, which has even some of its promoters concerned: 'national systems of supervision and regulation—to say nothing of tax and accounting policies—that were created many years ago were not designed for a marketplace of worldwide dimensions in which firms with differing charters and national

---

17 The case involves Brothers Industries Ltd, a Japanese concern assembling typewriters in Bartlett, Tennessee, and Smith Corona, the US concern doing the same offshore. Adding another element of globalisation, Smith Corona is owned 48 per cent by Hanson PLC, a British group (Reich 1991b; Sanger 1991). Sanger's story also points out that Chrysler inadvertently may have filed an ITC claim against *itself* when it charged Japanese firms with dumping minivans in the US market—one of the vehicles covered by the definition is made for Chrysler by Mitsubishi. The Brothers Industries request subsequently was denied, the firm not being enough of a domestic producer to claim injury.

18 Helen Milner's case studies of selected US firms in the 1920s and 1970s, and a cross-sectional comparison of US and French firms today suggest that the more extensive the multinationality of firms becomes, the less likely they are to demand protection and the more likely they are to resist it, even if their industry is under pressure from import competition. At the same time, she points out that these firms may increase demands for 'strategic trade policy'. Some of the most advanced industrial sectors, including semiconductors, commercial aircraft and telecommunications, exhibit this pattern (Milner 1988; Milner & Yoffie 1989; Yoffie & Milner 1989).

origins compete head-to-head with each other around the clock and around the world' (Corrigan 1987, p. 2; see also Ohmae 1990; and Spero 1988–89).[19] And novel financial instruments, which are designed to reduce or diversify risks for individual firms and investors, at the same time can increase the system-wide transmission of destabilising factors such as stockmarket crashes.[20]

In the absence of a solution to the eroding efficacy of standard national policy instruments through more effective international policy coordination, for example (of which there is as yet little sign), we can expect governments to try to find more unconventional ways to cushion their domestic economies from unexpected shifts and swings in currency values and import levels. Indeed, the liberalisation of capital markets is central to any explanation of the recent increase in the 'new protectionism' in trade (Bhagwati 1988, p. 71). But cross-border corporate ties and market forces now are undermining the efficacy of that well-established domestic compensatory move as well.

Orthodox economists welcome this development on the assumption that it will increase economic efficiency while decreasing government intervention. In point of fact, however, it may have just the opposite effect. If the relatively benign option of the 'new protectionism' ceases to provide effective relief, then there is no telling what measures governments might turn to in exasperation. Such a move would not be 'correct' or 'efficient' by the standards of economic theory, but governments in the industrialised countries are elected by their constituents, not by the keepers of the economic faith. The very success of uncompensated liberalisation—or disembedded liberalism, if you will—could generate precisely the kind of economic nationalism that embedded liberalism was designed and was able to contain.

There is a particular Japan/Asia–Pacific angle to this story as well. Not surprisingly, it concerns whether Japan's pattern of globalisation conforms to the general pattern or is distinct and possibly detrimental to the multilateral trading system as a whole. The basis for this concern is Japan's rapidly expanding foreign investment in the East and Southeast Asian region, reflecting the need to source offshore as a result of the appreciation of the yen and rising domestic labour costs. Indeed, since the Plaza Agreement of 1985 realigning the yen and the dollar, that investment has risen from less than $2 billion per annum to nearly $8 billion projected for

---

[19] Steps have been taken to coordinate the supervision of international banking, but international securities trading, and the international banking and securities clearance and settlements systems are weak and vulnerable.

[20] Empirical studies of the 1987 stockmarket crash find, however, that direct international linkages, that is, cross-border equity investment, do not explain the worldwide decline in equities markets; what was transmitted was panic, and cross-border investment is not necessary for that to have occurred (Bennett & Kelleher 1988; Aderhold et al. 1988).

1990 (Sterngold 1990c; Sanger 1990b); and Japanese manufactured imports from the region increased by some 200 per cent from 1985 to 1988 (*The Economist* 1990d).

There is a benign reading of where this could lead to, and one not so benign. In the benign variant, Japan's investments would contribute to the industrialisation of the entire area and lead to its active participation in the multilateral trading system. In the less benign variant, Japan merely expands its own industrial structure over a more broadly based manufacturing platform, stretching from South Korea to Singapore. The home-country sourcing preference that Japanese multinationals have exhibited to date would remain in place, and Japan's imbalance in intra-industry trade with the rest of the industrial world would continue unabated. As one study of this phenomenon has concluded, Japanese firms 'are tightly controlled by the respective parent company, procure their equipment mainly in Japan and own and operate mainly Japanese machinery' (Kreinin 1988, pp. 540–1).[21] If this less benign scenario were to materialise, the European Community would likely respond by turning more decisively inward and the United States by turning its bilateral free-trade areas into more airtight trading blocs.

4. Conclusion

When US policy-makers sat down with their foreign, largely British, counterparts to negotiate the post-war economic regimes, the practices they sought most to banish from the repertoire of international trade relations were various beggar-thy-neighbour policies—and for the United States, British imperial preferences—together with exclusive currency blocs and other restrictive practices in the monetary realm. Put positively, they sought to institute the principle of economic openness. A return to pre-World War I *laissez-faire* liberalism was not a viable solution, however, no matter how much the New York banking community and some export-oriented industries agitated for it, because between the two wars governments throughout the industrialised world had become subject to new domestic political demands and constraints. Thus, the post-war economic regimes were designed to achieve progressive liberalisation internationally without, however, subordinating the domestic economy to the

---

21 Kreinin's work is a comparative study of procurement practices by Japanese, European and US multinationals in Australia. Japanese multinationals operating in the United States imported over $71 billion worth of goods into the United States in 1987, overwhelmingly from Japan, while exporting $21 billion—the difference being roughly equivalent to the size of the US trade deficit with Japan that year (Lehner & Murray 1990). Of course, it is possible that Japanese firms simply have not yet matured as transnationals, and that over time this pattern will change—an argument made by Bhagwati (1991a, pp. 30–2).

strictures of external parity; and to allow for and even facilitate governmental intervention in the domestic economy, without, however, triggering the mutually destructive consequences of inter-war practices.

For what they were designed to achieve, these regimes have performed remarkably well. They have contributed to an expansion of international trade and capital flows that is historically unprecedented in its magnitude and duration. They have withstood the most severe economic dislocations the world has experienced since the Great Depression. They have accommodated and even facilitated the emergence of new entrants such as Japan and the Asian newly industrialised countries, whose pace of evolution from relatively poor countries to newly and even leading industrialised countries also is unprecedented in recent history. Lastly, the institutional adaptations invented by countries by and large have been designed not to gain unacceptable unilateral advantage but, at one and the same time, to respond more effectively to the changing international economic environment without abandoning the fundamental normative understandings that animated the regimes in the first place.

Yet still the trade regime is in trouble today. In part the trouble is rhetorical in origin, and that part ought to be solvable without undue difficulty. It concerns the irrelevance of much of free-trade discourse in deciphering the meaning of the so-called new protectionism. Practices that arguably fall within the *actual* post-war institutional compromise, which I have termed embedded liberalism, must be distinguished from instances of illiberal protectionism if total obfuscation and rancorous debate is not to destroy what is left of the trade regime. Their difference lies, as suggested above, in their intent and result. To claim that governments have tried to achieve effective protection via VERs and similar instruments makes it necessary to assume that they are either stupid, or perverse, or both—so bad a job would they have done for so extended a period of time. The instruments of 'managed trade', on the other hand, which are designed to fix or allocate market shares, are clearly violations not only of the letter but of the spirit of post-war norms and, therefore, should be resisted and undone.

A second part of the problem is more institutional in character and also more difficult to solve. The major institutional changes that have taken place in the domain of trade have pushed domestic economic structures to centre stage. That is true of the decline of formal trade barriers, the growth in global service transactions, and the phenomenon of globalisation itself. But GATT was designed to achieve a balance of *external* rights and obligations, not to achieve *internal* restructuring. Moreover, it is in any case impossible to achieve symmetrical results by symmetrical means from asymmetrical starting points. Now, no one can oppose the recommendation that GATT be strengthened. But in the meantime, governments can be forgiven if they do not stand by and watch entire industrial sectors collapse while negotiations go forwards. Moreover, it makes as much if not more sense, in the light of our discussion also to strengthen the policy harmonisation roles of the OECD. Much as in the arms-control field, greater transparency would result on which mutual and balanced confidence measures could be built, leading ultimately to more serious negotiations on a multilateral basis concerning the adverse external effects of asymmetries in domestic structures.

A third part of the problem is fundamentally intellectual in character, and it may be the most difficult to resolve. The construction of the post-war regimes and their operation for many years was sustained by a broad, quasi-Keynesian consensus on what made the public economy tick (Ikenberry 1992). That consensus, of course, has long since been shattered, and none has yet taken its place. No comprehensive and systematic reconstruction of the post-war economic regimes is conceivable without such a consensus.

But even partial reform will require major intellectual stretching by the economics profession. Not being trained as an economist, my characterisation of what is needed perforce is unschooled and may be off the mark. It seems to me, though, that to understand institutional change in the global economy ultimately will require a model of the global economy that treats it as an entity in its own right: a non-territorial, decentred yet singular space-of-flows, which exists alongside the various national spaces-of-places that we call national economies. These conventional spaces-of-places will continue to engage in 'external' economic relations with one another, which we will continue to call trade, foreign investment, and the like, and which are more or less effectively 'constrained' by the state. In the model of the global non-territorial space-of-flows, however, which needs to complement the national-economies model, 'exterior' relations become internal transactions, and the state is endogenised. I am sure that this is a difficult challenge, but in the long run it should not be insuperable.

I am somewhat less sanguine about the ability of mainstream economists to come to come to grips with the issue of Japan, not because it is inherently more difficult, but because there is so much more at stake for the profession itself. If the 'revisionist' Japanologists are even partially right, and if the theory of scientific revolutions à la Kuhn has any bearing on this matter, then economists would be the last to admit that Japan represents a different type of capitalist economic formation. And before so doing, they would be expected to go to some lengths to ignore or discount contrary evidence, invent circuitous logics to account for anomalies, and deploy a variety of rhetorical strategies to discredit the opposing position. The recent strategic trade policy debate, in fact, exhibited some of these patterns, but in the end it successfully raised related issues and is, therefore, a welcome development irrespective of who ultimately proves right or wrong (see Richardson 1990a; Cohen 1990). Understanding the domestic economic structure of Japan, and thereby helping to attenuate the inevitable trade disputes with Japan that lie ahead, will require similarly detailed empirical studies, informed by models of strategic rationality, and which explicitly test for, not simply assume, what Albert Hirschman has called the 'mono-economics' claim that pervades the conventional theory (Hirschman 1981, ch. 1).

3 History Restarted: Japanese–American Relations at the End of the Century

CHALMERS JOHNSON

The peculiar Cold War relationship between Japan and the United States lasted from approximately 1950 to 1990. Today it continues only through inertia, without any foundation in grand strategy or in response to a common threat, despite a high degree of economic interdependence. Japan and the United States are today, as Nakanishi Terumasa puts it, merely 'paper allies' (Etō & Nakanishi 1991, p. 113). Both the Japanese and the Americans have profited greatly from their forty-year alliance, but they have also deluded themselves about its foundations and are emerging from it crippled in certain major respects. One of the most striking asymmetries between Japan and the United States in the aftermath of the Cold War, and largely caused by it, is Japan's weakness in taking a larger role in world affairs and the United States' weakness in re-establishing the industrial and economic foundations on which its claims to global leadership rest. To talk about Japanese–American relations at the end of the century, then, means first of all to understand the delusions and dependencies with which they are emerging from the fog of the Cold War.

Amid the welter of political and academic verbiage concerning the collapse of communism and the end of bipolarity, two theses stand out for their insight and originality. One is Francis Fukuyama's 'The End of History?' and the other Alan Tonelson's 'What is the National Interest?' (Fukuyama 1989; Tonelson 1991). Both reflect diametrically opposite views of the nature of the Cold War, and they therefore differ on the significance of its end.

After one strips away the Hegelian camouflage, Fukuyama's argument can be reduced to an unabashed American victory cry: we won! According to Fukuyama, the Cold War was not simply a political and military contest between the Soviet and American empires; it was, above all, a contest

39

between advocates of the primacy of the state and advocates of the primacy of society. In terms of economic ideology, the battle was between V.I. Lenin and Adam Smith, between a state-led command economy and a state-as-referee *laissez-faire* economy. 'The triumph of the West, of the Western *idea*', Fukuyama writes, 'is evident first of all in the total exhaustion of viable systematic alternatives to Western liberalism'.

Looking out of the corner of his eye, Fukuyama can see that Japan does not fit this schema. But he defines the problem away (just as many Japanese critics of the United States think that Americans are also doing): 'Many Americans are now aware that Japanese industrial organization is very different from that prevailing in the United States or Europe, and it is questionable what relationship the factional maneuvering that takes place with the governing Liberal Democratic Party bears to democracy. Nonetheless, the very fact that the essential elements of economic and political liberalism have been so successfully grafted onto uniquely Japanese traditions and institutions guarantees their survival in the long run'. This is, of course, a restatement of the official American position that Japan was reborn in the image of the United States during the Allied Occupation and that in the long run the two will converge as liberal democratic countries. If one accepts Fukuyama's proposition that the bedrock of modern history was a struggle between Leninism and liberalism, then liberalism (including Japan's version) won, and history—at least until some new dialectical paradigm emerges—is over.

By contrast, Alan Tonelson is more in the neo-realist mode. He would agree with Gilpin that the Western strategy in the Cold War encompassed (i) a series of alliances (NATO and the Japan–US Security Treaty) based on 'a common assessment of the Soviet threat'; (ii) extended deterrence that 'united the industrial democracies militarily'; and (iii) the Bretton Woods system of economic cooperation, its last vestige today being GATT-style 'free trade', which was intended to overcome 'economic nationalism' (Gilpin 1989b, pp. 3–5). However, Tonelson goes further and argues that the essence of American policy was a 'strategy of smothering the foreign policy (and economic) independence of Western Europe and Japan'. During the Cold War, the United States sought to meet 'all the major needs—principally those for security and prosperity—that historically led the Western European countries and Japan to conduct their own foreign policies in the first place'. The intent of this policy, most clearly evident in the Bretton Woods arrangements, was twofold: to rehabilitate Western Europe and Japan as markets for American goods and as allies against the USSR, and to prevent the reappearance of a pre-1914 multipolar balance of power, 'which had proved highly unstable and in fact had collapsed into two terrible conflicts'. In contrast to Fukuyama, Tonelson stresses that the Western strategy in the Cold War was aimed above all at preserving a bipolar world.

Today, Tonelson believes the 'smothering strategy' of the United States has become completely unsustainable because (i) it requires the continued 'hemorrhaging of U.S. economic strength' and (ii) Western Europe and Japan are no longer interested in going along. Contrary to James Fallows' important argument that with the end of the Cold War, the United States must 'contain Japan', Tonelson thinks that this is precisely what the United States has been doing for the past forty years (cf. Fallows 1989). Kissinger made a similar case to Chou En-lai in 1971; and many Americans see the Security Treaty today as a safeguard for the rest of Asia and the Pacific 'against the possibility of a more assertive Japanese profile in the region backed by military force' (see LaFeber 1989, p. 105; Ginsburg 1991, p. 20). In Tonelson's conception, the Cold War amounted to a smothering of history (its suspension if not its literal end), and the revolutionary events of 1989–91 portend its restarting. He concludes that 'increased Western European and Japanese independence will undoubtedly make the world less stable' and that the United States should 'focus on coping with the consequences of a less stable world' (Tonelson 1991, p. 46). Tonelson's article is a work of policy advocacy; he does not dwell on whether the United States *can* wean itself away from its Roman pretensions (even though it can no longer afford them) or on what grand strategy Japan might pursue, if it is capable of formulating one.

I believe that the mode of thought exemplified by Fukuyama's article characterises what passes for strategy in Washington these days, and that the mode of thought exemplified by Tonelson's piece characterises what passes for strategy in Tokyo. If my contention is even close to the truth—and as we shall see there are many serious people in Tokyo other than the stridently neo-nationalist Ishihara Shintarō who subscribe to it—then it is reasonable to conclude that during the 1990s Japan and the United States are on a collision course (see Morita & Ishihara 1989; Ishihara et al. 1990; Ishihara 1991; cf. Carbaugh Jr & Kase (eds) 1991). Needless to say, just as the navigator of a ship who warns of a collision course is not predicting a collision, I am not *predicting* a collision. But I want to lay out the perceptions, capabilities, lack of capabilities, and asymmetries that the Cold War relationship between Japan and the United States fostered. And I want to point out that, other things being equal, without reform in both countries they portend conflict. Let me disaggregate this complex whole into three subdiscussions: (1) the New World Order; (2) the movement from the GATT to economic regionalism and perhaps toward a new version of the Greater East Asia Co-Prosperity Sphere; and (3) the problem of what the Japanese call 'emotional friction' (*kanjō no atsureki*) (Okamoto 1991, p. 155), or the possibility that the Japanese and Americans do not *want* any longer to be allies.

1. New World Order

One of the ironies of the Persian Gulf War 1990–91 is that (although it did not look like it) Japan actually supported the United States in an international military venture more fully than it had ever done in the past. Never before—during the Korean War, the defence of Taiwan, the defence of South Korea, the fight against the communist insurgency in the Philippines, the defence of South Vietnam, the Arab–Israeli war of 1973, and the Iran–Iraq war of the 1980s—had Japan concretely supported the United States' use of force in areas where its own national interests could also be said plausibly to be involved. Nonetheless, it was during the Gulf War that Americans concluded from Japan's reluctant contributions that the Japanese were not serious allies and that the Americans and the Japanese harboured different values concerning the 'New World Order'. The Gulf War thus served as a catalyst in Japanese–US relations, turning numerous impressions and irritations that each country had about the other into more hardened stereotypes. As William Watts put it, 'The picture many Japanese have of America is one of a society beset with internal problems and at times virtually out of control, while the counterpart American image of Japan is one of a nation of humourless workaholics, bowing before higher authority' (Watts 1991a, p. 4). These views colour what each side thinks is a plausible version of a post-Cold War international system and of Japanese–American relations now that the threat of communism no longer unites them.

The basic Japanese position is well and candidly stated by Ogura Kazuo of the Ministry of Foreign Affairs:

> The United States has lost a considerable amount of economic influence in the world. The United States no longer has the money or the manpower to see its global ideals realized. In order to realize its own global dreams, the United States must now turn to other countries...[But] the United States is too proud to admit that it relies on other nations. For better or worse, the nations of the world are becoming more dependent on each other economically and politically. This is only now beginning to sink in. However, the people of the United States refuse to accept their new predicament...The American people do not want to be dependent on the Japanese (Ogura 1991, pp. 4–11).

The question remains why the United States has lost economic influence and must rely on others to help it out. Is it merely because Western Europe and Japan have caught up with the United States, or is the United States in actual decline?

Today virtually all Japanese seem convinced that the United States is in decline, even though they differ on what Japan should do about it. Until the Gulf War, there were roughly three schools of thought in Japan: those who felt it was in Japan's own interest to help prop up the United States; those who had read Paul Kennedy's *Rise and Fall of the Great Powers* closely and concluded that it was a waste of resources to try to prop up the United States; and those who took the position that even though the United States was in decline, since it refused itself to admit it or do anything about it, Japan should continue to profit from the old relationship as long as possible (Kennedy 1988; see also Johnson 1990a). The Japanese are aware that any real programme of domestic reform in the United States would involve costs to them: a genuine American 'peace dividend' would mean a reduction of US military commitments in the Western Pacific; the development of a US economic strategy would mean serious American demands for reciprocity in market access, investment, and environmental protection on the part of its trading partners; and a true free-trade agreement with Mexico might mean some strategic closing of the US market to Asian exporters. But so long as the United States continues to waver on these issues, the Japanese believe they must work on the proposition that America's days as a superpower are numbered.

For years Japanese leaders and analysts have been hammering away at conditions in the United States that they think disqualify it from continuing to exercise leadership. These include Washington's fiscal deficits, the country's low economic competitiveness, drug-ridden cities, violent crime, and a miserable public education system. Former Prime Minister Nakasone, for example, merely reflected the common wisdom when he remarked that 'drug abuse [in the United States] has reached alarming proportions' (Nakasone 1991a). A 1991 symposium of distinguished Japanese officials, professors, and industrialists, some of them educated in the United States and all of them familiar with it, contended that credit-card abuse in America was causing 'middle class families to give up', that the 'homeless live in tents put up even near the White House in Washington', and that the Harvard Business School was only good at training financiers for Wall Street, that is, for 'hollow work' (*kyogyō*).[1] Professor Saitō Seiichirō of Rikkyō University summarised the opinions of the group: 'I believe that the United States is a "vegetating nation" [*shokubutsu kokka*]. The troubles are seen by everyone, but they are not healed by anyone. The situation is worsening. It is not worsening all at once but it is worsening gradually. The Americans have grown used to it. But then they coerce us into lending them money. The United States is heading in the direction of a vegetating nation' (*Voice* 1991, p. 117).

Even though some of the popularity of these views can be ascribed to the nationalistic pleasure of comparing conditions in the United States with those in Japan, today they are widely held by Japanese opinion leaders, not just by neo-nationalist fringe groups. Some authorities on the United States, such as Homma Nagayo, emeritus professor of the University of Tokyo and former head of that university's American Studies Center, even warns of a possible 'U.S. collapse from internal problems', a

---

[1] Discussion among Kojima Akira, member of the Editorial Board of the *Nihon Keizai Shimbun*; Iida Tsuneo, member of the International Japanese Culture Research Center; Terasawa Yoshio, Director General of the Multilateral Investment Guarantee Agency; Yakushiji Taizō, professor of Keiō University; Saitō Seiichirō, professor of Rikkyō University; and Yamamoto Takuma, Chairman, Fujitsū, Inc., on 'Zento tanan no Amerika keizai' (The Many Future Difficulties of the American Economy) (*Voice* 1991).

development he fears the Americans might blame on Japan. In Homma's view, Japan should try to find a 'graceful exit' (*hanamichi o tsukuru*) for the United States from its role as hegemon (Etō & Homma 1991, p. 107).[2] Until that occurs, many Japanese regard the United States with growing contempt—as the world's 'credit-card policeman' or as what Christopher Layne has called a 'Potemkin-village superpower' (Asai 1991; Layne 1991, p. 80).

With these attitudes as a background, the spectacular success of the American-led *blitzkrieg* against Iraq came as a shock to Japan. Nonetheless, the combination of 'smart bombs but dumb VCRs' simply caused many influential Japanese to conclude that the United States and the former USSR had more in common than they had previously thought: both countries overtaxed their domestic economies to support their privileged military-industrial complexes. For example, Funabashi Yōichi of the *Asahi Shimbun*, sees parallels between the disintegration of the European communist economies and the 1987 collapse of the New York stock exchange (Funabashi 1990, 1991a, p. 220). The Japanese are well aware that their intervention prevented the stock market collapse from turning into a panic. On the Gulf War itself, Funabashi vacillates between seeing it as America's Suez or as an example of 'macho unilateralism' aimed at disguising weakness and at intimidating the Japanese (Funabashi 1991a, pp. 93, 96). Other Japanese writers have taken a similar line. In a recent discussion, Nakanishi Terumasa of Shizuoka University argued that President Bush's decision to use force in the Persian Gulf was 'a kind of historical *coup d'état* against the new order, an attempt to reverse the trend toward multilateralism in the post-Cold War world'. Etō Jun added that, 'The United States is now becoming dependent on Japan at an accelerating rate for the advanced technology that it needs to sustain its military interventions' (Etō & Nakanishi 1991, pp. 115, 118).

Before considering the Japanese prescriptions for a New World Order in light of these conditions, let me turn briefly to the corresponding American impressions of the Japanese. These are, in essence, that Japan is a 'unidimensional economic superpower' which fails 'the test of good global citizenship, much less leadership' (Arase 1991, pp. 23, 29). In William Barnds' view (and it should be noted that he is a recent past president of the Japan Economic Institute, one of the Japanese Government's prime information agencies in Washington): 'Japanese policy [in the Gulf War]—and the government went beyond what most of the public supported—demonstrated that Japan remains insular, still sees its role in the world largely in terms of its narrow economic self-interest, and remains politically unwilling and unable to assess and act on its interests

---

2 Only a few years ago Homma was arguing that '...we should be free from cultural nationalism, pernicious symptoms of which are now found in Japan' (Homma 1989, p. 219). It seems that Professor Homma has himself become a 'pernicious symptom'.

in a broader international context, especially during a crisis. When one of the world's key nations fails to set policies that help maintain the international system, the system is in trouble' (Barnds 1991).

Why do the Japanese behave this way? For many Americans the answer is that the Japanese and the Americans see the world and the maintenance of order in it differently. The Americans hold to 'principles' whereas the Japanese respond only to pressure, such as the notorious American *gaiatsu*, or what many Japanese masochistically delight in calling 'Japan-bashing'. A good example of these views comes from former Assistant Secretary of Defense Richard Perle:

> Even before the question of sending Self-Defense Forces to the Gulf became an issue, what surprised the American people is that even when the Japanese government had decided to send some medical teams, there were hardly any volunteers. Doesn't 'contributing' mean realizing one's own international responsibilities and then trying to meet those responsibilities, not just doing something because the United States wants you to? I find it hard to understand why Japan doesn't realize this (*Asahi Shimbun* 1991, p. 1).

From a Japanese point of view, the Gulf War virtually began with an outburst of *gaiatsu* (foreign pressure). According to the *Yomiuri Shimbun*, a letter from US Secretary of Defense Dick Cheney dated 10 August 1990, eight days after Saddam Hussein's invasion of Kuwait, to Director General of the Japanese Defense Agency Ishikawa Yōzō stated, 'At this time evidence is needed to show that the U.S.–Japan relationship continues to be firm...[Without such evidence, the U.S. government cannot refute the argument that] the two nations no longer have a relationship' (*Yomiuri Shimbun* 24 October 1990, p. 1). In the *Yomiuri*'s assessment, the then Prime Minister Kaifu's cabinet read this letter as a threat, one that moved its members much more profoundly than the menace of Saddam Hussein.

Japanese political scientists explain this reliance on *gaiatsu* as a consequence of the United States' smothering strategy during the Cold War, a strategy that was implemented most forcefully against Japan in the wake of the Security Treaty riots of 1960. In the analysis of Professor Sasaki Takeshi, post-war Japanese politics should be divided into three phases: (i) 1945–1960; (ii) 1960–1985; and (iii) 1985–present. In the first phase, 'politics retained its ideological dimension'; but in the second phase, when Japan put further constitutional development on hold and devoted itself to high-speed economic growth, 'Japanese politicians began to lose interest in the high politics of diplomacy and national security, and competition among political parties became a mere formality, adding momentum to the political apathy of the people'. During the third phase, changes in Japan's external environment, and its own growing wealth, forced it to think about reforming its political system. But its politicians, literally having forgotten their function, persisted in their factional battles, or in arranging for their sons and grandsons to succeed them, or in 'pork-barrel politics'. Japan's 'foreign policy continued to be oriented exclusively to economic issues and it took virtually no initiatives in other fields' (Sasaki 1991).

A major unintended consequence of the United States' hegemonic smothering strategy, then, was the atrophy of the Japanese political system. To quote Sasaki again, in responding to the demands of the Gulf War Japan's political leadership

> found itself in serious conflict with the deeply entrenched domestic interests catered to over the decades. Stable though it might outwardly seem, Japanese politics began to suffer from chronic, structural instability...Japanese political leaders today are a product of the second phase...In the second phase...the role of politics actually contracted, and systems emerged through which the burdens of politics were taken over to a considerable degree by other organizations and actors [the bureaucracy, big business, and the U.S.]...The bureaucracy has cultivated involvement in the people's daily lives incomparably deeper than that attempted by politicians, and the structures of that involvement are firmly established.

Reliance on *gaiatsu* is thus one Japanese adaptation to American hegemony, and Japanese officials themselves often invite and orchestrate it by prompting their normally uninformed American counterparts. 'It is often said that the Bush Administration has acted at times like an opposition party and even at times like the ruling party itself' (Sasaki 1991, p. 6). During the Gulf War, a common pun in Tokyo was that Prime Minister Kaifu was busy using his 'Bush-button phone' to call the White House. As we shall see, the Americans do not normally acknowledge that this situation exists because it contradicts their view that Japan is a democratic ally which has freely joined in a 'global partnership' based on Japanese–American 'burden-sharing'. But the leading external, non-American analyst of *gaiatsu*, Aurelia George, concludes:

> U.S. pressure has become a powerful catalyst for change in the Japanese economy, polity, and society...U.S. pressure is now penetrating the inner reaches of the Japanese policymaking process. Almost all the government's major decisions are held up for scrutiny in terms of their possible impact on Japan's relations with the United States...In many respects the United States is itself an actor in the Japanese policy process: as a surrogate opposition party presenting the only true set of alternative policies to the government's, as an interest group representing the voice of Japanese consumers, and as an alternative power base for Japanese prime ministers seeking to overcome both shortfalls in their factional strength and domestic resistance to change (George 1991, pp. 17, 18).

During the Cold War, Japan and the United States learned roles that they played opposite each other quite successfully, but these roles have become anachronistic. Nonetheless, most Japanese and Americans are not ready to give them up and learn new ones. The Japanese still like leaving their external security needs to the Americans, and the Americans still enjoy the Roman appurtenances of power. The situation is comparable to the last decades of the Edo *bakufu*, when the samurai were still deferred to by the merchants who were simultaneously their financiers. 'In Washington', writes Thomas Ginsburg, 'those who continue to see the United States as the global hegemon are reluctant to share international decision-making' (Ginsburg 1991). Joseph Nye subtly reinforces their position by his arguments that even though the Americans are making no efforts to check their decline, they still control a vast reservoir of 'soft power' with which to keep their erstwhile allies in line (Nye Jr, 1990a).

In Tokyo too, even such neo-nationalists as Nakanishi change their tune when writing in English: 'No matter how much may be said and written about the end of the Cold War, there will be no fundamental change in the Japan–U.S. relationship unless there are basic changes in the strategic political and economic context governing the relationship' (Nakanishi 1991, p. 11). But, of course, it is precisely those 'basic changes in the strategic political and economic context' that have started to occur: the Russians want a deal on the Northern Territories; both Koreas are now members of the United Nations and on their way towards a probable nego-tiated unification; and a combination of Mount Pinatubo and the Filipino Senate have closed down the United States' last outposts in its former colony. The time for a New World Order is now.

Japanese thinking about what kinds of institutional arrangements should replace those of the Cold War is actually more advanced than that of the Americans. They call these new arrangements 'pax consortis', a concept invented by Professor Inoguchi Kuniko and now widely used although with varying definitions throughout Japanese policy-making circles (Inoguchi 1987). Former Prime Minister Nakasone defines it as 'peace achieved through the cooperation of many nations led by the United States' (Nakasone 1991b, p. 76). In a different context, Nakasone added that the specific members of the consortium should be the Group of Seven (G-7) advanced industrial democracies. 'Despite the spectacular allied victory in the Persian Gulf', he wrote, 'a new world order is nowhere in sight...Superpower America is in economic decline...We are entering the age of Pax Consortia...[a] transition from economic to com-prehensive summitry...The Group of Seven will have to serve as the world's banker, gendarme, and environmentalist' (Nakasone 1991a). Satō Hideo agrees with this formulation, but he warns that it will not be easy to achieve: 'The United States would have to reject hegemony' (Satō 1991, p. 146).

Inoguchi herself does not include a leadership role for the United States. 'The shape of the world order', she writes, 'will not be a unipolar Pax Americana; it will be a system of joint management by a consortium of industrial nations' (Inoguchi, K. 1991, p. 27). Unfortunately, there are several obvious objections to this sort of reasoning. It fails to specify *why* the various nations should cooperate with each other, and is therefore as flawed as the original idealism that prompted the so-called neo-realist school to develop the theory of hegemonic stability (see also Gilpin 1987). For example, why should not the UN Security Council, with of course the addition of Japan and Germany as members, play the role given by these theorists to the G-7 democracies? Is not any global pax consortis already upstaged by the emergence of the expanded European Community (EC), the North American Free Trade Zone, and the probable re-creation of the Greater East Asia Co-Prosperity Sphere? Given the prolongation of the negotiations over the Uruguay Round to modernise the GATT rules because of European and Japanese obstruction, a pax consortis seems as likely a prospect as a smoothly functioning United Nations.

The US response to these proposals has been ambiguous. Americans thus far seem to prefer the term 'burden-sharing' in talking with their former Cold War clients about future relations, but this phrase tends to alarm the Japanese who see it as a ploy to get them to pay for US foreign policy without participating in its formulation. In any case, proposals for burden-sharing (*futan no wakachiai*) sound to the Japanese like invitations to join a sinking ship, and they violate Japan's oldest instinct about foreign affairs: *nagai mono ni wa makareyō* 'move with the powerful' (see Welfield 1988, p. 2). It should be recalled that Japanese foreign policy in the twentieth century has been based on bilateral alliances with the nation that Japan deemed to be the most powerful in every sense, including cultural. This led to the Anglo–Japanese Alliance, 1902–22; the Axis Alliance with Germany, 1940–45; and the Japanese–American Security Treaty, 1952–present. Japan has never been drawn to alliances with nations in decline. The Americans would, therefore, be wise to abandon the term 'burden-sharing', because it both reeks of American self-righteousness and amounts to a self-advertisement of America's declining ability to carry out an independent foreign policy.

Another dubious concept favoured by some Americans in dealing with Japan is 'global partnership'. The term is prominently featured in a so-called policy consensus report of August 1991 on 'the future of U.S.–Japan relations', which was endorsed by a large number of former American officials who reside in Washington, including Alexander Haig, Melvin Laird, Charles Percy, William Proxmire, Paula Stern, Robert Strauss, and Paul Volcker. References to an 'equal partnership' (allegedly established by Reischauer when he was ambassador), or a 'potential partner' (as co-builder of the FSX and supplier of advanced technology to the Department of Defense), or a 'global partnership' (undefined) are all mixed up (Foreign Policy Institute 1991). No one knows exactly what 'global partnership' means except that the two nations should continue to get along so long as neither has to make any sacrifices.

More than a year after the end of the Gulf War, the New World Order was quite recognisably the old world order continuing through inertia but visibly slowing down. Ambassador William Gleysteen summarised the situation as follows: 'Certain inherent American strengths and Japanese liabilities are working against a radical switch in global influence from the United States to Japan in the foreseeable future…[Japan will temporarily remain an] almost equal ally [even though it has] largely replaced the United States as the [Asia–Pacific] region's creditor and provider of assistance, as the source of the most useful technology, and as an appropriate model for economic development' (Gleysteen Jr, 1991, pp. 27–33).

2. Economic regionalism

In talking about economic issues in the Asia–Pacific region, one must begin by largely discounting or ignoring the opinions of economics professors in English-speaking countries. This is because they failed to anticipate the growth of great wealth in the area, still cannot adequately explain it, and are today concerned more with defending their arcane theories than with studying the nature and potentialities of Asian capitalism. It is more than likely that history will come to judge English-language academic economics as having the same relationship to Asian capitalism that academic Marxism–Leninism taught in the former USSR until August 1991 had to the Soviet economy.

I raise this issue at the outset because one of the major controversies at the heart of the various economic disputes between Japan and the United States is what theory applies and whether the East Asian and North American capitalist economies even belong to the same species. And the answer has direct implications for policy. If the two economies belong to the same species of capitalism, then there is every reason to suppose that problems might be solved or ameliorated through such measures as macroeconomic coordination, exchange and interest-rate adjustments, deregulation, market-opening agreements, and foreign direct investment. If they are not members of the same species, then such measures are likely to make the situation worse—which arguably has been the case since the so-called Plaza Agreement of 1985.

GATT and the Uruguay Round are a case in point. If the economists' doctrine of free trade actually has some validity, then the attempt to extend and force a conclusion to the Uruguay Round after the negotiations collapsed in Brussels in December 1990 makes sense. But if GATT, during the most recent past two decades, was really based on a political doctrine—the willingness of a hegemonic power, the United States, to exchange economic benefits for political and security backing as part of a grand strategy against the Soviet Union—then the Uruguay Round collapsed because the Cold War is over. As Lawrence Krause has observed, 'The rest of the world has seen the U.S. make too many mistakes—both in the economic and political arenas—to comply with U.S. desires now that they no longer require a protective U.S. military umbrella' (Krause 1991, p. 4; see also Prestowitz Jr, et al. 1991). It is as plausible to conclude that this was the calculation made by Japan and the EC at Brussels in 1990 as to contend that they have benightedly missed the point of the lessons taught by Adam Smith, David Ricardo and their followers.

The Japanese are extremely well informed about 'the nearly fanatical loyalty to "free trade" that has characterized America's bipartisan foreign policy establishment' (Chang 1991, p. 51). In the past they have verbally respected it and tried to turn it against the Americans whenever the latter sought reciprocity in bilateral economic relations. But times have changed. The Japanese no longer care what the Americans think. When, in March 1991, Japanese government officials threatened to 'arrest and prosecute' American rice exporters for merely displaying three different kinds of rice that are grown in the United States at a privately sponsored International Food and Beverage Fair held in Chiba city, Japan, the Cold War relationship between the two countries was clearly over (*Aera* 1991). As John Ruggie has pointed out, 'A very different and much more politicised international trading game is emerging, one that is not well illuminated by the conventional free-trade/protectionism discourse' (Ruggie 1991b, p. 15).

Trade between Japan and the United States will of course continue, but it will now be managed trade—something that has long been true for the Japanese side but that the Americans must now learn. Interestingly enough, the 1991 Japanese–American agreement concerning trade in semiconductors is an excellent example of successfully managed trade. Article 10 of the agreement states, 'The Government of Japan recognizes that the U.S. semiconductor industry expects that the foreign market share will grow to more than 20 percent of the Japanese market by the end of 1992 and considers that this can be realized'. The very definition of managed trade is negotiated market shares. Nonetheless, in order to protect their ideological *amour propre*, the Americans inserted into the preface:

> The purpose of this Agreement is to enhance free trade in semiconductors on the basis of market principles and the competitive positions of the U.S. and Japanese industries and in accordance with established principles of the General Agreement on Tariffs and Trade.[3]

More intellectually serious than the trade issue is the problem of structural differences between the Japanese and US economies. 'To what extent', asks I.M. Destler, 'is major systemic variation politically tolerable, consistent with the notion of a "fair" overall relationship?' (Destler 1991, pp. 24–5). It is unnecessary here to rehearse the extensive attacks on and defences of *keiretsu*, administrative guidance, structural corruption, infringements of intellectual property rights, industrial policy itself, and many other features of the Japanese economic system that have com-

---

3 US–Japan Semiconductor Trade Agreement, signed 11 June 1991, Washington DC, by Ambassador Murata Ryōhei and US Trade Representative Carla Hills (text from the Office of the United States Trade Representative). See also Stokes (1990b).

manded the attention of Japanese and Americans for the past two decades (see Pyle (ed.) 1987; Yamamura (ed.) 1989; Yamamura (ed.) 1990). Actually, it has long been recognised that structural differences need not in themselves be an obstacle to economic exchange, as the years of expanding trade and investment among the command economies, the reformed command economies, the capitalist developmental states, and the *laissez-faire* economies demonstrate. The question of structural differences between Japan and the US has become salient because it embarrasses the United States Government's economic advisers. Their advice has been based on the idea that structural differences did not exist, or that evolutionary change was reducing them, or that such tactics as the Structural Impediments Initiative (aimed at Japan's retail trade industry, its lax antitrust laws, spending on public works, and other more or less innocent bystanders) would take care of the problem.

The fighting issue at the heart of the structural differences question is 'revisionism', and the possibility that those whom the Japanese Government and American hangers-on label revisionists may turn out to be correct. Peter Ennis recently defined revisionism as the

> view that Japan's economy and society are not organized around classical notions of free markets, in which the direction of the economy is determined by the independent actions of consumers and corporations, all operating to maximize their profits and incomes. This challenges the conventional wisdom (hence 'revisionism') among American policymakers that Japan is fundamentally similar to the United States and other Western capitalist democracies (Ennis 1990, p. 30).

Until the early 1990s, the Japanese establishment stigmatised the views of anyone who suggested that Japan had a different history of industrialisation, a different role for the state in the economy, a different evaluation of economic affairs in the overall scheme of things, and different ways of financing industry or dealing with labour-management problems than was taught in English-language textbooks. Even today some Japanese writers warn of revisionism's dangers. Iida Tsuneo, for example, himself a staff member of the primary semi-official agency for contending that Japan is incomparable, the International Japanese Culture Research Centre in Kyoto, still wants the economy declared off limits for discussion. He also insists that Japan's economy is just like other capitalist economies: its trade surpluses are temporary, *keiretsu* are not important, and the revisionists who 'say the Japanese economy is capitalist in form only and actually operates on non-market principles' are 'polemical and overdrawn' (Iida 1991, p. 15).

But what is new and important is that many Japanese writers and economists are beginning to acknowledge that there are major differences between Japan and the United States. This is important for international relations because it puts the Japanese–American relationship on a new ideological footing, one that in my opinion is more realistic than the old one and that will have to abandon the condescending efforts of American *gaiatsu* to force the Japanese to reform their economy using the US economy as a model. As Harry Gelber puts it, 'Marx was clearly wrong—at least so far—in arguing that "the mode of production of material life determines the general character of the social, political, and spiritual processes of life", for neither industrialism nor post-industrialism have made Japanese society akin to Germany or France like Britain' (Gelber 1991, pp. 35–6). Some Japanese are starting to agree.

Former Foreign Minister Ōkita Saburō, one of Japan's most distinguished economists, in what may also be a mild parody of President Bush's rhetoric, writes: 'There are many rooms in the house of capitalism... [Japan may occupy] some kinder gentler middle ground between a centrally controlled economy and a *laissez faire* market-driven economy. The Japanese experience is thus studied as one point of light' (Ōkita 1991; see also Ōkita 1990). Sakakibara Eisuke in a new book characterises Japan as a 'non-capitalist market economy' (Sakakibara 1990). Noda Masaaki lists seven principles that he believes distinguish Japan's 'samurai capitalism' from its Anglo–American relatives, number seven being that 'national prosperity is in the hands of state bureaucrats' (Noda 1991). Terasawa Yoshio confesses that 'Japan is not really the pure survival-of-the-fittest American-type of capitalism. It is half socialism... and the government is in control...On the surface Japan is a capitalist system like that of the United States, in other words a free competition, survival-of-the-fittest system; but on the inside it is different' (*Voice* 1991, p. 110; see also Nakatani 1991).[4]

Not all of this new candour will please Americans. Every once in a while a Japanese writer contends that Japan's superior economic performance *vis-à-vis* the Americans was not just a matter of market forces and getting the prices right but a form of retaliation against the United States for its hegemony. Or neo-nationalist writers argue that Japan's economic performance demonstrates the superiority of the Japanese 'race', while deriding 'mongrel' nations such as the United States and Brazil. For example, Professor Aida Yūji of Kyoto University has suggested that 'Iberian and African cultural traits seem to impede industrialization' and that the United States 'with its vast human and technological resources... could become a premier agrarian power—a giant version of Denmark, for example—and the breadbasket of the world' (Aida 1990).

---

4   At the 1991 Annual Meeting of the Board of Governors of the World Bank and the IMF, Mieno Yasushi, head of the bank of Japan, said, 'Experience in Asia has shown that although development strategies require a healthy respect for market mechanisms, the role of the government cannot be forgotten. I would like to see the World Bank and the IMF take the lead in a wide-ranging study that would define the theoretical underpinnings of this approach and clarify the areas in which it can be successfully applied to other parts of the globe' (World Bank 1991a, p. 6).

These views are important for international relations, I believe, because they signal that Japan is consciously drawing away from the American example and beginning to see itself as a model for other Asian economies (and perhaps Eastern Europe and Russia as well). It seems significant that when in September 1991 the Russians suggested that they might be willing to return the Northern Territories to Japan, International Trade and Industry Minister Nakao Eiichi replied that his ministry was ready to offer Moscow the benefit of its own post-war reconstruction experience in rebuilding the economy (*Daily Japan Digest* 11 September 1991, p. 1). Such advice might be more valuable than any currently being proffered by the International Monetary Fund (IMF) or the World Bank.

Japan is not, of course, a *potential* model for East Asia. It is already the prototype of the capitalist developmental states—Taiwan, South Korea, and Singapore in the first tier, the Association of Southeast Asian (ASEAN) states in the second—that have transformed Pacific politics. The most important fact about the post-Cold War Asia–Pacific region is Japan's growing economic dominance and the degree to which it is integrating all the nations of the region (including mainland China) through trade, direct investment, aid, financial services, technology transfer, and Japan's continuing role as a developmental model. The high yen (*endaka*) caused Japan to enter for the first time into a genuine horizontal division of labour with the other nations of East Asia. Today there is no doubt that Japan has the capacity to create a yen-based regional economic grouping in the Asia–Pacific region and that it has been moving in that direction as a way of responding to the expanded market that the EC will form in 1993, and to the North American Free Trade Zone. Japan understands, without openly acknowledging it, that the European and North American agreements came into being when they did in part as responses to the challenge of Japan's own neo-mercantilism; but it does not want to exacerbate the situation by a precipitate move towards a yen-bloc. Moreover, many Japanese leaders warn against any action that could disrupt relations between Japan and North America and Europe. Former Prime Minister Nakasone has declared, 'It is impossible to imagine a secure Asia without a U.S. presence' (Nakasone 1991b, p. 79).

There are many speculative aspects to the growing trend towards economic regionalism. Europeans, Latin Americans and Southeast Asians all ask themselves whether they can really trust putting their respective destinies in the hands of Germans, Americans or Japanese. Equally importantly, existing institutions have the capacity to transcend or redirect regionalism in potentially less exclusive directions. NATO, the OECD, the G-7 democracies, APEC, and PECC already exist and are functioning. Nonetheless, I believe that these considerations are not strong enough to stand in the way of regionalism, and that by the end of the century the world is likely to be reduced to a G-3: a Japan-dominated Asia–Pacific region in which the United States has only observer status; a German-dominated Europe that includes Austria, Scandinavia and probably

Poland, Czechoslovakia and Hungary; and a US-dominated North American region that may well be preoccupied with economic and demographic disasters in Mexico and elsewhere (see Johnson 1991). But I acknowledge that there are many contingencies that could alter this prediction, and that the world of the future might be only G-2: Europe and an Asia–Pacific region that includes both Japan and the United States. There are powerful influences promoting this configuration, including the fact that two-fifths of Japan's overseas direct investment is in North America. There is also the negative factor that whereas the United States is feared and envied in Latin America, Japan is feared and envied in Southeast Asia, making each an ideal counterweight for the other.

There is one further question that has not received enough attention but that constitutes perhaps the most important intellectual issue in assessing Japan's future role in the world. What are Japan's intentions, or is Japan even capable of having strategic intentions? All governmental intelligence estimates are based on a combination of three sets of data—past behaviour, current capabilities, and future intentions—with a conscious attempt to avoid all forms of theorising since these may skew or warp the data. In the case of Japan, past behaviour and current capabilities are so extraordinary and so formidable as to cause any other nation or people to be concerned about its future intentions. As we have already noted, many of Japan's allies and trading partners believe that during the Gulf War, and with regard to the Uruguay Round of GATT negotiations, Japan displayed an inexplicable inability to discern its own national interest. This aspect of Japan, of course, contrasts markedly with its well-known ability at the level of industry and finance to develop and pursue long-term strategies with intense competitiveness.

Perhaps the most articulate proponent of the view that Japan is incapable of formulating strategic intentions is Karel van Wolferen. He comes to the same conclusions as Professor Sasaki Takeshi quoted earlier, but he sees the paralysis of the Japanese Government as more serious and less easily corrected than do Sasaki and other Japanese political scientists. For van Wolferen, Japan is without a compass and without brakes. He writes:

> I distinguish administrative decisions, which involve adjustments to an existing policy, from political decisions, which introduce new commitments or major changes in the way a country orders its domestic affairs or relates to the rest of the world. Japan's administrators (government bureaucrats as well as the bureaucrats in the industrial federations, the financial institutions and the corporate groupings) are among the world's most capable administrators. But like bureaucrats anywhere in the world, they can of necessity only be concerned with very limited areas of policy-making. What makes Japan special is the inability of its politicians to come up with the necessary political input, even when that would seem to serve the national interest (van Wolferen 1991, p. 27).

I basically agree with this analysis. In my opinion, this political paralysis is an unintended consequence of the way in which the United States exercised its hegemonic role in the Cold War, what Tonelson earlier called the 'smothering strategy'. But when it comes to Japan's movement towards a new Greater East Asia Co-Prosperity Sphere, I believe that Japan may know exactly what it is doing, that its bureaucrats are quite capable of guiding the nation in this direction, and that its seeming indecision merely reflects a delicate sense of timing and excellent camouflage for its long-range intentions. Since 1987, according to *The Economist*, 'Officials at MITI, the Ministry of International Trade and Industry, have been studying the economic prospects of the Pacific basin. They have concluded that greater political and economic integration of the region is inevitable. They are groping for a way to harness that development for Japanese interests' (*The Economist* 1988, pp. 35–6). As mentioned earlier, former Prime Minister Nakasone opposes such a grouping if it would exclude the United States, but others such as Kakizawa Kōji, the ruling party's leading foreign affairs specialist, favour it (Funabashi 1991b). Japan has already supported the floating of two different trial balloons. In Seoul in January 1989, it backed former Australian Prime Minister Bob Hawke's original proposal for an APEC without the United States. And at the end of 1990, Malaysian Prime Minister Mahathir Mohamad proposed an East Asian Economic Group that, in Hadi Soesastro's terms, 'is perhaps the first time after World War II in which a leadership role in East Asia is handed to Japan on a silver platter by another Asian country' (Soesastro 1991, p. 14).

Japan has not (yet) formally endorsed any proposal that would start to separate it from the markets of North America and Europe. But it is clearly thinking much harder about this issue than it is about, for example, the Uruguay Round of the GATT talks. In a speech in Los Angeles during the summer of 1991, then Japanese Ambassador to the United States Murata Ryōhei issued this warning:

> I'd like to tell you that there is an apprehension in Asia that the EC and a North American free-trade area might form introverted, less open economic entities. This is why some Asian leaders have proposed the formation of economic entities in Asia, which would exclude non-Asian developed nations such as the United States. However, I sincerely hope that the North American free-trade area will be an open, extroverted system, rather than closed and introverted. If the latter is pursued, it may lead to inattention on the part of the United States regarding the Asia–Pacific region. This inattention could conceivably result in the advocacy of economic regionalism in Asia (Murata 1991, p. B7).

In my opinion, much more important than the European single market or the North American free-trade agreement as an influence on Japanese thinking was the Plaza Agreement of 1985. It raised the value of the yen from 235 yen to one US dollar to approximately 135 yen to one US dollar. Although this devaluation of the dollar was expected to give North American and European firms a window of opportunity to compete with Japan, they failed to capitalise on it and the opportunity has now passed.

At the same time Japan undertook a major restructuring of its industries, including massive investments domestically and overseas. Out of this experience came Japan's proposal for a new regional order, a new and much more prosperous version of the Greater East Asia Co-Prosperity Sphere; and it has not been distracted from that goal by Americans harping on the failed GATT negotiations or the Persian Gulf War. If I am right, it may be that just as the people of Moscow and East Berlin now joke that socialism was the shortest route from capitalism to capitalism, the people of the Pacific will soon be saying that Asian capitalism was the shortest route from the Greater East Asia Co-Prosperity Sphere to the Greater East Asia Co-Prosperity Sphere.

3. Emotional friction

One further reason why I think the future may see three distinct economic regions rather than a renewal of the Japanese–American alliance is that Japanese writers have begun to prepare the public emotionally for a rupture of that alliance. This is not a bilateral initiative but primarily a Japanese initiative. It started in Japan in the wake of the Gulf War. Despite a growing interest in and fear of Japan as an economic competitor, most Americans have, until recently, paid little attention to Japan. They supposed that Japanese–US relations were at least as good as those with Europe and considerably better than with some long-standing American friends such as Israel. But from Japan come cries of alarm and an outpouring of emotionalism that William Watts sees as a 'communications disconnect' (Watts 1991b, pp. 4–5; see also Hasegawa 1991). Murakami Kaoru warns that, 'The watchword of the Congress is bash Japan, but meanwhile in Japan a new nationalism is gathering strength' (Murakami 1991). Some of this writing deserves serious consideration, even if evaluating its influence is still quite difficult.

Ogura Kazuo, the head of the Cultural Exchange Department (*Bunka Kōryū Bu*) of the Foreign Ministry, is interested primarily in the differences in values held by Japanese and Americans and the place of value judgements in relations among foreigners. He writes:

> Both countries are democratic and have market economies...However, that is not the point. These two countries have taken an entirely different *approach* to these values at home and abroad...Many Japanese find the concepts behind personal liberty, democracy, and free market economics to be outlandish [*batakusai*, exotic, foreign]...The Japanese people do not have a common set of ideals and values. They do not share any 'universal' religious beliefs or political ideals with other peoples in the world. The Japanese have not exported their 'gods' to other countries...Japan has been interested only in earning respect and status in the world community. Will Japan ever change its mind and sacrifice human life for other causes? The answer is no (Ogura 1991, pp. 4–11).

Without doubt this argument is overdrawn; the ethical principles involved in *on*, *giri*, and *ninjō* (roughly translated, 'obligation', 'duty', and 'human emotions') are as ubiquitous in Japan as any set of ethics ever can be in a given society. But the essence of Ogura's argument is that Americans *expect* the Japanese to adopt their values. The Japanese, however, are not interested in American values, are not trying to proselytise their own ones, and resent America's trying to make Japan a 'psychological colony' (Ogura 1991, p. 9). The idea that Japanese do not have 'fundamental' values, only situational ones, is an old theme of Western writers about Japan from Ruth Benedict to Karel van Wolferen. One writer, who refers to Japan as a 'secular superpower', goes so far as to say:

> In international settings, Japanese never seem to know what is going on.
> Even at home, our mass media often miss the significance of world
> events. Lacking a system of principled beliefs—call it religion or
> ideology—we misjudge the values and motivations of other people. We
> have a superficial, sometimes distorted view of global politics. The sim-
> ple truth is that we are uncomfortable with philosophical concepts.
> Japanese love making money, but if you ask us why we toil, we shrug
> our shoulders; hard work and affluence seem to be ends in themselves.
> Questions about the meaning of life elude us (Izawa 1990).

These views are relevant to the alliance because, as Iriye and Cohen observe, in the post-war world the Japanese have defined themselves in relation to the United States whereas Americans perceive Japan only insofar as it reflects American values. Americans are actually little interested in Japanese realities (Iriye & Cohen 1989, p. 189). These conditions have existed throughout the post-war period, but the disparities in power between the two countries and their common interests in the Cold War kept any tensions thus generated under control. The Gulf War shattered the old complacency. 'One must realize', writes Okamoto Yukio (formerly of the Ministry of Foreign Affairs):

> that American expectations toward Japan had risen considerably under
> the concept of 'global partnership'...[Japan failed to live up to these
> expectations]. But there's more to the situation. Unfortunately, Japan's
> basic posture was questioned. Americans interpreted Japan's actions as
> being completely void of any human convictions about the need to
> defend peace and order...In addition, Japan decisively left the impres-
> sion that it reacts only when pressured by the United States and never
> takes the initiative in coping with problems as if they were its own
> (Okamoto 1991, p. 149).

A particular virulent form of the rising concern with value differences among Japanese and Americans is racism. Ishihara Shintarō has long harped on American racial prejudice as 'the root cause of Japan-bashing', and in the Persian Gulf War many Japanese felt that the differences in American criticisms of the Japanese and the Germans reflected racism (Ishihara 1991, pp. 26–32). There may be some truth to this, but it also ignores and deflects attention from the differences between Germany and Japan. Germany has real political parties compared with Japan's façade of political accountability; Germany is embedded in the European Community whereas Japan has hardly begun to respond to its neighbours' concerns; Germany is actively engaged in helping a distressed area of the world, East Europe, whereas much of Japan's foreign aid is as valuable to its general trading companies as it is to the designated recipients; and Germany clearly expressed its differences with the Bush Administration's strategy towards Iraq while the Japanese debate centred only on what would satisfy the Americans. In light of these considerations, Americans are tired of being called racists or Japan-bashers for trying to understand accurately what is going on in Japanese policy-making circles.

At the same time Americans suspect that Japanese charges of American racism reveal a Japanese preoccupation with race. The long series of racial slurs uttered by former Prime Minister Nakasone Yasuhiro, by LDP faction leader (and during 1992 Foreign Minister) Watanabe Michio, and by former Justice Minister Kajiyama Seiroku are only the most obvious examples. But this preoccupation with racial categories is revealed in many other, more subtle ways. For example, the *Asahi Shimbun* recently noted that a Japanese citizen, Professor Iriye Akira, was in 1988 elected president of the 18 000-member American Historical Association and then added, 'It is inconceivable that a similar thing [that is, a foreign national assuming such a position] could happen in Japan any time soon' (*Asahi Shimbun*, 9 January 1991, p. 1). Another example was the statement by Sassa Atsuyuki, the former head of the Cabinet Security Office and a strong critic of Japan's lack of military cooperation in the Gulf crisis, that Japan 'underestimated the ferocity of the Anglo-Saxons' (*angurosakuson no sugosa no kashō-hyōka*) (Sassa 1991). An American is tempted to respond that it is not accurate to refer to American citizens as Anglo-Saxons, since the United States is a polyethnic society. But the Japanese might also have noticed that neither the chairman of the American Joint Chiefs of Staff, nor a field commander with the surname of Schwarzkopf, nor many of the troops can plausibly be thought of as Anglo-Saxons. Japan may have underestimated the ferocity of the Americans, but it is alarming that they conceive of this in racial terms.

I do not believe that the Japanese–American alliance is unravelling because of value differences alone. The comments quoted here are, however, symptomatic of the changing emotional and psychodynamic foundations of the relationship. My own position is much like that of Ogura Kazuo: I expect foreigners to have 'foreign' values (Ogura 1991, p. 8). As for Japan's lack of involvement in the Gulf War, I agree with Henry Kissinger when he wrote:

> I told a highly educated and sophisticated friend that I could not imagine any American rationale that would encourage Japan to place its forces at a great distance from its home islands when there was no Japanese urgency to do so. He didn't understand. He said that any nation as

powerful economically as Japan had a duty to participate, otherwise it is taking a free ride. Now that is an approach to foreign policy that might work if everybody had the same interests, but it is also historically unsound (Kissinger 1990).

Nonetheless, it seems to me that the emotional tinder discussed here has a potential for fuelling the larger, more substantive disputes between Japan and the United States discussed earlier. As Barnds puts it:

What appears likely is not a rupture or a complete breakdown of the relationship, but a gradual drifting apart in terms of psychology, trust, and political cooperation. There is as little evidence of American willingness to accommodate Japan's growing (potential) power as there is of Japanese willingness to exercise a measure of leadership (Barnds 1991).

One sample of the possible future course of the US–Japan relationship was President Bush's disastrous visit to Tokyo in January 1992. Bush had earlier cancelled a November 1991 trip to Japan because of American criticism that he was neglecting domestic policy, a cancellation that had the incidental effect of weakening the new Prime Ministership of Miyazawa Kiichi. When the trip was rescheduled for January 1992, the President decided, as an act of political expedience, to link Japan and the issue of American unemployment; and he took with him 21 leaders of American industry, including the outspoken chairman of Chrysler, Lee Iacocca.

On 19 January 1992, Sakurauchi Yoshio, the Speaker of the Japanese House of Representatives, replied that 'It is really pathetic that America is becoming a subcontractor to Japan. The reason for the trade imbalance is that U.S. workers won't work hard and are unproductive and often illiterate' (*Los Angeles Times* 1992; Sanger 1992). This was followed by Prime Minister Miyazawa's remark that the United States had lost its 'work ethic', sparking a retort from Senator Ernest Hollings of South Carolina that American workers should 'draw a mushroom cloud and put underneath it: made in America by lazy and illiterate Americans and tested in Japan' (UPI 1992).

Perhaps more significant is the growing evidence in both Japan and the United States that such political epithets and stereotypes are gaining greater currency among normally uninterested sectors of the two populations. In Japan, the Gakken Company, a publisher of popular and sensational books, brought out a heavily illustrated mass market paperback called *Nihon basshingu ron* (On Japan Bashing), subtitled in English 'Latest Trends in Japan Bashing', which plays to the Japanese public's sense of grievance that it is merely being used as a scapegoat for the failings of others. As if in retaliation, Japanese sports enthusiasts launched an openly racist attack on a Hawaiian contender for the rank of *yokozuna* (grand champion) in sumo wrestling merely because he is a foreigner.

Meanwhile in the US, Americans were objecting strenuously to efforts by the Nintendo Company of Japan to buy a Seattle baseball team. And in

Los Angeles, a popular revolt from below stopped city authorities from completing a contract to buy Japanese-made trolley cars. In many regions of the US a campaign to buy American automobiles showed unexpected strength. And across the nation a new novel by Michael Crichton entitled *Rising Sun*, which deals with the challenge of Japan, became an instant bestseller. Crichton's novel carries as a final epigram a statement by Morita Akio of Sony: 'If you don't want Japan to buy it, don't sell it'.

These sorts of developments can be read as symptoms of the intrinsic situation that has developed between the two countries because of the end of the Cold War and the ability of vested interests—intellectual, military, and economic—to block needed reforms. As I stated at the outset, the Japanese–American relationship continues today only through inertia, without any foundation in grand strategy or in response to a common threat. Obviously, the spread of *kembei* (contempt for the United States) in Japan and so-called Japan-bashing in the United States beyond the circles of policy specialists, and largely because of their myopia and neglect, complicates any attempt to find solutions.

According to one important scenario, the situation is already beyond repair. In their wrongly neglected book (neglected in the United States but not in Japan, where by early 1992 it had sold around 400 000 copies[5]), Friedman and LeBard write:

> It is easier [for the US] to force Japan to limit its exports of cars to the U.S. and to increase its purchase of U.S. cars than to increase the efficiency of Detroit. This is the trap of empire. Empire is first won by the most efficient and industrious. It is then maintained by political and military efforts, not economic efficiency. Thus, economies atrophy while armies and navies grow. This military power is used to transfer wealth from colonies and allies, rather than going to the political effort of rebuilding the domestic economy. At each point, the imperialist power has a choice of solving an economic crisis through internal effort or increased exploitation. The latter, being the path of least resistance, is the usual choice. The result is frequently a vast military force with a hollow socio-economic center, an empire in collapse (1991, p. 401).

This view, of course, owes a great deal to Paul Kennedy's *The Rise and Fall of the Great Powers*, although it stresses the consequences of the decline of the American economy for the Pacific. Whether the failure to correct this decline leads to a US policy of extortion to maintain its superpower status and eventually to war is an open question, but Friedman and LeBard are neither wrong nor sensationalist to draw attention to the possibility.

In my opinion it is not hard to imagine a renewed alliance between Japan and the United States, one based on their current interests and strengths and not on those that existed when the Security Treaty was first negotiated. Such a renewed alliance would first and foremost attempt to

---

5 Sales figures are given in *Los Angeles Times*, 16 February 1992.

institutionalise the economic interdependence of the two countries while recognising their political and ideological differences. On the American side, two things at least are needed: first, a legal framework for managing our trade with Japan (Section 301 of the Trade Act of 1988 would do; if the administration had implemented the law against Japan over its closed rice market, we would probably today have a successfully completed Uruguay Round and much more friendly relations with Japan). Second, we need an industrial policy to ensure that American manufactured goods are attractive to American (and overseas) buyers, thereby avoiding protectionism, which would merely cheat everybody.

But although a newly-formulated Japanese–American alliance is not conceptually difficult to imagine and is clearly in the economic interests of the peoples involved, it would be politically difficult to forge. It would require fundamental changes in the systems of corporate governance, antitrust law, education, and political representation of both countries and an intense analytical effort on the part of the United States. It may well turn out that the two different states, the one military and regulatory and the other economic and developmental, cannot overcome their differences. In any case a renewed alliance would require leadership of at least the 1949 variety, and that, unfortunately, is in short supply on both sides of the Pacific.

4 Japan and the Region: Leading From Behind

ALAN RIX

As Japan's international economic position strengthens on the back of rising trade surpluses, growing technology exports, enhanced creditor status, and a massive aid profile, calls for Japan to show 'leadership' have increased. These have come from within Japan from those wanting to see Japan take a more positive stance on global issues, those who think Japan again deserves a position of world prominence, and those frustrated at Japan being blamed for the economic ills of other countries. Calls for leadership, or at least greater global involvement, have also arisen outside Japan, especially from those who want Japan to bear a larger burden in trade liberalisation, in the Western effort to shore up alliance activities in the various global hot spots, or in rebuilding the economies of Eastern Europe and the former Soviet Union. Thus, this chapter examines what Japan is doing to create the conditions for a more active Japanese role in the Asia–Pacific region. We are interested particularly in this from the perspective of international 'leadership'.

The then Australian Foreign Minister, Bill Hayden, addressing the subject of 'Leadership in the Asia–Pacific Region' in 1988, pointed to continuing American material and moral leadership, but also to the expectation that Japan's success and power carried 'expanded responsibilities', that Japanese public attitudes were adjusting to this transition, and that regional leadership involved trade, diplomatic and financial commitments (Hayden 1988). On the other hand, the *Wall Street Journal* asked:

> ...is this seemingly invincible economic engine destined in the next generation to roll over the world, establishing unchallenged supremacy? Or do Japan's limits—its scarcity of natural resources, its narrowness of

political vision and the animosity it stirs—foreclose true global leadership? (cited in *Australian Financial Review*, 3 March 1989).

Japan and 'leadership': the debate

The single most dominant issue in the debate hitherto about the future role of Japan has been the question of whether Japan can, or will, rival the United States as the dominant hegemonic power. Much of the debate is based on an assumption that Japan actually aspires to this form of global leadership. Some Japan hands predict what Morse (1987) called Japan's inexorable 'drive to pre-eminence', and Ezra Vogel (1986) has foreseen over the coming few years 'a pattern of limited and uneven Pax Nipponica'. This would involve great *de facto* Japanese power, exerted but not with confidence. A recent contribution to the debate about Japanese leadership argues that 'having evolved toward greater international leadership, Japan—the incipient leader of tomorrow —has found itself on the same path as hegemons of yesteryear', providing public goods and running the risk of having to support and meet the costs of the international economic system by itself. The ultimate cost of hegemonic leadership is hegemonic decline (Rosecrance & Taw 1990).

Against these views are ranged a dominant perspective that Japan will *not* emerge as a dominant power. Kindleberger (1981) foresaw 'a superfluity of would-be free riders'. Japan, he argued, had no appetite for world responsibility. Rostow (1985) feels that Japan's capacity to lead is 'restricted by its incomplete acceptance of the trade responsibilities that leadership demands', although the world economy needs the leadership of both the United States and Japan. Gilpin takes a similar stance: 'the nature of their economy has made it difficult if not impossible for them to carry out hegemonic responsibilities' (Gilpin 1987, p. 376). Kent Calder (1988) is also doubtful about Japan's capacity to become 'an overarching hegemon in the international system'. Calder's theory of the 'reactive state' has received much attention, as he focuses on Japan's unwillingness and inability to take independent leadership positions on international economic issues, its relatively weak armed forces, and domestic restraints. Calder argues that Japanese leadership will be 'technical and sector-specific rather than broadly political', if it is to occur at all.

A process of cooperative regime-change involving Japan and the United States is widely supported as the most likely of outcomes. Russett (1988) takes this approach, although Drysdale (1988) argues the case for a more conscious process of collective leadership at least in global economic management, since Japan's growing influence, notably in the Asia–Pacific region, is not dominant or exclusive. Amongst Japanese observers, the model of 'cooperative hegemony' based on the US–Japan relationship is the dominant one. One of the main analysts of Japan's world role, Takashi Inoguchi (1986 and 1991), sees what he calls 'Pax Americana

Phase II' and 'bigemony' as 'the most feasible scenarios over the next 25 years'. The former involves 'the United States retaining its leading position in the world, deftly prodding and cajoling its allies into an enlightened joint action', something that was exemplified in the Gulf Crisis of 1990–91. Bigemony, in contrast, involves closer Japan–US economic policy integration in the joint management of the world economy. Inoguchi clearly prefers the former scenario as it is more manageable, less risky to the world as a whole, and can flow over into a more coalition-based arrangement of states. For Inoguchi (1986), Japan remains a 'supporter', although it must 'adopt a positive policy of contribution as a long-term strategy and carry it out steadily and prudently'. 'Supporter-ship' can, although Inoguchi does not say so, also avoid the penalties and costs associated with leadership.

These contrasting approaches prompt questions as to whether Japan would be content with a cooperative hegemonic structure, whether it aspires to leadership, whether it is demonstrating 'leadership' and, if so, what sort. Furthermore, how limited is its leadership? Is it 'sector-specific' or regional? And what forms does it take? Is there a 'Japanese style' of international leadership? The model of Japan as a cooperative partner is not entirely supported by the evidence of Japan's regional policies, or of Japan's approach to leadership. Let us examine some elements of this approach.

The nature of Japanese regional and global leadership

What most commentators mean by 'greater Japanese responsibility' or 'an enhanced Japanese world role' is never entirely clear, but they are generally seen as involving one or more of the following: speaking up more in international forums, taking greater initiative in multilateral or bilateral contexts, taking more regional responsibility, accepting an increased burden of cost-sharing in international collaborative efforts (such as aid-giving), working towards achieving global objectives (such as environmental protection), or providing intellectual input into debates about management of the global economic and political systems. One possible example of the last is the 'strategic pragmatism' approach said to be the typical Japanese model of action (Schmiegelow & Schmiegelow 1990). This is a form of pragmatic, state-guided economic dynamism, and one that has had a marked demonstration effect on the development strategies of a number of Third World countries, notably the newly industrialising countries of Asia (the NICs): South Korea, Taiwan, Singapore and Hong Kong.

Some of the discussion on the prospects for Japanese leadership is inherently dubious about Japanese capacity to lead. Political leadership in the Japanese domestic context is highly personalised, in many ways still a 'patron–client' mould (Stockwin 1982), but certainly one where power is brokered and interests balanced through close-knit personal networks. Thus, the most likely model of action envisaged for Japan, a cooperative and supportive one, fits more comfortably with the notion of leadership put forward by Oran Young (1989, 1991). He argues that hegemonic dominance, or imposition, is less relevant in today's environment than negotiated leadership:

> ...leadership is not simply a matter of motivation. Nor is leadership merely a form of benevolent behaviour exhibited by the principal members of privileged groups who act in such a way as to supply public goods to others regardless of their unwillingness to contribute toward the supply of such goods. Rather, leadership in connection with the formation of international regimes is a matter of entrepreneurship; it involves a combination of imagination in inventing institutional options and skill in brokering the interests of numerous actors to line up support for such options. A leader in this context is an actor who, desiring to see a regime emerge and realizing that imposition is not feasible, undertakes to craft attractive institutional arrangements and to persuade others to come on board as supporters of such arrangements (Young 1989, p. 355).

Young further points to the role of such entrepreneurial leadership in determining outcomes arising from institutional bargaining in international society. He later specifies leadership in more detail, suggesting forms of structural, entrepreneurial and intellectual leadership, although confining them to the actions of individuals rather than states (Young 1991). There is still confusion about whether collective entities such as states can exhibit this range of leadership characteristics.

I argue in this chapter that Japan does, indeed, exhibit some characteristics of the forms of leadership identified by Young, but they do not add up to a distinctive Japanese play for power or grab for hegemony, although they clearly constitute a limited type of leadership at the state level under conditions of regime formation. This is Japan's 'leadership from behind', its efforts to shape (in the case studied here) an Asia–Pacific order that accepts Japan as an economic power on its own conditions, but abjures the concept of Japanese leadership through overtly dominant behaviour. Attempts to maximise the conditions for effective Japanese action do not constitute a style of leadership in the Washington mould, nor one designed to satisfy Western expectations of what Japan should be doing to raise its international profile or increase its international contribution—to 'pull its weight' and 'lift its game'. It is a style of leadership that aims at creating long-term Japanese influence in the region, and has been a successful form of long-standing 'entrepreneurial' leadership that has carved out a regional role for Japan as investor, trader, aid donor and political actor.

The main issue is the entrepreneurial nature of Japan's approach to the region. Though not yet a recognised leader, over time Japan has been able to 'broker' acceptance in the region of appropriate limits to Japanese international behaviour, limits that suit both Japan and its neighbours.

Achieving consent has been uppermost in Japanese minds. The phenomenon rebuts recent criticism of Japan that it is lacking in leadership. Japan in the Asia–Pacific region is a clear example of the development of leadership over time through ideological convergence, growth of shared values, and tolerance of the limits of behaviour.

There are, however, questions to be asked. What are the preconditions and parameters of this process? Has it worked effectively, and how deliberate has it been? To what extent has it represented merely a flow-on of responses to domestic priorities into the international arena? How has this approach affected particular countries? Has Japan's status in a particular policy area (and here we look at the case of foreign aid) impacted on its leadership? We shall address these issues below.

Preconditions: Japan and the regional context

The Asia–Pacific region is no *tabula rasa* for Japanese leadership aspirations. It is changing quickly under the influence of a range of new pressures. First, US–Japan economic competition is affecting not only the traditionally rather stable relationship between the two powers, but also public attitudes in each country towards the other and the status of each in the region.

Second, alongside the heightening of Japanese economic strength and the creation of a regional Japanese economic presence, has been the appearance of other strong and rapidly growing economies in Asia, and the rise of new players in the regional political economy, as Schmiegelow and Schmiegelow (1990) indicate, modelled closely on Japanese economic development patterns. This has led to more pressing demands for trade and investment by the NICs, notably for large-scale Japanese investment, and joint venturing; and to responses within Japan for industrial restructuring to escape direct NIC–Japanese competition and heavy trade, coupled with intensive trade competition in third markets.

Third, Japanese historical links with the region continue to plague Japanese attempts to assert its views regionally. The visit of the Japanese Emperor to Southeast Asia in October 1991, and the criticism by Queen Beatrix of the Netherlands of Japan's past policies in Southeast Asia, are symptomatic of the Japanese need to mend historical bridges. Buzan's (1988) argument that Japan has to come to terms with its history before it can play an effective part in shaping the future is something of which we are continually reminded. The textbook issue has been a nagging irritant in relations with South Korea and China, and there has never been any committed Japanese response to rectifying the problems that textbook approval raises on a regional level. The potential solidarity of the Asian NICs with Japan, based on its model of development, is undermined by the unresolved tensions of Japan's history.

Fourth, altered power relations within the region are now a major challenge for Japan's capacity to demonstrate leadership. The changes in the former Soviet Union present a grand opportunity for Japan to capitalise on what has been the most intractable problem in its foreign relations since 1952. Yet the process of change is incomplete. Japan's domestic political leaders have been too absorbed with their internal struggles to give much attention to pressing foreign-policy issues. Further south, the resolutions in Cambodia pave the way for renewed relations between Japan and the Indochinese nations, while the questions of China's longer term approach to domestic transformation and the potential for a more liberalised relationship with other countries are yet unclear.

Fifth, the question of Japanese methods is a lively topic. The Japanese 'strategic pragmatism' approach does not, according to Gilpin (1987), qualify it for a leadership role. The approach involves 'state-guided, private polypolistic supply-push innovation' (Schmiegelow & Schmiegelow 1990, p. 572), but it has led to massive Japanese trade surpluses and a continuing reluctance to open its own markets despite strong pressure from the Structural Impediments Initiative and other negotiations. Rosecrance and Taw (1990), in fact, see some evidence of Japan as the world's largest creditor recognising that it has the greatest stake in the maintenance of the world trading and financial system, and beginning to respond to pressure from the economic system over which it has so much influence. This can be seen most starkly in the impact of the 'Japanese model' on the development strategies of industrialising countries, especially in the Asia–Pacific region. Its current policies towards Southeast Asia and the NICs are geared to an export-growth strategy for that region. This is already placing pressure on Japan to move towards hegemonic 'sacrifices' for the sake of regional economies.

Sixth, a final element of the regional context is the question of the Japanese domestic political system and its capacity to produce clear international policies. The most recent testing period in Japanese diplomacy has been marked by continuing domestic leadership instability, and the ineffectiveness of the political system in forging and articulating a Japanese response to international pressures. There are no major developments in the domestic political context which would suggest a change to this process, especially given the defeat of Mr Kaifu's political reform bill in October 1991, Mr Kaifu's own stepping-down as Prime Minister, and his successor Mr Miyazawa's continued stalling over the proposal for Japanese participation in international peace-keeping forces. The Peace-keeping Organisation bill was passed by the Diet in June 1992, despite continuing intense debate in Japan about its implications. It marks a clear new initiative by Japan to assist in international peace-keeping efforts.

Taken together, these conditions constrain Japan's international leadership role, and reinforce the relevance of Japan's entrepreneurial approach towards the Asia–Pacific region. In this context, the sixth point, concerning the capacity of the domestic system to provide a basis for international leadership, has particular relevance. Several studies (Stockwin (ed.) 1988; Calder 1988) have pointed to domestic constraints on Japanese foreign policy, and events surrounding the selection of a new prime minister in November 1991 have reconfirmed the limits of prime ministerial authority in the Japanese political system, and the importance of both party and parliamentary support for international initiatives. Furthermore, the sensitivity of the domestic Japanese constitutional debate touches the heart of the international leadership question, given the potential for both extremely narrow and extremely broad interpretations of the concept of 'self defence', and the intensity of discussion between supporters of those two poles. The Japanese political system has yet to address seriously the problem of changes in Japanese defence policy following the breakdown of communism in Europe and the former Soviet Union, and the process of nuclear-weapons reductions.

Regional economic development: Japan and ASEAN

A key feature of Japan's regional leadership is its impact on regional economies, such as the NICs. The relationship with the Association of Southeast Asian Nations (ASEAN) is an important element of this, since Japan is undoubtedly the major influence on Southeast Asian economic development. Japan's relations with ASEAN have always been governed by Japan's recognition of its own economic and security interests determined by resource supply and geopolitical factors, particularly the threat of regional political instability. This has led successive post-war Japanese governments to lay special emphasis on close relations with the nations of Southeast Asia, and the ASEAN group in particular. Sueo Sudo (1988a) has pointed to the attempts by Fukuda in the 1970s to imprint a Japanese policy perspective on bilateral dealings, and the activist manoeuvrings of the Ministry of Foreign Affairs to give Japan a political role in the region, 'one step further in attaining its role of a regional leader in Southeast Asia'. He went on to suggest that it was the ASEAN policy that could provide a core for a larger international role (Sudo 1988b).

Certainly, the ASEAN relationship has remained central to Japan's regional initiatives, especially in the foreign-aid field (Rix 1992). The Japanese approach to managing ASEAN relations remains centred on economic cooperation, but backed up by cultural exchange and cooperation in such areas as Indochina policy. The centrepiece of Japanese economic assistance to ASEAN is the new Asian Industries Development (AID) plan, involving enhanced investment by Japan, stimulation of small and medium industry in ASEAN using official loans and export promotion policies, and enhancement of technology transfer through both government- and private-sector mechanisms. The programme has been criticised as heralding Japanese attempts to strengthen control over the Asian regional economy and integrating the Asian economies under Japanese leadership (Arase 1988), although it has not yet gone far enough to be drawing such conclusions.

At the same time, the AID plan is a major advance in Japan's activating the benefits of closer industrial cooperation with the economies of Southeast Asia and China. It is a joint public–private-sector programme, exploiting the horizontal division of labour between Japan and Asia, and targeting industrial rather than resources or infrastructure development. It indicates a clear Japanese intention to establish for itself a central position in financing Asian industrial growth. However, success in this objective will depend greatly on the capacity of the administrative system in Tokyo to deliver effective country planning, and on ASEAN responses to Japanese initiatives.

The priority given to ASEAN countries in Japan's regional approach to managing international relations is the result of long-standing ties and a massive concentration of Japanese aid policy mechanisms on delivery of assistance to ASEAN countries. There is no radical new agenda, although Japan has been attempting to play a more assertive regional role since the late 1980s by considering the discussion of a new security framework for the region (*Far Eastern Economic Review* (hereafter *FEER*), 1 August 1991). This involved a proposal for the ASEAN post-ministerial conference to be used as 'a process of political discussions designed to improve the sense of security among us'. Japan did not press the issue much further. Japan's style of regional political action is still couched in the cautious passivity criticised by ASEAN observers in the past. It is not a moralistic style of action, nor one given to grandstanding despite posturing by some Japanese leaders.

Japan's economic leadership in the Southeast Asian region derives from its steady build-up of aid, trade, investment and cultural ties over thirty years and more. Japan has pursued its own discrete objectives into which ASEAN nations fitted quite neatly as targets for economic growth and political stabilisation. There is a strong interdependence factor in Japanese policies towards Southeast Asia that colours the Japanese approach, a factor which bolsters domestic support for the emphasis on ASEAN. At the same time, Japan's dominance of the development priorities of the ASEAN countries is a strong object lesson in the power of historical and cultural ties. It also reminds us of the security priorities for Japan, and of a renewed emphasis on more local security issues with the greatly altered status of the former Soviet Union as the major perceived threat to Japan. As the focal point of Japan's ASEAN policies, relations with Indonesia most closely reflect the Japanese concern for strategic security (*FEER*, 27 September 1991).

Political initiative: Japan and China

The same interdependence lies in Japan's relationship with China; this was central to Japan's negotiating a more pragmatic international response to Chinese action in the Tienanmen Square incident of 4 June 1989. Economic links with China focus also on aid—a link that did not remain affected for very long by Tienanmen. The urgency with which Japan attempted to put suspended aid ties back on a normal course, and persuade others to do the same, speaks loudly of the very practical concerns of the Japanese Government not to interrupt its own aid programme and to remain on sound terms with the Chinese rulers. Japan was certainly activist in its arguing for an early resumption of aid against other powers, and helped change the climate of international opinion in pursuing its plans to recommence aid ties. Its desire to assert its own priorities did work to shift the parameters of international debate.

In late May 1989, contracts were signed on 97.1 billion yen worth of bilateral loans, and these and other ongoing aid activities were not interrupted by the reaction to Tienanmen. The third round of loans for the 1990–95 period, worth 810 billion yen and agreed on with great fanfare during then Prime Minister Takeshita's visit to Beijing in August 1988, was postponed beyond the scheduled start of the loans in September 1989. However, the Japanese Foreign Minister was quoted as already calling in mid-June for a resumption of aid, in order to assist China's economic infrastructure and standard of living (*Australian*, 14 June 1989). By August, continuing aid projects were operating again smoothly, and official cultural relations were back on track. A new grant-aid package for equipment for the Shanghai hospital, a Beijing television station, and a nursing school was announced in December 1989, and aid in the transport field was also resumed in December.

Japan took the opportunity to reconsider its options openly following the visit to China of President Bush's adviser Brent Scowcroft in December 1989, and with the end of martial law in Beijing on 11 January 1990. Takeshita's successor Prime Minister Kaifu had hinted in December 1989 at aid resumption, and bilateral talks with China were set down for late January 1990. These talks produced agreement to begin preparations for loan resumption, including some official surveys. Senior Foreign Ministry officials, and two senior government-party delegations visited China in July 1990, following Kaifu's success in gaining a softer wording on China sanctions in the communiqué of the Group of Seven (G-7) summit at Houston in early July (*Japan Economic Survey*, August 1990; *FEER*, 19 July 1990). Former Prime Minister Takeshita visited China in September to convey Japan's views to the Chinese Government and, with a World Bank decision to resume normal lending to China in October 1990 (as a result of the G-7 decisions on China aid), the loans package was unfrozen. A visit by Prime Minister Kaifu to China in the northern summer of 1991, the first by a leader of the major industrial nations since the events of June 1989, sealed the return to normal relations in aid. The visit was warmly received by Chinese leaders. Anxious to restore relations with the West, they announced China's agreement to sign unconditionally the Nuclear Non-Proliferation Treaty. Kaifu maintained pressure on China over linking aid to arms production and export, but did not press the issue of human rights.[1]

Japan was clearly able to influence Western opinion on the China issue, through a process of summit negotiation and a firm demonstration that it was impatient for a change in the international climate of opinion. Even so, Japan was unable to take unilateral action, but moved instead to try to influence international opinion more quickly towards its own position. It was successful in this, in a rare example of Japan's pre-paredness to bargain for its preferred outcome. It was of enormous significance for Japan to achieve a resumption in the China aid package, for it was crucial to Japan to maintain a high level of disbursement of aid funds to meet promised aid targets. As China's largest aid donor, Japan also had an institutional stake in the maintenance of close relations with the Chinese leadership.

Negotiating the agenda: Japan and Indochina

Japan has shown the same willingness to take part in ongoing international negotiations over the future of Cambodia, although it has been less conspicuous than in its *démarche* over China. The relationship with Vietnam has in the past been solid, based on aid and trade, reflecting the strategic importance of Vietnam in the region (Shiraishi 1990). Vietnam was one of the main recipients of Japanese grant aid in the 1960s, an indicator of Japan's support for American policy in Vietnam. Aid has been suspended since the invasion of Kampuchea in 1979, although Japan has given a small amount of official aid in the form of technical assistance (equipment and expertise), emergency relief, and medical and cultural restoration assistance ($US4.8 million in 1988 and $US1.6 million in 1989), and Japanese organisations are involved in a range of non-official activities (Gaimushō 1990 and 1991).

Speaking in Jakarta in May 1989, the then Japanese Prime Minister, Mr Takeshita, pledged that there would be 'positive consideration to extend financial cooperation, dispatch personnel and provide necessary non-military materials to assist the introduction of an effective control mechanism to facilitate the peace process in Indochina' (Gaimushō 1989). In addition, Takeshita said that 'it is our intention, after a political settlement has been reached, to cooperate in the reconstruction and

---

[1] Details of these events are found in the Japanese newspapers of May–August 1991.

development of Indochina'. Japanese businesses are preparing for renewed economic ties with Vietnam, and the Director-General of the Asian Affairs Bureau of the Ministry of Foreign Affairs was quoted in an official journal as saying that 'with aid to Vietnam frozen, various forms of exchange cannot proceed. Trade is carried out very timidly. I'd like to return this situation to a more natural one in due course' (*Gaiko foramu*, November 1989).

Japan is adopting a strongly supportive bilateral stance *vis-à-vis* Vietnam, although it has not taken any unilateral position on the resumption of aid. Foreign Minister Nakayama pledged further cultural and humanitarian assistance (*Japan Times Weekly* International Edition, hereafter *JTW*, 5–11 November 1990), and acknowledged Vietnam's importance in regional peace and prosperity. At the same time, Japan has strongly supported the UN process to bring the warring parties in Cambodia together, and took an active part in the 1989 Cambodian Peace Conference in Paris and later negotiations. Part of the difficulty that Japan has faced in its Indochina policy has been its close ties with ASEAN (Shiraishi 1990, p. 97); indeed, Shiraishi argues, Japan's scope for initiative in seeking a resolution of the Cambodian problem was determined largely by the attitude of ASEAN. This type of constraint was not present to the same extent in Japan's relations with China, given Japan's dominant position as an economic partner of that country. In fact, China's rapid rise to become one of the top recipients of Japan's bilateral aid was at the expense, and over the protestations, of the ASEAN countries which were fearful of being downgraded in their hitherto major-recipient status. Japan was able to cement its ties with China over ASEAN opposition, but did not have the same freedom of action in relation to Vietnam. Nor was Japan prepared to attempt to move ahead of ASEAN opinion on the Indochina question. Events are moving quickly, however: investors (including ASEAN firms) are keen to shift into Vietnam; Japanese trading houses are already well established there, have proposed major projects, and are urging the Japanese Government to restart Official Development Assistance (ODA) (*Daily Yomiuri*, 8 November 1991; *Yomiuri Shimbun*, 5 November 1991).

The historical agreement in October 1991 between Cambodia's warring factions has opened the way for an active Japanese role in assisting Cambodian reconstruction. There is doubt about whether Japan will take part in any peace-keeping force, although some editorials have strongly supported such a move (*Yomiuri Shimbun*, 24 October 1991). Japan has been laying the groundwork, however, for a substantial economic impact on Vietnam, with Japanese companies poised to be involved in investment and resource exploitation, and with aid ties to be resumed soon. Japan has also taken a creative role in preparing for Cambodian reconstruction and sponsored a conference on this topic in Tokyo in June 1992. This will go with renewed Japanese ODA to Cambodia, stopped after January 1974 except for some minor humanitarian relief. As a first step, Prime Minister Miyazawa has promised a study mission in early 1992, saying that 'we must make an appropriate contribution' (*Yomiuri Shimbun*, 13 November 1991). Undoubtedly, the main expectation from the region is for Japan to put up the funds for reconstruction. Acceptance of this responsibility would be a minor imposition on Japan's aid funds, but it would significantly expand Japan's stake in directing the future of economic development in Indochina, and Japan's authority in international approaches to the region.

Policy leadership: the case of foreign aid

To a great extent, Japan's relations with ASEAN, China and Indochina revolve around matters of Japanese foreign aid. Aid is the single most visible and most controllable means of Japanese international economic management in the Asia–Pacific region. It is because of Japan's standing as the largest aid donor in the region, and its potential for economic influence over so many of the countries of the region, that we cannot say anything meaningful about Japanese international leadership without considering Japan's contribution in the aid field. That can be assessed by asking the following questions:

- is Japanese aid the prime vehicle for less-developed countries' economic development?

- does Japanese aid support Western alliance efforts to manage the Third World?

- is aid the basis of a global shift in power towards Japan?

- is Japanese aid setting a new agenda for Western donors?

Impact on economic development

Through official aid, Japan's impact on economic development in the less developed countries is undoubtedly significant. In 1989 Japan was the largest donor to thirty 'developing countries' (OECD classification), including such nations as Brazil, Nigeria, China, Indonesia and the Philippines. For half of those 30 nations, Japan provided over half the aid received and for five of them (Myanmar, Paraguay, Qatar, Bahrain and Brunei) over three-quarters. In the same year, Japan was the second largest donor to 27 countries. Therefore, of the 144 nations to which Japan gave aid in 1989, it was the leading or next-to-leading donor for over 40 per cent of them (Gaimushō 1991). This gives Japan significant potential influence in economic decision-making in those recipient nations, and on the economic growth potential of regions such as Southeast and East Asia, South Asia and the South Pacific.

Although there has been no large-scale study of the development impact of Japanese aid, and the evidence that we have relates mainly to individual projects or countries, outcomes are obviously mixed.[2] Recent debate argues that Japan's aid has been unquestionably successful in assisting development, especially in Asia, because of the growth of the Asian economies. 'On balance', writes Islam in a recent and widely read book, 'Japanese aid has been effective in fostering economic development, as Tokyo has consistently applied this model of development aid' (Islam (ed.) 1991, p. 213), that is, the model of aid as a support to self-help on the part of the developing-country recipients. Yet such conclusions are not strongly supported by evidence.

Japan has largely avoided the moral debate on the issue of aid and development impact. The stated social vision of Japanese aid has been one of 'economic self-reliance' and 'self-help' on the part of recipients, and Japanese officials have not been greatly troubled by the finer points of the debate about 'who benefits'. This has had the effect of keeping Japan out of meddling in recipient domestic economic and political systems, and out of ideological arguments about which countries should or should not receive aid. Rhetoric about the economic development benefits for recipients of Japanese aid is therefore premature. It is not yet possible for Japan to be a new development vehicle for the Third World because, despite Japan's large aid flows, about one-third of bilateral aid went to only three countries in 1990 (Indonesia, China and the Philippines), and just under one-half went to only five countries (the above three plus Bangladesh and Thailand). One-third of *all* Japanese ODA was spent on these five countries. Japan's aid has certainly shaped the economic future of these nations. Thus, there is potential for significant influence in the future over the development directions of other Asia–Pacific economies, but the evidence is not yet available.

Given the inflexibilities of the Japanese aid system, the slow adoption of country and sector programming, and the limited number of staff in the Japanese aid bureaucracy, the prospects for a rapid diversification of the types and direction of Japan's aid are poor. Nonetheless, for both sides of the debate about benefits there is a need for more data. It would help to have the Japanese aid style more seriously tested in the context of recipient growth and development experience. Even an analysis that both Japanese and American aid has greatly assisted the Philippines economy, points out that with improvements in aid delivery and mechanisms the contribution could have been much greater (Inada 1990).

---

2   The Foreign Ministry publishes an annual collection of project evaluation reports. A series of articles assessing the impact of Japanese aid was published in *Yomiuri Shimbun* in July and August 1989.

Japan's use of strategic aid to support the Western alliance system

Japan's use of strategic aid to support the Western alliance system is well documented (Yasutomo 1986). There has also been some strengthening of Japan's political rationale for aid in recent years, notably 'aid for democratisation', firstly for Eastern Europe, but more generally for those nations that 'adopt freedom and democracy as a fundamental value' (Gaimushō 1990, pp. 47–50). However, this does not yet mean that aid is *withheld* from those countries not holding to these principles, although the then Prime Minister Kaifu proposed in 1991 that aid be limited towards those countries exporting or spending excessively on arms (*JTW*, 18–24 March and 15–21 April 1991). This policy has not been firmly applied to date and was specifically ruled out by Tokyo in the case of aid to Indonesia following the Dili incident of late 1991 (*FEER*, 27 February 1992).

While there is a publicly acknowledged basis for applying political principles in aid-giving, in Japan there is no generally agreed formula on how this might be put into practice more widely. Japan has tended to follow the lead of the United States in giving strategic aid, except insofar as Japan itself has used comprehensive security as a rationale for aid priorities. Japan's use of aid to help manage Third World affairs is governed by several factors: pressure from the United States for Japan to act on its behalf (Orr 1990); aid interdependence with individual countries; broader economic relations; historical ties and Japanese sense of international responsibility; desire for kudos; and the bilateral power balance. Looking broadly at these factors, we are only beginning to see Japanese activity in Third World management. It is as yet unsophisticated, springing more from a desire to manage its own aid programmes and bilateral or regional ties, than from a strategic view of its global responsibilities or a measured philosophy of its preferred world order of which developing countries are a part.

Global power shift

Do we see a global power shift arising from Japan's aid role? As a tool of national policy, aid is effective and extremely flexible. It has helped Japan to a position of economic dominance and political eminence in Southeast Asia (and is heading that way in the South Pacific and perhaps South Asia). It has helped smooth some of the tensions in relations with the United States, provided Japan with a next-to-leading place in multilateral banks and financial institutions, and given Japan some purchase in dealing with Latin American and African nations. However, because aid has not yet been used widely by Japan as a means of political bargaining or diplomatic coercion (except in the broadest sense), we cannot yet say that it has made Japan a major player in global aid politics, although there is some basis for seeing Japan as a more active regional player with its aid as demonstrated above.

International aid debate

Japan's arrival at the top of the Organisation for Economic Cooperation and Development (OECD) aid table has important potential implications for the international aid debate. Traditionally, the United States and European donors have dominated the Development Assistance Committee (DAC), the aid donor group within the OECD. There is as yet no evidence that this has changed, although we have seen greater Japanese influence within the World Bank and the International Monetary Fund (IMF). A firmer Japanese leadership position within the DAC would require not only demonstration of a Japanese commitment to the dominant 'Euro-centric' notions of the purposes of foreign aid, and the broad 'development first' philosophy that has traditionally emanated from the DAC, but also some effective persuading of other DAC members about the merits of the Japanese philosophy of aid. While there are signs that the Japanese may be moving towards incorporating more emphasis on development issues in its aid programme, notably global problems with implications for foreign aid (the environment, population and drugs), there is no strong evidence that the Japanese are negotiating new international positions on these problems.

These initiatives do not, however, add up to anything like a leadership status in defining a new international aid agenda. The role of Japan within DAC itself is still not prominent. Japan does not take a high profile in policy discussions, and tensions remain between European and Japanese representatives. The present Japanese role in the DAC is one where Japan's extensive aid activities are out of alignment with its input into DAC policy.

In foreign aid, therefore, Japan is the key player in the region, but this does not yet extend globally in either structural or intellectual terms. Japan's regional aid role is a major one, and its capacity to influence events in countries throughout the region is considerable. There is, however, no Japanese drive to stamp its presence on the aid debate or to reorder the political economy of international aid relations, even in Asia. Nonetheless, Japan has been unswerving in its adherence to a highly instrumentalist aid policy in the region; coupled with its current dominance of aid flows themselves, Japanese aid will certainly be able to have an ongoing impact on regional development and attitudes to development policies.

Managing a new regional power structure: Japan and the former USSR

Japan's regional leadership has always been based on a policy of avoiding overt dispute with the former USSR. Japan's regional position has not been threatened by Soviet policy. Now its relations with the former Soviet Union are central to the direction of future Japanese policy in the Asia–Pacific region, because of the scale of Russian economic needs, the changed strategic alignments in North Asia, and the scope for Japan to be closely involved in forging a new arrangement of economic and political power. While the issue of who owns the Kurile Islands is currently of concern to the Japanese, that is of less long-term significance than matters of Japanese economic and technological relations with its new neighbours. At this stage there is little to show of Japanese initiative in the relationship, but it is early yet in the evolving post-socialist Soviet order.

When President Gorbachev visited Japan in April 1991, Japanese hopes for some resolution of the northern territories dispute were high. But while the resulting communiqué at least acknowledged for the first time since 1956 the existence of a problem, no agreement was reached. Fundamentally, Japan was reluctant to aid the Soviet Union given the extreme uncertainty about the country's future as a united federation (*FEER*, 9 May 1991), and Japanese investment in the Soviet Union is exceedingly small (about 0.05 per cent of total overseas direct investment). At the same time, it was recognised that Japan would have to go along with other G-7 nations if it were decided to assist the Soviet economy in a major way. While trying to maintain a tough line on linking economic assistance to Soviet territorial concessions, senior Japanese officials were reported noting that 'Japan will no doubt be obliged to play a leading role if the summit nations reach a consensus on providing financial help to Moscow, since Germany is largely side-lined by its need to channel funds to the eastern part of the nation' (*JTW*, 10–16 June 1991).

President Bush urged the Soviets to settle the Kuriles dispute with Japan (*FEER*, 8 August 1991), but it was not until after the failure of the August coup and a rearrangement of the Soviet political order that support was expressed in Moscow for the legitimacy of Japanese claims to the islands, and for the notion of a territory–aid trade-off. In a letter to the Japanese Prime Minister, Boris Yeltsin offered the islands in exchange for large-scale Japanese aid. Deputy Chairman of the Soviet Union's interim Cabinet, Georgy Yavlinsky, referred to the 1885 Japan–Russia Treaty (which allocated the four islands in question to Japan) as 'a good moral and legal starting point to solve the dispute' (*Australian*, 11 September 1991).

Despite a lack of firm agreement with the Soviet Union on sovereignty over the northern islands, the Japanese agreed in October to provide an emergency aid package of up to $US2.5 billion, including humanitarian aid, technical assistance and trade insurance (*FEER*, 17 October 1991). The reason for the package was linked to the G-7 discussion on Soviet aid, and the push from European members for Japan (and Canada) to contribute to the overall support (*Australian*, 9 October 1991).

Japanese negotiations with the old Soviet Union both on territory and aid delivery still lie ahead. Likewise, decisions on the longer term involvement of Japanese investment in the ex-Soviet economy (particularly in the Far East) have yet to be addressed. Unless there is improved stability in these economies over the coming few years, it is likely that direct investment on any large scale (akin to that in China) is a long way off. Japan's objectives at this stage are still short-term. The leader who can bring home the northern islands will gain great domestic political kudos; for the first time in the post-war period Japan is in a position to extract concessions from Russia and, so far, has used its financial strength as a crude bargaining tool, even to the point of some resistance to G-7 decisions on aid. As of early 1992, however, Prime Minister Miyazawa is moving carefully, de-linking the question of aid from that of territory (*Yomiuri Shimbun*, 7 November 1991).

It is too early to be definitive about Japan's future relationship with Russia and the Commonwealth of Independent States. This is partly a result of the Commonwealth's own instability and uncertain economic and political future, but there are a range of constraints on the Japanese side as well. To begin with, Japan remains a solid treaty partner of the United States and has a defence profile that is still dependent on American support, even if this dependence is diminishing.

Second, reforms do not eliminate regional tensions. North Korea still remains an unpredictable player, even though there have been contacts with Japan, some indications of flexibility on the part of the North Koreans, a Japanese Government decision to consider recognition of the North (*Nihon Keizai Shimbun*, 11 September 1991), and constructive talks between the two Koreas.

Third, political manoeuvrings within the Japanese governing party deflect attention from the policy issues, and lay open the party to factional disputes over foreign policy questions.

Fourth, Japan's improved relationship with China (despite the continuing Chinese hard line on human rights issues) could conflict with a softer Japanese approach to Russia and support for democratisation in that country. The stronger moral component in Japanese aid policy is aimed primarily at the Chinese, even though it is not applied to the aid itself; this policy runs counter to the strongly affirmative stance shown towards democratisation in Eastern Europe and the former Soviet Union, which is being backed up by economic assistance.

Fifth, the relations between the international community and the former Soviet Union have not given Japan great scope for international leadership, except in providing certain levels of aid. Japan was ultimately unable to exert its voice urging caution on the question of support for the

Soviet economy, and bent to the majority opinion in the G-7 following the August coup. The test of Japanese leadership on this issue will come over the Kurile Islands and the longer term Western contribution to the rehabilitation of the economies of the former Soviet republics.

Political partnership and economic dominance: Japan and Oceania

Japan's relations with Oceania are essentially economic in their implications for Japanese leadership. With the nations of the South Pacific the link is aid, with Australia it is trade and investment. In the South Pacific Japan has such a large and growing aid presence, with the potential for massive over-presence (given the imbalance between Japanese aid funds available and the lesser needs of the Pacific nations), leadership will depend on Japan's ability to adapt its aid profile to the needs of the recipient countries.

The Australian connection is one where Japan's creative diplomacy has been somewhat lagging. For many years Japan has been content to let economic issues drive its Australia policy, although a brief high point of then Foreign Minister Kuranari's incumbency was his 1987 Pacific cooperation initiative, aimed primarily at arousing some Pacific agreement about the need to control the Soviet presence in the South Pacific. The major bilateral issue remains that of the damage to third countries such as Australia from Japan's economic disputes with the United States and Europe. Japan has publicly agreed to avoid such impacts, but the political reality is that ultimately such assurances cannot be guaranteed.

A more active component of Japan's dealings with Australia in recent years has been in the area of political cooperation. Japan's interests lie, according to the recent Foreign Minister, Mr Nakayama, in the need to 'tailor our policies in a cooperative effort' (Nakayama 1991). This has extended to greater defence contacts, and former Australian Prime Minister Hawke expressed his view that Japan's world stature should be recognised by a permanent seat on the Security Council of the United Nations, to mark the greater world leadership that was Japan's 'as of right' (*Sydney Morning Herald* and *Australian Financial Review*, 20 September 1990). Japan will occupy a rotating seat for two years from January 1992. The current Prime Minister, Mr Miyazawa, has himself called for a restructuring of the UN Security Council, seeking a permanent seat for Japan (*Yomiuri Shimbun*, 1 February 1992).

But does that leadership extend to Japan's policies towards Australia itself? In many ways Japan's global economic position depends on its assumption that Australia (and similar major resource-exporters) will remain stable and reliable across the range of mineral and agricultural resources that Japan dominates as a market. A key factor is the heavy level of investment that Australia depends on from Japan, and the growing influx of tourists. Japan's approach to Australia is still one of rather tired tolerance and linkage maintenance.

Leadership is more likely to arise in relation to multilateral initiatives such as the Asia–Pacific Economic Cooperation (APEC). The concept of Pacific cooperation is one that has its roots in Japanese discussions of the 1960s, and a series of cooperative mechanisms put in place mainly with the assistance of former Prime Minister Ohira and his Foreign Minister, Dr Okita, over a decade ago. Japan has added its support to the APEC process that began with the initial ministerial meeting in Canberra in November 1989, and the second in Singapore in July 1990. Dr Nakayama's approach is that 'we attach importance to and support APEC as a process of cooperation open to the world and contributing not only to the Asia–Pacific region but to the global economic prosperity' (Nakayama 1991). Similarly, Japan has not shown great enthusiasm for the counter-proposal from Malaysia's Dr Mahathir for an East Asian Economic Caucus (EAEC), concerned that it would be too exclusionist and sub-regional (*JTW*, 13–19 May 1991). The United States is strongly opposed to the Caucus and has urged Japan to reject it. At the third APEC meeting in Seoul in November 1991, Japan expressed its firm support for the APEC process, emphasising as a reason for such support its own unique status as Asia's dominant economic power and G-7 summit member (*Yomiuri Shimbun*, 14 November 1991).

Japanese leadership in the Pacific region will depend ultimately on its contribution to negotiating a regional economic cooperation process that can embrace the South Pacific nations, Australia, New Zealand and Southeast Asia. There is indeed an opportunity here for Japan to adopt active intellectual and structural leadership in directing the evolution of successful regional economic cooperation. This involves issues of environmental management just as much as resource trade and industrial development. There is still some way to go in Japan adopting a firm position in international environmental policy development, despite the very strong initiatives that Japan is making in its aid programme directed towards environmental protection.

What is Japanese leadership?

There is clearly an image abroad of Japan as a non-leader, an expectation that Japan is not willing or able to take, or is prevented from taking, the sorts of leadership actions that might constitute the imaginative, broker-ing, persuasive role that we outlined early in this chapter. A great deal of media attention in recent months has been devoted to assessing what is wrong with the Japanese system, and what prevents the creative and swift policy responses necessary for effective international leadership. Much of this analysis stemmed from the inability of Japan to come up with rapid and effective reactions to the Gulf Crisis. Yet despite former Prime

Minister Kaifu's unequivocal apology for Japan's past misdeeds, and his forthright explanation of its developing political role in the region, the media reported that Kaifu's Southeast Asian trip in May 1991 'reminded Japan less of its political clout in world affairs than of the high expectations pinned on the nation by Asian neighbours seeking economic assistance' (*JTW*, 13–19 May 1991).

One writer argued that it is 'bureaucratic gridlock' that prevents the formation of appropriate policy, the lack of a unified, centralised management of government decision-making, even despite the notional supremacy of Cabinet over the bureaucracy (*JTW*, 13–19 May 1991). Lack of intelligence was another drawback, as was bureaucratic infighting within the Cabinet's Information Research Office, the main intelligence-monitoring agency of the government (*JTW*, 20–26 May 1991). Likewise, the Foreign Ministry has come in for sustained criticism, some critics arguing that 'it has lost its credibility completely', 'the Ministry is in chaos', or that it is unable to compete with its bureaucratic rivals in management of economic diplomacy (*JTW*, 5–11 August 1991 and *FEER*, 18 July 1991).[3]

A number of Japanese commentators, concerned at renewed US–Japan tension following the Gulf War, have argued for a more realistic Japanese approach to its world role. Hitoshi Hanai has put the case for a 'Japan as No. 2', helping the United States to reduce its trade deficits and debts, because 'Japan has neither the strength nor the wish to become [the dominant] power' (*JTW*, 15–21 July 1991). Others, such as the Chairman of Keidanren, Gaishi Hiraiwa, urge a distinctive Japanese contribution, economic in its basis and founded on 'principles and a framework of rules acceptable to the international community' (*Keidanren Review*, August 1991). He suggests Japan act as a 'coordinator' in the Asia–Pacific region to help the integration of local economies into the world market. To say that there is confusion and argument amongst Japanese commentators would be an understatement; the key point is, however, that there is some groping towards agreement about an appropriate role for Japan.

The body of this chapter analyses Japan's current regional influence and initiatives. Japan is a regional presence of enormous stature and influence. Its economic impact on ASEAN, China, Indochina, the former Soviet Union and Oceania is, either already or potentially, unparalleled in scope and intensity. Its foreign-aid profile is regionally dominant and likely to continue to grow. Japan's present status has a long history of accumulated regional responsibilities, in spite of domestic political and administrative limitation, its reputation as a reluctant leader, and argument at home about what is best for Japan to do. Japan's leadership role is already established, but there is clearly scope for it to continue a Japanese-

---

3   Recent proposals for strengthening the Ministry include the creation of a broad policy bureau and an intelligence/information bureau (*Yomiuri Shimbun*, 26 October 1991).

led programme of regional economic growth and development, to sponsor policy collaboration through regional institutions, and to create a longer term agenda for resolution of regional tensions.

There is ample evidence in Japan of the 'structural leadership' that Young describes, bringing the possession of material (mainly financial) resources to bear in the form of bargaining leverage. But there are some intellectual aspects of Japanese leadership at work as well, influencing the perspective of those participating in institutional bargaining (aid to China and Indochina is a good example). Japan has been at pains to shape an Asian order that accepts it as a power without military force, working to prescribe conditions for economic development that place major emphasis on the need for reasonably stringent guidelines for economic assistance (the principle of 'self-help'), and arguing firmly for a process of regional cooperation in regime-building, rather than overt domination by one power or another.

Japan's intellectual leadership has been subtle in its achievement of a broadly held view that Japan should play a soft political role in the region. Its structural bargaining has focused mainly on bilateral relationships and overt dominance of multilateral forums has been avoided. On a case-by-case basis, Japanese bargaining can be insistent; but its intellectual position has meant that Japan has been unable, because unwilling, to exert that strength forcefully at the multilateral level. A related problem in that context has also been the institutional impediments in the Japanese political and administrative system to a higher profile at the multilateral level.

This suggests that Japanese aspiration towards international leadership has been focused on creating the conditions for such a role, consistent with the economic strength, political influence but military weakness of its present international profile. It is a truly 'entrepreneurial' (in Young's terms) leadership style because Japan has laid the basis for structural leadership through sustained impact on the regional consciousness about the most effective and beneficial limits of Japanese international behaviour. This 'leadership from behind' has tried to maximise the conditions for effective Japanese action.

A dominantly influential Japan is now accepted and encouraged by the region because of regional benefits. Japan has engaged the countries of the region in an economic interchange that is now inescapable. It has helped develop economic performance in its own image within some of the region's economies, and alongside this economic influence its political role is also now entrenched. This has not been the result of a master plan, but the accumulation of domestic priorities that included resources policy, export promotion, industrial development, comprehensive security and a low-profile diplomacy. It has brought about a distinctive Japanese style of international leadership 'from behind'.

5 'New' Trade Theory and Policy a Decade Old: Assessment in a Pacific Context

J. DAVID RICHARDSON

This chapter characterises and evaluates what has come to be called variously the 'new', 'new-view', 'strategic', or 'industrial organisation approach' to international trade and trade policy. This approach, now more than ten years old, analyses trade in 'strategic environments'. Strategic environments feature small numbers of large, self-consciously interdependent agents who interact in activities that are themselves often interdependently (strategically) linked. The new view's perspectives have been controversial, but often because they have been misunderstood—like many ten-year-olds; and many of its subtler strengths have remained hidden. These misunderstandings and subtler strengths of the approach are the main themes of this chapter. A secondary emphasis is on applied and empirical work in the new tradition and its policy implications, with special regard to Pacific trade and investment.

Worldwide industrial organisation, and patterns of international trade and investment, have changed markedly since the 1950s. In parallel the economics sub-disciplines of industrial organisation and international trade have both undergone significant intellectual evolution. The policy implications of the changes and evolutions have been initially arresting. The new approach to trade policy is essentially an arranged marriage between new trade perspectives and new industrial-organisation perspectives.

The new approach to industrial organisation and regulation[1] has, for example, called into question traditional regulatory maxims such as that

---

[1] The theory is surveyed by Bonanno and Brandolini (1990), Jacquemin (1987), Schmalensee and Willig (eds) (1989), and Tirole (1989). The practice is surveyed by Areeda (1992) for the United States, and by Boner and Krueger

'big' and 'concentrated' are *per se* 'bad'; that vertical restraints, such as those on distributors' prices and client networks, inhibit competition (Coate & Kleit 1990); and that predatory practices are rarely seen in reality. It has also called into question the traditional treatment of the government regulator as an enlightened agent of the general public, viewing the regulator instead as a self-concerned maximiser. Especially when future private-sector jobs beckon, *that* maximiser is exposed to strategic private-sector influence, and perhaps capture.

Likewise, the new international-trade theory, building on the new approach to industrial organisation, has called into question traditional trade-policy maxims: 'free' trade is best except for irrelevant optimal-tariff arguments; subsidising exports shoots a nation in its own foot; most-favoured-nation non-discrimination has dominant strategic value; and infant-industry protection rarely succeeds in reality.

With challenges like these, it is no wonder that the new trade approach has inspired a counter-evolution, with appeals to the authority and wisdom of traditional perspectives, and disparagement of the new academic adolescents for naivety, myopia, inexperience and worse (see, for illustration, Bhagwati 1989b, Corden 1990, Haberler 1990).

Yet the new trade theory properly appreciated is both simpler and subtler than it appears. In essence, it proposes marriage—specifically that the new approach to industrial organisation and regulation (competition policy) be wedded to trade policy. The new theory argues that the two are not as distinct as they used to be, and insists that neither trade policy nor competition policy be evaluated independently of the other. This means that every trade policy initiative should account for its effects on national and international market structure, corporate conduct, and competitive performance. Likewise, every competition policy initiative should account for its spillover effects on trade, on foreign investment, and on the efficacy of foreign competition policies.

It is more than a little ironic that the marriage should be considered new at all, or evolutionary. It was arranged long ago. The Havana Charter of the stillborn International Trade Organisation contained an eight-article chapter on restrictive business practices with a remarkably modern ring— it covered fair competition and market access in both goods and selected services, by both private and state-owned firms. Both the Organisation for Economic Cooperation and Development (OECD) and the United Nations

---

(1991) for the United States, Canada and Australia, Japan and Korea, and more than the usual sample of European countries (Sweden and Spain, as well as France, Germany, the United Kingdom and the EC as a whole). Boner and Kreuger's comparisons have less focus on new-view industrial organisation alone, but Ordover (1990) and other contributors to Comanor et al. (1990) blend discussions of the new theory and practice for the United States and major European countries. Viscusi et al. (1992) is a textbook that does the same for the United States alone.

through the United Nations Conference on Trade and Development (UNCTAD) have developed voluntary codes to cover some of these concerns. The OECD, in fact, maintains an ongoing discussion of them (OECD 1984a, b, c, d; 1985; 1987a, b; 1988a, b; 1989a, b, c; 1991a; see also Willig 1983; Goldberg & Ordover 1991; Government of Canada 1991).

Recently, however, circumstances have been forcing trade and indus-trial-organisation perspectives even closer together (Barton 1990; Brittan 1992; Davidow 1991; Feketekuty 1991; Holmes 1991; Matsushita 1988; Montagnon 1990). Multinational corporate penetration and alliance-building (Graham & Ebert 1991; Julius 1990; Kravis & Lipsey 1989; Lipsey & Kravis 1986; Lipsey 1989, 1991; Ostry 1990a) have put pressure on governments to rationalise their competition policies and to consider negotiating GATT-like (General Agreement on Tariffs and Trade) agree-ments for international investment (Bergsten & Graham 1991; Committee for Economic Development 1990; Julius 1991; and Ostry 1990a). The European Community (EC) is forging a common competition policy, without respect to borders, in part to avoid circumvention of lower border barriers (Brittan 1992; EC Commission 1989, 1991; Rosenthal 1990). Japanese competition policy has raised unique trade and investment issues (Fung 1991; Ichikawa 1990; Lawrence 1991; Petri 1991a; Sheard 1991). Accentuated anti-dumping activism (Brooms 1990; Feltham et al. 1991; Lexenomics 1990; Messerlin 1991a, b; Nicolaides 1991a, b), voluntary export restraint arrangements (Barton 1990; Holmes 1991), and increased trade protection for intellectual property and high-technology industries (Jorde & Teece (eds) 1992) have all begun to come into conflict with competition policy. Liberalisation experiments in developing countries (Frischtak et al. 1989; OECD 1991a) have usually involved inter-dependent mixes of trade-policy and competition-policy reform, and have propelled these countries towards negotiating agreements on intellectual property protection and technology transfer (Barton 1990; Deardorff 1990; Maskus & Eby Konan 1991) in order to enhance their competitive structure.

The present survey of these trends and the new thinking about them is organised as follows. Part 1 is a meta-survey: it surveys the many surveys of the new approach. Part 2 updates them. Part 3 attempts to correct mis-impressions that have sprung up about the new view, and Part 4 attempts to highlight some of its subtler charms. Part 5 then assesses its importance to Pacific area trade relations.

1. A survey of the surveys

The broad character of new perspectives on trade theory and policy is now familiar to many in the academic and policy communities. A plethora of surveys in the past five-to-seven years has helped to impart this character.

Since the purpose of this chapter is to examine both prejudices and hidden virtues in the common characterisation of the new view, I will not attempt another survey. Rather in this section, I will briefly survey the surveys before moving on to refine the character sketch.

It seems helpful to do the meta-survey in tabular format. One feature that is immediately evident from Table 5.1 is that there is a considerable amount of *empirical* research on aspects of the new view. Much of this is relatively simple in its methodology: for example, case studies and simple numerical simulations figure prominently. But there is a long history of econometric approaches as well, summarised most completely by Globerman (1988), Goldberg and Ordover (1991), Lipsey and Dobson (eds) (1987) (see especially Geroski 1987), Markusen (1985), and Richardson (1989, 1990a). The consensus of the econometric research[2] surveyed there is that indicators of trade liberalisation such as export growth and import penetration: (i) correlate[3] negatively with measures of corporate market power, such as the proportion by which a firm can raise price above (marginal) cost; (ii) correlate positively with measures of productivity growth; but (iii) have little correlation with rates of entry into or exit from industrial activity. The first two correlations suggest that trade liberalisation is, indeed, still in the national interest, even under conditions of imperfect strategic competition. The third (lack of) correlation is anomalous. Expectations are that liberalisation stirs up creative Schumpeterian ferment, but there is little evidence of this so far.

Table 5.1 Surveys of new-view trade theory and policy

Survey	Distinctive Audience	Emphases	Distinctive Features
Baldwin (1991)	General economist, student (G)	Continuity of new view and traditional	Illustrative general equilibrium setting of new view, using 'Baldwin envelope'
Brown & Garman (1990)	Specialist economist (labour)	Labour-centred versions of new view	Implication for international factor migration and investment in human capital /contd

---

2 The best examples, often based on panels of industrial plants (that is, data with variation both across plants and over time), are: Caves (1988); de Ghellinck et al. (1988); Morrison (1989); Roberts (1989); and Tybout (1989). Roberts and Tybout (1991) is an update and extension of the earlier papers.

3 All these correlations control for relevant determinants of the variable under investigation *besides* trade liberalisation.

Table 5.1 cont.

Survey	Distinctive Audience	Emphases	Distinctive Features
Dixit (1984)	Specialist economist (IT, IO)	IO precursors of new view; Cournot algebra	One of the earliest surveys
Globerman (1988)	Specialist economist (IT, IO)	Partial equilibrium diagrammatic summary, empirical evidence surveyed	Review of new-view precursors in the Canadian literature, Eastman–Stykolt Case study of telecommunications subscriber equipment
Goldberg & Ordover (1991)	Specialist economist (IT, IO)	Non-tariff trade barriers and effects, especially voluntary export restraints (VERs) and cartels	Survey of empirical research on effects of VERs in agriculture, autos and textiles
Grossman (1990)	General economist	Welfare economics of sectoral policy in new-view settings; infant-industry arguments for high-technology activities	Cogent algebraic/graphical decomposition of new-view welfare effects Brief surveys of empirical studies Discusses implications of informational asymmetries
Grossman & Richardson (1985)	General economist	Welfare economics of strategic profit-shifting trade policies	Brief discussion of strategic-government-vs-government literature
Helleiner (1989)	Specialist economist (development)	Comparison and contrast to traditional infant-industry themes —learning, scale, externalities; applicability to developing countries	Case studies and empirical work on related themes in other chapters of the book

/contd

Table 5.1 cont.

Survey	Distinctive Audience	Emphases	Distinctive Features
Helpman (1984)	Specialist economist (IT)	Trade patterns and gains from trade (not trade policy) under scale economies	Technical treatment of foundational distinctions: national/international scale economies; homogeneous/differentiated products; no/free entry; segmented/integrated markets
Helpman (1989a)	Specialist economist (IT)	Trade policy with monopolistic competition and endogenous growth	Intra-industry trade; multinational corp.; North-South terms of trade
Helpman (1989b)	Specialist economist (IT), policy community	Trade policy with oligopoly and with endogenous growth; consideration similar to Helpman & Krugman (1989)	Anticipatory survey of Grossman & Helpman (1991)
Helpman & Krugman (1985)	Specialist economist (IT)	Patterns of trade, welfare gains with scale economies and product differentiation	Norm of integrated global economy; market contestability
Helpman & Krugman (1989)	Specialist economist (IT), student (UG, G)	Partial equilibrium, traditional perspectives with monopoly; new-view strategic perspectives under various scenarios	Empirical chapter Could be textbook
Krishna & Thursby (1990)	Specialist economist (IT)	Strategic profit shifting, effects of export restraints and other indirect policies	Agricultural illustration
Krugman (1989)	Specialist economist (IT, IO)	Similar to Krugman (1985) and Helpman & Krugman (1989)	Special attention to free entry and import protection as export promotion
Krugman (ed.) (1986)	General economist, policy community, political scientist	Varied	Industrial-activist school represented; highly readable

/contd

Table 5.1 cont.

Survey	Distinctive Audience	Emphases	Distinctive Features
Krugman (1987a)	General economist	Strategic profit shifting, externalities	
Levinson (1988)	Policy community	Summary more than survey	Brief, accessible
Lipsey & Dobson (eds) (1987)	General economist, policy community	Evaluation of industrial-activist school from new-view perspective	Multiple discussants of highly readable overview by Brander; useful synthesis by Lipsey
Markusen (1985)	General economist, student (G, UG)	Gains from trade with scale economies; impact of entry conditions	Simple general-equilibrium diagrammatics Canadian research and empirical evidence starting from Eastman–Stykolt
Pomfret (1991)	Specialised academic (IT)	Welfare economics of trade policy	Extensive references Discussion of selected empirical studies Similar sequence, treatment to Helpman & Krugman (1989)
Richardson (1989)	General economist, student (UG, G)	Results of empirical studies of welfare, dislocation effects	Bibliographic completeness Algebraic, diagrammatic summary similar to Markusen (1985)
Richardson (1990a)	General economist	Same as (1989) plus survey of econometric work by industrial-organisation economists on margins, total factor productivity, and entry/exit	

/contd

Table 5.1 cont.

Survey	Distinctive Audience	Emphases	Distinctive Features
Richardson (1990b)	General economist, political scientist	Critical, comparative review of Cohen & Zysman (1987), Krugman (ed.) (1986) and Lipsey & Dobson (eds) (1987)	
Vousden (1990)	Student (G, UG)	Textbook, economics of protection under perfect then imperfect competition	Political economy chapter; economics of adjustment, preferences, piecemeal reform

General economist = professional economists without regard to field.

Specialist economist = international trade (IT) or industrial organisation (IO) interest.

Political scientist = political scientists and academic specialists in international relations, political economy, etc.

Policy community = government officials, journalists and other commentators.

Student = graduate (G) or undergraduate (UG).

More recent econometric research, summarised in Part 2, supports and refines these findings. From all of it, the first prejudice in the common characterisation of the new view becomes clear. The prejudice is that the new view is entirely theoretical, unsupported by empirical evidence. Part 3 of this chapter discusses several more prejudices.

Part 2 also attempts to allay one other suspicion of the new view: that its theoretical support derives from simple-minded, old-fashioned, static models of oligopoly and monopolistic competition. The Table 5.1 catalogue suggests that there is much more than this to the new view (see especially Helpman 1989a, b). Dixit, Grossman, and Helpman notably have pioneered pathbreaking *dynamic*[4] analyses of trade policies and other governmental intervention under imperfect competition, to which we now turn.

---

4 Even so informed a contributor to the industrial-activism school as Laura D'Andrea Tyson seems to neglect the new-view 'dynamic models', though some of their conclusions support the industrial activists' policy recommendations. See, for example, the lack of attention in Tyson (1991).

2. Recent research

Analytical, empirical and policy-relevant research in the new approach continues at a rapid rate.

Of recent analytical contributions, Grossman and Helpman's (1991) book-length synthesis of a number of their own papers is especially noteworthy for its synthetic scope. It develops a realistic-but-stylised model of endogenous innovation, growth and trade, and explores its policy ramifications. The model features the kind of Schumpeterian process that is often alleged to undermine traditional policy perspectives based on assumptions of perfect competition. Thus, in Grossman and Helpman's treatment, successful innovators earn the right to price above cost, but need to expend resources, especially human capital on research and development (R&D) or reverse engineering, and are under constant pressure from new entrants to the production of information. Some specific information can be appropriated, but more general information cannot. The latter creates a positive spillover from R&D activities that can sometimes be kept within national boundaries, but may also spill over internationally. Merchandise trade involves both inter- and intra-industry flows of goods. The assumption that the marginal product of additions to the knowledge stock does *not* diminish creates a form of economies of scale from simultaneous additions to all inputs. Expectations matter, and historical accidents and temporary government policies can all matter forever.

Out of this structure comes an ordered cornucopia of scenarios in which trade (and industrial and technological) policies matter, sometimes along traditional lines (free trade is often wise[5]), sometimes along the lines of the industrial-activist school (strategic government promotion of selected activities is sometimes wise).

The more impressive contribution of the monograph is the order—the systematic organising principles for the cornucopia of dynamic policy options. This is not just another new-view contribution in which 'anything can happen' (see the discussion of that quip in Part 3). Grossman and Helpman show 'on average':

- how countries that are large in size, knowledge base, and/or abundance of human capital tend, indeed, to grow faster than others and to specialise in high-technology activities;

- yet how R&D (with large pro-growth spillovers) and high-technology manufacturing (with smaller pro-growth spillovers) often 'compete' with each other for the same human capital, so that a country that favours the latter over the former will often be *inhibiting* its growth;

---

5 See Rauch (1991) for the beginnings of empirical work along these lines, examining the growth patterns of Chile before and after trade liberalisation in the 1980s.

- how the case for trade-policy intervention becomes weaker as spill-overs become more and more internationally diffused and less and less nationally self-confined;

- how policy promotion of R&D in countries without comparative advantage in it can slow down growth world-wide, and therefore how much stronger the case is for policy promotion of R&D in locations where it is done most efficiently.[6]

The most noteworthy recent empirical contributions to the new view are econometric.[7] Levinsohn (1991) is a contribution in the same vein as Roberts (1989), Tybout (1989), and Roberts and Tybout (1991). For a sample of Turkish plants in industries of varying imperfect competition over the period 1983–86, Levinsohn finds the familiar responsiveness of the price/cost margin to trade liberalisation: plants' market power, measured by the degree to which they can raise prices above costs, is constrained by the extent of trade openness. Caves and Barton (1990) also find results of the familiar kind—specifically a fairly tight negative correlation between import penetration ratios and organisational *in*efficiency in a number of US industries[8], controlling for other determinants.

Yet several recent econometric contributions cut across the grain of these traditional conclusions. Dick (1991a, b), for example, takes the observation from new-view industrial organisation that horizontal co-operation (collusion) may be *pro*-competitive on balance, and applies it to respective panels of US and Japanese export trading companies (legally sanctioned cartels).[9] In both cases, many industries show significant

---

6 Grossman and Helpman are more careful than my summary to draw the distinction between policies that increase growth rates and those that increase national economic welfare. Not all that do the first do the second, and conversely.

7 Numerical simulation continues, e.g., Norman (1990), Venables (1990), and Klepper (1990), all in the same issue of the *European Economic Review*; R. Harris (1989); Norman (1989); Hunter et al. (1991). Case-study approaches also continue, e.g., Industry Commission (1990), Tyson (1991), OECD (1991b). Irwin (1990) represents an approach to economic history from the new-view perspective. In general, the conclusions from these varied approaches replicate the conclusions from earlier empirical work in the same tradition.

8 Their measure of organisational inefficiency is distance from a production-function frontier, estimated across several industries and time. They have to impose a similar structure across disparate industries because they lack the plant-level observations used by Levinsohn, Roberts and Tybout in the studies discussed above.

9 The US panel is made up of sixteen homogeneous commodities for which Webb-Pomerene Associations existed for certain (but not all) years in a full-time series of data running from the 1920s through to the 1960s. The Japanese panel is made up of a full-time series of data from 1950 through to 1984 on twelve homogeneous commodities for which Japanese export cartels were formed at various times during the 1950s and 1960s.

correlations of export price and volume in a pro-competitive direction, rather than in an anti-competitive direction (always controlling for other determinants of export supply and demand). Dick interprets this as consistent with the view that horizontal cooperation lowers the overseas marketing costs of exporters and improves the credibility of their quality guarantees.

These recent econometric papers illustrate an important trait of the new view. It is pragmatic—in exactly the same way as industrial organisation is pragmatic. Competition and open markets are on balance good things. But there *are* exceptions, and these exceptions may warrant policy intervention.

3. Mis-impressions about the new views

Even a cursory reading of the surveys in Table 5.1 corrects some obvious mis-impressions about the new view. For example, it is immediately clear that the new view reasons from the traditional perspective of overall national economic welfare, not from the mercantilistic perspective of producer interests or export competitiveness.[10]

The two most fundamental mis-impressions about the new view are, however: (i) that it is not new at all, but tired and irrelevant; or, almost perpendicularly to the first impression, (ii) that it has sealed the theoretical case for active industrial policy (along Japanese lines, of course). Three other mis-impressions as well as these are discussed below.

(i) *It's old hat.* It is easy to form the frustrating suspicion that new-view contributions are merely old mercantilist and federalist arguments—about optimal tariffs, infant industries, rent seeking, and the strategic importance of manufacturing—all decked out in the emperor's new clothes of strategic international competitiveness. The new views admittedly do encompass those old arguments.

But they also add considerably more: richer analyses of power, threat and commitment; tighter reasoning about entry, exit, research and development, reverse engineering, inter-temporal incentives, and economic dynamics—reasoning that allows statistical hypothesis testing on at least some questions; and instructive, if not compelling, metaphors from arms races, deterrence, retaliation, bargaining and coalition formation.

(ii) *It's the greatest thing since sliced bread.* It is easy to become carried away with the persuasive stories of successful industrial targeting, especially in high-technology sectors, especially by Japan and other Asian high-growth economies. Cautionary distinctions are rare—to many North Americans, the Ministry of International Trade and Industry (MITI) and

---

[10] This sometimes sets the new view apart from, and at odds with, the industrial-activist school represented by Cohen and Zysman (1987) or Tyson (1991) or contributors to OECD (1991b).

the Ministry of Finance are monolithic, and *chaebol* and *keiretsu* are the same thing in different languages, and equally successful too. Stories of grave targeting failures are forgotten—commuter airliners for Japan, supersonic airliners for Britain and France, Synfuels projects for the United States, endless failures for developing countries.

If the new view concludes anything, it is that the case for targeting is complex and necessarily pragmatic. Indeed, since the new view always carries along at least one distortion to the perfectly competitive norm (imperfectly competitive market structure, production externalities, informational asymmetries, or some combination), its assessments necessarily apply to a second-best situation, in which information and pragmatic judgement are necessary to draw any normative assessment about trade policy.

The new view has hardly killed the case for free trade; if anything, it has probably strengthened it (see Richardson 1989); what *has* been killed though, is the ability to defend free trade on the basis of ideology alone—and that may be just as well.

No single issue illustrates this as well as trade policy towards intellectual property, where the pragmatic case for granting (patent) protected market power in order to facilitate innovation (via appropriability of its rewards) is in constant tension with the equally pragmatic case for gains from free trade in presently protected products and processes. Should intellectual property protection be strengthened, say by trade sanctions authorised by the Trade-Related Intellectual Property negotiations of the Uruguay Round? If so, innovation would be probably enhanced in innovating countries, and increased rents earned by them. But those same innovating countries might gain even more under weaker intellectual property protection if innovations abroad could be imported or copied more quickly and easily, and with less risk and cost (fees, royalties, etc.). Imitator countries might be better off with strengthened intellectual property protection if the global pace of innovation were sufficiently speeded (albeit with slower dissemination), or with weaker intellectual property protection, if the pace of dissemination were sufficiently speeded (albeit from a smaller base of innovations). There is no way to resolve any of these issues in principle or ideologically. Factual, objective, pragmatic analysis is the only way, and that analysis could as easily suggest more managed trade in intellectual property as freer trade![11]

(iii) *It may be new, but it's practically irrelevant.* Still another mis-impression, more like the first than the second, is that because industrial competition is fairly workable after all, there is little practical relevance to new-view perspectives. This mis-impression observes how rarely markets are truly monopolised, and how rare even duopoly or triopoly is; this,

---

11 See Maskus and Eby Konan (1991) or Deardorff (1990) for more detailed discussions of various opposing criteria in issues concerning intellectual property protection and free trade.

coupled with deductive and empirical evidence that markets of four, five or more firms begin to behave very much like perfect competitors (see Bresnahan & Reiss 1991), leads to the verdict that the new views are practically irrelevant.

One trouble with this impression is its obvious inconsistency with the perceived need in every major country for *some* form of competition policy. Another is the short shrift it gives to the competitive economics of innovation, R&D and product cycles, discussed in Part 2 above, where monopoly ownership of patents and privileged market position are the rule and the reward for innovation. Another trouble is that new-view perspectives also apply in a perhaps more relevant case, where market power is passed down to labour through monopolistic agents. For example, excess profits may be passed along to workers in the form of wages that are higher than competitive norms. This is especially likely if workers are represented by a union or professional organisation which has power comparable to that of the employing firms, and which is able to protect its constituency (incumbent membership) from competitive pressure by free entrants (rival workers). Since inter-industry wage differentials are, in fact, much larger than can be explained using the model of perfect competition, there may be sizeable excess profits hidden in the wage and professional salary structures of the United States and many other developed countries, even though the industrial structure appears workably competitive (see Brown & Garman 1990; Dickens & Lang 1988; Katz & Summers 1989; Salinger 1984; and Thaler 1989).

(iv) *It's at least relevant to our leading-edge firms.* And still another mis-impression, more like number (ii) than number (i), is that new-view targeting should identify strategic firms not just strategic sectors, encouraging 'national champions'. Here those who are confused seem to have France in mind rather than Japan, which has vigilantly insisted on diffusion of information and technological innovation to small firms, precisely to avoid problems of accentuating competitive imperfections and creating unhealthy identification of government with a single corporate interest.

Contrary to this impression, there is surprising agreement among all new-view commentators—and even among many of the best known industrial-policy activists—that *firm*-focused government intervention creates some of the *worst* economic and political economic incentives for all parties. Thus, for example, the preference ranking for types of government microeconomic policies is virtually the same between the activists Cohen and Zysman (1987) and among the economists contributing to Krugman (ed.) (1986) and Lipsey and Dobson (eds) (1987): market-perfecting infrastructure first; government promotion of saving, education and R&D second; trade and industrial policies towards whole sectors third; firm-focused policies fourth, if at all (see Richardson 1990b, pp. 117–18).

(v) *It's a hopeless, helpless thicket of special cases.* Some commentators confronting the complexity of saying sensible things about trade policy in the new view conclude that nothing can be said! But this is an overreaction. The reaction gives inadequate credit to constructive contributions such as the agreement over policy ranking under (iv) above; or Grossman and Helpman's organising principles in trade policy for innovation and growth (Part 2 above); or the clear consensus of new-view empirical research and case studies of developing countries that, on balance, open trade and competition policies are more beneficial than the traditional view implies, not less (see Richardson 1989, 1990a and Frischtak et al. 1989).

4. Under-appreciated implications of the new views

Many attractive features and conclusions of the new perspective on trade policy are subtle, and not immediately apparent on first encounter:

(i) *The value of reciprocity, variety, even dumping.* The new views create appreciation for certain features of trade regimes that never fit the traditional perspectives well at all. Thus, for example, reciprocity in the new perspective should make trade wars less likely. It can be a convention that heightens the stability of a sequence of cooperative trade agreements among governments, and reduces the chance that recurrent negotiations will devolve towards noncooperative equilibriums.[12] Or, for example, variety in the new perspective is no frivolity. It contributes directly to welfare or productivity, filling niches that precisely match consumer preferences or input specifications, niches that would otherwise be unoccupied. Variety in capital goods and intermediate inputs lowers costs and improves productivity. Intra-industry trade can be as welfare-enhancing as traditional trade (see, for example, Ravenhill 1992). Or, for example, dumping has certain natural *pro*-competitive features, as described below.

(ii) *The hidden costs of traditionally sanctioned trade remedies.* The new view creates new concern about the costs of anti-dumping remedies and recourse to 'voluntary' agreements (see Davidow 1991 and Feltham et al. 1991). Anti-dumping remedies can be invoked in many countries as a result of import pricing below constructed cost, no matter what the product price is in the source country. The new view shows, however, how often pricing below apparent cost is an efficient business tactic (see Deardorff 1989). New-view dynamic models show the desirable effects of allowing new generations of products to succeed old, a process that is attenuated or cut off entirely if firms producing the old products can bring

---

12 The language conveys the proper feeling, although the point being made is, in fact, fairly technical and game-theoretic. See Axelrod (1984) for a seminal contribution in a stream of research that continues to be extended and refined (*Science News*, 18 January 1992, p. 39, reports on one strand, for instance).

successful anti-dumping suits on the grounds of predation. Predation by new and better generations of products is, from this point of view, a quality that enhances productivity, and anti-dumping activism may undermine growth as well as static efficiency. [13]

For different reasons, the new view raises caution about 'voluntary' practices that fall into grey areas on the fringe of the GATT. Price undertakings permitted to settle anti-dumping suits, for example, have all of the characteristics of price fixing. Voluntary export restraints that set market-share ceilings have all of the characteristics of cartels. [14] Trade-related performance requirements for investors may often involve anti-competitive export market sharing or exclusive links to local suppliers at the expense of competitive imports. [15]

Finally, all of these traditionally sanctioned practices can be barriers to entry. Free entry is, in fact, a trait the benefit of which is better appreciated in the new view than in the traditional, where it gets taken for granted.

(iii) *The advantages of maximally free entry*. One of the central lessons of industrial organisation is that the potential for entry disciplines market power. [16] Yet many of the more arresting interventionist conclusions of new-view trade analysis rest in some fashion on barriers to competitive entry. One example is the well-known potential for strategic trade policy to shift oligopolistic profits towards one's own firms—*incumbent* firms to be exact. When new firms are allowed, the same policy merely causes excessive entry in pursuit of the policy-generated rents—resource-wasting rent seeking of the classic kind. Such entry in the face of scale economies may, furthermore, drive each individual firm 'up' its average cost curve, thereby imposing a productivity penalty as well from the 'inefficient entry' (see Horstmann & Markusen 1986). Another example is the well-known potential for import protection to serve in some circumstances as a means of export promotion. It is not widely appreciated that the fundamental mechanism here is that trade policy serves as a barrier to foreign entry, and that when domestic entry is allowed it is often inefficient, and wasteful rent seeking dissipates the export-promoting advantage of the policy.

---

[13] Areeda's (1992) comment with respect to antitrust is relevant here as well '...without a more disciplined test for predation...litigation may chill the impulse, perhaps already weak, toward price competition in oligopolistic markets'.

[14] Price fixing and cartels are the practices least tolerated or rationalised by all nations' competition policies. In the United States, they are *per se* illegal.

[15] Pomfret (1991) has an excellent new-view survey of trade policies as 'facilitating practices', the term from industrial organisation that describes practices that facilitate *anti*-competitive behaviour.

[16] Even the mere potential for entry is sometimes enough, as the literature on contestable markets shows.

It is important to appreciate that the higher-profile interventionist results from new-trade analysis subtly promote support of one's own incumbents and suppression of foreign entrants, thereby undermining the general understanding of how important entry is *in general* for markets to work well, for avoiding oligopolistic rigidity and turgidity, and for achieving workably competitive outcomes, even with imperfect competition. New-view analyses that make these counter-interventionist points are unfortunately lower in profile but should not be. New-view analysis without free entry almost *invites* the proliferation of entry barriers that would justify further policy activism on behalf of incumbents. This would be a devolutionary vortex of the classic rent-seeking, resource-wasting kind.

New-view analysis with free entry has a number of policy implications that need highlighting. One of the most important is the entry-facilitating value of minimal transparent barriers to cross-border merger and acquisition, which is often a means by which new entry takes place (or by which exit is avoided[17]). Another is the pro-competitive value of wide access to the bureaucratic trade-policy process, which is otherwise weighted in favour of incumbent firms. For example, to promote access, anti-dumping and countervailing duty cases might be required to include economic impact evaluations that would calculate injury to domestic users from the remedy, as well as injury to domestic producers from the offence (see, for example, Finger & Dhar 1991). Or, for example, new firms (as well as consumers) might gain from a weakening of the sovereign compulsion doctrine that insulates incumbents from antitrust suits brought in opposition to voluntary restraint arrangements.

(iv) *A cautious analysis of externalities, with emphasis on their scope and appropriability.* Comparative advantage in the new view is less deterministic and more influenced by policy than in the traditional view. Trade patterns among countries, for example, are indeterminate under economies of scale and imperfect competition. That is, for purposes of the political economy of strategic trade policy, there are many alternative geographical concentrations of production for scale-intensive goods that each feature the same relative prices, global supplies and global demands. Countries can inherit shares in a given alternative by historical accident or can stake claims to shares by policy aimed at getting there (that is, reaching some preferred alternative) first. The controversial question is why one pattern of comparative advantage is better for a nation's standard of living than another.

The broadest answer is externalities, and the new view has more things to say about them than is commonly acknowledged. Externalities are hard-to-appropriate spillovers from one economic activity to another, or

---

17 The proposed co-ownership of McDonnell-Douglas' commercial division by Taiwan Aerospace and other Asian investors is a good example.

linkages among them. 'Hard-to-appropriate' means that it is hard to assign property rights to them, and thus hard to buy or sell them.

One particularly provocative perspective that the new view casts on externalities can be summarised as follows (see also Richardson 1990b, pp. 119–21):

a. Many spillovers and linkages are detectable, if not precisely measurable.

b. They are most accurately detected by information gathered efficiently by private-sector agents such as stock analysts, commercial and investment bankers, and strategic planning groups of firms contemplating merger.

c. Therefore, they are more and more internalisable; and

d. less and less a valid ground for government intervention aimed at capturing their benefits.

This perspective on externalities has been shaped by the new economics of information. Information, like technology, is a kind of product that can be produced (like others) by devoting resources to it. Information describes and detects many things including interdependent linkages. Banks, brokers, analysts, accounting firms, venture capitalists, shareholders and potential joint-venture partners are all in the business of producing information for the market. The market for information works about as well as any other, and has been the beneficiary of impressive technological innovation in informatics and telecommunications. As a result, it is increasingly true that even subtle complex products and services can be defined well enough, made appropriable enough by assigning property rights, and thereby made marketable. True externalities are increasingly the exception. They are the spillovers and linkages that cannot be appropriated, priced and marketed. Thus, instances of government intervention justified by externalities will be exceptional too. They will have to rely on the government's information being better than that of banks, brokers, analysts, accountants and so on. Otherwise the rule will be that there is very little that deters any firm from joint ventures with firms in sectors that are somehow vitally linked to it.

In an era of growing alliances and information then, many more intersectoral spillovers are appropriable. They are not externalities and give no suggestion of the need for policy. The distinctive role of a government as an identifier and corrector of growth and competitiveness externalities, and as a shaper of comparative advantage, is being filled by firms and banks that are able to do so very well for themselves.

From this perspective, there are hidden costs in government barriers to cross-border mergers and to trade in services such as accounting, brokerage, investment banking and underwriting. The hidden cost is the inefficiency introduced into information markets and the constriction of markets that would otherwise work to internalise spillovers and linkages among sectors.

The broader new view is not, however, dogmatic on the issues of externalities. The particular perspective described above is not yet a consensus. Detection of technological spillovers and linkages *is* incomplete; their appropriability and, therefore, marketability *is* only partial. Thus, Grossman and Helpman (1991), for example, include extensive theoretical treatment of the extreme in which spillovers *are* nationally containable, as well as the extreme in which they are diffused internationally. And Caballero and Lyons (1989, 1990, 1991 jointly with Bartelsman) find significant empirical evidence for inter-sectoral externalities, in both short and long runs, for both Europe and the United States.[18]

(v) *A cautious analysis of political economy, with warnings about regulatory capture.* The broader question underlying several new-view issues is how different the political economy of the new view is from the political economy of the old, and how different it may be from polity to polity.

Krueger (1990), a new-view sceptic, presents one provocative answer to this broader question: 'not much', she says in essence. She appeals to the regulatory-capture tradition in industrial organisation (see Stigler 1971 and Peltzman 1976), in which political and economic pressures turn regulators increasingly towards viewing the industry being regulated as a constituency to be served. Her first step is a careful exposition of the parallels between post-war infant-industry arguments for developing-country protection—now largely discredited because of wasteful and inequitable government failure; and more recent technological-infant arguments for industrial-country protection—often accepted blithely as something governments can, *should*, *MUST* do. Krueger reminds her readers of how unlikely it would be for governments to fail so miserably in the first instance and succeed in the second. She discusses the daunting information requirements that confront any government attempt to pick promising infants of any kind; the rent-seeking opportunities that often proliferate as a result; the informational advantages that industry has over government with inevitable incentives to misrepresent; the consequent inability to conduct any form of realistic cost-benefit evaluation (well accepted as a precondition for other government programmes); and the inherent irreversibilities and time–consistency problems in all infant-industry protection—that mere legislative promises of temporary-protection-until-the-industry-matures are often inconsistent with both government and industry incentives when the time actually comes to remove the protection.

---

18 Their findings, however, do not deny that such externalities can be captured internally by firms that operate in many sectors.

Yet Krueger's is not the only possible answer to the broad question. Industrial activists often claim that Northern European corporatism and the East Asian culture of business–government cooperation are alternative and better models of political economy. If so, then Krueger's questions need to be answered directly. Was such success in spite of capture? Or was capture, in fact, helpful in some regards? If so, how were informational problems overcome, rent seeking and misrepresentation minimised, and time–inconsistency avoided? What were the sectoral failures, and why did they fail? The new view virtually invites new study of the political economy of industrial policy in Germany, Japan (see Yamamura & Yasuba 1987; and Inoguchi & Okimoto 1988), Korea, Taiwan, and Singapore, compared to the same in selected English-speaking and in developing countries.

(vi) *The advantages of an international agent for competition policies.* Reporting, monitoring, mediating and rule-making in the matter of 'fair' competition are important functions that every government carries out domestically. Often this is done with some degree of structural independence built between the competition authorities, politicians, and the industries subject to the rules, precisely to avoid the abuses of regulatory capture and 'crony capitalism'. At the international level, however, no competition authority exists, and the new view can be easily misconstrued to be a form of crony capitalism writ large, in which 'my cronies are my country's firms'. Properly construed, however, the new view points to the need for an international ordering of competition policies, with at least some harmonisation, and possibly with an institutional structure possessing some degree of independence from industry and national politics, though, of course, chartered by national politicians. Such an institution could be like the GATT, for example, a general agreement on competition policies. Or it could be a code to the GATT, to be negotiated in a future multilateral round. In any event, the new view provides ample reason to contemplate this sort of institutional change.[19]

The GATT is concerned principally with border policies, and has less to say about non-border policies. Among other things, the new view highlights the ability of a government to create the moral equivalent of a border policy by its choice of non-border policies. This is, of course, true in traditional perspectives as well, where a tariff or export subsidy, for example, could be replicated by a combination of production subsidy and consumption tax. But the importance of the point is greater in the new view, since the firms concerned with international market access are not atomistic but have profiles, and since under some circumstances permanent sectoral displacements can be achieved by temporary and/or pre-emptive policy decisions.

---

[19] See Brittan (1992) and Graham and Richardson (1991) for more discussion along these lines and Camps and Diebold (1986) for prescient anticipations of these concerns.

5. Pacific policy implications

For better and worse, Pacific countries have been centrally involved with practical experiments in new-view trade policy for many years. Pacific experimentation has included activist national initiatives, reactivist national responses, bilateral 'grievance negotiations', and pragmatic bilateral cooperation.

Many Europeans and North Americans believe that Japan, Korea, Singapore and Taiwan have been the most active practitioners of new-view trade policies. They fear that Thailand, Malaysia and perhaps others will follow. Out of that perception has come questionable dependence on anti-dumping defences and voluntary restraint arrangements, and also more constructive experimentation with special bilateral, sectoral and 'structural' negotiations over integrated trade and competition policies aimed at establishing new ground rules and more level playing fields.

Australians and New Zealanders seem to share these beliefs and perceptions. Out of that has come a promising experiment in bilateral integration and harmonisation of their respective trade and competition policies.

(i) *Activist national initiatives and reactivist national responses.* It is not at all clear, according to some of the best recent studies of Asia–Pacific growth and development, that strategic new-view trade policies have been really all that important. Both Noland (1990) and the Industry Commission of Australia (1990), for example, put much greater weight on a stable, predictable policy environment, on high rates of investment, saving, and education, on opportunities for inexpensive technological catch-up, and on a relatively even internal distribution of the gains from growth.[20]

In fact, if any consensus exists on Asia–Pacific trade policies, it is that they have been on balance outwards oriented. The same cannot be said of European and American defences against Asia–Pacific competitiveness. Both anti-dumping barriers and recourse to voluntary restraint arrangements are inwards oriented and facilitate oligopolistic distortion, extortion and waste, as described in Part 4 above. Furthermore, their facilitation of competitive imperfections occurs worldwide, enabling exporter firms as well as importer rivals to fix prices and market shares. New-view analysts of every ideology find much to worry about in such trends.

But it is also true that whatever their trade posture on balance, Asia–Pacific countries have in some instances aggressively substituted or maintained non-border policies for border policies. Production subsidies and support, coupled with high taxes on luxury goods and inefficient distribution systems between consumer and producer, have many of the

---

20 The Industry Commission's research covers Japan, Korea, Taiwan, Hong Kong and Singapore. Noland's research covers the last four plus Indonesia, Malaysia, the Philippines and Thailand.

same effects as import protection and export promotion. Barriers to foreign direct investment, whether by takeover or greenfield means, insulate domestic incumbents from entry by foreign firms behind the effective border barriers. In addition to the obviously protectionist policies towards merger, acquisition and establishment by foreign firms, such barriers to foreign direct investment include tightly regulated, closed financial-service markets, and permissive policies towards domestic 'recession cartels' among weak firms facing reduced business. New-view analysts worry about these trends too.

Two recent experiments in Pacific area trade policies meet new-view concerns in novel and constructive ways. They also illustrate new-view integration of trade and industrial policy issues.

(ii) *The Structural Impediments Initiative* (SII) (see Cooper 1991, and Noland 1991). The Structural Impediments negotiations between the United States and Japan arose out of the recurrent grievance bilaterals of the 1980s[21], all concerned with US complaints about Japanese barriers to market access. These grievance bilaterals were first carried out sectorally under normal US 'Section 301'[22] auspices, then under the multisector approach of the Market-Oriented Sector-Selective (MOSS) negotiations, and (almost) under the pattern-of-unfair-trade-practices approach that would have been associated with the naming of Japan under US Super 301 procedures. Japan was named only narrowly, of course, because agreement was reached to experiment with the SII approach to the broad issues.

Among other things, SII negotiations touch on exclusive business practices, distribution, and pricing by Japanese firms, and on inadequate R&D, inadequate export promotion, and burdensome official export controls in the United States. Each country draws up a list of perceived structural impediments to market access in its counterpart, then negotiates reciprocated commitments to reduce impediments. The goals of the enterprise are faster growth, improved market access, reduced trade imbalance, and less perceived inequity between the two trading partners—precisely the concerns of most new-view reasoning. SII borrows from standard trade negotiations the strategic principles of horizontal bargaining over multiple issues, cross-issue trade-offs, (implicit) request/offer procedures, and (implicit) nondiscrimination.

The jury is still out on whether SII commitments have been successfully implemented (the exercise is slated to continue for three years). But it is likely that the substance, if not the exact structure, of SII will appear again in relations between the United States and its Pacific trading partners.

---

[21] Richardson (1992) contains a fuller account of what follows.

[22] Section 301 in US trade laws allows the US Government to initiate negotiations with any trading partner over practices that create discriminatory, unjustifiable or unreasonable barriers to US goods and services, and ultimately to impose sanctions if the negotiations are unsuccessful.

If SII-flavour negotiations were to be seen as a desirable way to merge negotiations over trade policy, industrial policy and technology policy, three big issues would need to be resolved:

a. What scope? Would continued bilaterals along SII lines be wise? Or all that was feasible? Would a broader multilateral approach be possible? A new GATT round (see Brittan 1992)? An OECD-centred negotiation? A Pacific-area minilateral? Do Asian countries, Australia and New Zealand need to worry about possible bilateral deals on competition policy and access between the United States and the EC that would be aimed at insulating them from Pacific-sourced market disruption?[23] How could smaller countries with uniquenesses and grievances of 'less weight' be represented?

b. What role for the legislatures? The US Congress did not officially authorise SII negotiations, nor ratify the outcomes so far. It remains to be seen whether US SII commitments can really be substantive or credible without Congressional backing and implementation, or whether Congress would have any interest at all in authorising further exercises.

c. What fit, if any, to national styles of political economy? It is not at all clear that the priority given to commercial interests in SII-flavour negotiations matches the priorities, traditions or desires of voters. Voters in the United States, in particular, still cling to populist suspicions of all 'big' business, whether foreign or domestic. Americans, more than most, fear corporatist co-option of government (see Richardson 1987, pp. 104–7). On the other hand, Americans do seem to be wondering whether US management as well as government couldn't learn a thing or two from Asian success stories.

(iii) *The Australia–New Zealand Closer Economic Relations (CER) Agreement* (see Brooms 1990; Thomson 1989; and Thomson & Langman 1991). The CER Agreement has been in force since 1983, but was buttressed by new commitments as a result of a 1988 review, and is currently under review again. It is in many ways a comparable effort to the European Community's attempt to complete a single internal market, only without the bureaucratic superstructure of the European Commission or any designs on political or monetary union.

In addition to bilateral free trade in most services as well as goods, the CER commitments that illustrate new-view perspectives most directly are: the replacement of anti-dumping and other trade remedies with harmonised competition guidelines for fair business practice; the attempt to establish a common business law more generally, as well as common

---

23 Early reports of the September 1991 agreement on competition policy cooperation between the United States and the EC included this as an implicit motivation for the agreement.

rules on standards and technical specifications; disciplines over non-border subsidies to industry; and cross-country standing for each nation's regulatory authority to investigate and enforce the new agreements.

The jury is also still out on how these CER commitments will be maintained through the deep macroeconomic downturn of the early 1990s. Assuming that they are maintained, the CER experience, like EC experience, may help to shape wider Pacific and global negotiations along these lines in the future. The key issues, however, are:

a. How special is the CER experience? Australia and New Zealand began with many parallels—language, history, legal and political systems. How much is transferable to the experience of other nations?

b. How open could the CER arrangements be or become? In particular, what sort of accession would be possible for other important trading partners, Pacific or otherwise? And what sort of evolution would be possible for the various rules of origin that govern the eligibility of goods, services and establishments for provisions of the CER Agreement?

It is interesting to consider the parallels between CER features and issues and those that confront the North American Free Trade Agreement (NAFTA) currently being negotiated between Canada, Mexico and the United States. In what areas, for example, could the CER ever become open to Indonesian accession in the way that the Canada–US agreement became open to Mexico? Could the NAFTA and CER agreements ever come together across the Pacific without further participation by Asian or Latin American Pacific countries?

Big questions such as these are worth asking, of course, but begin to depart from the practical, pragmatic attempt of the new view to integrate the perspectives of trade policy and competition policy because the global environment for trade and investment has forced such integration. A smaller and more rhetorical question is perhaps a useful way of summing up the contribution that new-view trade analysis makes: isn't it significant that *no* important regional trade agreement today is concerned with border measures alone, and virtually all include provisions for 'fair' industrial competition? That is what the new view is about.

6 The 'Japan Problem' in Pacific Trade

JOHN RAVENHILL

The Pacific, we are often reminded, is the most dynamic region of the world economy. The sustained rapid economic growth of the economies of Japan and the region's newly industrialising countries (NICs), and more recently of China and most of the Association of Southeast Asian Nations (ASEAN) countries, caused the Pacific's share of world trade to grow from 43 per cent in 1969 to 53 per cent in 1988.[1] Trade *within* the Pacific has accelerated markedly, increasing from 17 to 26 per cent of world trade over this period (Petri 1991b).[2] Intra-regional trade consequently has become relatively more important for the Asia Pacific Economic Co-operation group (APEC), and for the member countries individually (see Tables 6.1 and 6.2).

APEC markets now account for more than two-thirds of all exports originating within the region, a marked increase over the last decade. Regional trading partners also consume a similar proportion of APEC-manufactured exports; again a rapid growth in their share was recorded in the 1980s.[3] Even without intra-regional trade preferences, economic inte-

---

1 From 1965 to 1987 the NICs' (Hong Kong, South Korea, Singapore and Taiwan) share of world income rose from 0.5 to 1.9 per cent. The combined share of Indonesia, Malaysia, the Philippines and Thailand rose from 1.0 to 1.3 per cent. In the same period, Japan's share of world income increased from 5.4 to 16.5 per cent (Noland 1990, Table 1.1).

2 For the purposes of this chapter, the Pacific is defined as the fifteen members of the Asia Pacific Economic Co-operation grouping: Australia, Brunei, Canada, China, Hong Kong, Indonesia, Japan, South Korea, Malaysia, New Zealand, the Philippines, Singapore, Thailand, Taiwan, and the United States.

3 APEC markets became more important in the 1980s for all members, save for the two major oil exporters, Brunei and Indonesia. A similar pattern holds true

106

gration within the Asia–Pacific region has reached levels approaching those within the European Community.

Table 6.1 Share of APEC countries in APEC total exports 1980–90 (%)

	1980	1984	1990
a. All commodities			
APEC 15	54.2	64.0	66.4
APEC 13 to APEC 13	38.7	37.0	42.1
APEC 13 to North America	23.0	32.4	29.2
b. Manufactures*			
APEC 15	51.4	64.1	65.4
APEC 13 to APEC 13	28.8	27.4	35.9
APEC 13 to North America	27.4	39.7	33.7

Note: * Manufactures are defined as Standard Industrial Trade Classification 5–8 less 67 and 68.

APEC 15: Australia, Brunei, Canada, China, Hong Kong, Indonesia, Japan, South Korea, Malaysia, New Zealand, the Philippines, Singapore, Taiwan, Thailand and the United States.

APEC 13: The above less Canada and the United States.

Source: Calculations by International Economic Data Bank, ANU using UN trade tapes.

The data in Table 6.1 also underline the importance of the North American market for the region's exports: the United States and Canada account for close to one-third of all of the exports of the other thirteen APEC members (Western Pacific). In the 1980s, overall exports from the Western Pacific countries to North America increased more rapidly than trade *within* the Western Pacific region. Similarly, the share of other APEC countries in US exports rose dramatically during the 1980s. By the end of the decade, more than half of all US exports were being absorbed by other APEC countries (30 per cent in the Western Pacific). An Asian economic grouping which excludes North America, along the lines of that

for manufactured exports, although some levelling off occurred in the second half of the decade in the region's share of manufactured exports from three of the NICs (Hong Kong, Singapore, and Taiwan), with the share of Singapore and Taiwan's manufactured exports going to other APEC markets actually declining. This fall in the rate of growth was perhaps a reflection of the proliferation of voluntary export restraints and other trade barriers within the region to their manufactured exports in this period; it may also have reflected attempts at market diversification.

proposed by Malaysian Prime Minister Mahathir, would be a much less significant and less dynamic actor.

Table 6.2 Share of APEC markets in members' exports 1980–90 (%)

Member	Total exports			Manufactures*		
	1980	1984	1990	1980	1984	1990
Australia	58.5	57.6	69.6	46.3	45.2	72.9
Brunei	95.0	97.7	86.9	99.8	100.0	5.8
Canada	73.5	83.6	86.1	79.8	90.6	90.8
China	68.8	79.3	81.0	62.9	77.8	80.1
Hong Kong	51.8	68.7	69.9	51.3	68.7	69.0
Indonesia	87.3	87.1	82.0	67.7	78.3	67.7
Japan	55.2	66.0	66.5	54.7	65.2	65.6
South Korea	59.5	66.3	69.1	56.8	63.3	67.4
Malaysia	71.4	74.9	81.1	71.8	79.1	78.6
New Zealand	54.0	58.2	64.3	75.3	80.8	80.0
Philippines	72.8	79.4	79.9	67.0	78.1	78.2
Singapore	61.2	67.8	70.9	66.5	73.6	70.2
Taiwan	67.6	79.4	78.1	67.2	79.6	76.2
Thailand	54.6	56.7	63.2	58.7	64.4	63.1
USA	38.2	46.2	50.3	38.0	48.0	50.0

Note: * Manufactures are defined as SITC 5–8 less 67 and 68.

Source: Calculations by International Economic Data Bank, ANU using UN trade tapes.

The acceleration of economic integration in the region, its overall welfare benefits notwithstanding, has produced a new set of political frictions. These have centred around bilateral trade imbalances, differences in national economic structures and concomitant trade composition, and continuing (and in certain instances increasing) barriers to intra-regional trade. Among the most important of these impediments are restrictions on trade in agricultural products, and the use of voluntary export restraints and orderly marketing arrangements by the region's industrialised countries in efforts to constrain the growth in exports of 'sensitive' manufactures from regional trading partners.[4]

The desire of Northeast Asian countries to maintain existing barriers to trade to protect politically influential domestic groups has complicated efforts to reach agreement on agricultural issues in the Uruguay Round. But from the perspective of their *systemic* repercussions, by far the most serious disputes in intra-regional trade concern differing economic structures, their associated trading patterns, and the imbalances in bilateral trade that they produce. In particular Japan's unusual trading pattern,

---

4 For discussion of these barriers to intra-regional trade see Drysdale and Garnaut (1989), Stern (ed.) (1989), and Anderson and Tyers (1987).

especially its relatively low levels of imports of manufactured products, has generated frictions which threaten to develop into trade wars. The primary aim of this chapter is to examine how trading patterns within the region have evolved since the conclusion of the Plaza Agreement in 1985.[5] In particular the chapter explores the changes that have occurred in Japan's trading relations with other Asia–Pacific countries since 1985, and the extent to which these have contributed to reducing trade frictions within the region.

Trading anecdotes: is there a 'Japan problem'?

Much of the discussion of the problems arising from Japan's trade with other countries in the region, particularly the United States, has been disingenuous, its focus being on largely irrelevant or inappropriate indicators. Three such indicators stand out: trading anecdotes; the extent of formal barriers to access to the Japanese market; and the aggregate trade imbalance.

Trading anecdotes

Trading anecdotes have added some colour to what is often otherwise a turgid debate but throw little light on the real problems involved. The sorry story of the efforts to exclude American-made aluminium baseball bats from the Japanese market may or may not be indicative of more general problems. A count of the number of McDonalds' golden arches on the Tokyo skyline, on the other hand, is equally uninformative about import penetration of the Japanese market (although it may be a partial answer to those who rely on culturally based arguments to deny that the Japanese have a taste for Western goods). Such anecdotes tell us as little about overall trade problems as the Honda story tells us about the overall effects of industrial policy in Japan. To see these anecdotes repeatedly brought up in supposedly serious academic studies of Japan's trade structure is surprising and, indeed, disturbing.

Formal trade barriers

The second irrelevance is data on formal barriers to market access. Here commentators often appear to be engaged in a schoolboy-like, 'I'm holier than thou' competition. One Japanese economist (Miyoshi 1987, p. 46) is probably correct in claiming: 'The Japanese market is just as open as any

---

5 The Plaza Agreement took its name from the Plaza Hotel New York where a meeting of the Group of Five (France, Germany, Japan, the United Kingdom, and the United States) agreed on a coordinated strategy to push down the value of the dollar *vis-à-vis* the currencies of its major trading partners. For details see Funabashi (1988).

other market in the industrialised world if differences in social custom and legal and administrative systems are taken into account'.[6] But the sting of this statement lies in the tail: it is precisely the 'differences in social custom and legal and administrative systems' that are the most important barriers to other countries' exports—especially if the retail system and the structure of business groupings are included under the social custom rubric.

Continuing focus on Japan's levels of tariffs and the number of its formal non-tariff barriers in comparative perspective is simply beside the point. The contentious issue in the trade debate is the various structural impediments to import penetration, discussed below.

Bilateral trade imbalances

The third irrelevance on which much attention has been focused is the size of overall bilateral trade imbalances. There is no good economic reason why any bilateral trade relationship should be balanced. And, indeed, Petri (1984) has shown that even if the *overall* external trade accounts of both Japan and the United States were in balance, the *bilateral* trade between them would still be unbalanced in Japan's favour.

To be sure, such imbalances have profound importance in the political frictions they generate. But the magnitude of such imbalances is more likely to reflect differences in macroeconomic policies and factors than the presence of trade barriers. As we have often been reminded (for instance, Cooper 1987), the basic accounting identity $X - M = G + (S - I)$ demonstrates[7] that the trade gap is equal to the overall savings deficit (surplus)

---

6   Japan's post-Tokyo Round tariffs, weighted by the 1976 import shares which were used for Tokyo Round calculations, average 6.2 per cent. The figure for the United States is 3.3 per cent; for Canada 4.6 per cent; for Germany 5.7 per cent; and for Australia 14.8 per cent. Agricultural products and petroleum weigh heavily in the Japanese average.

The estimated *ad valorem* equivalents of non-tariff barriers are Japan 8.2 per cent; the United States 2.4 per cent; Canada 1.9 per cent; Germany 2.5 per cent; and Australia 4.0 per cent. These estimates appear in Saxonhouse and Stern (1989, pp. 302–3 and 308–9).

The claim by Komiya and Irie (1990, p. 83, fn. 16) that 'Japan has not formally requested trade-partner countries to impose a single [VER]' is particularly disingenuous. As Petri (1991b, p. 15) points out, Japanese VERs are not publicly announced. They are widely reported to include restrictions against Korean knitwear (implemented February 1989 for three years), and against raw silk, and silk yarn and fabrics (Balassa & Noland 1988, pp. 54–5). The Korean Spinners' Association instituted voluntary restraints on exports of cotton yarn to Japan in the 1983–86 period (Takeuchi 1990a, p. 114). But Japan's record on VERs is certainly no worse than that of other industrialised countries, and in recent years, is probably better than that of the United States.

7   Where X = exports, M = imports, S = savings, G = government revenue less government expenditure, and I = investment.

plus the deficit (surplus) in the government budget. This accounting identity is of course *ex post*, and protection will indeed have various effects on levels of domestic savings and investment. But in which direction the net aggregate effect will operate is unclear on an *a priori* basis (Bhagwati 1978).

Even those who have argued that Japan's import volume is abnormally low in comparison with those of other industrialised countries do not believe that a reduction in its trade barriers will necessarily lead to a removal of its trade surplus. Lawrence (1987), who estimated that Japan imports about 40 per cent fewer manufactures than it would if its markets were as open as those of the average Organisation for Economic Cooperation and Development (OECD) economy, calculated that the removal of barriers would reduce the trade surplus in manufactured goods by only 17 per cent. A successful liberalisation of imports would also promote exports unless domestic savings were reduced. The principal impact would be to increase intra-industry trade. A similar point is made by Krugman (1987b), McCulloch (1988), Balassa and Noland (1988), and Cooper (1987).

In the absence of major changes in the savings, investment, and government budget balances of Japan and the United States, therefore, no major reduction in the bilateral trade imbalance would be expected. The US trade deficit with Japan is largely a self-inflicted wound.

Given the chronically low savings ratio in the United States, and political immobilism over the budget deficit, it is puzzling why some economists believed that a devaluation of the dollar against the yen would be sufficient to bring about a substantial change in the trade balance. Saxonhouse (1983, pp. 279–80) described 'a massive amount of empirical work' which 'with perhaps a number of minor exceptions all...suggests that a change in the price of the yen relative to other currencies will result in a substantial change in the Japanese current account balance. All the major econometric models of the Japanese economy come to this conclusion regardless of the detail or lack of detail in their treatment of the foreign sector and its linkages with the domestic economy and abroad'.

How wrong can one (or one's econometric models) be! The period since the Plaza Agreement has seen no reduction in Japan's overall trade balance in current dollars; only a modest reduction in US deficits, and a continuous increase in Japan's surplus with the East Asian NICs. This is not to suggest that no changes in Japan's trading pattern have occurred since the Plaza Agreement; some of these will be detailed in the second half of this chapter. Overall trade balances mask changes in trade volumes—which responded more quickly to changes in the exchange rate than the value of exports and imports (Corker 1990; Petri 1991a)—and in both the commodity and partner composition. But the adjustment of exchange rates has yet to make a major dent in Japan's trade surpluses with the United States (Figure 6.1) or with its other major trading partners.[8]

Figure 6.1 Indexes of US–Japan trade balance and yen–dollar exchange rate (1985=100)

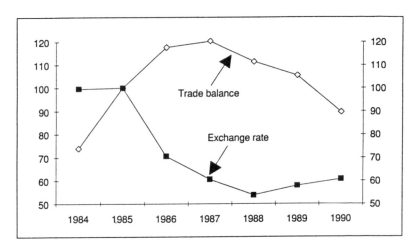

Source: Calculated from data in IMF, *Direction of Trade Statistics*; IMF, *International Financial Statistics*.

Is Japan an outlier in international trade?

In one sense, this question can easily be answered. Japan's pattern of imports is quite unlike those of other industrialised countries. In particular the share of manufactured imports in Japan's gross domestic product (GDP) is much lower than that of other countries. Japan's ratio of manu-

---

8   Other factors which have been suggested as contributing to the limited change in the bilateral US–Japan trade balance following exchange rate realignment include the low pass-through rates in Japan's import and export prices (Baldwin 1988). This effect has been attributed by some to uncompetitive domestic markets in Japan which enable abnormal profits to be earned both on imports and on domestic manufactures; the latter enables Japanese companies to practise price discrimination and underwrite less profitable exports from their domestic sales (Yamamura 1990). Marston (1991) provides an extensive review of the evidence that Japanese firms engage in such discriminatory pricing. Bhagwati (1990) argues that voluntary export restraints on a number of Japanese imports ensured that they were selling at a premium; adjustment to the exchange-rate changes has come through cutting into these premiums; price rises have thus been avoided. Komiya and Irie (1990) suggest that full employment in the United States reduced the potential for devaluation to lower the trade deficit.

factured imports to GDP has hovered around 2.5 per cent since 1970, whereas that for the United States has increased from 2.5 per cent to over 7 per cent in the same period. The ratios for other industrialised countries showed a similar increase over these years: by the second half of the 1980s the weighted average for industrialised countries was over 10 per cent (Takeuchi 1990a, p. 100). The contrast between Japan and other industrialised countries is even more stark when imports of manufactures are measured against the share of manufacturing in GDP: whereas the ratio for the United States in 1987 was 38 per cent, for West Germany 45 per cent, and for France 59 per cent, that for Japan was a mere 8 per cent (Lincoln 1990a, p. 19).

A more difficult question, however, is whether this pattern is unusual once account is taken of Japan's economic structure. In particular Japan's heavy dependence on imported raw materials and its distance from other industrialised countries' markets are often cited as reasons for why Japan in general has relatively low levels of imports and, in particular, why it imports comparatively small volumes of manufactured goods.

This issue has been the subject of protracted debate among economists who have employed a variety of econometric models in attempting to assess the impact of Japan's economic structure on its trade pattern. As Saxonhouse and Stern (1989, p. 313) acknowledge, the models that underlie all of these studies make 'highly unrealistic assumptions' about the nature of industry structure and international trade. All of the findings must, therefore, be interpreted with considerable caution.

Those studies that have found that Japan's pattern of imports is not different from that which would be predicted, once economic structure is taken into account, most often have employed a factor-endowment model based on the Heckscher–Ohlin theory of comparative advantage. The problem with such models is that they are based on net rather than gross trade in individual products; in other words they do not permit observation of intra-industry trade[9], which many perceive as the most dynamic element in world trade. Hufbauer and Chilas (1974) (see also Lipson 1982) suggested that because the GATT pattern of mutual concessions fostered intra-industry trade then, gross trade in manufactured goods has expanded at a far faster rate than net trade.

Saxonhouse's studies (for example, 1983, 1986, 1988), which use this approach, are often cited by those who argue that Japan's unusual trade pattern can be explained by its economic structure. But these studies have a number of other serious flaws. One of the most important concerns the nature of some of the countries used in the sample against which Japan is

---

[9] Intra-industry trade refers to the simultaneous export and import of products belonging to the same 'industry'. An example would be automobile trade between Sweden and Germany in which Sweden imports BMWs and exports Volvos. Intra-industry trade thus often involves the exchange of goods differentiated by brand name.

compared—these include developing countries such as India and Indonesia, and/or countries such as Australia, which for the years covered by the data used in the study had high levels of protection of their domestic manufacturing industries. For non-econometricians, perhaps the most basic test of a model is whether it produces results which are in accord with general knowledge. Saxonhouse's work fails this simple test for, as Balassa and Noland (1988, p. 252) point out, his studies fail to identify Japan's rice sector as being protected!

Most of those studies that have employed methodologies based on Chenery (1960) or the Helpman–Krugman (1985) model, and that have not excluded intra-industry trade, have found that Japan is an outlier, even after taking into account economic structure and distance from markets (Lincoln 1990a, p. 20).[10] Japan is estimated to import substantially less— as much as 40 per cent less (Lawrence 1987)—than it would if its trade pattern corresponded to that of other industrialised countries.

As Krugman (1991, p. 4) concludes: 'it seems fair to argue that, in the general debate, the view that Japan does import less than one might have expected wins on points…On the whole, then, the conventional wisdom survives crude empirical testing more or less intact'. Krugman had earlier suggested that Japan could reasonably be expected to have a ratio of imported manufactured goods to GNP at least equivalent to that for extra-EC imports into the European Community: Japan's relative disadvantage in natural-resource endowment, which would tend to count against manufactured-goods imports, should be offset by its smaller market size, which would normally be reflected in higher ratios of imports. But in 1984, Japan's manufactured imports-to-GNP ratio was 2.9 per cent, less than half the 6.5 per cent share of EC GNP accounted for by extra-EC manufactured imports. Srinivasan and Hamada similarly suggested, using models of imperfect competition, that the import penetration ratio for manufactures in Japan should be 24 per cent higher than that for the United States whereas Japan's ratio, as discussed below, was substantially below the US figure (cited in Lawrence 1991).

There is, however, a methodological problem with all of the studies that have examined Japan's overall pattern of trade: they do not explicitly model the alleged barriers to imports in Japan. Numerous lists of such barriers have now been compiled (for instance, Balassa & Noland 1988; Lincoln 1990a; Okimoto 1987; Rapp 1986; Saxonhouse & Stern 1989). The impediments identified range from government actions such as 'administrative guidance', inadequate protection of intellectual property rights, delays in granting patents, procurement practices, customs proce-

---

10 Besides Lincoln's useful review, other surveys of the econometric studies of Japan's trade include Takeuchi (1989), Balassa and Noland (1988, Appendix C), and Saxonhouse and Stern (1989).

dures, and testing and certification procedures for imports, to the import-restricting effects of *keiretsu*.[11]

Empirical work is beginning to be published which estimates the trade-impeding effects of some of these barriers. Petri (1991a) found that:

(i) markets where businesses account for a large share of purchases tend to have relatively low import penetration;

(ii) markets where the government accounts for a large share of purchases similarly tend to have relatively low import penetration; and

(iii) distribution margins are negatively related to import penetration—supporting the widespread belief that the structure of the retail system is an impediment to imports.

Furthermore, a study by Lawrence (1991) estimates that *keiretsu* lowered the imports of the industries in his sample by as much as 50 per cent. These aggregate studies are reinforced by Kreinen's (1988) survey which found that the purchases of the Australian subsidiaries of Japanese transnationals were directed overwhelmingly towards Japanese products. No similar bias towards home-country products was observed for subsidiaries of US transnationals.

If Japan's level of manufactured imports is abnormally low, the explanation, it is generally agreed, lies in its unusually diminutive rates of intra-industry trade, a factor first discussed in detail by the Japanese economist Sazanami (1981).

Lincoln (1990a) makes a persuasive case that Japan's intra-industry trade is 'startlingly different' from that of other countries at similar levels of economic development. This cannot be attributed alone to Japan's dependence on imported raw materials, as other countries which similarly lack abundant domestic supplies of raw materials have far higher levels of intra-industry trade. As Lincoln points out, apart from coal Germany's dependence levels on imported raw materials are very similar to those of Japan, but the intra-industry trade index for Germany, nevertheless, is more than double that of Japan.[12] Japan's ratio also diverges significantly

---

[11] Other countries, of course, have similar impediments. See, for instance, the list of US structural impediments produced by the European Community, which is reprinted in Saxonhouse and Stern (1989).

[12] All references to the intra-industry trade index in this chapter are to the formulation originally proposed by Grubel and Lloyd (1975). The formula for calculating this index is:

$$IIT = \Sigma_i [IIT_i \times (x_i + m_i)/(X + M)]$$

where

$$X = \Sigma_i x_i$$
$$M = \Sigma_i m_i$$
$$IIT_i = [1 - |x_i - m_i|/(x_i + m_i)]$$

from those of the resource-poor NICs of East Asia, which would be expected to have lower levels of intra-industry trade given their lower levels of economic development. Japan is unique among advanced industrialised countries in the way it imports materials and components in their least refined forms.[13]

A second striking characteristic of Japan's intra-industry trade is that it decreased at a time when an increase would have been expected. A cross-national study by Balassa (1986) of 38 developed and developing countries showed that intra-industry specialisation increases with the level of economic development and the size of domestic markets. Yet in a period in which the Japanese economy was growing rapidly, and its export composition (as measured by 'revealed comparative advantage' in Balassa's (1965) terms) was changing towards skill-intensive products, its overall intra-industry trade index first decreased then stagnated (Table 6.3). Furthermore, as Lincoln (1990a, p. 49) shows, Japan diverges from its industrialised country trading partners in this period: not only did it conduct distinctly less intra-industry trade with them than they do with one another, but the gap widened. The explanation can probably be located in Balassa's (1986, p. 40) other major finding: that intra-industry specialisation is positively associated with the openness of national economies.

Corroboration for this argument is provided in a study by Lowe (1991). He found that the growth in intra-industry trade among OECD countries has been associated with the convergence of their resource bases. Japan has been the exception to this rule: as its resource base became more like those of other OECD countries, its intra-industry trade ratio failed to increase. Lowe's study is unusual among those that have focused specifically on intra-industry trade in that he attempts explicitly to model Japan's resource endowment and its effects on such trade. He suggests that until the early 1970s Japan's low levels of intra-industry trade could be explained by the country's resource dispersion and size. From the mid-1970s onwards, however, the dummy coefficient for Japan entered into the regression equation increased in absolute size and became statistically significant; that is, attributes of Japanese economic structure

---

13 Japan's trading structure is also obviously affected by its location—further away from its principal markets than most of its competitors. How the effects of distance might best be incoporated within an econometric model of Japan's trade has been a matter of considerable controversy. Transport costs for many goods have fallen substantially in recent decades, sometimes in response to technological changes, such as the use of bulk carriers, that Japan has pioneered; a model which employs physical distance as the variable is unlikely to reflect such changes. And there is evidence that Japan's transport costs for its single most significant import, petroleum, are less than those faced by most major industrialised countries. For further discussion of this issue see Balassa and Noland (1988, Appendix C pp. 240–2).

other than resource endowment were associated with the abnormally low levels of intra-industry trade.

Table 6.3   Intra-industry trade indices, manufactures 1970–90, all trading partners

Country	1970	1975	1980	1984	1990
Japan	.32	.26	.29	.26	.36
United States	.57	.62	.60	.61	.70
France	.78	.78	.82	.80	.85
South Korea	.19	.36	.38	.46	.47
Taiwan	-	-	.35	.40	.48
Singapore	-	-	.67	.75	.72

Note: Manufactures defined as SITC categories 5–8 less 67 and 68, aggregated at the 3-digit level.

Source: For 1970 and 1975, Lincoln (1990a), Table 3.2; for 1980, 1984, and 1990 calculations by International Economic Data Bank, ANU using UN trade tapes.

A third peculiarity of Japan's intra-industry trade that Lincoln (1990a) demonstrates is that such trade is lowest in those sectors where Japan has enjoyed most success in exporting. Given the way in which the index of intra-industry trade is calculated, this may appear to some extent to be a tautology. Nevertheless, Japan's pattern is again distinct from that of other industrialised countries, which have much higher levels of intra-industry trade even in those sectors where their exports are concentrated. As Petri (1991a) shows, Japan's intra-industry trade is greatest for its declining sectors where segments of their activities have been abandoned to foreign producers. Again the contrast is with other industrialised countries where intra-industry trade has developed as a consequence of exchanges of different brand-name goods within the same product line.[14]

Lawrence (1991) suggests that market imperfections are a significant source of the low levels of intra-industry trade, in particular the dominant role that Japanese trading companies have in Japan's import trade, a role that has increased in importance over the last decade. Whereas the nine

---

[14] A focus on intra-industry trade is sometimes attacked for its assumption of homotheticity, that is, that tastes do not vary across industrialised countries. Defenders of Japan's trading structure argue that it is the uniqueness of Japanese tastes and the inability of foreign corporations to cater to them that explains the trade imbalances. Komiya and Irie (1990, p. 88) for instance, assert that 'European and US enterprises generally...do not yet know well the kinds of products and services wanted by Japanese consumers and enterprises'. As Wolff (1990) points out, the claim that foreigners do not produce goods that Japanese want is belied by observation of the overseas purchases of Japanese tourists once they are given the opportunity to buy such products at prices which are not drastically inflated by the Japanese distribution and retail system.

major trading companies handled 56 per cent of all of Japan's imports in 1980, their share rose to 65 per cent by 1983 and to 77 per cent by 1987 (Gerlach 1992, p. 111). Japanese subsidiaries in the United States ship two-thirds of US exports to Japan (Encarnation 1992, p. 118). Drawing on earlier work on *keiretsu* by Gerlach (1989), Lawrence suggests that it is unlikely that Japanese trading companies will import products that compete directly with those produced by their domestic affiliates. Trading companies are more interested in preserving their relationships with domestic suppliers than with enhancing short-term consumer welfare by passing on cost savings from lower-price imports. The trading patterns in turn rest on what Encarnation (1992) has termed the pursuit of 'strategic investment policies' by Japan, that is, policies intended to prevent US corporations from establishing majority-owned subsidiaries within Japan. Japan's abnormally low levels of intra-industry trade are the consequence.

Variations between countries' patterns of intra-industry trade not only have important economic but also very significant political consequences. As Balassa (1966) argued more than a quarter of a century ago, the systemic advantage of intra-industry trade is that it tends to reduce the adjustment costs of trade liberalisation. Countries are not faced with the prospect that entire industries will be forced out of production. And as Ruggie (1982, p. 399) argued, the essence of the embedded-liberalism compromise that has sustained the post-war international trading regime was a pattern of trade which 'promised to minimize socially disruptive domestic adjustment costs as well as any national economic and political vulnerabilities that might accrue from international functional differentiation'. This pattern of trade was based on intra-industry exchange: a shift occurred in the post-war years in the pattern of functional differentiation in international trade from the level of the country and sector to the level of product and firms (Cooper 1968).

The absence or low levels of intra-industry trade in many sectors in which Japan has been most successful intensifies the costs of adjustment for its trading partners, and renders Japan vulnerable to accusations that it engages in 'adversarial trade' in which it sets out systematically to destroy the industries of its competitors (Drucker 1987). And the low levels of intra-industry trade tend to deprive Japan of potential domestic allies in its foreign markets (companies that export to Japan), who might otherwise oppose protectionist measures against Japanese exports.

Japan's low levels of intra-industry trade generate trade frictions in the Pacific not just because of their immediate impact on the United States through the bilateral trade pattern, but also because of their effects on trade with third parties. In particular, the low levels of Japan's imports of manufactured goods in the 1980s ensured that the United States bore the main burden of adjustment to the East Asian NIC's rapid expansion of exports of manufactured goods.[15]

Penetration ratios (the ratio of imports to domestic production minus exports plus imports) for Japan and the United States for specified manufactures are presented in Table 6.4. Whereas the penetration ratio for East Asian exports of all manufactures including textiles, clothing and footwear was higher for Japan in the 1970s, by the first half of the 1980s the ratios were higher for the United States. Except for textiles, clothing and footwear, the gap between the penetration ratio for the United States and that for Japan continued to widen *throughout* the 1980s, testimony to the relative closure of the Japanese market from the mid-1970s onwards.

Table 6.4 **Penetration of industrialised countries' markets by East Asian manufactures (%)**

	$\bar{x}$ 1970–74	$\bar{x}$ 1975–79	$\bar{x}$ 1980–84	1985	1989
a. **All manufactures**					
North America	0.53	0.95	1.56	2.05	2.98
Japan	0.75	1.07	1.32	1.38	1.92
b. **Textiles, clothing, footwear**					
North America	1.99	4.19	7.22	9.84	12.31
Japan	2.81	3.91	4.73	5.36	9.51

Note: Categories derived from Drysdale (1988), Table 6.7, pp.166–7. East Asia is China, South Korea, Taiwan, Hong Kong and the ASEAN countries.

Penetration is defined as imports divided by apparent consumption (production plus imports minus exports).

Source: Calculations by International Economic Data Bank, ANU using UNIDO data.

[15] Whereas Japan was the single most important market for South Korea, Taiwan and Thailand in the mid 1960s, the United States had assumed this role by the 1980s (Noland 1990). A case can be made that there are economic benefits to be derived from more rather than less rapid adjustment through a process of 'creative destruction'. For the political economist there are a number of problems with this reasoning. The more rapid the pace of adjustment, the more likely that there will be significant political costs for a government arising from the social changes that inevitably accompany rapid industrial change. Governments may be forced into additional expenditure on social protection and/or retraining measures. Second, the more rapid the increase in imports, the less possibility there is for the domestic industry to undertake the necessary restructuring which, under a slower pace of adjustment, might ensure its survival. Third, the GATT regime has an implicit norm of 'burden sharing' under which the costs of adjustment to imports from developing countries are expected to be divided among all industrialised member states.

The remainder of this chapter examines the extent to which the peculiar pattern of Japanese imports has changed in the years since the Plaza Agreement, and the implications for both the emerging regional division of labour and for trade frictions. Why should the Plaza Agreement and associated changes be expected to have any impact on Japan's intra-industry trade? Three principal arguments might be put forward. First, intra-industry trade will increase as a consequence of the price effects on competitive commodities arising from exchange-rate changes. A plausible case can be made that imports of competitive commodities will be more price elastic than those of goods for which Japan has no domestic substitutes—exchange-rate changes are thus likely to have their greatest impact on *intra*-industry trade. Second, the Plaza Agreement may be taken as a symbol of more general efforts under pressure from the international community to liberalise access to the Japanese market and to increase the volume of imports. Third, the dramatic increase in the value of the yen in the two years after Plaza (from 250 yen to the dollar in September 1985 to 120 in 1987) would be expected to produce a surge in Japanese foreign direct investment (FDI)— and FDI in general has previously been associated with the growth of intra-industry trade. The magnitude of the exchange-rate change is particularly important in that it would be likely to overcome previous inertia effects, and tilt the scales towards a decision to invest overseas—or to import goods that previously were only marginally competitive.

Post-Plaza changes in intra-Pacific trade

The Plaza Agreement produced a rupture with Japan's previous pattern of trade as Corker (1990) and others have shown. The volume of manufactured imports more than doubled in the second half of the 1980s. Impressive changes also occurred in the composition of Japan's imports in these years. This was particularly true of trade with other APEC countries (Table 6.5). The share of exports of manufactures in total APEC exports to Japan nearly doubled during the 1980s, with most of the increase occurring in the 1985–89 period.[16] Nevertheless, Japan's trading pattern continues to be distinctly different from that of its industrialised-country trading partners.

By 1990, Japan's aggregate index of intra-industry trade (IIT) had exceeded levels recorded in the last twenty years. The declines experienced in the 1970s and first half of the 1980s were reversed (Table 6.3). But Japan's intra-industry trade index still lags a long way behind those for other industrialised countries, and even those for resource-poor NICs

---

16 A similar substantial increase was recorded in the share of manufactures in APEC exports to the United States but in this case the biggest rise occurred during the first half of the decade.

such as South Korea and Taiwan. The increase in manufactures in Japan's imports from the Pacific is reflected in the rise in its IIT index for trade in manufactures with other Pacific countries in the 1985–90 period—but only slightly to exceed the level recorded in 1980 (Table 6.6). When the North American countries are excluded, however, a more substantial increase is recorded, a subject discussed at greater length below.[17] Apart from Australia, whose IIT ratio declined, most of the other APEC members recorded marked increases in their ratios. The levels of intra-industry trade within the Pacific are still substantially lower, however, than those within the EC—the obverse of the 'natural complementarity' that is often said to underlie the dynamism of intra-Pacific trade.

Table 6.5   Exports of manufactures as a percentage of total exports from APEC countries to Japan and the United States

Destination	1980	1984	1990
Japan	23.3	27.6	43.6
US	66.5	77.7	82.0

Note: Manufactures defined as SITC 5–8 less 67 and 68.

Source: Data from International Economic Data Bank, ANU using UN trade tapes.

A more detailed breakdown of changes in intra-APEC intra-industry trade is provided in Table 6.7. The major sources of the increase in Japan's overall IIT index with other APEC countries are evidently changes within Standard Industrial Trade Classification (SITC) 6 (basic manufactures) and 7 (machinery).

Within SITC 6, disaggregated data show that the largest percentage increases in imports occurred in SITC 61 (leather and fur manufactures, major sources the United States and South Korea), SITC 62 (rubber manufactures—the United States), SITC 63 (wood and cork manufactures—especially from ASEAN 4), SITC 65 (textiles—China, South Korea, Taiwan and the United States), SITC 66 (non-metal mineral manufactures such as china, glass, and cement—Thailand, South Korea, and the United States), and SITC 69 (other metal manufactures—US, Taiwan and South Korea). Large percentage increases in imports disguise the low absolute values involved in trade in some of these products. By far the largest increases in the value of Japanese imports came in textiles and in non-metal mineral manufactures.

---

[17] In passing it is worth noting that the US IIT index for trade in manufactures with other APEC countries remains substantially higher than that of Japan even when trade with Canada is excluded: this is not the result that economic theory would predict given the size differential of the US and Japanese economies, and the greater distance of the US from other APEC countries.

Table 6.6 **Intra-industry trade indices, manufactures 1980–90, APEC only**

APEC Country	APEC 15			APEC 13		
	1980	1984	1990	1980	1984	1990
Australia	.28	.21	.27	.34	.23	.31
Brunei	.00	.06	.06	.04	.06	.04
Canada	.61	.70	.69	.27	.20	.20
China	.31	.34	.43	.33	.40	.52
Hong Kong	.47	.51	.47	.30	.33	.30
Indonesia	.08	.12	.17	.10	.17	.19
Japan	.31	.27	.34	.21	.20	.27
South Korea	.41	.47	.51	.44	.49	.56
Malaysia	.47	.57	.62	.38	.42	.62
New Zealand	.30	.31	.32	.34	.34	.36
Philippines	.19	.38	.44	.25	.38	.41
Singapore	.66	.76	.74	.62	.66	.69
Thailand	.30	.32	.42	.24	.29	.40
USA	.55	.55	.59	.39	.35	.42
Taiwan	.38	.41	.51	.50	.51	.63

Notes: Manufactures defined as SITC 5–8 less 67 and 68, aggregated at the 3-digit level.

APEC 15 is all countries listed above; APEC 13 is all countries less United States and Canada.

Source: Calculations by International Economic Data Bank, ANU using UN trade tapes.

Table 6.7 **Intra-Pacific intra-industry trade indices 1980–90**

Country/ group	SITC 5			SITC 6*			SITC 7			SITC 8		
	1980	1984	1990	1980	1984	1990	1980	1984	1990	1980	1984	1990
Japan	.66	.62	.63	.37	.38	.44	.21	.19	.28	.39	.29	.36
US	.54	.65	.63	.58	.50	.60	.63	.64	.65	.34	.22	.37
NICs	.41	.53	.62	.75	.74	.79	.62	.69	.75	.43	.43	.70
ASEAN 4	.16	.21	.39	.33	.37	.46	.31	.45	.54	.39	.36	.38

Notes: * Excludes 67 and 68.

NICs = Hong Kong, Singapore, South Korea, Taiwan.

ASEAN 4 = Indonesia, Malaysia, the Philippines, Thailand.

Source: Calculations by International Economic Data Bank, ANU using UN trade tapes.

Intra-industry trade between Japan and selected partners in six categories of manufactured goods where imports grew most rapidly was isolated for further investigation. These products were textiles; clothing and footwear; chemicals; non-electrical machinery; electrical machinery; and transport equipment. The indices of intra-industry trade are presented in Table 6.8.

Table 6.8   Intra-industry trade indices for specified manufactures for Japan

Trading partners		Textiles	Clothing & footwear	Chemicals	Machinery		
					Non-electric	Electric	Transport equipment
USA	1980	.49	.55	.45	.75	.51	.04
	1984	.34	.17	.50	.46	.38	.02
	1990	.54	.62	.60	.49	.51	.08
EC	1980	.81	.34	.59	.65	.26	.24
	1984	.82	.33	.55	.41	.20	.30
	1990	.74	.14	.66	.42	.23	.65
NICs	1980	.57	.11	.33	.07	.28	.04
	1984	.47	.13	.29	.09	.24	.08
	1990	.49	.08	.30	.22	.33	.15
ASEAN 4	1980	.23	.25	.20	.01	.17	.02
	1984	.36	.50	.25	.04	.15	.01
	1990	.37	.03	.29	.17	.30	.01

Source: Calculations by International Economic Data Bank, ANU using UN trade tapes.

For the selected products, the balance of trade with the United States (reflected in the intra-industry trade ratios) became more even over the course of the 1980s only in textiles, clothing and footwear, chemicals, and (from an extremely unequal starting point) transport equipment. In electrical machinery, the IIT ratio by the end of the decade had recovered to the level recorded at the beginning. This was a consequence of a doubling of Japanese imports from the United States in the second half of the decade, while exports to the United States rose by only 50 per cent in these years. Japanese exports at the end of the decade, however, remained three times the level of imports from the United States.[18] For textiles, the rise in the index came from both an increase in Japanese imports from the United States (a doubling in the years 1984–90), and a decline in Japanese exports to the United States (down 14 per cent). But at the end of the decade, Japanese exports still exceeded imports from the United States by a two-to-one margin. In transport equipment (which at the two-digit level of

---

[18] The curvilinear nature of the graphical representation of the Grubel–Lloyd index should be kept in mind when examining the IIT ratios. Thus, whereas the index has a value of 1 when trade is balanced, if imports are one half of exports (or vice versa) the index has a value of .66; when imports are four times exports the index is .4; and when imports are seven times exports the index is .25.

aggregation includes aircraft as well as road vehicles), imports from the United States increased more than four-fold in the period, a time when Japanese exports increased by only 50 per cent. Yet at the end of the decade, Japanese exports in this category were still more than seven times those of the United States.

The most marked change in the IIT ratios reported in Table 6.8 came in trade in transport equipment with the EC. Here the IIT ratio more than doubled in the years after Plaza. This reflects a more than six-fold increase in Japanese imports at a time when Japan's exports to the European Community increased less than three-fold. This may attest to the new Japanese fondness for European luxury cars and, for instance, to the success of BMW and Volvo in establishing their own sales networks in Japan. Europe currently exports to Japan more than ten times the number of cars than does the United States. It should be noted, however, that the more even balance in trade in transport equipment between the EC and Japan also reflects the much lower level of Japanese vehicle exports to the EC than to the United States which can be attributed to a considerable extent to barriers protecting the European market.[19] Nevertheless, Japan's sales of transport equipment to the EC in 1990 were still double its imports from Europe in this category.

Other notable changes in the ratios were for most categories of trade with ASEAN countries, and for trade in the three types of machinery with the Northeast Asian NICs. For both groups of countries, imports of machinery rose substantially in the post-Plaza period. Japan's imports of non-electrical machinery from the NICs increased more than eight-fold in the years after 1985; imports of electrical machinery were up by more than 3.5 times (although in both cases the trade balance in these products was still substantially in Japan's favour). Similar increases (although from a much smaller base) were recorded in imports from the ASEAN 4. These changes reflect a new division of labour in East Asia, driven in large part by increases in foreign direct investment both from Japan and from the Northeast Asian NICs (for further discussion see Bernard & Ravenhill 1992). For the purposes of this chapter, the main interest is in the recent increases in Japan's investment in countries in East Asia.

If there is substance to the critics' suggestions that the access of foreign firms to the Japanese market is restricted by such factors as the distribution system, the role of large trading companies, restrictions on sharemarket takeovers, and lifetime employment conventions making it difficult for newcomers to attract quality management and labour, then there may be considerable advantage to foreign companies if they arrange

---

19 In 1990 Japan exported cars to the value of $8.3 billion to the EC compared to sales of over $21.2 billion to the US.

affiliation with Japanese corporations through, amongst other means, accepting Japanese equity participation.[20] Although there are considerable difficulties in collecting comparable data on foreign direct investment because of differences in national methods of calculation, incomplete recording, and hidden flows through transfer pricing (DFAT 1990; Hyun & Whitmore 1989), some recent trends are now very clear. By the end of the 1980s, Japan was the world's single most important source of FDI. Japan's FDI has increased dramatically since the Plaza Agreement—outflows in yen terms have more than doubled.

Table 6.9   Japanese manufacturing FDI in Asia, by major host country 1973–90

Period (inclusive)	Hong Kong	Sing- apore	Korea	Taiwan	China	Thai- land	Malay- sia	Indon- esia	Philip- pines	Asia Total
				Millions of current US dollars						
1973–76	64	146	292	111	0	71	154	550	78	1 496
1977–80	85	467	295	134	1	120	251	843	143	2 353
1981–82	30	323	59	96	8	99	77	476	55	1 230
1983–84	19	342	69	130	22	118	227	268	20	1 258
1985–86	66	198	178	385	46	112	97	93	57	1 265
1987	108	268	247	339	30	210	148	295	na	1 679
1988	85	179	254	303	203	625	346	298	na	2 370
1989	116	678	257	360	206	784	471	167	na	3 220
1990	114	270	147	513	161	714	592	536	na	3 053

Source: Except for Taiwan, data are from Japan, Ministry of Finance, *Zaisei Kinyo Tokei Geppo*, various issues. Data until 1986 reproduced from Takeuchi (1990b). I am grateful to Mitchell Bernard for supplying me with data for subsequent years, and the Taiwan data from 1987, which is derived from *Keizai Gaigyo, Koryu Kyokai* (1991), p. 32.

The major beneficiary of these flows has not been developing countries, however, but North America: the share going to North America in the 1985–88 period is variously estimated to be 47 per cent (DFAT 1990) and 62 per cent (Takeuchi 1990b). Less than 20 per cent of the total has been directed towards Asia. Nonetheless, flows to Asia have risen significantly and now constitute over 80 per cent of total FDI in less developed countries. Originally the focus was primarily on Northeast Asia but as comparative advantage has changed, so Japan has invested increasingly in ASEAN countries (Pasuk 1990) and China. Japan is by far the single most important investor in South Korea, Thailand, and the non-oil and non-

---

[20] An exclusive focus on foreign direct investment underestimates the links between Japanese corporations and overseas affiliates through such ties as technology licensing. But Japanese corporations have increasingly preferred to take a majority share in projects in Asia (Encarnation 1992, p. 178).

financial sectors of Indonesia. In Taiwan, Hong Kong and the Philippines it is second behind the United States, and in Malaysia it is the second most important investor (after Singapore) in manufacturing (DFAT 1990). Details of the country breakdown of Japan's FDI in manufacturing in Asia are presented in Table 6.9.

Local sales have traditionally been more important than exports for Japanese FDI affiliates in less developed countries. Again there is a contrast with US transnational affiliates which, contrary to arguments that have often been made about Japanese transnationals (Kojima 1986), export a higher percentage of their production. Both US and Japanese affiliates in Asia have higher exports-to-sales ratios than in any other region, but even in Asia, US subsidiaries exported approximately twice as large a percentage (60 per cent) of their production in the early 1980s than Japanese FDI affiliates (Hyun & Whitmore 1989, p. 36).

Japanese FDI, therefore, given its sectoral focus and its primary orientation towards local markets, would not have been expected to have had a major impact on the overall regional trade balance in manufactures in the 1980s. There is some danger, however, of drawing conclusions on data which do not fully reflect production from the most recent wave of Japanese FDI; this has been far more export-oriented than previous investments. In Thailand, for instance, Petri (1991c) found that the export-orientation of post-1986 Japanese investments was more than three times higher than that of pre-1983 investments. And important changes in the composition of FDI in manufacturing are occurring.

In particular, the share of labour-intensive and natural resource-related industries in Japan's FDI has fallen, while that of machinery has risen spectacularly (from less than 20 per cent in the early 1970s to over 60 per cent by the mid-1980s). A larger percentage of production in the machinery sector (with the exception of transport machinery) is exported in general, and exported to Japan in particular. And of those exports back to Japan, Takeuchi's (1990b) data show that a large part (over 75 per cent for many types of machinery) are sold through intra-firm trade by affiliates to their parent companies. Imports from affiliated companies accounted for over two-thirds of all Japanese machinery imports from Asia in the mid-1980s (Takeuchi 1990b, Table 12). For Asian companies interested in exporting to Japan, it pays to have a Japanese partner.

A changing division of labour within the Pacific is thus taking place, driven in part by Japanese FDI. But to what extent has this helped to decrease regional trade frictions by reducing trade imbalances? To date the answer appears to be very little.

One reason for this is that Japanese FDI tends to be import-intensive: Japanese subsidiaries overseas rely more heavily on imported machinery and components from their home country than do other countries' Transnational Corporations (TNCs) (Kreinin 1988; Krugman 1990a). The evidence suggests that this is not a one-off phenomenon associated with the initial import of capital goods. Rather Japanese affiliates overseas continue to depend heavily on the home country for intermediate inputs (Petri 1991c). MITI data for the late 1980s show that Japanese subsidiaries that manufactured machinery in the NICs and ASEAN countries imported over 40 per cent of their components from Japan (Bernard & Ravenhill 1992, Table 3).

A second reason is that a substantial part of the production from the subsidiaries may be exported to the United States or other third countries; indeed, the investment may have resulted from a desire to circumvent voluntary export restraints or other barriers to imports from the home country. Unfortunately, no detailed data are available on the exports from Japanese overseas affiliates to the US market. Petri (1991c, p. 2) reports data, however, which show that in 1988 Japanese affiliates in Asia exported $35 billion worth of goods; their imports were valued at $39 billion; they ran a trade *deficit* of $13 billion with Japan and a trade *surplus* of $9 billion with other countries. Japan's EXIM Bank reports that in fiscal year 1989, 'even in ASEAN, where the re-export ratio was highest, only 10.4 per cent of sales were to Japan' (Takaoka & Satake 1991, p. 17). The aggregate trade data discussed below suggest that new trade triangles are developing, in which ASEAN countries import components from Japan and the NICs yet rely on third-country outlets—primarily the United States but also the European Community—for their new manufactured exports.

Table 6.10 US and Japanese bilateral trade balances with East Asian NICs ($US billion)

		Hong Kong	South Korea	Sing-apore	Taiwan	Total NICs
a.	**United States**					
	1984	-5.84	-4.04	-0.45	-11.09	-21.42
	1985	-6.21	-4.76	-0.94	-13.06	-24.97
	1986	-6.44	-7.14	-1.50	-15.73	-30.83
	1987	-6.51	-9.89	-2.34	-18.99	-37.73
	1988	-5.16	-9.91	-2.48	-14.21	-31.76
	1989	-3.93	-7.07	-1.83	-14.31	-27.14
	1990	-3.11	-4.89	-2.08	-12.36	-22.44
b.	**Japan**					
	1984	5.71	3.01	2.83	2.78	14.33
	1985	5.79	3.02	2.29	1.65	12.75
	1986	6.14	5.22	3.14	3.18	17.68
	1987	7.37	5.17	3.98	4.25	20.77
	1988	9.60	3.62	5.97	5.62	24.81
	1989	9.27	3.56	6.26	6.44	25.53
	1990	10.92	5.76	7.16	6.96	30.80

Source: IMF, *Direction of Trade Statistics Yearbook*, 1991.

Despite the increase in the IIT ratios for Japan's trade with the NICs in machinery, and despite the more than three-fold rise in the value (in current dollars) of Japan's imports in manufactures from the NICs in the 1985–89 period[21], Japan's trade surplus with each of the NICs has risen (in current dollars) in every year since the Plaza Agreement (Table 6.10). The picture is almost a mirror image of that of the US balance with these countries. The United States continues to run a huge trade deficit with the four (although by 1990 this had fallen back to the pre-Plaza levels).

Table 6.11 US and Japanese shares in East Asian exports of manufactured goods (%)

Exporter	1980		1984		1990	
	US	Japan	US	Japan	US	Japan
Hong Kong	34.13	2.76	45.98	3.29	30.71	4.93
South Korea	28.90	13.28	38.56	10.12	32.45	15.43
Singapore	20.96	8.12	32.52	3.58	28.35	5.54
Taiwan	38.37	7.31	53.66	6.30	39.49	8.89
China	9.04	11.02	18.68	10.79	22.92	8.79
Malaysia	31.66	5.70	41.28	5.91	28.31	5.35
Thailand	17.46	7.14	29.39	6.77	27.81	13.29

Note: Manufactures defined as SITC 5–8 less 67 and 68.

Source: Calculations by International Economic Data Bank, ANU using UN trade tapes.

Japan's share of the manufactured exports of three of the NICs (the exception is Singapore) increased somewhat during the 1980s. But even at the end of the decade, its share was minuscule compared to that of the United States (Table 6.11). Not all of this can be attributed to the relative size of the two economies—Japan's GDP in 1989 was estimated to be 55 per cent of that of the United States. Only for South Korea does Japan come close to absorbing half the level of exports that the United States does—for the other NICs the ratio is less than a quarter. A similar pattern is emerging for the ASEAN countries and China. Only in the case of Thai exports does Japan absorb half the level of the United States. Despite the realignment of currencies, despite the increase in Japan's intra-industry trade with other East Asian countries, and despite their success in increasing their manufactured exports to the Japanese market, the United

---

21 Care has to be taken in interpreting data on changes in the value of Japanese imports since the Plaza Agreement, especially when they are expressed in current dollar terms, as these reflect the large changes in the dollar–yen exchange rate after 1985. When trends are expressed in yen values or in volumes they may be quite different. Unfortunately, data on import volumes are notoriously unreliable.

States continues to bear the bulk of the burden of adjustment to the industrialisation of the countries of the Western Pacific rim.

Conclusion

The 'Japan problem' continues to threaten the stability of the international trade regime. An acknowledgement that Japanese capitalism is different in form from that of other countries (just as New Zealand capitalism differs from that of Australia, as one commentator suggested at the symposium at which the chapters of this volume were first presented), misses the important point entirely. It is not just that Japan is different, but the negative consequences that these differences have for an increasingly fragile trade regime. The objective of this chapter has not been to engage in a Japan-bashing exercise but to attempt to identify more carefully the sources of the 'Japan problem', and to assess to what extent they have been ameliorated by forces driven by changes in exchange rates since the Plaza Agreement.

As was suggested at the beginning of the chapter, a significant part of what is popularly perceived as the 'Japan problem' is in fact a 'US problem'. The US aggregate balance-of-trade deficit with Japan is largely a self-inflicted wound: the product of political inertia, which is reflected in the failure of both Congress and successive presidents to tackle in any serious manner the burgeoning budgetary deficit and the country's low rates of savings.[22] But part of the current US discontent in its trading relations with Japan rests not on the aggregate trade balance but on perceptions that Japanese markets are closed to those products for which the United States is a very competitive exporter.

The period since the Plaza Agreement shows that Japan's trade and investment patterns are indeed responsive to changes in the exchange rate. Japan's ratio of intra-industry trade has risen to levels beyond the peak of the early 1970s; Japan's imports of manufactures from the East Asian NICs (measured in current dollars) increased three-fold from 1985 to 1990. What we do not know as yet is whether these changes are a one-off shift in Japan's trading pattern or whether they are the first part of a trend that will lead to a major restructuring of this pattern. And we also need to inquire as to what shape the emerging division of labour in the Pacific is taking.

---

[22] The United States is also, of course, damaging trade relations within the region by its increasing resort to voluntary export restraints and other grey-area trade-restricting measures, and through its Export Enhancement Program for subsidised agricultural exports. These US measures, damaging though they may be to the interests of other countries in the region, do not pose as serious a threat to the trading regime as the dispute with Japan.

The marked expansion of Japanese imports of manufactured goods that occurred following the Plaza Agreement undoubtedly owed much to changes in price relativities following the rapid revaluation of the yen by close to 50 per cent. The inflation of asset prices in Japan in the second half of the 1980s also stimulated demand for imported manufactures. Both of these factors may be viewed as unique events rather than ongoing trends. The yen floated downwards in value in 1989; asset prices have crashed in the early 1990s. As a consequence, the processes set in train by the Plaza Agreement have slowed and even in some instances been reversed. In 1990, for instance, the value of Japan's manufactured imports from the Northeast Asian NICs fell by 5 per cent compared to the 1989 level.[23] In 1991 Japanese imports of consumer durables were estimated to have fallen by over 20 per cent compared with the previous year (Wickes 1992, p. 21). Japanese foreign direct investment in 1991 was also substantially lower than in the immediate post-Plaza period. To suggest that the trend towards higher levels of intra-industry trade has halted would be premature at this stage; nevertheless, the recent data are more supportive of the idea that a new plateau in the IIT index may have been reached rather than of notions of the index's continuing rapid upward movement.

A second set of issues concerns the nature of the new division of labour emerging in the Pacific in the post-Plaza era. Aggregate data on manufactured imports, for instance, conceal the extent to which increases have been concentrated in a small number of products. For instance, the largest single increase in the overall value of manufactured imports by Japan over the period 1985–90 occurred in SITC 89, miscellaneous manufactured goods, a category which includes jewellery, antiques, works of art, and musical instruments. These alone accounted for 13.4 per cent of the increase in Japan's manufactures in these years.[24] The second largest increase occurred in chemicals (10.7 per cent of the total), followed by clothing (10.1 per cent) and road vehicles (9.9 per cent—mainly luxury European cars) (calculated from data in Wickes 1992, p. 27). These four categories alone accounted for 44 per cent of the increase in the value of Japan's total imports of manufactures in the years 1985–90.

---

23 One reason for this fall was a reaction by Japanese consumers to the perceived low quality of some consumer electronics products from the NICs. Korean and Taiwanese companies now realise that they will not be able to penetrate the Japanese market on a substantial scale until they improve the quality of their products and build up a service network. The surge in sales to the Japanese market in 1988–89 thus represented a false start which may, by having damaged the reputations of products from these countries, have set back their export efforts for some considerable period.

24 In 1990, for instance, Japan's imports of artworks and jewellery exceeded the value of its textile imports, and of its iron and steel imports; they were three-quarters of the value of all road vehicle imports, and nearly double the value of all imports of telecommunications and sound equipment.

These data again reinforce the perception that Japan is importing primarily those products that do not compete with domestic production. Similarly earlier in this chapter the data on increases in Japan's intra-industry trade index for trade with other Pacific countries showed that much of the change was the result of growth of imports within SITC 6, basic manufactures. The particularly noteworthy characteristic of products in these categories is that they are all usually classified as raw material-intensive, unskilled labour-intensive, or human capital-intensive. *None* of them fall into the capital- or technology-intensive categories. These data suggest that the rise in Japan's intra-industry trade in recent years has followed its well-established pattern: intra-industry trade has grown most rapidly in those declining sectors where domestic production is being phased out. A similar conclusion is reached in a study by Park and Park (1991) of manufactured exports from the Asian NICs to Japan. They find that unlike the experience in the United States where the NICs have had increasing success in selling capital- and technology-intensive exports, these countries have improved their position in the Japanese market mostly by selling labour-intensive manufactures.

Even with the changes in the second half of the 1980s, Japan remains very much an outlier in its trading structure in comparison with other industrialised countries. Japan's ratio of intra-industry trade still lags substantially behind that of other industrialised countries, as does its ratio of manufactured imports to manufacturing's share in GDP (for 1988, the most recent year for which World Bank (1991b) data are available, Japan's ratio was 9.5 per cent compared with 37.8 per cent for the United States, 47.6 per cent for Germany, 62.5 per cent for South Korea, and 64.3 per cent for France).

Further investigation is required to locate the sources of Japan's low levels of intra-industry trade. While this chapter is at odds with much of Bhagwati's (1991a) analysis of Japan's trade, his suggestion that we need more industry-level studies to determine the reasons for Japan's low level of manufactured imports is a compelling one. There are some industries where Japan undoubtedly enjoys such a competitive advantage that one would expect its exports to greatly exceed imports. The automobile industry is an obvious example. Furthermore, changes in Japanese manufacturing practices, such as the widespread utilisation of Just-in-Time techniques, may reduce the possibilities for intra-industry trade in some sectors. The argument that there are substantial informal barriers to imports in Japan, on the other hand, is most persuasive in those instances where it can be shown that other industrialised countries sell disproportionately less of their products in Japan compared with their sales in third-country markets where they are competing with Japanese products (Christelow 1985–86; Krasner 1987). There was a certain irony in a recent issue of *The Economist* (11 January 1992) where an article that was generally derisory about US claims that there are substantial non-official barriers to exports to Japan was set adjacent to an article on the Japanese computer industry.

This reported that personal computers cost 20 per cent more in Japan than in the United States, and that Japan's 'Big 3' producers (Fujitsu, NEC, and Hitachi) hold three-quarters of the Japanese market but only three per cent of other world computer markets. Clearly some segments of the Japanese market remain closed by non-official barriers.

Where government procurement practices or the retail system play a significant role in impeding imports then there is a strong case for continued foreign pressure to overcome Japanese political immobilism to bring about greater liberalisation of the market. Without such liberalisation and a further increase in Japan's intra-industry trade, there is a real danger that the frictions caused by Japanese exceptionalism will fracture the international trading regime.

7 The Triad and the Unholy Trinity: Lessons for the Pacific Region

BENJAMIN J. COHEN

Economic cooperation is now on the agenda of the Pacific Region. As the chapters in this collection testify, governments throughout the area are becoming increasingly aware of the many interests they share in common; even more importantly, there is now growing appreciation of the value of collective approaches to help promote regional objectives or to resolve tensions where mutual interests differ. Until now, understandably, most attention has focused on the high-profile issues of trade and investment. But as the countries of the Pacific move into the 1990s, the challenge of cooperative management of monetary relations is taking on increasing salience as well. The question addressed in this chapter is: what are the prospects for successful monetary cooperation in the Pacific Region in the 1990s? Since to date there has been little experience within the region itself to draw on, the analysis of this chapter will focus primarily on implications that can be drawn from the most prominent example of monetary cooperation elsewhere—specifically, the regularised process of 'multilateral surveillance' that has recently been developed and refined by the governments of the Group of Seven (G-7).

Among the G-7 countries (the United States, Britain, Canada, France, Germany, Italy and Japan), procedures for monetary cooperation have been gradually intensified since the celebrated Plaza Agreement of September 1985, which formally pledged participants to a coordinated realignment of exchange rates. Ostensibly the aim of these evolving procedures is to jointly manage currency relations and macroeconomic conditions across Europe, North America and Japan—the area referred to by many simply as the Triad. Finance ministers from the G-7 countries now meet regularly to discuss the current and prospective performance of

133

their economies; policy objectives and instruments are evaluated for possible linkages and repercussions; the principle of mutual adjustment in the common interest is repeatedly reaffirmed in official communiqués (for details see Dobson 1991, chs 3–5). Yet for all their promises to curb unilateralist impulses, the governments involved frequently honour the process more in word than deed. In fact, if there has been one constant in the collaborative efforts of the Triad, it has been their lack of constancy. Commitments in practice have tended to ebb and flow cyclically like the tides. In its essence, G-7 monetary cooperation has had a distinctly episodic quality to it.

The main premise of this chapter is that international monetary cooperation, like passionate love, is a good thing but difficult to sustain. The reason, I argue, is systematic and has to do with the intrinsic incompatibility of three key desiderata of governments: exchange-rate stability, capital mobility, and national policy autonomy. Together these three values form a kind of 'Unholy Trinity' that operates regularly to erode collective commitments to monetary collaboration. The impact of the Unholy Trinity has been evident in the experience of the G-7. The principal implication for the countries of the Pacific Region is that the conditions necessary for a serious and sustained commitment to monetary cooperation are not easy to satisfy and, without major effort, appear unlikely to be attained any time soon. The irony is that even without such a commitment most regional governments will find their policy autonomy increasingly eroded in the coming decade—in a manner, moreover, that may seem even less appealing to them than formal cooperation.

The organisation of this chapter is as follows. Following a brief evaluation in Part 1 of the basic case for monetary cooperation, Part 2 reviews the experience of the G-7 countries since 1985 noting, in particular, a distinctly cyclical pattern in the Triad's collective commitment to policy coordination. Reasons for the episodic quality of monetary cooperation with emphasis on the central role of the Unholy Trinity are explored in Part 3, and the question of what might be done about the resulting inconstancy of policy commitments is addressed in Part 4. The chapter concludes in Part 5 with possible lessons for the Pacific Region.

1. The case for policy cooperation

Conceptually, international cooperation may take many forms, ranging from simple consultation among governments, or occasional crisis management, to partial or even full collaboration in the formulation and implementation of policy. In this chapter, following the lead of standard scholarship on international political economy (e.g., Keohane 1984a, pp. 51–4), cooperation will be identified with a mutual adjustment of national-policy behaviour in a particular issue-area, achieved through an implicit or explicit process of inter-state bargaining. Related terms such as 'coordination' and 'joint' or 'collective decision-making' will, for our purposes, be treated as essentially synonymous in meaning.

In the issue-area of international monetary relations, the theoretical case for policy cooperation is quite straightforward (see e.g., Cooper 1985; Artis & Ostry 1986, ch. 1). It begins with the undeniable fact of intensified interdependence across much of the world economy. In recent decades, states have become increasingly linked through the integration of markets for goods, services and capital. Structurally, the greater openness of economies tends to erode each country's insulation from commercial or financial developments elsewhere. In policy terms it means that any one government's actions will generate a variety of 'spillover' effects—foreign repercussions and feedbacks—that can significantly influence its own ability, as well as the ability of others, to achieve preferred macroeconomic or exchange-rate objectives. (Technically the size, and possibly even the sign, of policy multipliers is altered both at home and abroad.) Such 'externalities' imply that policies chosen unilaterally, even if seemingly optimal from an individual country's point of view, will almost certainly turn out to be sub-optimal in a global context. The basic rationale for monetary cooperation is that it can *internalise* these externalities by giving each government partial control over the actions of others, thus relieving the shortage of instruments that prevents each one separately from reaching its chosen targets on its own.

At least two sets of goals may be pursued through policy coordination. At one level, cooperation may be treated simply as a vehicle by which countries together move closer to their individual policy targets. (In the formal language of game theory favoured by many analysts, utility or welfare-seeking governments bargain their way from the sub-optimality of a so-called Nash equilibrium to something closer to a Pareto optimum.) Peter Kenen (1988, pp. 75–7) calls this the *policy-optimising* approach to cooperation. At a second level, mutual adjustments can also be made in pursuit of broader collective goals, such as defence of existing international arrangements or institutions against the threat of economic or political shocks. Kenen calls this the *regime-preserving* or *public-goods* approach to cooperation. Both approaches derive from the same facts of structural and policy interdependence. Few scholars question the basic logic of either one.

What is accepted in theory, of course, need not be favoured in practice—however persuasive the logic. As Martin Feldstein (1988, p. 3), a sceptic on the value of policy cooperation, has written:

Although [theory] might suggest that international coordination is unambiguously better than the uncoordinated pursuit of national interest, it is important to distinguish between the theoretical possibilities of idealized coordination and the realistic potential gains of practical coordination. In practice, despite its aspirations, international coordination may produce results that are not as satisfactory as those that result from each country's uncoordinated pursuit of national self-interest.

Few scholars question the logic of Feldstein's scepticism either. Quite the contrary, in fact. Samuel Brittan (1991, p. 37) may be correct when he asserts that 'being in favor of coordination is like being in favor of virtue or motherhood'. But even virtue and motherhood can be said to have their drawbacks. In recent years there has been a virtual avalanche of formal literature citing various qualifications to the basic case for monetary cooperation and casting doubt on its practical benefits. The irony is evident: even as policy coordination since the mid-1980s has ostensibly become fashionable again among governments, it seems to have gone out of style with many analysts. At least five major issues have been raised for discussion by economists working in this area.

First is the question of the *magnitude of the gains* to be expected. Although in theory the move from a Nash equilibrium to Pareto optimality may seem dramatic, in practice much depends on the size of the spillovers involved. If externalities are small, so too will be the potential benefits of cooperation.

Many analysts cite a pioneering study by Oudiz and Sachs (1984) designed to measure the effects of monetary and fiscal policy coordination by Germany, Japan and the United States, using data from the mid-1970s. Estimated gains were disappointingly meagre, amounting to no more than half of one per cent of GNP in each country as compared with the best noncooperative outcomes. Although some subsequent studies have detected moderately greater income increases from coordination, most tend to confirm the impression that on balance very large gains should not be expected (Kenen 1989, pp. 23–9; Currie et al. 1989, p. 25–7).

Second is the other side of the ledger: the question of the *magnitude of the costs* to be expected. Theoretical models typically abstract from the costs of coordination. In reality, however, considerable time and effort are needed to evaluate performance, negotiate agreements, and monitor compliance among sovereign governments. Moreover, the greater the number of countries or issues involved, the more complex are the policy adjustments that are likely to be required of each (Artis & Ostry 1986, pp. 17–18). All this demands expenditure of resources that may loom large when compared with the possibly meagre scale of anticipated benefits. For some analysts, this suggests that the game may simply not be worth the candle. For others, it implies the need for a more explicit framework for cooperation—some formally agreed set of rules—that could substitute for repeated negotiations over individual issues, such as the Williamson–Miller (1987) extended target-zone proposal or Jeffrey Frankel's (1988) plan for nominal-income targeting. The advantage of an articulated rule-based regime is that it would presumably be more cost-effective than endless *ad hoc* bargaining. The disadvantage is that it would require a greater surrender of policy autonomy than many governments now seem prepared to tolerate (a point to which I shall return below).

Third is the so-called *time–inconsistency* problem: the risk that agreements, once negotiated, will later be violated by maverick governments tempted to renege on policy commitments that turn out to be inconvenient (e.g., Canzoneri & Gray 1985). The risk, in principle, is a real one. In relations between sovereign states, where enforcement mechanisms are weak or nonexistent, there is always a threat that bargains may be at some point broken. But whether the possibility of unilateral defection constitutes much of a threat in practice is hotly debated among specialists, many of whom stress the role of reputation and credibility as deterrents to cheating by individual governments (e.g., Kenen 1989, pp. 29–33). In the language of game theory, much depends on the details of how the strategic interactions are structured, for example, the number of players in the game, whether and how often the game is iterated, and how many other related games are being played simultaneously. Much depends as well on the historical and institutional context, and how the preferences of decision-makers are formed—matters about which it is inherently difficult to generalise. In the absence of more general specifications, few definitive judgements seem possible *a priori*.

Fourth is the possible *distortion of incentives* that might be generated by efforts at policy coordination. In an early and influential article, Kenneth Rogoff (1985) argued that international cooperation could actually prove to be counterproductive—welfare-decreasing rather than Pareto-improving—if the coordination process were to encourage governments collectively to choose policies that are more politically convenient than economically sound. Formal coordination of monetary policies, for example, could simply lead to higher global inflation if governments were all to agree to expand their money supplies together, thus evading the balance-of-payments constraint that would discipline any country attempting to inflate on its own. More generally, there is always the chance that ruling élites might exploit the process to promote particularist or even personal interests at the expense of broader collective goals. This risk too is widely regarded as realistic in principle and is hotly debated for its possible importance in practice. And here too few definitive judgements seem possible *a priori* in the absence of more general specifications.

Finally, there is the issue of *model uncertainty*: the risks that policymakers simply are badly informed and do not really understand how their economies operate and interact. Frankel and Rockett (1988) in a widely cited study demonstrated that when governments do differ in their analytical views of policy impacts, coordination could well cause welfare losses rather than gains for at least some of the countries involved. For some analysts, this is more than enough reason to prefer a return to uncoordinated pursuit of national self-interest. For others, however, it suggests instead the value of consultation and exchanges of information to avoid misunderstandings about transmission mechanisms and the size and sign of relevant policy multipliers. As Holtham and Hughes Hallet (1987) and Ghosh and Masson (1988) have each shown, the success rate of policy cooperation can be expected to be much higher if governments design their policies cautiously to take explicit account of the possibility of model uncertainty.

Where, then, does all this discussion come out? None of the five issues that have been so thoroughly aired in the literature is unimportant; sceptics have been right to raise and emphasise them. But neither do any of these qualifications appear to deal a decisive blow to the underlying case for cooperation, which retains its essential appeal. For this reason most analysts, myself among them, still remain disposed to view policy cooperation for all its imperfections in much the same light as virtue or motherhood—an inherently good thing. Net gains may be small; motivations may get distorted; outcomes may not always fulfil expectations. Nonetheless, despite all the risks the effort does seem justified. Robert Solomon (1991, p. 51) said it best when he wrote:

> Serious obstacles stand in the way of effective macroeconomic coordination…Nonetheless, there have been occasions when the world economy would clearly have benefited from coordination, and such occasions will undoubtedly arise again. On balance, therefore, coordination of macroeconomic policies is worth pursuing.

2. The ebb and flow of policy commitments

A problem remains, however. To be effective, the collective commitment to cooperation must appear credible; and to be credible, that commitment must above all be *sustained*. Individual governments may play the maverick on occasion (the time–inconsistency problem); a little cheating at the margins is after all hardly unexpected, or even unusual, in international relations. But the commitment of the collectivity must be seen to be enduring: there can be no room for doubt about the continuing relevance, the *seriousness*, of the process as such. Otherwise incentives will indeed be distorted for state and non-state actors alike, and outcomes could well turn out to be every bit as counterproductive as many analysts fear. As Peter Kenen (1991, p. 31) has warned, 'Sporadic management may be worse than no management at all'. Yet, as noted at the outset, that is precisely the pattern that policy coordination has tended to display in practice. The history of international monetary cooperation is one long lesson in the fickleness of policy fashion.

During the early inter-war period, for example, the central banks of the major industrial nations publicly committed themselves to a cooperative attempt to restore something like the pre-World War I gold standard, only to end up in the 1930s energetically battling one another through futile rounds of competitive devaluations and escalating capital controls. And similarly during the Bretton Woods era, early efforts at cooperative institution-building and joint consultations ultimately terminated in mutual recriminations and the demise of the par-value system. In the middle

1970s, endeavours to revive some kind of rule-based exchange-rate regime were overwhelmed by policy disagreements between the Carter administration in the United States and its counterparts in Europe and Japan, leading to a record depreciation of the US dollar. At the turn of the decade renewed attempts at joint stabilisation were cut short by the go-it-alone policies of the new Reagan administration, leading to the record appreciation of the dollar which, in turn, set the stage for the Plaza Agreement of 1985. The broad picture of monetary relations in the twentieth century is clearly one of considerable ebbs and flows in the collective commitment to policy cooperation.

Moreover, the big picture—much in the manner of Mandelbrot fractals—tends broadly to be replicated in the small. (A fractal is an object or phenomenon that is self-similar across different scales.) Often super-imposed on longer waves of enthusiasm or disillusionment with policy cooperation have been briefer 'stop–go' cycles of commitment and retreat, such as the short-lived attempts of the London Monetary Conference and later Tripartite Agreement to restore some measure of monetary stability in the 1930s. In the 1960s and early 1970s, even as the Bretton Woods system was heading for breakdown, the major financial powers cooperated at one point to create a new international reserve asset, the Special Drawing Right (SDR), and then at another to temporarily realign and stabilise exchange rates in the Smithsonian Agreement of December 1971. And even before the Plaza Agreement in 1985 there were already regular meetings of finance ministers and central bankers to discuss mutual policy linkages, as well as of lower-level officials in such settings as the Organisation for Economic Cooperation and Development (OECD) and the Bank for International Settlements (BIS). The now-fashionable process of multilateral surveillance was, in fact, first mandated by the leaders of the G-7 countries at the Versailles summit in 1982.

Most significantly, the same cyclical pattern has been evident even during the brief period since the announcement of the Plaza Agreement. The appetite for mutual accommodation in the Triad continues to wax and wane episodically; inconstancy remains the rule. Formally the G-7 governments are now fully committed to the multilateral-surveillance process. In actual practice, despite regular meetings and repeated reaffirmations of principle, policy behaviour continues to betray a certain degree of recurrent recidivism. At least four distinct rounds of stop–go motion can be identified in the trend of events since 1985.

Round I: September 1985–February 1987

This round, lasting from the Plaza Agreement up to the so-called Louvre Accord, was typical in starting promisingly but ending raggedly. The Plaza Agreement itself was, of course, responsible for making policy coordination formally fashionable again after several years of disrepute. But it did not take long for the process in practice to begin losing momentum as policy divergences reasserted themselves. As has so often occurred in monetary history, the governments involved found it difficult to sustain their collective commitment to cooperate in the common interest.

The key to the Plaza Agreement was the willingness of the Reagan administration, at the start of its second term under the leadership of incoming Treasury Secretary James Baker, to abandon its earlier unilateralist impulses, owing above all to the accelerating deterioration of the US balance of trade. The story is well known and has been well described elsewhere (e.g., Funabashi 1988, ch. 3; Destler & Henning 1989, ch. 3). Suffice it to note here that Secretary Baker was determined to head off protectionist pressures in the Congress, first and foremost by engineering a sharp depreciation of the dollar from the astronomical heights it had reached by early 1985. Quite understandably, he also wanted to ensure that his policy strategy would not be compromised by offsetting actions elsewhere. Emphasis was placed, therefore, on negotiating the concurrence of the other major financial powers, using the forum conveniently provided by the informal meetings of the finance ministers of the so-called Group of Five (the United States, Britain, France, Germany and Japan) that had already been going on for nearly a decade. It was the G-5 ministers that had been directed by the Versailles Summit to develop a process of multilateral surveillance of one another's policies and performance. It seemed only natural to build on that emerging process to implement a critically needed realignment of exchange rates.

Fortunately, the other governments involved were in accord and joined enthusiastically in setting out to burst the exchange market's speculative bubble. Although in retrospect it appears that the dollar may already have peaked by mid-1985, fears were widespread throughout the northern summer that a new rebound might be imminent. Thus, after meeting at the Plaza Hotel in New York in September, the G-5 ministers declared in a widely publicised communiqué that an 'orderly appreciation of the main non-dollar currencies is desirable', and pledging to 'stand ready to cooperate more closely to encourage this' outlined a series of explicit policy initiatives to be undertaken by each country. By the standards of diplomatic discourse, these commitments amounted to an unusually unambiguous signal of policy intention. The Plaza Agreement was also unusually successful, helping to consolidate and accelerate a shift of market sentiment that in less than two years wholly reversed the dollar's previous appreciation.

Initially the goal of the Agreement could be considered essentially regime-preserving—in Kenen's words (1988, p. 77), 'to defend the trade regime rather than alter the exchange-rate regime'. But soon the goal of policy optimisation came to be included too as US officials, flush with their achievements in exchange-rate management, pressed the other governments to strengthen their still-embryonic multilateral-surveillance procedures. In May 1986 the G-7 summit in Tokyo formally directed finance ministers to articulate a new framework for cooperation, including the use of so-called objective indicators of economic performance (for example, growth, interest and exchange rates, current-account balances and fiscal deficits) to review and evaluate the 'mutual compatibility' of national policies. Summit leaders also added Italy and Canada to the coordination process, effectively making the G-7 ministerial group rather than the G-5 the central forum for decision-making (although, in practice, outcomes not surprisingly tend to be determined largely by the views of the Big Three—the United States, Germany and Japan).

At the time, this new-found zeal for policy cooperation seemed quite remarkable. In retrospect it is clear that the turnabout largely resulted from a rather fortuitous coincidence of national preferences. No government in the Triad wanted to see a damaging resurgence of protectionism in the United States.

A depreciation of the dollar, achieved in part by a reduction of US interest rates, also promised to serve broad macroeconomic needs at a time of comparatively low inflation and weak growth, by providing room for greater monetary ease in both Europe and Japan to stimulate internal demand. In effect, no major conflict existed for the moment between the aims of domestic policy and the goal of realigning exchange rates—in the words of Yoshio Suzuki (1990, p. 566), a former executive director of the Bank of Japan, 'a rare case of a happy harmony between autonomy and coordination'. As Robert Keohane (1984a, pp. 51–5) has reminded us, however, there is an enormous difference between harmony (understood as a situation in which actors' policies pursued in their own self-interest happen automatically to facilitate attainment of others' goals as well) and cooperation (understood as an active process of mutual accommodation). Declaring a collective commitment to policy cooperation seemed innocuous enough when no real compromises of national interests were required.

Unfortunately, such a happy harmony was bound to prove fleeting. By the end of 1986, it was already evident that the interests of the major players were beginning to diverge again as the dollar's depreciation carried beyond what many regarded as desirable. In September, the first formal meeting of the finance ministers of the full Group of Seven agreed that there was no need for 'further significant exchange rate adjustment', in effect declaring that the realignment had now gone far enough. Yet over the following months the dollar continued to weaken, exacerbating concerns in Europe and Japan about the harm being done to the competitiveness of their export industries. Tensions were further aggravated by calls from Washington for more expansionary policies in the major surplus countries, in particular Germany and Japan, despite fears in these countries of renewed inflationary pressures. The idea was to give further impetus to an improvement of America's current balance. For the Europeans and Japanese, however, the cause of the US trade deficit lay in

America's low savings rate—due especially to the Reagan administration's massive fiscal deficits—rather than in the performance of others. Conflicts between domestic objectives and exchange-rate policies were clearly on the rise.

Round II: February 1987–October 1987

The response of the Triad countries was the Louvre Accord announced in February 1987 after another ministerial meeting, this time at the old headquarters of the French Treasury in Paris (Funabashi 1988, ch. 8; Destler & Henning 1989, ch. 4). Once again the goal was essentially regime-preserving (Dobson 1991, p. 61)—to demonstrate anew the Triad's collective commitment to the principle of policy cooperation as such. Indeed, for many observers the Accord represented a new high-water mark in the multilateral-surveillance process. Yet again, however, national divergences quickly re-emerged to undermine faith in the process, and ultimately to contribute to the 'Black Monday' stockmarket crash in October.

Although the Louvre Accord, unlike the Plaza Agreement, aimed to stabilise exchange rates rather than realign them, the two pacts were similar in outlining a series of explicit policy initiatives to be undertaken by each country. Asserting that currency values were now 'broadly consistent with underlying economic fundamentals', the G-7 governments 'agreed to cooperate closely to foster stability of exchange rates around current levels'. Central to this were the formal policy commitments of the Big Three—Germany and Japan on the one hand promising new fiscal stimulus; the United States on the other pledging again to cut its budget deficit. As at the Plaza, ministers were determined to send an unambiguous signal of policy intentions.

In terms of its exchange-rate objective, the Louvre Accord was reasonably successful. Despite some renewed dollar weakness in the months March to May and again in September, a fair degree of currency stability was in fact attained. Most of this achievement, however, could be attributed to massive exchange-market interventions rather than to internal fiscal or monetary adjustments. In terms of its domestic objectives, the Louvre Accord only managed to highlight policy tensions in the Triad. By the end of the northern summer, Washington was again calling on Germany and Japan for more expansionary measures including, in particular, lower interest rates to prevent a further depreciation of the dollar; and once again the Germans and Japanese were resisting for fear of rekindling inflationary pressures. In September, the president of the German central bank openly repudiated the US approach by insisting 'that prevention of inflation should be priority over the achievement of exchange rate stability'. In early October, Secretary Baker equally openly rebuked Germany's Finance Minister for his country's high interest rates. What had begun at the Louvre as a proud reaffirmation of common purpose ended little more than a half year later in public bickering and recrimination.

The denouement, of course, came with the stockmarket crash in the middle of October. The Louvre Accord contributed directly to the arrival of Black Monday by setting a goal of exchange-rate stabilisation without firmly ensuring the requisite mutual adjustments of domestic policies. German and Japanese resistance to lower interest rates, at a time of continuing pressure on the dollar, inevitably meant the prospect of higher rates in the United States; and this, in turn, widened the differential between bond and stock yields to the point where some adjustment of equity prices had to be expected. Overt policy conflict among the G-7 governments, by adding to the atmosphere of uncertainty in financial markets, only made matters worse. In the words of *The Economist* (24 October 1987), Secretary Baker's public criticism of German interest-rate policy 'put the market in the mood to crash'. Destler and Henning (1989, p. 63) call his remarks 'the greatest mistake that Baker made as Treasury Secretary...Open verbal warfare among the G-7 apparently undermined the markets' confidence...when the markets were already anxious... fearful...and shaken'. In the event, it did not take much more to trigger the steepest meltdown of global stock values since 1929.

Round III: October 1987–September 1990

Once more, the response of the G-7 was to demonstrate anew their collective commitment to policy cooperation—first by concerted intervention to support the dollar, which quickly came under accelerated selling pressure following the crash; and then, after some hesitation, by a new exchange of domestic policy commitments outlined in late December in yet another ministerial communiqué (the so-called 'Telephone Accord'). And once more policy divergences eventually emerged to strain faith in the process.

Currency intervention began almost immediately and remained substantial until the dollar, after hitting new lows, finally bottomed out in January 1988. The goal, as at the Plaza and the Louvre, was again clearly regime-preserving, as minds were concentrated by the spectre of a possible worldwide financial collapse. And when it became evident that more than just intervention alone would be needed to fully restore stability of exchange rates, additional domestic measures were announced in the Telephone Accord in December, reaffirming 'the basic objectives and economic policy directions agreed in the Louvre Accord'. As in the earlier agreements, policy pledges included more fiscal stimulus by Germany and Japan, and implementation of a new deficit-reduction plan in the United States. Endorsements of these mutual commitments have been ritually repeated at virtually every G-7 meeting since the Telephone Accord.

Six months later, currency intervention picked up again and continued until after November leading to the first strengthening of the dollar after nearly three years of decline. Whether this renewed activity was in any way directly related to the US presidential election in 1988 is unclear (although it does seem evident that a healthier dollar did nothing to hurt the prospects of candidate George Bush, then the incumbent Vice President). What is clear is that the stronger dollar gradually enabled the other G-7 nations to shift their concerns from the exchange market to the increasingly critical problem of resurgent inflation. Interest rates, which had been cut sharply in anticipation of possible liquidity problems following the stockmarket crash, were now starting to rise again in the Triad countries, particularly after the middle of the year. A stronger dollar meant that governments in Europe and Japan no longer felt so compelled to hold down asset yields to deflect purchases of their currencies. By the time of the first G-7 ministerial meeting of 1989 in February, it was clear that policy-makers now wished to concentrate more on domestic price stabilisation. As in 1985, for the moment at least no real compromises of national interests seemed required. Once again so long as the dollar remained buoyant, a happy harmony could exist between the aims of domestic policy and the demands of exchange-rate management. But as before such a fortuitous conjuncture of preferences was bound to prove fleeting. As time moved on, differences over interest-rate policy gradually intensified into more and more open conflict.

In April 1989, for example, tensions were provoked when Germany suddenly raised its interest rates without giving any warning to others in the Triad. 'There was some degree of surprise', admitted one US official (*New York Times*, 12 May 1989). And a month later feelings were further soured when the Germans then declined to join Japan and the United States in an additional coordinated adjustment of rates to help stem an escalating appreciation of the dollar. 'There appears to have been a breakdown in collaboration on interest rates', commented the *New York Times* (12 May 1989) drily. Said one private commentator: 'They have a common preoccupation with inflation, and they can dress that up as a common international concern and say they're fighting inflation together. But they're not. They're fighting it separately' (*New York Times*, 12 May 1989).

A year later at a ministerial meeting in Paris in April, even greater strains were generated when Germany and the United States rejected a Japanese request for a concerted rate cut to help bail out the yen, which was then under attack. Both the German and US governments were evidently too preoccupied with their own inflation problems at the time to worry about the Japanese, who in turn were so infuriated that they refused to send any representative to the next ministerial meeting in Washington in May. The collective commitment to multilateral-surveillance was visibly weakening. Indeed, by the northern summer of 1990, many observers were openly questioning the relevance of the whole process. Commented one analyst: 'Active macroeconomic policy coordination currently appears to be in abeyance' (Webb 1991, p. 334). It was certainly becoming difficult to take the G-7's ritual reaffirmations of principle very seriously.

Round IV: September 1990–present

And then came Saddam Hussein's invasion of Kuwait in August, triggering a sharp spike of oil prices and fears of a new global economic crisis. Once again, in the interest of regime-preservation, ministers sought to project an impression of determined and coordinated action; and once again policy divergences among the G-7 governments soon reasserted themselves.

The main challenge facing the G-7 was a renewed run on the dollar after two years of relative strength. The group's main response, as in the aftermath of the 1987 stockmarket crash, was to reaffirm the members' mutual commitment to exchange-rate stability. At their next meeting in September, ministers declared that 'exchange rates were now broadly in line with continued adjustment of external balances'. They also insisted that they would 'continue to cooperate closely on exchange markets in the context of the economic policy coordination process'. Over the following months, however, few actions were taken to back up their determined words. In the delicate phrasing of the International Monetary Fund (IMF), the statements of the G-7 'indicated a preference for exchange rate stability. On the other hand, the extent to which this preference affected policy actions may at times have seemed unclear; the decline in the dollar …encountered virtually no resistance from official operations in foreign exchange markets…and the objective of exchange rate stability may have appeared not to have had a major influence on monetary policy actions' (IMF 1991, pp. 91, 95). In short, credibility was quickly strained. By January, *The Economist* (26 January 1991) was openly questioning whether policy cooperation could still be considered *à la mode*.

During 1991, conflicts over interest rates dominated relations in the Triad. In February, German rates were raised, despite US objections and the continued weakness of the dollar. And then in April, after the dollar began to rebound, a new battle erupted when Germany and Japan rejected a proposal by Nicholas Brady, who had succeeded James Baker as Treasury Secretary in 1988, for a coordinated easing of monetary policies. In June, efforts to achieve a new consensus at the G-7 meeting in London ended inconclusively, with ministers in effect agreeing to do little more than disagree. By the time of their next meeting in October, members found it more convenient to talk about the disintegrating Soviet Union than haggle over interest rates, but they once again 'reaffirmed their continued support for economic policy coordination'. By the end of the year in December, the Deutsche Bundesbank felt free to tighten policy again without even consulting Germany's G-7 and EC partners, in a move that had the *New York Times* talking of 'economic warfare, 1991 style' (22 December 1991, Section 3, p. 1F). What October's words now meant in terms of practical commitments was no longer very clear.

Summary

It is obvious that the G-7 governments do, indeed, find it difficult to sustain the collective commitment to cooperation. Recidivism does recur. This is not to suggest that the multilateral-surveillance process has been utterly without redeeming social value. On the contrary, one can reasonably argue that for all its episodic quality the effort has on balance been beneficial, both in terms of what has in fact been accomplished and in terms of what has been avoided (Dobson 1991, pp. 126–30). Anecdotal evidence seems to suggest that policy-makers have had their consciousness genuinely raised regarding the foreign externalities of their domestic actions; in any event, the regularity of the schedule of ministerial meetings now clearly compels officials to integrate the international dimension much more fully than ever before into their own national decision processes. At the same time potentially severe challenges to regime stability have been successfully averted, including in particular the rising wave of US protectionism in 1985 and the stockmarket crash of 1987.

Collective initiatives have been designed cautiously to avoid the pitfalls of model uncertainty and have not typically been chosen simply for their political convenience. Overall, gains do appear to have outweighed costs.

The gains might have been larger, however. One can also reasonably argue that the positive impact of the process might have been considerably greater than it was had there been less inconstancy of behaviour. That is perhaps the chief lesson to be learned from this brief recitation of recent monetary history. Governmental credibility has undoubtedly been strained by the cyclical ebb and flow of commitments since 1985. With each retreat to unilateralism market scepticism grows, requiring ever more dramatic *démarches* when, once again, joint initiatives seem warranted. *Net* benefits, as a result, tend to be diminished over time. Multilateral surveillance may have redeeming social value, but its stop–go pattern makes it more costly than it might otherwise be. In a real sense we all pay for the fickleness of policy fashion.

3. The influence of the Unholy Trinity

Why is international monetary cooperation so episodic? To answer that question it is necessary to go back to first principles. Blame cannot be fobbed off on 'karma', accidental exogenous 'shocks', or even that vague epithet 'politics'. Consideration of the underlying political economy of the issue suggests that the dilemma is, in fact, systematic—endogenous to the policy process—and not easily avoided in relations between sovereign national governments.

The central analytical issue, which has been well understood at least since the pioneering theoretical work of economist Robert Mundell (1968, chs 16–18), is the intrinsic incompatibility of three key desiderata of governments: exchange-rate stability, private-capital mobility, and monetary-policy autonomy. As I wrote in the introduction to this chapter my own label for this is the 'Unholy Trinity'. The problem of the Unholy Trinity, simply stated, is that in an environment of formally or informally pegged rates and effective integration of financial markets, any attempt to pursue independent monetary objectives is almost certain, sooner or later, to result in significant balance-of-payments disequilibrium, and hence provoke potentially destabilising flows of speculative capital. To preserve exchange-rate stability, governments will then be compelled to limit either the movement of capital (via restrictions or taxes) or their own policy autonomy (via some form of multilateral surveillance or joint decision-making). If they are unwilling or unable to sacrifice either one, then the objective of exchange-rate stability itself may eventually have to be compromised. Over time, except by chance, the three goals cannot be attained simultaneously.

In the real world, of course, governments might be quite willing to limit the movement of capital in such circumstances—if they could. Policy-makers may say they value the efficiency gains of free and integrated financial markets. If polled 'off the record' for their private preferences, however, most would probably admit to prizing exchange-rate stability and policy autonomy even more. The problem, from their point of view, is that capital mobility is notoriously difficult to control. Restrictions merely invite more and more sophisticated forms of evasion, as governments from Europe to South Asia to Latin America have learned to their regret. More than a quarter of a century ago, quite early in my professional career, I asserted an Iron Law of Economic Controls: once implemented, I contended, limits on capital mobility must be multiplied at a rate at least equal to that at which means are found to circumvent them (Cohen 1965). Although the labelling may have been pretentious, the thought is arguably even more valid today in an era when financial markets have become more ingeniously innovative than ever. As an alternative James Tobin (1982, ch. 20) has proposed a tax on financial transactions, to limit capital mobility by 'putting some sand in the wheels' of the markets. But this idea too poses problems for practical implementation, as Rudiger Dornbusch (1988, pp. 220–2) and others have pointed out. Not only would such a tax be costly to administer, to be effective it would also have to be applied jointly by financial centres everywhere—a very demanding condition. More realistically most governments, in the area of the Triad at least, have tended to resign themselves to the inevitable if not always welcome presence of a high degree of capital mobility.

In practice, therefore, this means that in most instances the Unholy Trinity reduces to a direct trade-off between exchange-rate stability and policy autonomy. Conceptually, choices can be visualised along a continuum representing varying degrees of monetary-policy cooperation. At one extreme lies the polar alternative of a common currency or its equivalent—full monetary integration—where individual governments sacrifice policy autonomy completely for the presumed benefits of a permanent stabilisation of exchange rates. Most importantly, these benefits include the possible improvement in the usefulness of money in each of its principal functions: as a medium of exchange (owing to a reduction of transaction costs as the number of required currency conversions is decreased), store of value (owing to a reduced element of exchange risk as the number of currencies is decreased), and unit of account (owing to an information saving as the number of required price quotations is decreased). Additional gains may also accrue from the possibility of economies of scale in monetary and exchange-rate management as well as a potential saving of international reserves due to an internalisation through credit of what would otherwise be external trade and payments (Mundell 1973; Robson 1980, ch. 6). Any saving of reserves through pooling in effect amounts to a form of seigniorage for each participating country.

At the other extreme lies the polar alternative of absolute monetary independence, where individual governments sacrifice any hope of long-term exchange-rate stability for the presumed benefits of policy autonomy. Most importantly, as Mundell demonstrated as early as 1961 (Mundell 1968, ch. 17), these benefits include the possible improvement in the effectiveness of monetary policy as an instrument to attain national macroeconomic objectives. Today, of course, it is understood that much depends on whether any trade-off can be assumed to exist between inflation and unemployment over a time horizon relevant to policy-makers—technically, whether there is any slope to the Phillips curve in the short-term (Robson 1980, ch. 6). In a strict monetarist model of the sort popular in the 1970s, incorporating the classical neutrality assumption ('purely monetary changes have no real effects'), such a trade-off was excluded by definition. The Phillips curve was said to be vertical at the so-called 'natural' (or 'non-inflation-accelerating') unemployment rate, determined exclusively by microeconomic phenomena on the supply side of the economy. More recently, however, most theorists have tended to take a more pragmatic approach, allowing that for valid institutional and psychological reasons Phillips-curve trade-offs may well persist for significant periods of time—certainly for periods long enough to make the preservation of monetary independence appear worthwhile to policy-makers. From this perspective, any movement along the continuum in the direction of a common currency will be perceived as a real cost by individual governments.

The key question is how this cost compares with the overall benefit of exchange-rate stabilisation. Here we begin to approach the nub of the issue at hand. My hypothesis is that for each participating country both cost and benefit vary systematically with the degree of policy cooperation, and that it is through the interaction of these costs and benefits that we get the episodic quality of the cooperation process we observe in practice.

Assume absolute monetary independence to start with. Most gains from exchange-rate stabilisation, I would argue, can be expected to accrue 'up front' and then decline at the margin for successively higher degrees of policy cooperation. That is because the greatest disadvantage of exchange-rate instability is the damage done to the usefulness of money in its various functions. Any move at all by governments to reduce uncertainty about currency values is bound to have a disproportionate impact on market expectations and, hence, transaction costs in foreign exchange; further steps in the same direction may add to the credibility of the collective commitment but will yield only smaller and smaller savings to participants. Most of the cost of stabilisation, on the other hand, can be expected to be 'back-loaded' in the perceptions of the relevant policy-makers. That is because governments have an understandable tendency to discount the disadvantages of foreign agreements until they find themselves really constrained in seeking to attain their domestic objectives — at which point disproportionate importance comes to be attached to the compromises of interests involved. Where initial moves towards coordinated decision-making may be treated as virtually costless, further steps in the same direction tend to be seen as increasingly threatening. Thus, the marginal cost of policy cooperation for each country tends to rise systematically even as the marginal benefit may be assumed to fall.

The relationship is illustrated in Figure 7.1. Points along the horizontal axis represent successively greater degrees of policy cooperation, from absolute monetary independence at the left to full currency union at the right. Points along the vertical axis represent successively higher levels of marginal cost or benefit (measured for convenience on the same scale). Curve BB measures the marginal benefit of exchange-rate stabilisation for a single country, assumed to decline as policy cooperation is increased. Curve CC measures the marginal cost for the country, assumed to rise as cooperation is increased. Static equilibrium is represented by point E, where the two curves intersect. If the country finds itself to the left of point E, it will have an incentive to commit itself to an intensified process of policy cooperation. If it finds itself to the right it will be tempted to retreat from its commitment, moving towards greater unilateralism in national behaviour instead. In political-economy terms point E may be understood as the degree of cooperation that maximises the utility of governments in the political marketplace, analogous to the level of production that maximises profit for competing firms in the economic marketplace.

Dynamics enter if we consider the stability of the positioning of the two curves. Curve CC may be considered to be stationary since it directly reflects governments' domestic policy preferences, which are determined exogenously. Curve BB, on the other hand, is more likely to shift about significantly since it largely reflects market expectations, which can be assumed to vary considerably over time. Anything that independently enhances confidence in the stability of exchange rates, and thus reduces the need for deliberate currency management, will shift curve BB to the left; anything that shakes market confidence, conversely will shift it to the right. Correspondingly, for each shift of BB along curve CC there will be a new static equilibrium, altering incentives for governments to agree to policy compromises. My argument is that it is precisely because of such shifts that we observe so marked a pattern of stop–go cycles in international monetary cooperation.

Figure 7.1 Benefits and costs of policy cooperation: static equilibrium

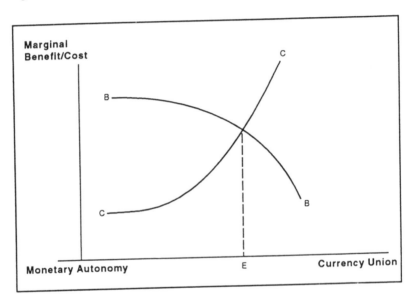

Consider, for example, the original impetus for the Plaza Agreement of 1985—the rising tide of protectionist pressures in the United States. The threat to the trading system was plainly adding to nervousness in currency markets, in effect shifting curve BB to the right where a renewed commitment to policy coordination seemed attractive to all the governments concerned. In turn, market confidence was independently reinforced by the growth-promoting easing of monetary conditions that followed, reflecting the fortuitous 'happy harmony' of policy interests at the moment. BB as a result drifted back to the left again completing the cycle, and by reducing the felt need for currency management, helping to account for the increasingly acrimonious policy divergences that began reasserting themselves before the end of 1986. And these policy conflicts, in turn, triggered Round II by renewing market concerns and tensions, shifting BB once more to the right and setting the stage ultimately for the Louvre Accord in early 1987. Similar rightwards shifts of the BB curve caused by the stockmarket crash later in 1987 and the Gulf crisis in 1990, each followed by a period of drift to the left, would appear to explain the subsequent Rounds III and IV as well. In all four instances the collective commitment to cooperation was initially stimulated by an exogenous or policy-induced, confidence-shaking shock. And in each instance the commitment was eventually undermined, once confidence was restored, by a growing discrepancy between the perceived costs and benefits of that commitment.

Figure 7.2 Benefits and costs of policy cooperation: dynamic equilibrium

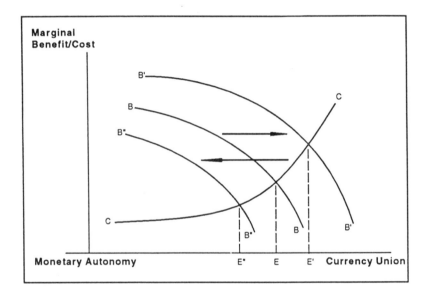

These four cycles were clearly no accident. Quite the contrary, they must be regarded as an endogenous feature of the ongoing policy process. The typical pattern is stylised in Figure 7.2. Starting at an initial equilibrium E, the cycle begins with some confidence-shaking shock that sends the BB curve to the right (B'B'), creating a new enthusiasm among governments for some form of policy cooperation (E'). It continues with a subsequent drift of curve BB back to the left again (B"B"), reflecting the confidence-building impact of the cooperation effort, and ends ultimately with a corresponding retreat by policy-makers from their collective commitment (E"). Point E", of course, may be either to the left or right of the original point E. The only exogenous element of the process is the shock that first triggers each cycle, which is by definition unpredictable. But this one random note in no way makes the overall pattern less systematic. In the real world, like it or not, shocks do have a nasty habit of repeatedly happening, even if we can know neither their nature nor their timing in advance. And once they do happen, they clearly seem to generate a distinct ebb and flow in the appetite for mutual accommodation. Recidivism not only recurs; it is explicable.

4. Can cooperation be 'locked in?'

The dilemma posed by the Unholy Trinity thus helps us to understand why international monetary cooperation is so episodic. The question remains: what, if anything, can be done about it?

One answer can be ruled out from the start: the proposition that the observed inconstancy of policy behaviour could be overcome if only governments could be educated to comprehend their own best interests. If my hypothesis is correct, governments are already acting in their own best interests and behaving in a manner consistent with a rational calculus of their own costs and benefits. The issue is not myopia: policy-makers surely are not unaware of the impacts of their behaviour on market expectations (as reflected in the cyclical movements of the BB curve), and would stick to their commitments if that seemed desirable. Rather, it is a question of how policy incentives change over time as a result of the shifting tide of events. Fundamentally, my reasoning may be understood as a variant of the logic of collective action first elucidated by Mancur Olson more than a quarter of a century ago (Olson 1965). A common interest is evident to all, yet individually rational behaviour can, at least part of the time, lead to distinctly sub-optimal outcomes. This is true whether the common interest is understood in terms of policy optimisation or regime preservation.

Moreover, my hypothesis has the advantage of being consistent with a wide range of alternative paradigms that have been employed in the standard international political-economy literature. It is certainly compatible with traditional realist or structuralist approaches in which the sovereign state, for reasons of analytical parsimony, is automatically assumed to behave like a rational unitary actor with its own set of well-defined national interests. It is also consistent with more pluralist models of policy-making, in which conceptions of interest are distilled from the interplay of differing combinations of domestic political and institutional forces; and even with models drawn from public-choice theory, in which policy behaviour is assumed to reflect first and foremost the personal interests of policy-makers (the principal-agent problem). For the purposes of my hypothesis, it really does not matter where the policy preferences of governments come from. It only matters that they act systematically on them.

Assuming education is not the answer, the crux of the issue becomes whether any collective commitment to cooperation once made can be 'locked in' in some way. If the problem is that governments find it difficult to sustain their enthusiasm for the process, can a solution be found that will effectively prevent them from retreating?

One obvious possibility is the extreme of a common currency, where individual autonomy is—in principle—permanently surrendered by each participating country. In practice, of course, not even full currency unions have proved indissoluble, as we saw in the case of the East African shilling in the 1970s or as evidently we are about to see in the case of the (former) Soviet Union today. But cases like these usually stem from associations that were something less than voluntary to begin with. When undertaken by consenting sovereign states, full monetary unification generally tends to be irreversible—which is precisely the reason why it is seen so seldomly in the real world. During the *laissez-faire* nineteenth century, when monetary autonomy meant less to governments than it does now, two fairly prominent currency unions were successfully established among formally independent nations—the Latin Monetary Union dating from 1865, and the Scandinavian Monetary Union created in 1873—each built on a single, standardised monetary unit (respectively the franc and the krone). Both groupings, however, were effectively terminated with the outbreak of World War I. In the twentieth century, the only comparable arrangement has been the Belgium–Luxembourg Economic Union, established in 1921. (Other contemporary currency unions, such as the CFA franc zone and the East Caribbean dollar area, had their origins in colonial relationships.) The recent difficulties experienced by the European Community (EC) in negotiating the details of a formal Economic and Monetary Union (EMU) illustrate just how tough it is to persuade governments even as closely allied as these to make the irrevocable commitment required by a common currency.

Short of the extreme of a common currency, an effective solution would require participating governments to voluntarily pre-commit to some form of external authority over their individual policy behaviour. The authority might be supplied by an international agency armed with collectively agreed decision-making powers—corresponding to what I have elsewhere (Cohen 1977) called the organising principle of supra-nationality. It might also be supplied by one single dominant country with acknowledged leadership responsibilities (the principle of hegemony). Or it might be supplied by a self-disciplining regime of norms and rules accepted as binding on all participants (the principle of automaticity). Unfortunately, neither experience nor the underlying logic of political sovereignty offers a great deal of hope in the practical potential of any of these alternatives. Supra-nationality and automaticity, for example, have always tended to be heavily qualified in international monetary relations. In the G-7 multilateral-surveillance process, the International Monetary Fund (in the person of its managing director) has been given a role, but limited only to the provision of essential data and objective analytical support, and public articulation of any sort of binding rules (regarding, for example, exchange-rate targets) has been strenuously resisted by most governments (Dobson 1991). Hegemony, in the meantime, may be tolerated where it is unavoidable, as in the sterling area during the 1930s or the Bretton Woods system immediately after World War II. But as both these historical episodes illustrate, dominance also tends to breed considerable resentment and a determined eagerness by most countries to assert individual autonomy as soon as circumstances permit.

The principal exception in recent years has been the joint currency float (the 'snake') of the European Community, first implemented in the 1970s by a cluster of smaller countries effectively aligned with West Germany's Deutschmark, and later extended and formalised under the European Monetary System (EMS) starting in 1979. Under the rules of the EC's joint float, national monetary discretion for most members has been distinctly constrained, despite relatively frequent realignments of mutual exchange rates and, until the end of the 1980s, the persistence of significant capital controls in some countries. German policy, on the other hand, has not only remained largely autonomous but has effectively dominated monetary relations within the group. In effect, therefore, the snake has successfully locked in a collective commitment to cooperation through a combination of automaticity and hegemony. Yet not only has the arrangement proved tolerable to its members, over time it has gradually attracted new participants; and now, despite the difficulties of gaining irrevocable commitments to a common currency, may be about to be extended again in the form of EMU.

The reasons for this success quite obviously are unique and have to do most with the distinctive character of the institutional ties that have developed among EC members. Over time, as Robert Keohane and Stanley Hoffmann (1991) have recently noted, the EC has gradually built up a highly complex process of policy-making in which formal and informal arrangements are intricately linked across a wide range of issues. Decisions in one sector are closely affected by what is happening elsewhere and often lead to the sort of inter-sectoral 'spillover' effects that were first emphasised in early neo-functional theory (Tranholm-Mikkelson 1991). (Note that these effects are quite different from those featured in the theoretical case for policy cooperation, which stresses spillovers in a single sector or issue-area.) More generally, member governments have come to fully accept a style of political behaviour in which individual interests are jointly realised through an incremental, albeit fragmented, pooling of national sovereignty—what Keohane and Hoffmann (1991, p. 13) call a 'network' form of organisation, 'in which individual units are defined not by themselves but in relation to other units'. And this, in turn, has been made possible only because of the existence of a real sense of commitment and attachment—of *community*—among all the countries involved. In this sense, the EC truly is the exception that proves the rule. Among states less intimately connected, resistance to any form of external authority over individual policy behaviour is bound to be correspondingly more stubborn and determined. Does this mean then that nothing can be done about the episodic quality of monetary cooperation? Not at all. In principle, any number of technical innovations can be imagined to moderate underlying tendencies towards recidivism by cooperating governments. As in the G-7 process, for example, meetings could be put on a regular schedule and based on an agreed analytical framework to help ensure greater continuity of policy behaviour. Much the same impact might also be attained by giving more precision as well as greater publicity to policy guidelines and commitments. And there might also be some benefit to be had from establishing a permanent, independent secretariat to provide an institutional memory and ongoing objective analysis of priorities and issues. The issue, however, is not administrative creativity but political acceptability. Each such innovation makes it just that much more difficult for policy-makers to change their minds when circumstances might seem to warrant it. Is the underlying relationship among the states involved sufficiently close to make them willing to take such a risk? This is not a question that can be answered *a priori*; as the exceptional case of the EC demonstrates, it is certainly not a question of monetary relations alone. Ultimately prospects for sustaining any cooperative effort in this crucial area on public policy will depend on how much basic affinity governments feel in other areas as well—in effect, on the extent to which they feel they share a common destiny across the full spectrum of economic and political issues.

5. Lessons for the Pacific Region

What lessons can be drawn from this discussion for the question of managing monetary relations in the Pacific Region in the 1990s? The principal implication is that a serious and sustained commitment to monetary cooperation requires a real sense of *community* among the countries involved, meaning, in particular, a real willingness to pool elements of state sovereignty across a range of issues, as in the EC's 'network' form of organisation. Unfortunately, the conditions necessary to establish such a style of political behaviour are not easy to satisfy and without major effort appear unlikely to be attained in the Pacific region any time soon. The irony, as indicated at the outset, is that even without such a commitment most regional governments will find their policy autonomy increasingly eroded in the coming decade—and in a manner that may seem even less appealing to them than formal cooperation.

We know that there is not much of a tradition of shared destiny in the Pacific Region. Indeed, it is not even clear how the region is to be defined. Is it to include all countries in or bordering on the Pacific—an enormously diverse group which, apart from geography, has almost nothing in common either economically or politically? Or are we talking about some less differentiated subgroup, including only a limited selection of states and excluding others? Are the United States and Canada part of the region? Latin America? China? (Which China?) The Russian Federation? The problems of defining the Pacific Region are well known and have long plagued efforts to promote economic cooperation in the area (Higgott et al. 1990; Harris 1991). Proposals in the past have ranged from a Pacific Free Trade Area (PAFTA) limited to just the five relatively developed economies of Japan, the United States, Canada, Australia, and New Zealand (Kojima 1971) to an idea for a far more comprehensive Organization for Pacific Trade, Aid and Development (OPTAD) modelled on the OECD (Drysdale & Patrick 1979). None of these schemes has ever come to fruition.

The challenge in fact is daunting. How can cooperation be promoted on any scale among countries more noted for their sustained antagonisms, ethnic and cultural conflicts, and border disputes? Many, having only recently emerged from colonial status, are understandably resistant to any surrender of their newly won political sovereignty. Most are more intent on individual nation-building than on regional interdependence. Few have yet demonstrated much inclination (borrowing from the language of Keohane and Hoffmann) to define themselves in relation to one another rather than in their own terms. Most still behave as if state interests can best be pursued unilaterally.

At present, the only institutionalised version of economic cooperation in the region is the so-called Asia Pacific Economic Co-operation (APEC) group, first proposed by Australian Prime Minister Bob Hawke in 1989. Participants include the six nations of the Association of Southeast Asian Nations, otherwise known as ASEAN (Brunei, Indonesia, Malaysia, the Philippines, Singapore, and Thailand), plus Australia, Canada, Japan, Korea, New Zealand and the United States. To date APEC has met three times: in Canberra in November 1989, Singapore in July 1990, and Seoul in November 1991. So far, however, little has been accomplished in terms of practical policy collaboration. If any serious affinity is beginning to develop among these states on commercial or financial issues, it has yet to be convincingly demonstrated.

Nor, focusing just on the issue of monetary relations alone, does there appear to be much *practical* basis for enhanced cooperation in the region. Financial links of Pacific countries have always tended to centre bilaterally on the United States, with the dollar still serving as the main currency of choice for both trade and investment purposes; direct connections among national capital markets in East Asia and Oceania remain rudimentary at best. Likewise, nearly all Pacific governments including Japan continue to use the dollar as their principal vehicle for exchange-market intervention; apart from the yen, no significant amounts of local currency are retained in reserves to help promote multilateral management of exchange rates. And, of course, any effort at coordination of domestic credit or fiscal policies would be severely hampered by the vast differences of economic, political, and institutional development that are evident in the region. These are all potent barriers to effective monetary collaboration.

This is not to suggest that such barriers cannot be overcome. With the appropriate will, initiatives could be designed to broaden financial links and permit more cross-trading of regional currencies. In lieu of existing exchange controls, for instance, a system of joint restrictions could be instituted on the model of the old sterling area to promote freedom of capital movement among Pacific countries. Likewise, in lieu of continued reliance on the dollar for intervention purposes, a network of reciprocal credit lines on the model of the European Monetary System's short-term lending facilities could be agreed to help efforts to stabilise mutual exchange rates. And in lieu of today's decentralised decision-making, a regularised procedure on the model of the G-7's ministerial meetings (preferably improved to include more publicity and a permanent secretariat) could be organised to ensure greater consistency of national macroeconomic policies. But does the will exist? As in the G-7, political acceptability remains the ticklish issue. To date, governments in the Pacific Region have seemed more impressed by the benefits of formal monetary sovereignty than by potential costs. Although in other issue-areas regional policy-makers may be showing increasing awareness of the limits of unilateralism (see the chapters by Higgott and Harris in this volume), none have yet shown any appetite for the major effort that would be required to reverse existing attitudes on monetary matters.

Unfortunately, such attitudes are short-sighted. Regional governments behave as if the choice in the monetary area is between autonomy and cooperation—and they still prefer autonomy. In fact, that behaviour overlooks two essential considerations, one analytical and one empirical. Analytically it overlooks the crucial message of the Unholy Trinity. If the recent experience of the Triad teaches us anything, it is that monetary independence in a world of growing capital mobility is increasingly illusory or else can be purchased only at the cost of greater and greater exchange-rate instability. Empirically it overlooks the spreading financial influence of Japan in the Pacific Region. More and more, the economies of East Asia and Oceania are finding themselves drawn into Japan's gravitational orbit by ties of trade, aid, and investment; and this in turn, as a recent award-winning study by Jeffrey Frankel (1991) clearly demonstrates, is making them increasingly sensitive to Japanese monetary conditions and policies. While as recently as 1988 local interest rates were still affected most by yields on dollar assets, Frankel shows that by 1991 yen rates had come to dominate in many local capital markets. Regional use of Japan's currency, albeit still second to the dollar, is also growing, and Tokyo is rapidly becoming the area's acknowledged financial centre. Over the course of the 1980s, the proportion of central-bank reserves held in yen rose from 13.9 per cent to 17.5 per cent, while the fraction of external debt denominated in yen nearly doubled to about 40 per cent. *De facto*, if not *de jure*, a kind of 'yen bloc' quite clearly is gradually coalescing in the region, in a manner not unlike the clustering of some of Europe's smaller currencies around the Deutschmark in the 1970s.

Together these considerations suggest that the choice for regional governments is not between autonomy and cooperation as such but rather between *different forms* of monetary cooperation or integration. In the 1990s countries can actively promote formal and mutually acceptable procedures for collective decision-making, perhaps building on the model of the G-7 multilateral-surveillance process. Or else they can procrastinate, which, in effect, would mean passively accepting the gradual emergence of a yen bloc instead. One way or another, they are bound to find their individual policy behaviour increasingly constrained. The question is where that external authority will come from—as a result of voluntary mutual accommodation (possibly incorporating elements of automaticity or supra-nationality) or from the unilateral decisions of an increasingly hegemonic Japan. Many in the region still remember Japan's role in World War II and remain suspicious of Japanese values and motivations; if history is any guide, many more would undoubtedly be resentful of a growing Japanese dominance in monetary affairs. It would be ironic, indeed, if they nonetheless soon find themselves part of a new version of a Greater East Asia Co-Prosperity Sphere by virtue of nothing more than their own indecisiveness and inaction.

8 Running on Empty? Complex Interdependence and the Future of Japanese–American Monetary Coordination

RICHARD LEAVER

Introduction

This chapter is concerned with future trends in the evolution of the balance between economic problems and economic solutions along the backbone of the nascent Pacific community, and specifically with the place that monetary cooperation might occupy within that matrix. It need hardly be said that the quality of multilateral or regional management which ultimately proves possible through the coming decade will, in large part, be shaped by the interaction between the world's two largest economies. If the dimensions of Japanese–American economic tensions can at least be contained, then the way remains open to new forms of management. If, however, problems overwhelm solutions, then 'squeaking by' might be the best that realistically could be hoped for.

Empirically, the following analysis is centred around the loosely institutionalised practice of Japanese–American financial coordination that provided the mainstay of the 1985 Plaza Agreement. The implementation of this agreement halved the value of the dollar in little more than eighteen months and, as Krugman (1988) has noted, made the fabled 'beggar-my-neighbour' devaluations of the 1930s look puny by comparison. This process of coordinated management, where Japanese public and private investors picked up the lion's share of costs, helped to curb trends in the foreign exchange market which were, at the time, generating widespread despair about the future of the international economy.

To the extent that Japanese activism within the framework of a G-7 agreement succeeded in dampening these fears about instability, the Plaza Agreement has gradually come to appear as a beacon of hope shining

159

through a fog of post-Cold War uncertainty. Many accept that any new order for our time will require, as it did in 1985, that Japanese financial strength be coupled to global projects as defined by those with the 'strategic vision' that Tokyo is alleged to lack. In that sense, the Plaza Agreement constitutes an important precursor to the kind of cooperative burden-sharing which many now summon to function as the heart of a post-Cold War international economic order.[1] This chapter therefore spends considerable time reflecting upon the conditions under which the Plaza strategy was implemented, the outcomes with which the strategy can properly be credited, and the prospects for future monetary coordination.

This empirical investigation is undertaken within a framework of 'complex interdependence' the lineage of which goes back to the early work of Keohane and Nye (1977). Many contemporary scholars of international political economy (IPE) are likely to regard that framework as a quaint anachronism which has been thoroughly transcended by more recent theoretical turns. It has, however, the virtue of bringing the issues of economic sensitivity and vulnerability into sharp focus. This focus draws attention to the salience of the social underpinnings of international power. Such 'domestic' considerations not only speak most clearly to the unanswered questions about the future possibilities of financial coordination which are my concern, but are, I believe, vitally necessary if the sub-discipline of IPE is itself to thrive through the more uncertain future.

Complex interdependence and lateral escalation

The evolution of 'dynamic economic problems' in the Pacific dates back to the period when the first visions of a Pacific community were received.[2] In the middle to late 1960s, those visions arrived just prior to the diagnosis of a cancerous growth along the commercial backbone of the Pacific economy. As noted in the Introduction to this volume, when the trajectories of the Japanese and American trade balances departed from their seemingly stable orbits and crossed each other's path—with Japan now accruing surpluses, and the United States, deficits—that malignant issue which we now know as the 'Japan problem' came into being.

That inversion of trade balances coincided with, and partially expressed, a series of broader changes which collectively marked 'the long decade' of the 1950s. In 1971, the system of fixed exchange rates conceived in the final days of World War II imploded under the weight of internal inconsistencies which were exacerbated by changed conditions, yielding in time a 'non-system' of floating exchange rates between the major economic powers. Two years later, the OPEC revolution dramati-

---

[1] For a variety of formulations of that role, see Bergsten (1990), Henning (1991), and Lewis (1991–92).

[2] A brief history of these visions is provided in Drysdale (1988, ch. 8).

cally reversed what hitherto appeared to be a secular trend to lower real energy prices. These changes led to an economic environment where the state was less central, where growth was less assured, and where the degree of politicisation of economic issues appeared more pronounced. In policy terms, these movements scripted a stagflationary menu of policy choices for the advanced capitalist world.

These serial developments in the extant 'regimes' in money, trade and oil fundamentally altered not only the nature of international interactions, but also the ways in which the dynamics of international relations were conceived by scholars. For academicians, they called forth the new sub-discipline of international political economy. Here the staple of professional debates quickly came to revolve around, and has remained transfixed by, the nature and implications of these transformations in the markets for money, traded goods and oil.

So far as the pattern of international economic interactions was concerned, at least one important and paradoxical implication could be derived from the new milieu. The enhanced permeability of national borders to economic forces increased the cost of 'national solutions' to low growth and made them less likely, but it simultaneously encouraged states to laterally displace those increased costs of adjustment onto others. In this sense, greater openness both increased the need for collective economic solutions and decreased the ability to arrive at such bargains. In short, these changes enhanced the scope for strategic behaviour within the economic domain. Consequently, 'the game which nations play' came to be distinguished by the attempt to manipulate short run sensitivities and longer run vulnerabilities to economic adjustment.

The pattern which subsequently came to characterise Japanese–American relations through the following decades exemplifies the main features of this 'new game' of complex interdependence. While Japanese manufactured goods clearly enjoyed a decisive competitive advantage across the more elaborate end of the spectrum of industrial competence, the full impact of this commercial dominance was diminished by other strategic weaknesses.

Some of these weaknesses had their origins in the formula which guided post-war Japanese reconstruction. In accordance with this design, Japanese exports relied heavily on the American market, and to that extent they were vulnerable to wilful manipulation of market access. The same formula saw the United States installed as the protector of Japan without any matching obligations—a division of labour which opened the way to American pressure for greater defence reciprocity. Additional counter-leverage came from the fact that it was American military might which secured Japanese access to, and safe passage for, the Middle Eastern oil that was indispensable to its 'economic miracle': indeed, the architect of containment, George Kennan, believed that Japan could be controlled by manipulation of its oil imports (see Cumings 1988, pp. 76–7).

Other countervailing weaknesses are of more recent vintage. After liberalisation of the Japanese capital market in the early 1980s, higher American interest rates proved so attractive to Japanese institutional investors that many believed that they had no alternative for placement of their funds. As Moffitt (1987, p. 574) expressed this point, '...the question is not whether...Japanese money will leave the US market and go elsewhere. There are no other money markets large enough to absorb it. They know it and we know it'.

Within this context, successive Japanese and American governments tried through the ensuing decades to at least contain the dimensions of the trade imbalance by consciously managing an ever greater share of their commerce. Beginning with the late 1960s restrictions on textiles trade, and continuing thereafter in regular half-decade intervals, the primary means of damage limitation were sought in the instruments of managed trade—voluntary export restraints, orderly marketing agreements, trigger price mechanisms, etc. In three respects, however, these attempts to manufacture a trade balance remained consistent with the structure of incentives emanating from the new environment of complex interdependence.

First, the instruments of managed trade simply failed to produce the intended result. The main cause of this repeated failure was the ability of Japanese exporters to use qualitative improvements to outflank quantitative restrictions—that is, to export higher value-added products while conforming to numerical targets. The instruments of managed trade can still be defended with the somewhat mystical counterfactual argument that the level of Japanese exports would have been greater in its absence, but this draws attention away from the unsavoury fact that the actual bilateral trade imbalance did not improve as each new generation of managed trade instruments was brought into play. As Tables 8.1 and 8.2 both suggest, the most pronounced movements towards more balanced trade came during periods when different, and more specific, forces were at work.

Second, while issue-specific commercial management returned, at best, a holding action, more impressive indications of a lasting trade reversal came through 'lateral shifts' in the terrain of economic conflict. When American administrations were able—either consciously or unconsciously—to link the issue of trade balance to domains where Japanese vulnerability was high, the gains along the trade front were much more striking. Movements in oil prices and exchange rates provide the most telling examples.

In 1971, for example, the Nixon administration delivered the first in a series of rolling blows against the newly expanding Japanese trade surplus. The 'New Economic Policy' which accompanied the American abrogation of Bretton Woods included a 10 per cent surcharge on all imports.[3] This remained in place until the allies had effectively revalued against the dollar. The 36 per cent revaluation of the yen that was

---

3   For a more complete discussion of Nixon's NEP, see Calleo (1982, ch. 4).

achieved by 1973 was greater than for any other currency—indeed, a movement in relative prices sufficient to lead to the virtual disappearance of the Japanese–American trade imbalance (see Table 8.1).

Table 8.1   Japanese exports to and imports from the US (billions of current US dollars)

Year	x	$\frac{x}{X}$ %	m	$\frac{m}{M}$ %	x–m	X–M	$\frac{x-m}{X-M}$ %
1990	91.1	31.7	52.8	22.4	38.3	52.3	73.0
1989	94.0	34.2	48.3	23.0	45.7	65.0	70.3
1988	90.2	34.0	42.3	22.6	47.9	77.5	61.8
1987	85.0	36.8	32.0	21.2	53.0	80.4	65.9
1986	81.9	38.9	29.4	23.0	52.5	83.0	63.2
1985	66.7	37.7	26.0	20.0	40.7	46.7	87.1
1984	60.4	35.5	26.9	19.7	33.5	33.6	99.7
1983	43.3	29.4	24.8	19.5	18.5	20.5	90.2
1982	36.5	26.4	24.2	18.4	12.3	6.9	178.0
1981	38.9	25.6	25.3	17.7	13.6	8.6	158.0
1980	31.9	24.4	24.6	17.4	7.3	-10.9	-
1979	26.5	25.9	20.3	18.5	6.2	-7.5	-
1978	25.4	25.8	14.9	18.7	10.5	18.4	57.0
1977	20.1	24.7	12.5	17.5	7.6	9.8	77.6
1976	15.9	23.6	11.9	18.3	4.0	-9.4	-
1975	11.2	20.2	11.6	20.1	-0.4	-2.1	-
1974	12.9	23.3	12.7	20.4	0.2	-6.6	-
1973	9.6	25.9	9.3	24.2	0.3	-1.4	-
1972	9.1	31.3	6.0	24.9	3.1	5.2	60.0

Notes: x = Japanese exports to the United States
         X = total Japanese exports
         m = Japanese imports from the United States
         M = total Japanese imports

Source: IMF, Direction of Trade Statistics, various issues.

The oil price rises of 1974 and 1979–80 worked in the same direction. During the 'long boom', the seemingly secular trend to ever-cheaper real oil prices constituted, as Keohane (1984b, p. 21) has observed, '…a peculiar sort of "invisible hand" in the form of improving terms of trade…' that benefited America's oil-importing allies in particular. The converse of that advantage was that those allies—and Japan in particular—bore the brunt of relative suffering associated with the transition to more expensive energy. The high energy intensity of Japanese hyper-growth, and the absence of any immediately available substitute for imported oil, gave the Tanaka Government no option during late 1973 but to pass on the full impost of higher prices to final consumers. This brought 'the Japanese miracle' to a screeching halt in the following year, when inflation temporarily exceeded 30 per cent—and the balance of trade plunged back into deficit.

Table 8.2   US exports to and imports from Japan (billions of current US dollars)

Year	x	x/X %	m	m/M %	m–x	M–X	m–x/M–X %
1990	48.5	12.4	93.1	18.0	44.6	123.9	36.0
1989	44.6	12.3	97.1	19.7	52.5	129.5	40.5
1988	37.6	11.8	93.1	20.3	55.5	140.4	39.5
1987	28.2	11.2	88.1	20.8	59.9	171.2	35.0
1986	26.9	12.4	85.5	22.1	58.6	169.8	34.5
1985	22.6	10.6	72.4	20.0	49.8	148.5	33.5
1984	23.6	10.8	60.4	17.7	36.8	123.3	29.8
1983	21.9	10.9	43.6	16.1	21.7	69.4	31.3
1982	21.0	9.9	39.9	15.7	18.9	42.6	44.4
1981	21.8	9.3	39.9	14.6	18.1	39.6	45.7
1980	20.8	9.4	33.0	12.8	12.2	36.2	33.7
1979	17.6	9.7	28.2	12.7	10.6	40.3	26.3
1978	12.9	9.0	26.5	14.2	13.6	42.3	32.2
1977	10.5	8.7	20.2	12.8	9.7	36.3	26.7
1976	10.1	8.8	16.9	13.1	6.8	14.5	46.9
1975	9.6	8.9	12.3	11.9	2.7	-4.2	-
1974	10.7	10.8	13.3	12.3	2.6	9.5	27.4
1973	8.3	11.7	10.2	13.9	1.9	2.2	86.4
1972	5.0	10.0	9.6	16.3	4.6	9.1	50.5

Notes: x = United States exports to Japan
X = total United States exports
m = United States imports from Japan
M = total United States imports

Source: IMF, *Direction of Trade Statistics*, various issues.

The central conclusion to take from this narrative is that the source of actual improvements in bilateral trade came not through direct management of the trade account itself; at best, the instruments of managed trade simply defended an already unfavourable ground. Real trade gains, such as they were, came through linkage to weak Japanese positions in other domains—notably, the markets in money and oil. In the short term, this demonstrated that the United States held most of the trumps within the new context of complex interdependence. It could offset a weak position in commerce against strengths in other domains, and make some headway at redressing the adverse trade balance. Put simply, Washington held the ability to strategically outflank its major commercial competitor.

The third point, however, is that even the trade-levelling effects produced by these flanking movements petered out through the medium term. By definition, a strategy of externalising the costs of adjustment is intended to preserve the freedom of action for those operating within the domestic economic domain. How they use that freedom of action—in particular, whether the privilege of enhanced independence is used wisely or not—then becomes a matter of great import.

In point of fact, these invaluable positions of strength which American administrations held in other domains came to be squandered in a variety of ways. The picture of waste is easiest to apprehend in relation to oil, where America's relatively high oil prices and high degree of self-sufficiency in oil afforded a priceless window of opportunity for moderating the pace of economic adjustment to the new world of higher real energy prices. Yet in the face of the OPEC revolution, the Nixon administration chose the path of least political resistance. It intervened to further moderate the costs of adjustment by holding down prices, so providing the cue to subsequent administrations which failed to impose significant consumption taxes in line with global trends. Consequently, during the era of oil shocks, the price paid by American oil consumers moved from the high end of the OECD spectrum to the rock bottom of the low end.[4]

MIT meets MITI

A similar combination of wishful thinking and political opportunism came to erode more of the positions of strength which initially encased American macropolicy. The supply-side revolution which was central to the Reagan administration placed blind faith in infinite market expansion at the heart of economic policy. By the middle of his first term in office, a perverse combination of tight monetary policy and loose fiscal policy had yielded what Epstein (1985) eloquently labelled 'a triple debt crisis': an internal American deficit, a Third World debt crisis, and an external American deficit. The external deficit was largely accounted for by a massive expansion of imports from Japan, where the monetary conservatism that was hardened by the oil crisis persisted well into the 1980s. As Table 8.2 shows, America's bilateral trade imbalance with Japan increased by 120 per cent between 1983 and 1985—a development that threatened to catalyse a protectionist backlash in Congress.

At this critical juncture, some particularly bleak assessments of the future of the global economy were made. One of the most influential came from Lester Thurow of the MIT. Looking both backwards and forwards, he argued that Japan, Europe and America each confronted rather different economic problems. Though he desired one common international solution to those different problems, he feared that 'the current degree of economic integration...[had]...outrun the world's collective political willingness to manage it' (Thurow 1985a), and that the divergent option of three national solutions was more likely.

Thurow painted the immediate conjuncture in a way which many found convincing. In America, the declining quality of inputs to the production process was, predictably enough, yielding low productivity growth, with

---

4   On the history of American energy policy through the post-war period, see Vietor (1984).

the vicious circle completed by the traditional American aversion to industrial policy.[5] In Europe, relatively rigid wages and conditions had generated a seemingly intractable employment problem that already stretched back two decades, while in Japan, the successful formula for post-war growth—written around the tight restriction of imports—now yielded an economic performance entirely dependent on exports that could simply not continue at current levels.

He then laid down a minimal list of preconditions which an internationalist solution to these heterogenous growth dilemmas would have to satisfy. First, it would be necessary to obtain agreement to dampen the fluctuation of exchange rates; second, the engine of global growth would have to be shifted off its current tracks of heavy reliance on expansion of the American deficit; and third, there would have to be an American willingness to resume 'the manager's job' of 'seeking consensus and making compromises', which it had thoroughly abdicated in the obsessive unilateralism of recent years. He clearly expected that each of these challenges would go begging, and that the political price entailed in nationalist solutions to each of these growth problems was lower than the price of a single internationalist one. Consequently, he predicted a gradual contraction in the overall degree of global economic integration.

In the face of these dire circumstances, the second Reagan administration arrived at a different opinion which again expressed its faith in the strategy of lateral escalation. Currency misalignment was deemed to be the major cause of the trade deficit and, consequently, dollar devaluation could again save the day. Hence, by the time Thurow's article saw the light of day in late 1985, a highly secretive plan cooked inside the G-5 meeting of finance ministers, explicitly targeted at devaluation and eventual stabilisation of the dollar, had already swung into action. Over the next eighteen months, the Plaza Agreement led the dollar sharply downwards under the tutelage of Reagan's new Treasury Secretary, James Baker. Then, as the dollar approached the 150 yen mark, Baker adroitly changed course, obtaining effective support for stabilisation at this lower level. Figure 8.1 captures these relative movements.

Throughout this period, all of Thurow's minimal requirements for an internationalist solution to the growth impasse were at least partially met. The fact that an agreement even existed about the direction in which the value of the dollar should move showed how far Baker had turned his back on the heavy unilateralism which had previously marked the Reagan adminstration's dollar policy; clearly some of Thurow's 'manager's agenda' had been taken up. Thurow's first precondition came to be discharged by the relative success which the agreement had over the longer run in marking out a new, lower, and ultimately more stable band for the dollar. Finally, during the course of implementing this agreement, Baker repeatedly broached the delicate issue of shifting the burden of growth to

---

5 These were the central themes of Thurow (1985b).

the surplus economies of Germany and especially Japan—Thurow's second precondition for an internationalist solution.

Figure 8.1 Exchange rate, yen and deutschmark

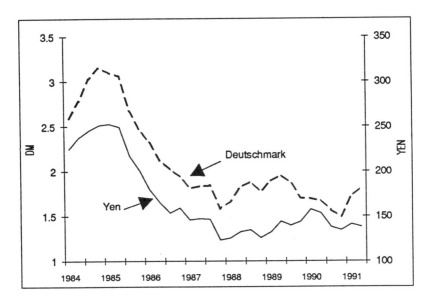

These three requirements, however, constituted only minimal standards, and their partial satisfaction only affords a weak hope that internationalist solutions to the problems of heterogenous growth will remain viable through the future. A better starting point for investigating this issue comes through the observation that the Plaza Agreement conformed to the pattern of challenge and response in Japanese–American economic relations noted previously. The strategy of lateral escalation had paid off relatively handsomely for Washington during its trade disputes of the previous two decades. On this occasion, the American response to a mounting Japanese trade surplus was another outflanking movement—namely, displacement of a trade issue to the monetary realm where Washington felt that the balance of vulnerabilities was more favourable to it. The question to ask is whether subsequent events and outcomes proved that appreciation to be correct: the answer will be an important index of the future prospects for post-Cold War monetary coordination.

The story of the Plaza devaluation has been told in full detail by Funabashi (1988) and in a more summary form by others (in particular, Destler & Henning 1989, and Putnam & Bayne 1987); consequently, there is no need to repeat it here. What is pertinent to our present concerns is a more limited, if concentrated, reflection on the outcomes (both positive and negative) which were achieved; the combination of instrumentalities employed (or not employed); and the environmental conditions under which the depreciation was conducted. These are the central matters so far as the future prospects for monetary coordination are concerned. They relate to the symbiotic effects between the agreement and the contextual structure of complex interdependence.

The outcomes from depreciation

Two potential crises were of direct concern to Baker in devising the Plaza strategy. The most immediate was posed by the rapidly declining US trade balance and the rising protectionist sentiment. With mid-term elections impending, the administration sought out ways to nip these sentiments in the bud. The second crisis was perhaps less pressing but potentially more dangerous, and revolved around the mounting appreciation that failure to lower the dollar through an orderly process would condemn it to fall later in a more haphazard manner. Almost all commentators accepted that the dollar was substantially overvalued, and that it must eventually fall. It had, indeed, commenced a downwards movement early in 1985, but when that stalled in mid-summer, Baker took the lesson that more comprehensive and coordinated government action was required to rectify this 'market failure'.

Congressional resentment congealed around the argument that the trade deficit represented lost American jobs. This concern with employment had some logic on its side during the earlier recession when the trade deficit first accelerated, but as recession gave way to boom, attendant increases in capacity utilisation deprived the case of much of its coherence. Nonetheless, the belief remained politically popular and powerful, and therefore it needed to be neutralised. A lower dollar created two possibilities—that American export and import-competing industries would become more competitive, so returning America's trade balances to a state of greater symmetry; and that evident cooperation by the allies would constitute a sign of good faith to Congress.

Over the longer run, the outcomes on the latter were more tangible than those on the former. As Table 8.2 indicates, the positive trade results which Baker sought from depreciation were slow in coming, and certainly far too late for the 1986 Congressional elections. Even at the end of 1988, and despite the exaggerated fall of the dollar against the yen, the best that could be detected in nominal terms was a small and slow decline in the size of the bilateral deficit. Against this, the value of Japanese exports to the US, and Japan's share of the multilateral American deficit, had both risen, while the share of American imports in total Japanese imports had decreased. J-curve and hysteresis effects accounted for much of the slow pace of improvement, while currency pegging practices in other East Asian economies helped maintain the multilateral American trade deficit (emphasised in Gordon 1988). However, Baker was unable to massage the improved trade figures required to fully relieve either Congressional tension or the Republican majority, though allied cooperation went some way to stalling more draconian proposals for dispensing with the Japanese threat.

The dangers arising from an unguided, possibly cataclysmic, crash of the overvalued dollar included a sudden boost to inflation and a regime of dramatically higher interest rates that would be required to maintain foreign funding of the internal deficit under these conditions. Fears along these lines were also held by the Federal Reserve and by then Secretary of State Schultz. The Plaza depreciation was at its best here, though success brought little political reward. Through the immediate post-Plaza period, foreign investment in dollar-denominated assets—particularly sourced from Japan—accelerated appreciably even though the decline in the dollar's value completely overwhelmed the higher yields available to the foreign investor.

Two features of the process of devaluation helped maintain the confidence of foreign investors; the appearance of a controlled process, and the absence of any indication of an acceptable floor to the dollar. Had the dollar been allowed to fall outside a framework of political coordination, investor confidence could have quickly evaporated, leading in turn to higher interest rates. Likewise, statements that indicated in advance the expected depth of the depreciation would almost certainly have encouraged foreign investors to postpone investment until the new floor had been reached, so eliminating their exchange rate risk.

But orderly process and political astuteness probably do not account for all of this success. The rising yen enhanced the foreign purchasing power of newly liberated Japanese investors by cheapening American assets. It may be, as Kawai (1991) has argued, that the enthusiasm of Japanese investors for American assets at this time was primarily governed by an appreciation of the desirable size of their strategic stake in American asset markets rather than the immediate yield of those investments—a hypothesis consistent with the long-run calculus frequently argued to lie behind Japanese investment.

As noted earlier, many were tempted by this apparently perverse behaviour to argue that Japanese investors had no alternative to the American market. If that were so, then the drying up of private sector Japanese investment in 1987 requires explanation, especially since the exchange rate risk had disappeared by then. As Destler and Henning (1989, p. 77) observed, some 80 per cent of the American current account deficit during 1987 was financed not by the private sector—which made a negative net contribution—but by foreign central banks. Interstate coordination was clearly crucial at this juncture for averting the higher interest rates that would have hastened the end of the Reagan boom at a politically inopportune time.

The instruments of depreciation

In theory, an international agreement to drive down and stabilise the dollar could be achieved by coordinated action through any one of three primary mechanisms—intervention in the foreign exchange market, fiscal adjustment and interest rate manipulation. In practice, coordination was easier in some domains than others, though not all G-7 participants agreed about which domains were easy or hard. The actions taken (or avoided) in the name of the agreed goal of devaluation therefore constitute a matrix which speaks to the issue of asymmetries in national vulnerabilities—the crux of future possibilities for monetary coordination.

A fighting fund was required to set the dollar tumbling, and at the Plaza, reserve authorities committed $US18 billion for coordinated interventions. This imparted initial downward momentum to the market and supported verbal indications of where the dollar should be headed. The fund proved sufficient for this preliminary task, though within two months it was almost expended. Stopping the fall, however, proved more difficult and much more costly. When the Louvre Accord was struck, the dollar nonetheless continued its downwards trajectory, and national authorities (mainly Japanese) are thought to have spent $US140 billion trying, without a great deal of success, to back up a succession of ever-lower post-Louvre reference ranges.

The huge size of that braking action highlights the difficulty which reserve authorities inevitably face in a market where the sheer volume of private transactions dwarfs the combined resources of states. Hence market intervention has to be backed up by coordinated monetary and fiscal policies that will get 'the economic fundamentals' of coordinating states in line with, and therefore able to support, the right kind of trade outcomes at pre-determined exchange rates. Lower interest rates and looser fiscal policies in Japan and Germany would shift the burden of global expansion away from the American economy and provide longer run positive support for the American trade balance. The former provides the cheaper money that induces higher levels of investment, while a looser fiscal mix more directly addresses the level of domestic demand. But on both of these important fronts, the post-Plaza experience was more mixed.

Since the early Reagan years had pushed real interest rates to record levels across the globe, coordinated interest rate lowering between the all-important G-3 was relatively easy. As Figure 8.2 shows, notably lower interest rate structures marked the post-Plaza period in Japan and Germany, with early and lasting reductions in Japan. Many of these discount rate movements were either hatched at G-7 meetings or the product of 'conscious parallelism' urged by Baker's Treasury. Looked at from another angle, this highlights the importance of speaking with one voice. In a market with a well-developed herd instinct, the shepherds have to work together if the flock is to be maintained. For the most part, dissension on interest rates within the G-7 was kept an exclusively private matter. Public bickering only became explicit in September 1987, when Baker's misgivings about a recent tightening of German monetary policy led him to accuse them of 'violating the spirit of recent understandings'— a spat that cued the October stock market crash (see Destler & Henning 1989, pp. 62–3).

Figure 8.2 Discount rates

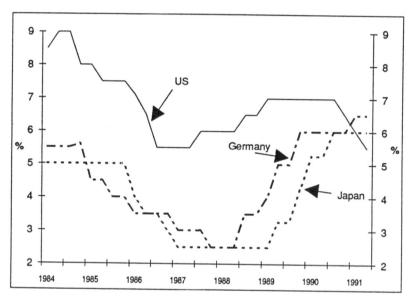

Fiscal policies, however, proved far more intractable in spite of sustained G-7 discussion of the need for coordinated action. In this domain, cooperation meant movement in opposite rather than parallel directions. In the United States, however, the goal of deficit reduction remained hostage to the same deadlock which had earlier cast Reagan in the unlikely role as 'the last of the Keynesians'. The Gramm–Rudman process of programmed deficit reductions was agreed by Congress in late 1985, and this was used by Baker in multilateral forums as a sign of American rectitude. But since the largest Gramm–Rudman cuts were always left for the future[6], the credibility of the programme never achieved great heights. There were no possible guarantees that Congress would prevail in a test of push and shove with the President, or that it would not subsequently reverse its commitment in the face of unknown exigencies.

---

[6] They were eventually tabled as part of the Louvre stabilisation.

None of this helped allay anxieties in Germany and Japan, where implementation of a fiscal stimulus was resisted for a variety of reasons. Both allies had relatively fresh—and sour—memories of Washington's earlier efforts to upgrade their economies to locomotives of world growth, and though the word 'locomotive' was studiously avoided through the post-Plaza period, in practice the call for stimulation amounted to the same thing. For relatively small economies, a commitment to set fiscal policy according to a requisition for global growth seemed to call for an extraordinary lax mix. Consequently, the best results remained promises rather than achievements, with the best of each emerging from the bilateral American–Japanese Structural Impediments Initiative (SII) negotiations rather than the multilateral process. One repercussion of these niggardly fiscal achievements was that Baker's determination to drive the dollar down became correspondingly greater.

The conditions for depreciation

In large measure, the Plaza devaluation confirms what we already know— namely, that coordinated action by independent national authorities is difficult at the best of times. It is important to emphasise that the conditions which confronted the coordinating parties in 1985 were, indeed, amongst the best of times. Three circumstances, in particular, cleared the path for joint action.

First, both Japan and Germany entered into the process of coordination from a baseline of, by their standards, relatively low growth; this created room for expansion closer to their more normal trajectory. Appreciation of their currencies worked in this direction by dampening the inflation that would have been associated with a purely national expansionary exercise of 'capitalism in one country'.

Second, as noted above, the high level of global interest rates associated with the early Reagan years—when both discount and prime lending rates rose everywhere by at least 50 per cent—created room for roughly parallel reductions through coordinated action which would simultaneously shift the point of application of global stimulus. The strong trend in American growth had been laid down by the asymmetric combination of lax fiscal policy and tight money. Domestic pressures for a more balanced mix of fiscal and monetary policy capable of sustaining the Reagan boom already existed before the Plaza Agreement, which partly made an international virtue out of this domestic necessity. In this sense, Baker's celebrated rejection of the 'unilateralism' of the first Reagan administration is not quite as dramatic as it appears to be. Nonetheless, had global interest rates not been so high, international coordination would have required a scissors movement of American increases and allied decreases—a divergent mix that would have been harder to orchestrate.

Third, the spectacular fall in oil prices during 1986 came to be important to the process of devaluation in two ways. It had a pronounced, once-off, deflationary effect across the oil-importing OECD world, so creating greater freedom for action on the interest rate front. In addition, falling oil prices temporarily attenuated the habitual Japanese concern with resource dependency that usually evokes an equally customary response of a drive for a trade surplus in manufactured goods.

These favourable conditions made it easier for the coordinating parties to do collectively what they would each like to have done separately. If that is so, then one unsavoury corollary may well be that the Plaza Agreement will never amount to more than a single, one-off episode, and in that sense, never constitute a realistic precedent for future coordination. Like Beamon's long jump record, it may stand for a long time.

That judgement may seem to stand in contradiction to Benjamin Cohen's chapter in this volume, where he demonstrates that G-7 members have, indeed, returned episodically to the well of policy coordination since the termination of the Plaza Agreement's life-cycle. About these later comings and goings, I would make only three observations. First, that they speak primarily about fluctuations in the will to summitry rather than material commitments to common projects; second, that many of the apparent 'successes' through the post-Plaza period—the role of the Japanese stock market in staunching the 'Black Monday' slide, for instance—owe little to summitry, and would have occurred in its absence; and third, that the very success of the Plaza process in managing the dollar's orderly devaluation established such high expectations about the prospects for future coordination that the expectations become independent causes of future crises when they are exposed as unrealistic. It was, for instance, G-7 disagreements over interest rates that touched off Black Monday.

Japanese–American coordination in a new world order

If this guarded judgement is correct, then it suggests that the hopes which have been invested in economic summitry as a guiding light to a post-Cold War order may be misplaced. The focus in the balance of this chapter tries to suggest reasons why this assessment can, in fact, be firmed.

As previously, the argument is cast in the language of complex interdependence—a language which speaks to some notable shifts in the distribution of medium-term vulnerabilities within the Japanese–American relationship. In the past, the Japanese strength in manufactured goods was offset against weakness in almost all other domains, and American lateral escalation of the trade dispute placed Japanese governments on the defensive by exposing these vulnerabilities. Today, however, the structure of vulnerabilities has fundamentally changed in ways which deprive

American administrations of the ability to outflank Japanese commercial strength.

Let us, therefore, turn to a contemporary investigation of the distribution of vulnerabilities in each of the three issue-areas that are the traditional home of IPE debates—trade, money and oil.

Trade restoration?

As the parameters of a post-Cold War world order slowly took shape, many analysts began to predict that the end-phase of the United States' trade problems with Japan had arrived. Between 1987 and 1989, as Bergsten (1990, p. 98) has observed, Japan's imports from the United States grew six times faster than its exports to it. Indeed, throughout the first half of the Bush administration's term, Baker's 1985 hopes for a more even Japanese–American trade balance seemed to be inching nearer to realisation. Trade outcomes moved in a direction broadly consistent with the radically revised structure of exchange rates. As Table 8.1 indicates, the rate of increase of Japanese exports to the US market continually slowed and then reversed, while the pace of American exports gathered momentum. By 1989, these opposed trends produced a small absolute reduction in the bilateral imbalance, and a more substantial 15 per cent reduction in 1990 as Japanese exports dropped 4 per cent while American exports rose 8 per cent.

This was the first time that the trade imbalance had contracted through successive years, and it seemed to many that the chickens of Plaza were finally, if slowly, coming home to roost. Noting that manufactured and high technology goods made up an increasingly large majority of Japan's American imports, Gordon (1991) added his preferred 'kinks' to the two export curves so that bilateral balance would be restored before the end of 1993. Others interpreted the Plaza exercise as the first tentative sign that coordinated political control was capable of being re-established over the hitherto free-wheeling foreign exchange market (see, for example, Gill 1991).

But even at the time when these favourable projections were made, there were already a number of signs suggesting that they might prove excessively rosy. First, the move back to an acceptable bilateral trade outcome was not as quick as many would have hoped. A year after the Plaza Agreement, when the 1986 oil price collapse had run its course, Krugman (1987b) did some back-of-the-envelope calculations on the conditions under which bilateral trade restoration might be achieved. Making allowance for the 'cleaning out effects' from prolonged over-valuation of the dollar, he came to the conclusion that a yen–dollar exchange rate below 140 combined with a 40 per cent reduction in oil prices should be sufficient.

However, by the end of 1990, five years of high yen had followed five years of high dollar, and the scope of oil price reductions had generally exceeded Krugman's assumption, yet the movement back to an acceptable trade outcome—let alone a balanced outcome—still had a considerable distance to travel. That could be interpreted in one of two ways. It suggests that the one factor abstracted from Krugman's analysis—the institutional factor—still has substantial life left in it as an explanation for the persistence of the trade deficit. It could also be taken as an indication of Japanese bad faith. One can assume that the temptation to lean to this side will be strong in a pre-election environment.

Second, the slow improvements in Japan's bilateral trade balance with the United States disguised the fact that Japan's surplus with the rest of the world was vanishing even more quickly. As Table 8.1 indicates, Japan's bilateral trade surplus with the US fell by 27 per cent during the last half of the 1980s, but its multilateral trade surplus declined by an additional 10 per cent. Consequently, the American share of Japan's total trade surplus actually rose from 63 per cent to 73 per cent through this period, even though the movement of relative prices was most pronounced along the dollar–yen axis. If, following Gordon, blithe forward projection of current trends is to be regarded as legitimate long-term analysis, then it was clear that existing trends would see the Japanese multilateral trade account reach equilibrium before the bilateral account with the United States. It would have to be doubted whether such an outcome could be squared with the political presumptions that moved Washington to call for ever-greater 'specific reciprocity' from Japan.

Third, the favourable tack in the bilateral trade balance recorded during 1989 and 1990 was achieved in a unique conjunction of relatively buoyant Japanese growth and a slow American slide into recession. American growth rates and the profit performance of its corporate sector both began to taper off from the moment Bush entered office, with the revised second quarter result for 1990 showing an economy already on the brink of recession. For the following three quarters, the annual decline of gross national product averaged nearly 1.5 per cent. Given this conjunction of growth and non-growth on different fringes of the Pacific, the really interesting observation is not that there has been a move towards greater trade symmetry, but why the move has not been more pronounced.

Previous recessions set something of a benchmark for the order of relative trade movement that might be expected. In the 1974–75 recession, there was a dramatic shift of more than 100 per cent in the bilateral imbalance of Japanese–American trade (see Tables 8.1 and 8.2), with the US recording its first (and last) trade surplus with Japan since the late 1960s. These Tables also show that a 10 per cent reduction in the Japanese bilateral surplus was achieved during the recession of 1981–82 against the ebbing tide of a sharply rising dollar. Since those were recessions of global scope, the direct impact on the relative magnitudes of

Japanese–American trade was minimised; nonetheless, the shift in bilateral trade balances was relatively large compared with the post-Plaza gains.

However, the combination of Japanese growth and American recession that marked the period of the Gulf War is unique to post-war recessions, and should be unusually favourable for trans-Pacific trade restoration. Even in the unlikely eventuality that Gordon's timetable for trade balance proves right, it would only confirm Destler and Henning's judgement that 'international adjustment achieved via a US recession would be a Pyrrhic victory' (Destler & Henning 1989, p. 54). Their verdict is a salutary reminder—if one was needed—that the purpose of economic policy is not singularly committed to the cause of trade balance, let alone any given bilateral account. Scholars once debated the issue of how low the dollar would have to fall to balance Japanese–American trade. Must we now ask the even sillier question of what level of American recession and Japanese growth would be necessary to balance their bilateral trade?

Finally, to make matters even worse, recent monthly trade outcomes suggest that Gordon's sanguine 'kinks' to the export curves were highly premature. In June 1991, just as the first hesitant signs of an American recovery were appearing, the American trade deficit reached a monthly low point of $4 billion. However, within that multilateral aggregate, the bilateral deficit with Japan increased both absolutely and relatively to account for 80 per cent of the total. Three months later, as the rate of Japanese growth began to fall and the American recovery showed signs of stalling, Japan's trade surplus stood 70 per cent over the previous year's figure, and projections began to point to absolute imbalances reminiscent of the vituperative days of 1985 (Martin 1991). At this point, it was hard to know what might be worse—a 'double dip' American recession that might at least suppress growth of the bilateral trade imbalance, or a recovery that could ignite it.

Monetary policies—a new disjunction?

As noted previously, the two preoccupations of the Federal Reserve through the course of the Plaza exercise were inflation and the consequences of a dollar free fall. Declining oil prices and a gradual slowdown of American growth helped clear the path to a more relaxed monetary policy, while the post-Louvre stabilisation (and upwards drift) of the dollar made inflation even less pressing. However, though the opening of President Bush's window of opportunity on a New World Order was marked by a resounding military victory, the American recession rekindled those two concerns, and created a domestic dilemma on the monetary front which has yet to abate.

Past experience suggests that war preparation should push the dollar up in 'the flight to quality'. It also suggests that the dollar should rise early in a recession as demand shrinks and the trade balance improves. But throughout the Kuwait crisis, the dollar moved against expectations in a downward direction, reaching a record low against the Deutschmark in February 1991 and near-record low against the yen. It rose only on the tide of military victory—even then, not as quickly as many expected (Gewirtz 1991)—and resumed its basic descent after mid-1991.

At the same time, the American inflation rate accelerated just when one might have expected the recession to induce a reduction. This upward movement was largely associated with the oil price spike of late 1990. Since American oil prices are not burdened with the heavy government taxes that are common throughout the OECD world (on which, see *Australian* 1990), they lack the heavy keel which yields price stability during oil crises. It was therefore notable that the inflationary spike associated with the fourth oil shock became most quickly manifest in the United States in spite of the recession, and that the rate of escalation in the American consumer price index kept pace with rises in Germany and Japan where economic growth remained relatively buoyant.

This imposed contradictory pressures upon interest rate policy. On the one hand, further interest rate reductions were required to reverse the trend to recession; on the other hand, the fight against inflation required a tight monetary policy. During the Kuwait crisis, this dilemma lined up national and international monetary authorities in favour of higher rates against an array of domestic interests labouring under inflationary conditions. The administration found itself isolated inside the G-7 (and from the Federal Reserve) by talking about the need for more growth through cheaper money. This stance prompted the first in a series of public lectures by the Managing Director of the International Monetary Fund (IMF) that spread well into the next year, all of which were focused around the steadfast need for monetary orthodoxy.[7]

As oil prices fell away in early 1991, the Federal Reserve proved more compliant with administration wishes, gradually reducing prime rates to 4.75 per cent—a full 3 per cent below the level at the commencement of the recession. These offerings, made in the expectation that the end of recession was nigh, have nonetheless been insufficient to pick the American economy up off the floor. As the decidedly sluggish recovery emerged and fears of a second dip gathered pace, the Bush administration has continued to push for even cheaper money against a somewhat reluctant Federal Reserve.

The heat which the administration has applied to monetary policy arises from the absence of a significant opening through the medium term for fiscal stimulation. The predictable effects of recession—reduced revenue take and increased pay-outs—combined with the costs of the S&L

---

7 See Camdessus (1990). The message was that efforts to push down interest rates too quickly would only succeed in raising both inflation and long-term interest rates, so choking off recovery. It was repeated the following April.

bail-out have produced a rapid escalation of the internal deficit. In the very year when Gramm–Rudman–Hollings is supposed to reinstate fiscal responsibility, the deficit is projected at $362 billion.[8]

Two recent studies from the Congressional Budget Office (CBO) suggest the magnitude of the medium term fiscal dilemma facing Washington. The first concerns the escalation of the annual cost of the S&L bail-out, which has risen from $22 billion in 1989 to $41 billion and $77 billion, with a projected $115 billion for 1992 (Pear 1991). The second CBO estimate deals with the cost savings associated with various levels of deep cuts in American strategic forces. A 6 000 warhead strategic arsenal—40 per cent below the negotiated START targets—would yield savings (in 1992 dollars) of $9.3 billion per annum over each of the next fifteen years, while reduction to 1 000 would produce a $17.4 billion annual saving (International Herald Tribune 1991). The appropriate conclusion is that through the medium term any positive fiscal effects from the 'peace dividend' will be totally out-gunned by the costs of the S&L bail-out, and that room for meaningful fiscal stimulation will be restricted.

Given fiscal recidivism, the call for cheaper money to stimulate dormant consumer spending is likely to appear attractive to an administration which now understands that the next election cannot be won on foreign policy alone. Whether that call will be answered—and, if answered, whether it will produce the right outcomes—is another matter. Indeed, given what he did when he delayed his planned 1991 Asian tour and stayed at home, President Bush now probably wishes he had stuck to his original travel schedule. Moving into populist mode, Bush casually issued a call for lower credit card rates that was picked up and amplified in Congress. This in turn led Greenspan to state that such a move would have 'serious adverse effects' on the American economy, so touching off the fifth largest one-day fall on Wall Street. When placed in the context of recent proposals by both Democrats and Republicans to revisit the wellspring of Reaganomics to draw out a middle-income tax break, it seems that the age of 'voodoo economics' has some life left in it.

This domestic dilemma over the direction of monetary policy becomes all the more complex when inserted into an international context. As noted earlier, one of the successes of the Plaza process lay in the maintenance of a healthy inflow of foreign capital over the course of dollar devaluation. A substantial 3 to 4 per cent interest rate premium in the American market helped sustain this inflow, and spurred the hope that what the United States had not quickly won on the trade account could eventually be recouped by harnessing Japanese finance to American domestic and international needs. For a brief moment in time, visions of a 'Nichibei economy' became the subject of enthusiastic inquiry (see, for example, Bergsten 1987, and Gilpin 1987, pp. 336–40).

---

8 Darman's projection from the White House is slightly lower at $345 billion.

More recently, however, the visions have clouded over. First, it has become ever more apparent that productive Japanese investment in the American economy touches upon raw political nerves. In theory, direct foreign investment offers at least a partial exit from the impasse of the trade dispute. In practice, as Kudrle (1991) notes, the American body politic is extremely sensitive to foreign sales of productive domestic assets. There is already acute political sensitivity to the possibility that Japanese direct foreign investment will merely export the *keiretsu* structure of Japanese industry to American shores, effectively locking American suppliers out of a closed network of inter-corporate linkages, or keeping the import component of American-hosted Japanese firms at current high levels (see Nakatani 1991). Such concerns could conceivably lead to a cumbersome process of vetting and screening inward Japanese investment, if not a lock out from the productive sector. The adverse knock-on effects to the trade account and to the general political relationship would not be negligible.

Second, the adequacy of the trans-Pacific interest rate premium and the direction of capital flow have come under question. Pressures for cheaper interest rates in the United States have coincided with higher rates in both Germany and Japan, as Figure 8.2 shows. Of particular relevance here is the collapse of the Japanese 'bubble economy', which has led Japanese investors to sell foreign assets to shore up uncertain financial positions at home. The inability of the Japanese Government to obtain G-7 support for the yen during the 1990 liquidity scare has probably served to increase the degree of caution shown by Japanese investors. Hence, while the dollar appreciation during 1988 renewed the confidence of Japanese investors, as from the first half of 1990, Japanese nationals became net sellers of US debt (*Australian Financial Review* 1990)—a behavioural pattern that has persisted ever since. So far as the American economy is concerned, the only means to ensure an adequate capital inflow through the future will be a higher structure of interest rates—which conflicts directly with the short-term domestic requirement for cheaper money.

There is no simple escape from these vexing trade-offs. At this stage, there must be a strong presumption that the Bush administration will favour a third turn of what Calleo and Allin (1990) call 'the Nixon cycle' of macroeconomic policy—cheap money in the context of an inflated internal deficit, with a policy of benign neglect towards the falling dollar. The crucial question which remains to be answered is whether the Federal Reserve, having expended its readily available ammunition, will give the administration what it will probably want in the run-up to an election, or whether it will set interest rates with a view to the longer term. If Greenspan accedes to immediate administration wishes, it may be necessary to engage in a dramatic lowering, since American financial institutions have fixed their attention on building up credit ratios by firming lending standards. Dramatic lowerings, however, would place equally dramatic downward pressure on the dollar, and sorely test the forbearance of the allies.

In such circumstances, coordinated action will be difficult. It is clear that the tough-minded Bundesbank will not be easily swayed from its present course; its focus is firmly set on the inflationary consequences arising from the ingestion of the East, even though Germany's current rate of inflation is well below American levels. By default, Japan seems destined to bear the brunt of American efforts to lay off a portion of this adjustment cost. The Bank of Japan has some scope for coordinated action, since interest rate reductions provide one way to stimulate the slowing Japanese economy. But because its economy is only half the aggregate size of the US economy, coordinated efforts that are deemed meaningful in Washington are always likely to appear excessive in Tokyo. The result could put the fragile G-7 mechanism through its most severe test.

The changing equation between energy and power

Historically speaking, the constitution of the international oil market has linked into 'America's Japan problem' as both cause and solution. Washington's trade dispute with Japan stems partly from Japan's raw materials deficit—epitomised in oil—which calls forth a corresponding surplus in manufactured trade. On the other hand, that same oil dependency has provided part of the means for alleviating symptoms of that trade problem. As noted above, the oil shocks of 1973 and 1979 both threw Japan's growth, inflation and balance of trade trajectories badly off course—so much so that many Japanese came to believe that these price rises were at least sanctioned by the United States as a means of reminding the economically more dynamic allies of their subordinate status.

This seemingly entrenched pattern of stereotypes figured prominently in Bush's Gulf War script for the New World Order. Though the short, sharp and finite oil 'price spike' associated with the Gulf War hardly compares with the experiences of 1973 and 1979[9], the episode demonstrated the continuing vitality of the popular presumption that the United States was engaged in an 'other-regarding act' on behalf of its major allies. On the right of the American political spectrum, it was taken as axiomatic that American self-interest did not require access to Middle Eastern oil; from this basis, many isolationists stood against the Gulf commitment. In internationalist circles, it was commonly believed that the import-dependent allies should at least pay generous tribute for secure access to the Middle Eastern fields on which they were manifestly dependent.

---

9 For a concise comparative outline of the previous oil shocks, see Hartshorn (1982).

However, beneath the rhetoric of perpetual allied dependence, new patterns of economic vulnerabilities which depart radically from the established mould were associated with the Gulf War. As I have argued at greater length elsewhere (Leaver 1992), these speak to future shifts in the underlying balance of economic power.

First, there have been important movements amongst the allies regarding their relative sensitivity to rising prices for imported oil. Naturally, both Germany and Japan continue to depend on oil imported from the Middle East in particular, and recent Japanese deals with both Saudi Arabia and Iran will probably increase that country's degree of external dependence through future years. However, this needs to be offset against increasing American import dependency. After a marginal rejuvenation early in the Reagan years, American domestic oil production has recently been falling at a rate of about 4 per cent per annum while demand (prior to the recession) was expanding at just under 2 per cent. Hence, on the eve of the Kuwait crisis, slightly more than half of total American oil consumption was imported, while at the margin, half of OPEC's incremental output was destined for the US market (Toichi 1990).

In addition, as Morse (1990) amongst others has documented, the international oil market now exhibits more of the characteristics of a genuine 'arms length' market, with notable declines in both vertical and horizontal integration through the last decade. In this context, the physical exposure of any single importing nation to any given source of supply is no longer so politically significant, since prices quickly equalise under competitive pressures that have global scope. In these conditions, the most salient political issue concerns the ability of national economies to adjust with minimal internal and external cost to higher oil prices.

Second, figures on national import dependency do not directly correlate with the degree of domestic economic suffering wrought by higher prices. Changes in the efficiency of use of petroleum mediate the relationship between import dependency and domestic economic outcomes. Here there is notable change that clashes directly with the common American political presumption of allied dependency on imported oil.

The earlier, more severe oil shocks taught Japanese and German governments lessons about energy efficiency that Washington has consistently refused to learn. Because they bore the burden of economic suffering, the allies were serious about energy conservation in a way that the United States has demonstrably not been. Since 1973, Japan has exported energy intensive industries offshore, upgraded the energy efficiency of its domestic industrial base, lowered energy consumption of the products which it yields, and substituted out of oil wherever possible. In the United States, while increased oil prices did initially induce some efficiency gains, these have receded since the oil price collapse of 1986 at a time when the share of imported oil in total American consumption has doubled. With prices the lowest in the world, the inflationary impact of any price rise is felt most acutely in the United States, while the structural nature of the current account deficit makes higher import prices hard to absorb. Every dollar rise in the price of oil currently adds more than US$3 billion to its trade deficit and subtracts twice as much from the level of domestic demand.

The overall result of these changes is best conveyed by the fact that recent Japanese growth has been achieved with one-third the energy intensity of American growth, while Japan now consumes 30 per cent less oil in absolute terms than it did in 1973 for an economy that is over twice as large (Koyama 1990). When Japanese oil imports are expressed as a percentage of domestic product, they are now only marginally higher than the corresponding American figure (*The Economist* 1990e).

Consequently, when charted against this social baseline, import dependency within the US–Japan relationship is no longer highly asymmetric, while the adjustment costs to higher prices in the future are focused on and within the American economy.

The political consequences of these divergent trends are likely to be profound so far as arguments for allied burden-sharing are concerned over the long run. They collectively suggest that one important basis for continuing Japanese political dependency has withered on the vine. These shifts may even be significant in the short run. With OPEC operating at 95 per cent of current capacity, and with increases now evident in both the rate of American consumption and external dependency[10], near-term oil price rises brought on by political chaos in the former Eastern bloc suppliers could further hamper the rate of the American recovery while nudging up inflation, so reinforcing the same dilemma which plagued American monetary policy during the Gulf War.

Conclusion

The interwoven stories dealing with the evolution of the markets for traded goods, money and oil which are told in this chapter all lead to one general, relatively strong conclusion—that the positions of strength which the United States enjoyed within all of them have eroded through time. More specifically, the ability which Washington once had to offset a weakness in one of these domains (traded goods) against enduring strengths in others (money, oil and security)—that is, the ability to pursue a strategy of lateral escalation—has also decayed. If this much is accepted, then it raises probing questions about the prospects for future American 'leadership'—questions which assume disturbing proportions when combined with an *a priori* assumption that any formula sufficient to secure Cold War victory should enjoy a long shelf-life.

---

10 In the first quarter of 1991, and in spite of reduced demand associated with the recession, American oil self-sufficiency slipped below 45 per cent. By October of that year, US petroleum demand turned upwards for the first time in thirteen months.

So far as the specific issue of monetary coordination and its future prospects is concerned, this chapter reaches two conclusions. The first emphasises diminishing returns. The initial round of post-Bretton Woods dollar devaluation virtually levelled out trans-Pacific trade for a short period. Even though the Plaza process unleashed a devaluation of much greater magnitude, the yield, measured in terms of the trade balance, has been lower. Those who bring the capital account into the picture might be tempted to say the yield has been negative.

The second conclusion concerns diminishing opportunities. Agreement about the Plaza strategy was facilitated by a uniquely favourable international conjuncture in which the short-term interests of all major states pushed in the same direction. Similarly, implementation of the Plaza strategy ultimately rested largely on the seemingly endless support of both public and private Japanese capital. If the underlying structure of national economic vulnerabilities has indeed shifted—our first, strong conclusion —then neither phase of a strategy of coordination should be so easy in the future, though the greater need for more effective coordination across the range of macropolicy is not in doubt. At the very least, future coordination will call for a more conspicuous American downpayment, and yet American administrations will not be in favourable positions to provide it.

9 The GATT After the Uruguay Round

G**ILBERT** R. W**INHAM**

Writing about the General Agreement on Tariffs and Trade (GATT) after the Uruguay Round is like contemplating the future of a couple thinking about marriage: much depends on whether the deal goes through. In the case of the GATT, the Uruguay Round would undoubtedly establish firmer trade rules and relations between the GATT contracting parties, but negotiating the Round has been torturous, and the result is by no means clear at the time of writing in late spring 1992. The state of play is that the major issue of agriculture is not resolved between the United States and the European Community (EC), and as well serious disagreements persist in other important areas ranging from industrial tariffs to trade rules. Most of all, the timetable for the negotiation is precarious, a point we will return to in the conclusion.

The Uruguay Round produced the most dramatic setback the GATT has experienced since its creation in 1947, in the failure of the Ministerial Meeting in Brussels in December 1990. Since that event, patient diplomacy has helped put the negotiation back on track. First, events in the GATT itself helped move the Uruguay Round along. It was widely felt at the Brussels Meeting that the Uruguay Round agenda had become too large to manage effectively. In response the GATT Director General, Arthur Dunkel, restructured the negotiation into seven working groups from the previous fifteen groups, and arranged the appointment of new chairs for working groups, as well as fresh faces from the GATT secretariat to support the administrative side of the negotiation. The smaller number of working groups helped to identify and facilitate the negotiation of trade-offs; furthermore, the working group chairs formed an informal steering group to assist the Director General in the political management of the negotiation. The chairs even took up offices in the GATT headquarters, which underscored their increasingly important role in the negotiation process.

By the northern autumn of 1991, the GATT had a negotiating machinery in place that seemed as well structured as possible to promote an eventual agreement in the Uruguay Round. At the Brussels Meeting in December 1990, it was probably true that the Uruguay Round was not ready for conclusion in many areas, and that a political agreement at the top would have resulted in chaos at the working level, especially in services and in market access. One year later this was much less the case. Improved organisation of the negotiation helped to highlight difficult issues and intractable parties, which at the time of writing continue to be agriculture, particularly between the United States and the EC.

A second factor in resuscitating the Uruguay Round was the appearance of movement on agriculture on the EC side. Following the Brussels Meeting, EC Commissioner for Agriculture Ray McSharrie openly criticised the EC's Common Agriculture Policy (CAP) on the grounds that it had advantaged only rich farmers and had utterly failed small-scale European agriculture. This undercut the legitimacy of the CAP, and accelerated the reform that was already under way in the EC. Further movement came from the German Government which indicated in October 1991 it would ease its support for the EC position in agriculture (*International Trade Reporter* 1991a, p. 1610). This was substantial change from the German position during the Brussels Meeting, and it left the French—as the major supporers of the CAP—in a more isolated position in the EC. The German action increased the probability that a changed position by the United States would actually lead to a meaningful negotiation on agriculture.

A third factor was the reduction of US demands on the European Community in agriculture. Until early November 1991, the United States had been demanding from the EC a reduction of 90 per cent in agricultural export subsidies and 70 per cent in domestic supports and border protection over ten years, while the EC offer was 30 per cent cuts in domestic supports counting from 1986. In a meeting on 9 November with EC President Jacques Delors, US President George Bush agreed that the United States would accept a cut in export subsidies of about 30 per cent over five years or 35 per cent over six years (Dulforce & Gardner 1991, p. 1). By everyone's account, these figures brought the negotiating differences between the two sides into a reasonable range and made agreement possible.[1]

---

[1]   A similar US negotiating tactic was followed in the Tokyo Round, when newly appointed US chief negotiator Robert Strauss substantially reduced US agricultural demands on the EC and thereby unblocked the negotiation which had been stalled for about two years (Winham 1986, pp. 164–7). As in the Tokyo Round, the characterisation of the US action differed between Europe and the

Negotiations continued at an intense pace through to late December 1991. When it became apparent no general agreement was possible, GATT Director General Arthur Dunkel submitted a draft agreement compiled by secretariat officials along with the chairs of negotiating committees (Draft Final Act 1991). The draft agreement is a remarkable and uncommon initiative by the GATT Secretariat, since international agreements are usually not drafted in precise treaty language in the absence of general agreement among major negotiating delegations. The draft reflects both the enormous accomplishments as well as the sense of desperation and uncertainty that underlie the Uruguay Round effort.

The Uruguay Round is a step in the evolution of the multilateral trade system. Success in this endeavour would deepen the system, which means that the rules and procedures of the GATT would be more firmly established in international trade policy. Failure would have the opposite effect. Not only would it dash the prospects of advancing the system, it would also call into question the value of continuing with the existing rules and procedures.

In the post-Uruguay Round period, there will be questions raised about the continuing relevance of the basic GATT contract. A critical problem is the impact of regional trade agreements on the GATT, a problem to which Canada and the United States have contributed by concluding a bilateral free trade agreement and by negotiating a trilateral agreement that would include Mexico. Other problems for the future are the development of new issues on the GATT agenda, such as those dealing with the interface between international trade and environmental protection. Finally, the GATT will have to contend with a challenge from neo-mercantile thinking that constitutes a fundamental threat to the international trade system.

Regionalism and the GATT

The current negotiation of the North American Free Trade Agreement (NAFTA) between Canada, Mexico and the United States underscores the importance of regionalism in the GATT system. It is widely expected this negotiation will produce an agreement-in-principle during the summer of 1992, despite the political difficulties this will create in the United States and Canada, which are distracted by electoral politics and constitutional politics respectively. That this agreement is going ahead despite political uncertainties is a reflection of frustration with GATT on the one hand, while on the other it is a response to a rapidly globalising economy that creates its own pressures to bring political structures like trade regimes into line with wider economic relationships. The NAFTA also reflects the

---

United States, and US publications such as *Inside U.S. Trade* and *International Trade Reporter* avoided the term 'concession', which was used by Dulforce and Gardner of the *Financial Times*.

fact that major trading nations have an easier time negotiating trade agreements with reform-minded developing countries than they have dealing with each other. The Uruguy Round is proof of the last assertion, where the longstanding impasse between the United States and the EC on agriculture, and more recently on intellectual property and services, has paralysed progress at the multilateral level.

In the late 1980s, regionalism received considerable impetus from the conclusion of the Canada–US FTA, which is ironic since neither government was particularly supportive of regionalism in principle. Canada by tradition was committed to multilateralism, while the United States, which since the 1930s had promoted the concept of nondiscrimination, was a strong defender of the universalistic GATT system. The reason the FTA was concluded is that the agreement was in Canada's economic interests and the United States' political interest. Canada's international trade was already substantially bilateralised before the FTA was signed, and the agreement was needed to ensure that trade rules safeguarded Canadian access to the US market. For the United States, which was under pressure in the context of a stalled Uruguay Round to demonstrate that trade liberalisation could work, the FTA offered an opportunity to carry out a policy of achieving trade liberalisation through bilateral agreements if it could not be achieved through multilateral agreements. When it was signed in 1988, the FTA appeared to be a unique and untroubling case of bilateralism. However, that uniqueness is now called into question by the NAFTA negotiation with Mexico, and the possibility that the addition of Latin American nations might eventually turn NAFTA into a hemispheric free-trade area. The fact that the United States is involved with all these initiatives means that they inevitably will have an important impact on the GATT (Schott 1989a).

Prima facie, regional groups are a threat to the GATT because they compromise universality and the nondiscriminatory treatment of traded products. While there is some debate about how serious this threat is, it is clear some analysts are unconcerned about the threat and are prepared to shift US trade policy in the direction of a bilateral strategy. For example, US Senator Max Baucus (D–Montana) has called for increased bilateralism on the grounds that progress in GATT negotiations is too slow, owing to the large number of interests that must be accommodated (Baucus 1989). On the other hand, bilateralism creates more flexible forums and a faster negotiating process, with the result that success becomes possible and not an apparently unreachable target, as in the Uruguay Round (Aho 1989).

Baucus argues the United States needs new bilateral rules with its closest trading partners, especially Japan and Mexico, and that it cannot afford to wait for the GATT to address these uniquely US relationships. Baucus' argument is realistic and even compelling, because he recognises the importance of the international economy to the US' economic future, and he seeks to improve the capacity of the United States to trade openly and effectively in that world economy. It is the tools of trade policy Baucus is concerned with, and he feels the GATT is no longer the most effective tool for the United States.

Senator Baucus' views amount to a call for a fundamental shift in US trade policy, and any such shift would constitute a serious threat to the GATT. The shift would come not so much from Baucus' goals, which are reasonably consistent with liberal trading relations, but rather from the consequences of the policies he espouses. A bilateral strategy risks breaking up what has been an undifferentiated system of contractual obligations into several parts. It has been argued by proponents of bilateralism that there is a difference between liberal trading relations and nondiscriminatory relations, and that an insistence on nondiscrimination (that is, the most-favoured-nation (MFN) procedures of the GATT) in international trade can slow progress toward further liberalisation that might be made on a piecemeal basis. This is undoubtedly true, but what is not taken account of is that preferential or discriminatory arrangements create a political structure wherein it is more difficult to pursue liberalism.

Preferential arrangements introduce alliance considerations into trading relationships. Preferences and discrimination ultimately introduce into trade policy a search for pragmatic side deals and trade-offs, which often have inimical consequences for trading partners not party to the deal. Preferential arrangements tend to break the association between free trade and internationalism, and it has been internationalist sentiments in the post-war periods that have been one of the attitudinal bulwarks behind free trade. Preferential or discriminatory relationships present a structural threat to the system of liberal international trade, and the probability is that one cannot threaten the structure of a system without threatening as well the values that help maintain it.

There are risks for the world trade system in a strategy of bilateralism, or even regionalism. One of the risks is the problem associated with rules of origin, or content requirements, that are needed to put a regional trade agreement into place. In any free-trade area, rules of origin are necessary to define the trade that is included in the area, and to prevent the transshipment of products that originate outside the area. Rules of origin are an old problem in regional trade associations, but they take on a new importance in the context of international competition for investment, because external parties may seek to access the market of one partner in a free-trade area by locating production (after receiving suitable incentives) in another partner. This can quickly become a political issue where investment incentives or production costs (especially wage rates) differ between members in a regional trade agreement.

The recent trade dispute between Canada and the United States over the North American content of Honda automobiles is an example of the difficulties rules of origin can produce (*International Trade Reporter* 1992, p. 384). Honda has located plants in the United States and Canada. It produces engines in the United States, assembles the engines in cars in

Canada, and then exports the finished cars to the US market. In a routine audit for North American content, the US Customs services determined the engines received too many foreign parts to qualify as a US product, which causes the finished cars to fail the 50 per cent North American content requirement mandated by the Canada–US Free Trade Agreement. The result was the United States applied the MFN tariff of 2.5 per cent to the imports of finished cars in lieu of normal duty-free entry. Honda (and Canada) vigorously protested this action.

This case has several ramifications. At the outset it is a dispute over technical audit regulations, and the possibility—suggested by some Canadians—that the implementation of the regulations was politically motivated. A dispute settlement panel will undoubtedly resolve the question of implementation in this case, but what remains will be the fact that the regulations themselves will be much more subject to dispute in future regional trade agreements, in addition to any disagreement that might exist over the level of content required in a free-trade area. More important is the underlying issue of foreign investment. The real issue in the Honda case is whether foreign investment and the jobs it creates will be located in Canada or the United States, and one would expect these issues to be even more difficult in future regional agreements that included both developed and developing countries. The unfortunate impact of regional trade agreements may be to increase the importance of regulation and cross-border inspection of trade, not only between members of regional associations and external trade partners, but even between the members of regional associations themselves.

Despite the risks associated with regional trade agreements, the world seems to be going in that direction. Are there any positive aspects to this development? An advantage of the development of regionalism—apart from the greater ease of negotiations as Baucus noted—is that it creates some intermediate organisation and structure to the international economic system. The international economy is overwhelmingly vast, and the number of nations is correspondingly large. This system has become too large to be dealt with on an undifferentiated basis. It could be argued that there is a need to 'decompose' the system in order to manage it effectively, and regionalism presents a kind of 'parts-within-parts' decomposition that is recommended by analysts who have studied complex systems (Simon 1969). The key point is perhaps not so much whether regional trading blocs are formed but whether they are internationalist in philosophy and are consistent with GATT obligations. In this respect the Canada–US FTA may serve as a model, for it was consciously negotiated within the GATT framework, and in some places such as the energy chapter it has simply incorporated GATT rules in order to promote Canada–US trade liberalism. If future trade groupings—starting with NAFTA—have as benign an effect on the GATT as did the FTA, then it is possible that regional blocs might improve the conduct and management of multilateral negotiations, while at the same time providing a mechanism that could effectively address uniquely regional problems.

New issues

The issues in the Uruguay Round will continue to occupy the GATT, whether they are part of a negotiated Uruguay Round settlement or not. However, a number of new issues are now crowding onto the agenda. These will have to be dealt with whether it be in multilateral negotiations or in more piecemeal politicking either inside or outside the GATT. These issues include the relationship of trade with environmental regulations, competition rules, immigration and security (*International Trade Reporter* 1991b, p. 1405).

The interface of trade with other seemingly unrelated issues (such as the environment) is an indicator that the world is becoming more of a single society instead of being only a group of separate and anarchic societies. The cross impact of one issue-area on another is commonplace in domestic politics, and national leaders routinely face questions of whether to support budget allocations for defence versus education, or to promote a reduction of environmental pollution at the expense of employment. However, national leaders that make international economic policy usually do not face as many issue conflicts in international relations as they have to handle internally, owing largely to the less complicated international system in comparison to domestic systems. Until fairly recently, the international system has been the stage for only occasional relations between the citizens of one country and those of others; now it is the main locus of economic activity for many people, and business and political affairs routinely spill over national boundaries to affect citizens in other countries. As a result, national leaders are increasingly confronting policy choices in the conduct of international policy (including trade policy), and they need to resolve priorities in international politics much as they do in domestic politics.

Nowhere is this better seen than in the new issues facing the GATT, especially environment. It is widely claimed that environment will be a major issue in GATT in the 1990s, and it has already become so in regional trade negotiations like the FTA and especially NAFTA. Environment and trade tend to interact at two levels: political and legal. At the political level, environment has been forced onto negotiating agendas by constituents who fear trade agreements will increase environmental abuse through increasing trade and economic activity. This occurred first in the Canada–US FTA, where environment was a highly charged issue that produced more heat than light in the Canadian 'free-trade election' of 1988. In the NAFTA negotiation, the concern is more focused, and deals especially with the alleged lower environmental standards in Mexico and the attraction such standards create for US businesses seeking to avoid the cost of environmental regulation. Environment has not been before the Uruguay Round negotiation; however, it has been dealt with recently in the GATT Council, and this body reactivated a long-standing but moribund committee charged with handling this issue. It seems clear that environment will appear prominently on the agenda of future GATT multilateral trade negotiations.

A concrete example of the conflict between trade and environment is the trade dispute between Mexico and the United States over tuna fish (*Inside US Trade* 1991). The dispute arose over the US Marine Mammal Protection Act (MMPA) which regulates the harvesting of tuna in US waters. The MMPA requires that fishermen catch tuna in a manner that avoids killing dolphins, which often swim in the vicinity of tuna. The MMPA also imposes a ban on imports of tuna from other countries which use fishing methods that result in a higher incidence of dolphin-kill than US methods. Further to the restriction on imports, the MMPA provides that the United States may ban imports of tuna products from other countries that have originally bought their tuna from an offending country; and the Act also states that the ban on tuna imports can be extended to all fish products if, presumably, the offending country does not change its practices.

In sum, the United States established an environmental regulation for US fishermen, which was extended more or less equally to foreign fishermen who sought to sell in the US market. The United States assumed the regulation was consistent with the GATT, on the grounds that—under Article iii—it accorded 'treatment no less favourable' to foreign products than it did to US products.

Not surprisingly, the Mexicans saw it differently. Instead of focusing on Article iii, the Mexicans rested their case on the prohibition against trade restrictions (other than tariffs) found in Article xi.[2] This constituted a strong case, because the language of Article xi is strong and unequivocal. The conflict between Articles iii (national treatment) and xi (quantitative restrictions) over tuna was a striking replay of an earlier case between the United States and Canada over lobsters (*Lobsters* 1990). The lobster case involved a US prohibition against the sale of 'short' lobsters, which was then extended to the importation of short lobsters from Canada. Canada took the position that the import ban on short lobsters was an illegal restraint under Article xi, while the United States saw the ban as an Article iii requirement fairly applied to nations and foreigners alike. The United States won the case, but the panel was badly conflicted, allegedly along national lines, and hence it is a poor precedent for future law. What is clear from these cases is that the inherent conflict between Articles iii and xi

---

2 GATT Article xi states: 'No prohibitions or restrictions other than duties, taxes or other charges, whether made effective through quotas, import or export licenses or other measures, shall be instituted or maintained by any contracting party on the importation of any product...'

will be the terrain for future battles over trade versus environment in the GATT.

The tuna panellists decided in Mexico's favour. They took the position that the ban on imports was a trade restriction that violated Article xi, and could not be justified under the concept of national treatment. The panel was particularly alarmed at the extra-territorial application of US law called for by the MMPA, and it argued that if other contracting parties were to follow the same course as the United States, then the GATT would be workable only among those countries that had identical internal regulations. The panel was sympathetic to the environmental objectives of the US legislation, but they recommended those objectives be achieved through international cooperative arrangements. Since the United States and Mexico are currently negotiating the NAFTA, it is probable the tuna issue will be settled bilaterally in order not to jeopardise a broader agreement.

The GATT ruling on tuna shocked the environmental movement in the United States, and it even surprised more experienced GATT hands who felt it unlikely GATT rules would ever impede a contracting party's capacity to enact domestic environmental regulation. In the fallout from the tuna affair, several issues are now clear. One is that the GATT is likely to be seriously troubled in the 1990s by inconsistent national regulations, which will be a stimulus for negotiation but also will serve as the greatest obstacle to negotiated agreements.

Second, there will be a need to separate serious environmental concerns on the one hand from a mixture of emotionalism and opportunistic protectionism on the other. For example, in the tuna case a cynic could argue that support for the MMPA was more an emotional response to the incidental killing of dolphins (inspired perhaps by the popular TV character Flipper) than by a concern for the environmental impact of tuna fishing on dolphin populations, since those populations have risen rather than fallen over the last decade. In these circumstances, protectionist interests are usually quick to take advantage of opportunities presented by the political process. Third, the conflict between environment and trade is likely to get worse as environmental regulations affect products with high trade flows. An example can be seen in the recycling regulations now being placed on paper and newsprint sales in the United States, which will deeply affect Canada's exports of a major traded item (*Globe and Mail* 1991). Canadians might object if the United States were to apply its recycling regulations to Canadian exports, but it seems unlikely that Canada would be able to get a 'tuna-like' policy from the GATT to avoid US regulations. As a result, Canada will likely have to comply with US legislation, or at least attempt to negotiate an alternative arrangement.

The environmental issue points out the growing importance of the judicial process in contemporary international trade policy. The GATT is a form of international regulation, but what often occurs today is a form of re-regulation: that is, the adaptation of existing regulatory rules of a regime to take account of new circumstances. The likely course that re-regulation takes is that problems get raised in the judicial process, and then they are moved into the negotiation process as nations seek general solutions to specific problems. All this tests the flexibility of the GATT, which to this point has been a remarkably flexible structure.

The neo-mercantilist challenge to the GATT

The failure to conclude the Uruguay Round negotiation on schedule has triggered criticisms that go well beyond that negotiation itself. The most prominent of these criticisms have been launched by Lester Thurow and Clyde V. Prestowitz and his associates (Thurow 1991; Prestowitz Jr et al. 1991). The conclusion reached by these writers is that the GATT is no longer relevant to today's economic realities, and it must be replaced by new treaty rules and/or new national trade policies. Their arguments amount to a fundamental challenge to the GATT in the 1990s.

Above all, these GATT critics are stimulated by the declining position of the United States in the world economy. They feel that the United States made the GATT work from 1947 by promoting a liberal milieu, and by accepting unequal outcomes in GATT negotiations. The capacity of the United States to do this stemmed from its preponderant (or hegemonic) position in the world economy after World War II. The United States supported freer trade because it genuinely believed in it, but it also had an economic position that allowed it to accept the inevitable cost of leadership. Today the alleged failures of the GATT bargain are traced to the loss of US preponderance, and the fact that the United States can no longer afford to accept an uneven deal in the GATT system.

These critics argue that the trade world is changing away from the ideal of liberal trade that is assumed by the GATT. There has been a steady move towards managed trade in the past two decades, which has reduced dramatically the proportion of world trade falling under GATT rules.[3] Examples of managed trade would, of course, include agriculture under the EC's Common Agricultural Policy, and textiles under successive Multi-fibre Arrangements; also included would be automobile trade which is governed by various voluntary export restraints (VERs), and trade in semiconductors, which is controlled by bilateral trade agreements. Another modern development that threatens the GATT is the aforementioned formation of trade blocs, starting with the expansion of the EC

---

[3] One critic's estimate of the fraction of global trade covered by GATT is as follows: 'approximately 25 percent takes place inside global companies (intra-company trade); approximately 25 percent is bilateral trade (by preference agreements); approximately 25 percent is barter trade; approximately 25 percent can be considered free trade, governed by GATT rules' (Ruigrok 1991, p. 77).

and now extending to regional arrangements such as the Canada–US FTA or the proposed North American Free Trade Agreement (NAFTA). The concern over managed trade has led Prestowitz and his associates to propose scrapping the concept of national treatment entirely on the grounds that sovereign nations will want in the future to manage their economies on a more preferential basis internally than national treatment will allow. Also, these analysts argue, the MFN principle should be dropped since, in a trading world already fractured by preference groups, MFN does not permit nations to respond to that diversity with selective or nuanced policies. Clearly, Prestowitz's criticism is a frontal attack on the GATT, for if national treatment and MFN were removed there would be little incentive to retain the rest.

Criticism is also voiced over the performance of GATT negotiators and the value of recent GATT agreements. The Tokyo Round, for example, is said to have produced meagre results for the United States, particularly in the Government Procurement and Civil Aircraft codes, which had the potential to achieve, but nevertheless failed to realise, tangible benefits for their signatories. As for the Uruguay Round, the critics argue that the agenda of the negotiation is too heavily weighted towards services and intellectual property, and does not deal sufficiently with manufactured products which are a more important source of national competitiveness and wealth. GATT negotiations, it is claimed, are legal crusades to standardise national trade policies, and they are conducted by trade officials more interested in creating rules rather than results, or, in short, in negotiating rather than acting. As a result, the rules that get negotiated inhibit rather than promote national competitiveness and strong national economies.

At the centre of these criticisms is a concern for the national economy, in this case the economy of the United States. Concern for the national economy is not a new phenomenon in the history of international trade policy. Since the eighteenth century, the normal trade policy of nations has been protectionist, with the exception of two periods of liberalism. The first was in the mid-nineteenth century when Britain, with a preponderant position in Europe following the Napoleonic wars, initiated free trade and encouraged other European countries to follow suit.[4] The second is the current period, which began at the end of World War II. In both cases, the period of liberalism was underwritten by the leading power of the era: Great Britain or the United States. As a result of those experiences there is a lively debate over whether hegemony is a necessary condition for a liberal regime (Keohane 1980). What seems likely is that where a leading nation (or nations) has the power to dominate the system, and it also views a liberal trade system as being in its own interest, then there is a high

---

4 This encouragement was accomplished through the expedient of an international trade agreement, namely, 'The Cobden–Chevalier Treaty of 1860' (Condliffe 1950, pp. 222–3).

probability the system will be liberal.[5] The liberalism of the nineteenth century ended in the depression that began in the mid 1870s. In the current period, things are less clear. About the loss of US hegemony there is no doubt, but whether the system is tilting from predominantly liberal to something else is a subject of some uncertainty.

What seems fairly clear, however, is that the critics of the GATT see the trade system as moving towards greater nationalism in trade policy; and in response, they recommend greater concern for the national interest in US trade policy. The philosophical background for this position can be traced back to the mid-nineteenth century writings of Frederick List, who attacked the cosmopolitan free-trade views of Adam Smith and Jean-Bapiste Say. For List, the nation was the central political reality, and he called for an economic policy of protectionism in order to strengthen the national unit. In the modern age, List's nationalist philosophy has been less attractive than the classical school of Smith and Ricardo, and it has been almost forgotten. However, one can see reflections of List in modern commentators like Thurow or Prestowitz, or even Robert Reich, who has argued that the United States should abandon its ideological opposition to government intervention in the economy and assist US manufacturers to move towards higher value and therefore more competitive production (Reich 1983). Reich's argument is not protectionist, because he opposes subsidies and other government policies that retard economic adjustment, but it is a competitive argument based on the performance of national economies as units. As such, it is not far from the national strategy advanced by List, who claimed in regard to the economic activity and wealth of a nations' citizens that 'nowhere have labour, economy, the spirit of invention, and the spirit of industrial enterprise, accomplished anything great, where civil liberty, the institutions and laws, external policy, the internal government, and especially where national unity and power have not lent their support' (List 1856, p. 178).

One indicator that nationalism is becoming more important in international trade policy is the trend toward mercantile policies (Hagelstam 1991). Mercantilism in trade policy can be defined either narrowly or broadly. Most narrowly, mercantilism calls for a nation to establish a surplus of exports over imports in order to assure an inflow of precious metals or specie, which in turn were associated with wealth. Mercantilism placed the focus on the balance of trade, it emphasised export promotion, and it placed restraints on imports above the level of export earnings. Implied in mercantile policy, and included in any broader definition of mercantile theory, was the use of an interventionist government to ensure that export capacity would be developed to its fullest. In broader terms, mercantile policy calls for a close relationship between government and

---

5   For example, Gilpin has noted: '…a liberal international economy cannot come into existence and be maintained unless it has behind it the most powerful state(s) in the system' (Gilpin 1975, p. 85).

business to promote national economic development. Implicit in this relationship was the use of government incentives to domestic production mixed with protectionism to avoid serious competition from imports. Regardless of whether defined narrowly or broadly, mercantilism ultimately was a matter of promoting national wealth and, therefore, power. It was a state philosophy that emphasised national institutions and the relative power position of nations in the international system.

There are indications now that trade policy in developed countries, especially the United States, has turned towards mercantilism in the past decade. One is that, as Lester Thurow has noted, all leading nations appear to be motivated not so much by comparative advantage, which might create diversified production, but rather by a desire to develop certain industries that are deemed to have especially high growth potential. As a result, nations are competing intensely in similar areas, such as microelectronics, biotechnology, and communications and computing. It is usually taken for granted that such industries will need government support and protection. It is also accepted that industrial competitiveness can only be achieved through access to international markets, with the result that governments—as well their industries—have now entered the race for external markets. The role of government is reflected, for example, in the repeated demands of the United States and other countries for better access to Japan's internal market (Bhagwati 1989c).

A second indicator of mercantilism is reflected in the continuing impact that producers have over trade policy at the expense of consumers. In the modern age, the views of Adam Smith that promoted economic rationalisation and free trade won the ideological battle over mercantilism, but mercantilism still influences government policy. The reason is that the economic efficiency of Smith and Ricardo applied to the economy as a whole: it was a theory that explained how overall consumption could be increased with a given number of inputs. However, governments are only indirectly motivated to improve overall consumption; usually, they are more concerned with who benefits relatively within the state, and whether those disproportionate benefits promote state interests or not. In the past decade, producer interests—ranging from farmers in Europe to industrialists supporting unilateralism in the United States—appear to have been gaining ground in their fight for influence over governments, at the same time that the world economy is becoming more integrated and in need of internationalist and not nationalist solutions. It is this problem especially that has made the Uruguay Round negotiation so difficult to settle.

A third example of mercantilism is reflected in the unilateralism that has become prominent in US trade policy, and that will likely be copied by the EC and others if it is not curbed in a Uruguay Round agreement. The most obvious example of unilateralism is Section 301 in US trade legislation. This provision gives the US trade representative the power to determine whether a foreign trade practice is unreasonable or discriminatory, and to remedy that situation through negotiations with the foreign country, backed up with the power to employ the sanctions of a with-drawal of benefits or the imposition of new trade restrictions (Bhagwati 1991a). While Section 301 is not GATT-consistent and therefore objectionable on those grounds, in fact the provisions have been used mainly to pry open foreign markets to US exporters rather than to close US markets to foreigners. Section 301 has been defended by the US Government on the grounds that it is a tool for trade liberalisation, but it will likely do more damage than good in the long run. For one thing, nations certainly can disagree over what constitute 'unreasonable' trade practices, and it is unlikely that the targets of Section 301 actions—like Japan—will long accept unilateral and unreciprocated demands by the United States to change their trade policies. For example, the resentment in Japan to US unilateralism can be seen in the book by Morita and Ishihara, *The Japan That Can Say No* (1989). Once resistance is encountered to Section 301, it is more likely the action will result in new trade restrictions than any opening of foreign markets.

A further and less obvious impact of Section 301 actions is the effect they have on reducing constituency support in the United States for multilateral trade negotiations. Usually trade negotiations succeed internally by mobilising a coalition of export-oriented industries to offset those import-competing industries that are disadvantaged by trade liberalisation. Section 301 provides an alternative to trade negotiations for export-oriented industries to achieve their goals, and thus leaves import-competing industries as the main constituents with which trade negotiators must deal. Whether one would agree with J. Michael Finger that Section 301 has fundamentally altered the philosophy of the Reciprocal Trade Agreements Act of 1934, it nevertheless seems it has upset the practical mechanism whereby the United States and other countries have carried out trade liberalisation in the past (Finger 1991).

An example of the effect of Section 301 can be seen in the reaction of the US Pharmaceutical Manufacturers Association (PMA) to the draft Uruguay Round agreement of December 1991 (the Dunkel draft). The PMA should be a major supporter of the Uruguay Round agreement: it has clear export interests, and it has lobbied for more than a decade over great odds to have an agreement on trade-related intellectual property (TRIPs) included in the Uruguay Round package. Given the difficulty of even getting TRIPs on the GATT agenda, one would have thought the Dunkel draft—which substantially increases the international protection given to intellectual property—would have been viewed as a major achievement by the developed countries. Industry in the EC does view it in this light. However, the PMA has rejected the Dunkel draft largely on the grounds that it offers developing countries a ten-year grace period before complying with provisions in the TRIPs agreement. At the present time, various nations such as India, Brazil and Thailand are subject to bilateral pressures mainly under Section 301. The effect of the Dunkel draft—as noted by PMA official Harvey Bale—would be to reduce those pressures: 'But under the Dunkel text offering the ten-year extensions, these countries can "thumb their noses" at the U.S. and Europe and say get "off my case", Bale said' (*Inside US Trade* 1992a, p. 2).

Commenting further on the effect of the Dunkel draft, Bale's statement was summarised as follows:

> Section 301 of U.S. trade law would in effect be gutted if the Dunkel text on TRIPs is accepted by GATT members, Bale said. He pointed out that section 301 has been extremely effective in combating violations of intellectual property, especially for pharmaceutical products. But a major objective of U.S. trading partners is to 'defang' this trade law, he said. If the language offering the grace period for developing countries is not substantially modified, section 301 would lose its significance even though it would still be on the books, he said (*Inside US Trade* 1992a, p. 3).

This statement substantiates the argument that Section 301 is viewed as an alternative by export-oriented industries to a multilateral agreement. Furthermore, the Section 301 alternative has produced an uncompromising attitude in those industries, even to the point that they oppose a delay of concessions which is entirely consistent with the 'special and differential' treatment normally accorded developing countries in GATT negotiations.[6]

Finally, a fourth indicator of mercantilism in contemporary trade policy is seen in the criticisms levelled by Prestowitz and his associates that GATT negotiators are more concerned with the rules whereby trade is exchanged than the results of those exchanges. In their attack on US trade policies, the authors state: '...it was more important to negotiate to save GATT than to save US manufacturing' (Prestowitz Jr et al. 1991, p. 134). Perhaps no statement summarises so succinctly the difference between 'neo-mercantilist' philosophy and the GATT regime as the notion that trade policy should focus on results rather than rules. In the GATT, as in most forms of limited government (including US democracy!), the essence of the regime is the rules and not the substantive results produced from one period to the next. Trade is a competitive system. GATT rules move this system one step away from anarchy in an essentially anarchic world, and they do so through creating constraints that all nations have found in their interests to respect. If one nation ignores rules to secure results, others will too, especially since results are sometimes zero-sum and, therefore, gains cannot be achieved without creating losses elsewhere. Despite the obvious threat to the stability of trade relations posed by Prestowitz's results-oriented formula, the formula, nevertheless, has become increas-

---

6 Even with a TRIPs agreement nearly completed, Section 301 continues to be the apparent instrument of choice for intellectual property trade lobbies. On 25 February 1992, the PMA, the International Intellectual Property Associations and the Motion Picture Association joined to call upon the US Trade Representative to launch a Section 301 investigation against eight developing countries (*Inside US Trade* 1992b, p. 3).

ingly popular in recent years in the US Congress and among influential industries in the United States.

To sum up, the GATT attempts to create a nondiscriminatory system of international trade. This system is fundamentally inconsistent with the combination of nationalism and neo-mercantilism implicit in some of the current critiques of the GATT. To the extent these critiques gain influence over national trade policies, they will essentially weaken the rules-oriented GATT regime. At this moment the major variable affecting the future influence of neo-mercantilism on the GATT is the Uruguay Round. If the Round is successful, it will demonstrate that the main GATT-governing mechanism—that is, multilateral negotiation—continues to be a viable and legitimate process in the GATT regime. Conversely, failure in the Uruguay Round would be tantamount to failure in government anywhere, and it would reduce the legitimacy and, therefore, the support for the system. In the event of failure, neo-mercantilist arguments will carry more weight than they otherwise would do; and they will be more persuasive in future national trade policies, with consequent risk to the stability of the overall system.

Conclusion

The importance of the Uruguay Round to the future of the GATT necessarily raises questions about the timetable and agenda of the Round. Specifically, does the timetable offer the prospect of enough time to complete the Round, and what are the major hurdles to be overcome?

The timetable for the Uruguay Round, as in past GATT efforts, has been effectively set by the grant of negotiating authority from the US Congress to the administration. The current legislative mandate obliges the US President to notify Congress no later than 1 March 1993 of his intention to enter a trade agreement, and to present that agreement to Congress no later than 1 June 1993, after which Congress would have 60 days to approve or disapprove the agreement without amendment. It is improbable this deadline could be extended; therefore, given the importance of the Unites States to a negotiated agreement, the Uruguay Round agenda effectively operates on the same deadline as that of the United States.

Politically, there is considerable support for the notion that the Round should be concluded as quickly as possible, in part because of fear that negotiating momentum would be irrevocably lost if the Round were to stretch into late 1992. At this time of writing in late spring 1992, agricultural negotiations between the United States and the EC have still not been settled; and, because of the trade-offs nations have made between agriculture and other issues, there are numerous other outstanding problems in the negotiation as well. Whether these various difficulties will be resolved remains uncertain.

Assuming negotiations go well and an ad-referendum agreement (including agriculture) is reached by the summer, there will still be a need for further negotiation in market access (especially tariffs) and in service access agreements. To this point, nations have been unwilling to negotiate seriously in these areas because the basic trade-offs on more important issues—such as agriculture, intellectual property, textiles, and rules—have not yet been settled. For example, in the service sector there is a large number of access offers on the table, but the final give and take of bargaining has not been completed. It is generally assumed that bargaining in tariffs could go quickly, because of the long experience of GATT in this area. However, there is little experience in negotiating access agreements in services, which leaves this area in some uncertainty. In sum, assuming the most favourable of scenarios, it now appears unlikely the Uruguay Round could be completed without considerable further effort.

Given this timetable, there are two major problems in concluding the Round, and they both lie with the United States. One is purely a question of timing, namely, that 1992 is a presidential election year in the United States and it is well known that serious attention to policy-making begins to wane in the northern spring of election years. It would be difficult under the best of circumstances to maintain the momentum needed to secure passage of a complicated foreign trade bill and, as the presidential campaign takes off, that momentum is likely to be lost.

Second and more serious is the combination of substance and timing. The final deals have not yet been put in place in Geneva, but it is unlikely the United States will be able to maintain its position on unilateral action (especially Section 301 actions) if it wants a multilateral agreement in the Uruguay Round. However, the influential private sector Advisory Committee for Trade Policy and Negotiation (ACTPN) in the United States stated flatly in its 1991 Report to Congress that it 'supports the U.S. position that we must retain our ability to use domestic law (including Section 301) to address unfair and injurious foreign trade practices' (Report 1991, p. 52). This represents a substantial distance to be overcome on an issue that is critical to both the negotiating partners of the United States as well as US internal constituents. Whether Congress would be an effective agent to broker this issue in the middle of a presidential election remains highly problematical.

As observed in the Tokyo Round, the key to the settlement of GATT multilateral negotiations is still the participation of the two economic superpowers: the United States and the EC. In its negotiating strategy, the EC is obliged to complete its main internal bargaining before it tables an offer, but in the case of the United States much remains to be done internally after an external agreement is signed. The attention to agriculture in the Uruguay Round has diverted attention from potential difficulties of reconciling important elements of the US public sector (which have genuine power in a Congressional system of government) to the evolving agreements in the Uruguay Round. If an agreement is reached in Geneva, the next test of the Uruguay Round will come in the US Congress, and the outcome is by no means assured.

10 Fortress or Free Market? NAFTA and its Implications for the Pacific Rim

LORRAINE EDEN AND MAUREEN APPEL MOLOT

Introduction

When the Canada–US Free Trade Agreement (FTA) was signed in the second half of 1987 and implemented in January 1989, a Canada–US–Mexico free-trade accord was not even considered a remote possibility. The announcement in June 1990 by Mexican President Salinas de Gortari and US President Bush of their intention to begin discussions on a bilateral Mexico–US free-trade agreement forced the Canadian Government to decide whether or not it wanted to participate in a new round of trade talks. With an affirmative Canadian decision accepted by the United States and Mexico, the three countries began discussions in mid-1991 to create a North American Free Trade Agreement (NAFTA).

State initiatives, such as the NAFTA negotiations and bilateral US trade accords with Canada and Mexico, are one critical factor shaping the evolution of an increasingly North American political economy. The other is the changing realities of global investment patterns which have over the last decade seen many multinational enterprises (MNEs) begin to organise production on a continental basis, and a concomitant rise in the levels of direct investment by MNEs in production facilities in Mexico.

These state and market forces are examined in this chapter through an exploration of the rationales behind government moves towards regional trading blocs in general, and the impact these state policies are having on how multinationals organise for production within and between these blocs. We are also interested in the effects that technological change, in particular the shift to 'lean production' techniques, is having on MNE locational patterns in North America. Investment decisions by Asian MNEs, particularly those from Japan, over the last decade have been

201

responsive to these same state and market forces. Asia–Pacific trade with and investment in North America are of significance to all three parties to NAFTA, and Asian firms consider these North American investments as crucial components of their globalisation strategies. As the three North American political economies negotiate to institutionalise the growing integration among their economies, Pacific Rim traders and investors have reason to be cautious about the impact of a NAFTA on their future trade and investment opportunities.

A North American regional trading bloc

Strong multilateral institutions are in the interest of all countries concerned about the stability of the global economy. For over three decades the General Agreement on Tariffs and Trade (GATT) was successful in promoting tariff reductions, thereby increasing international trade. The very successes of multilateral tariff negotiations generated tensions in an organisation insufficiently equipped to handle expanding global trade and the inevitable national adjustment pressures that resulted. An increase in membership and a more complex agenda now focused primarily on non-tariff issues have brought international trade negotiations to a point of uncertainty. Moreover, the globalisation of production and the growing importance of trade between related companies have reduced the relevance of GATT. The difficulties of launching the Uruguay Round of GATT talks turned out to be but a precursor of the problems that resulted in their failure to conclude any agreements well into 1992.

Frustration with the complexities of attaining agreement among so many members on a wide range of issues has prompted many states to seek alternative ways outside the global trading system to promote their individual and collective economic interests. In addition, the perception that other states are not playing by GATT rules encourages regionalism as a way of increasing leverage against these free riders. Regional, including bilateral trading arrangements are but one of these strategies, and some states are moving to ensure a position for themselves within trading blocs: the United States by negotiating the FTA with Canada, and now NAFTA with Mexico and Canada; the European Community (EC) by intensifying the integration process through the reduction of border controls and the mutual recognition of national legislation; the members of the European Free Trade Association (EFTA) by seeking EC membership; and Japan by establishing subsidiaries in many East Asian countries as well as in the other two blocs.

Regional trading agreements provide many of the advantages of the multilateral trading system. Moreover, they may be easier to negotiate, and may encompass issues that have not been resolved at the global level; for example, the FTA addresses investment and service issues that have not yet been the subject of broader international accords. The difficulties of the Uruguay Round, particularly when contrasted with the relative success of regional blocs, may simply reinforce the attractiveness of these regional entities.

Jeffrey Schott defines a trading bloc as 'an association of countries that reduces intra-regional barriers to trade in goods (and sometimes services, investment and capital as well)' (Schott 1991, p. 1). Despite significant differences in the level of economic development between Mexico and the other two NAFTA participants, Schott suggests that North America meets the other three criteria he identifies as requisites for a 'successful' trading bloc: geographic proximity; similar or compatible trading regimes; and political commitment to regional organisation (Schott 1991, pp. 2, 7–10). Although large, crossborder income disparities are likely to create difficulties both during and after the NAFTA negotiations because 'producers in the richer countries are inevitably seen as swamping those in the poorer countries' (Schott 1991, p. 2), Mexico's trade regime since 1986 has become quite similar to that of Canada and the United States, thus facilitating regional integration.[1]

Intra-North American trade and investment patterns

What exists in North America is a pair of bilateral trading partners characterised by the asymmetric dependence of one party in each dyad on the United States. Elsewhere (Eden & Molot 1991, 1992; Cameron et al. 1992) we have documented the 'hub-and-spoke' nature of the trade and investment linkages among the three North American economies. The pattern of intra-North American trade is shown in Figure 10.1 using 1988 data.

The United States is the hub—the major trading partner—absorbing roughly 70 per cent of merchandise exports from the two 'spokes', Canada and Mexico. The United States in turn, sells about 20 per cent of its exports to Canada and 6 per cent to Mexico. Mexico and Canada trade very little with each other: Canada may rank sixth among Mexico's trade partners but each country's exports account for less than 5 per cent of the other's imports.

Despite recent efforts to stimulate Mexico–Canada economic linkages, the increase in trade since 1989 has been one way, that is, a rise in Mexican exports to Canada: these increased by 23 per cent in 1989 (External Affairs 1991). In 1990 the trade balance in Mexico's favour grew as Canadian exports to Mexico fell by 4.2 per cent (Fagan 1992, p. A1); Canadian exports to Mexico fell again in 1991.[2] Moreover, Mexico

---

[1] See, however, Helleiner (1990) for a less sanguine view.

[2] The explanation for the decline in Canadian exports to Mexico in 1991 is in part due to a glut in the world sulphur market. Given the concentration of Canadian exports to Mexico in products such as raw materials and agriculture, which are subject to dramatic price fluctuations, the Canadian Government

exports a higher percentage of fully manufactured goods to Canada (69 per cent of exports) than Canada does to Mexico (24 per cent).

Figure 10.1   Intra-North American trade 1988 ($US billion)

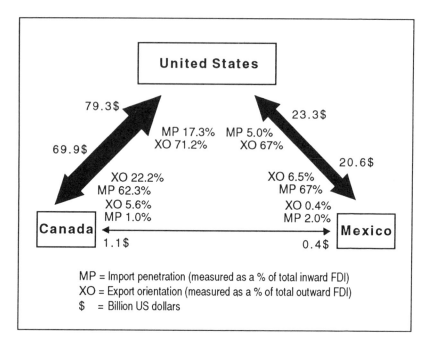

The composition of intra-North American trade in 1987 is shown in Table 10.1 and illustrated in Figure 10.2, using an economic grouping developed by Magun (1991). Canadian exports to Mexico consist primarily of raw materials, agricultural products and machinery and transport equipment (MTE), while Mexican exports are almost entirely in the MTE sector. Canada–US trade is also heavily dominated by this sector, as is US–Mexico trade.

One method for examining intra-North American trade relationships is the index of revealed comparative advantage (RCA) (Vollrath 1985, pp. 12–13). The RCA index measures the relative comparative advantage country i has in a particular commodity h, compared with countries j and k. An index over 1 implies country i has an RCA in exporting commodity h; an index below 1 indicates a comparative disadvantage in exporting the

---

hopes that Canada's exports to Mexico will move from commodity-based goods to manufacturing (Scotton 1991, p. 6). For an article critical of the composition of Canadian exports to Mexico see Godfrey (1992, p. 9) who entitles his article 'Mexico or Canada: which is developed?'.

commodity. Indexes over 1 thus indicate areas of trading strength for a country; indexes below 1 areas of weakness. RCA indexes should be treated cautiously, however, since they measure *actual* comparative advantage as distorted by trade and other barriers rather than underlying competitiveness. In addition, they tell us very little about *future* competitiveness. A clearer measure than RCA would perhaps be a measure of current export specialisation.

Table 10.1 **The structure of intra-North American trade 1987 ($US billions and percentage distribution)**

Direction of trade	from Canada	from Mexico	from Canada	from the US	from Mexico	from the US
Categories	to Mexico	to Canada	to the US	to Canada	to the US	to Mexico
1. Mineral fuels, lubricants and related products	0.001 0.33%	0.108 12.3%	8.614 11.6%	1.448 2.8%	4.056 19.8%	0.698 4.5%
2. Agricultural products	0.203 48.6%	0.087 9.9%	12.696 17.0%	3.902 7.5%	2.393 11.7%	1.609 10.4%
3. Resource-intensive manufactured goods	0.064 15.4%	0.033 3.7%	10.671 14.3%	3.798 7.3%	1.798 8.8%	1.227 7.9%
4. Labour-intensive manufactured products	0.004 1.0%	0.033 3.7%	1.501 2.0%	1.516 2.9%	0.845 4.1%	0.889 5.8%
5. Chemicals and related products	0.007 1.6%	0.011 1.3%	3.209 4.3%	3.246 6.3%	0.416 2.0%	1.425 9.2%
6. Machinery and transport equipment	0.132 31.7%	0.568 64.4%	34.783 46.6%	33.773 65.3%	8.716 42.5%	7.737 50.1%
7. Miscellaneous manufactured equipment	0.006 1.3%	0.042 4.8%	3.096 4.2%	4.041 7.8%	2.294 11.2%	1.855 12.0%
Total Exports	0.417	0.882	74.572	51.726	20.523	15.452

Source: Magun (1991, p. 6).

Figure 10.2 Structure of intra-North American trade 1987

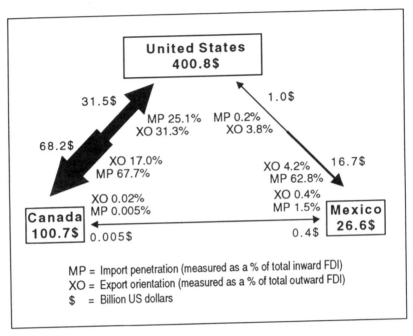

The RCA index is here defined relative to the other two North American trading partners. While normally one would calculate RCAs by summing exports over all countries in the world, due to data constraints we simply sum over the three countries in the North American triad.[3] Thus our index of revealed comparative advantage judges the comparative advantage of one of the three countries relative to the other two partners. The formula for the RCA index is:

$$RCA_i^{\,h} = \frac{X_i^{\,h} / [\,X_i^{\,h} + X_j^{\,h} + X_k^{\,h}\,]}{X_i / [\,X_i + X_j + X_k\,]} \quad (1)$$

where X is the dollar value of exports, i, j and k are countries, and h the commodity. The RCA of country i in commodity h is defined as the ratio of two fractions. The first is country i's exports of h as a percentage of all countries' exports of h; the second is country i's total exports as a percentage of total exports of all countries.

Table 10.2 calculates 1987 indexes of revealed comparative advantage for the three countries in terms of total merchandise exports based on the data in Table 10.1. An index over 100 shows the country has an intra-North American RCA in this category; an index below 100 shows a com-

---

3   The term 'triad' is used by Ohmae (1985).

parative disadvantage. Canada's RCA lies in the first three categories: fuels, agricultural products and resource-intensive manufactures; Mexico's in labour-intensive manufactures and miscellaneous manufactured goods; while the United States' RCA is highest in the more finished manufactured products, categories 4 through 7. In terms of the MTE sector, the US dominates with an RCA of 117.9, compared to RCAs in the 80s range for Canada and Mexico.

Table 10.2 Indexes of intra-North American revealed comparative advantage 1987

	Canadian revealed comparative advantage	Mexican revealed comparative advantage	US revealed comparative advantage
1. Mineral fuels, lubricants, and related products	125.8	213.3	35.0
2. Agricultural products	134.7	90.7	64.2
3. Resource-intensive manufactured products	133.1	79.5	69.6
4. Labour-intensive manufactured products	68.4	139.8	122.5
5. Chemicals and related products	84.4	39.2	136.8
6. Machinery and transport equipment	88.9	82.8	117.9
7. Miscellaneous manufactured equipment	59.7	157.5	126.6

Source: Calculated using data from Table 10.1

Although trade is obviously important in linking the three economies, the above noted statistics illustrate the uneven character of trade concentration. What is equally as important in the building of ties among Canada, the United States and Mexico is investment. Indeed, it is from this investment by multinational corporations that much of the bilateral trade is generated. In the contemporary global economy, trade and investment are complementary and cannot be separated.

The distribution of the stock of intra-North American foreign direct investment (FDI) is smaller but similar in direction to that of trade flows. The pattern of intra-North American FDI is illustrated in Figure 10.3. Approximately two-thirds of FDI in Canada and Mexico is controlled by US multinationals. The majority of the now over 1900 (Gereffi 1991a) maquila firms are owned by US multinational corporations and medium-sized US companies. At least 57 of the Fortune 500 largest US corporations have maquila plants, including the 'Big 3' US automobile producers and the major players in the consumer electronics industry. General Motors is now the largest employer in Mexico (SCEAIT 1990, p. 32).

Figure 10.3 Intra-North American investment 1989—stock of foreign direct investment ($US billion)

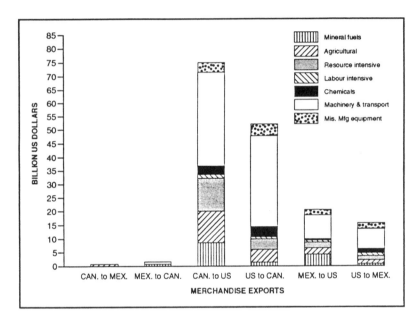

Canadians control about 25 per cent of FDI in the United States. In contrast is the level of Canadian FDI in Mexico which historically has been limited, and now is about $US400 million. This comprises 1.5 per cent of total FDI in Mexico, and places Canada seventeenth among countries with investments in Mexico.[4] In contrast to the huge numbers of US-owned maquila firms stands the less than a dozen such Canadian-owned companies, primarily in the automobile parts industry. There are also approximately 160 Canadian joint ventures in Mexico (Fagan 1990, p. B5).

---

[4] Four reasons can be given for the lack of Canadian investment in Mexico: (a) general lack of interest on the part of many Canadian-owned firms in outward FDI, except perhaps in the United States; (b) the lack of an FDI mandate for subsidiaries located in Canada; (c) distance between Canada and Mexico and therefore trans-shipment costs; and (d) the lack of Canadian provisions comparable to US tariff items 806 and 807.

In sum, the dependence of both Canada and Mexico on the US market and on US investment, and the limited nature of the economic ties between them clearly demonstrates both the hub-and-spoke nature of economic linkages with North America and the basis for an emerging trading bloc. In a global economy in which trading blocs are becoming critical, all three countries in North America have an interest in creating a trading unit which will enhance their economic opportunities. NAFTA would be larger in size, population and gross domestic product than the EC of the twelve.[5] However, unlike the EC, as we have illustrated in Figure 10.1, a North American trade and investment bloc would be dominated by the hegemon at its centre (Wilkinson 1991).

North American trade policies

The two pairs of 'hub-and-spoke' economic linkages analysed in the previous paragraphs have evolved without many formal agreements. Though there was periodic interest on Canada's part in the negotiation of free-trade agreements with the US, the last of which occurred in 1947[6], for the most part the two countries eschewed formal arrangements and the establishment of bilateral institutions (Molot 1974). Reasonably regular consultations at the official and political levels were for the most part seen as sufficient to maintain the increasingly complex economic relationship. Exceptions to the reluctance to negotiate formal agreements are the Trade Agreements of 1935 and 1937, the Hyde Park Agreement of 1941, the Defense Production Sharing Agreements of 1958–63, and the Auto Pact of 1965. The US–Canada economic relationship has been structured historically by the Canadian tariff (which made it attractive for US manufacturers to invest in Canada to serve the Canadian market), by the interest of US MNEs in Canadian resources, and by US and Canadian participation in the GATT.

Formal US–Mexican agreements are primarily a phenomenon of the 1980s.[7] Although there was a reciprocal trade agreement signed in 1942, it lapsed in 1950. The United States actively supported Mexican accession to the GATT both in 1979 and in 1986. The two countries signed a trade agreement in 1985 and two additional ones in 1987 and 1989 to promote consultation on and the resolution of trade disputes. Of far greater importance in promoting the development of bilateral US–Mexican economic

---

5   The relevant comparable figures are:

	NAFTA	EC (of twelve)
size	21 m sq k.	2.25 m sq k.
population	355 million	324 million
GDP	$5 trillion	$4.15 trillion

Source: World Bank 1989 (cited in Schott 1989b, p. 1).

6   Hart (1989) discusses the 1947 Canada–US trade negotiations.

7   This paragraph and the one following are based primarily on information contained in Hart (1990, pp. 62–4).

ties have been two US trade policies: the GSP (generalised system of preferences) adopted in 1976, and 1961 changes to US tariff regulations to permit the re-import into the US duty-free of US-made components sent abroad for assembly. Though Mexico is the fourth greatest beneficiary of the US GSP, it uses this system far less than do other states to promote their exports to the United States. It is tariff items 806 and 807 which lured US MNEs to locate in Mexico in the 1970s and 1980s. These tariff preferences form the basis for the close trade and investment ties between the two economies.[8]

Although both the United States and Canada continue to be supporters of the international trading regime, both are now advocates of a North American trading arrangement. The reasons for this US policy orientation lie in frustration with the complexities of multilateral trade negotiations, already noted, and in concerns about the economic and political stability of its southern neighbour (Morici 1991; Weintraub 1990a, 1990b). Worries about the international competitiveness of US firms relative, in particular, to Japanese multinationals have also prompted US policymakers to pursue a freer investment climate in Mexico. Lastly, NAFTA may be one step in the building of President Bush's plan for an 'Enterprise of the Americas', that is, a broader and deeper economic bloc centred on the United States that includes countries from both North and South America.

NAFTA is seen by the Canadian Government as a way to preserve and enhance the gains won in the FTA (External Affairs 1991). While concerns that NAFTA talks could lead to a reopening of this agreement and to the loss of hard-earned gains in the FTA were deterrents to Canada's participation in the talks, fear of not having a 'seat at the table' was the primary motivation behind its entry. The gains to Canada are expected to be small, and primarily in the form of Canadian exports to an expanding Mexican market (Investment Canada 1990; Eden & Molot 1991, 1992; Cameron et al. 1992; Molot 1991).

NAFTA is seen by the Mexican Government as the avenue to consolidate its economic liberalisation policies through guaranteed access to the United States, its most important export market (Bueno 1988; Weintraub 1990a, 1990b, 1990c). Mexican worries about trade diversion as a result of the first step in institutionalising the North American trading bloc, namely the FTA, was one of the major factors prompting Mexican President Salinas to propose a bilateral Mexico–US trading arrangement. Like Canada, securing and enhancing unrestricted market access to the United States was the major consideration in Mexico's free-trade calculus,

---

8 The US 806 and 807 tariff preferences levy US duties only on the difference between the value of goods imported from developing countries after subtracting US input costs. Thus US multinationals were encouraged to shift subassembly functions to maquiladora plants in the Mexican export processing zones.

since Mexico, like Canada, has faced continual and escalating harassment from US firms through countervailing and anti-dumping duty cases (Cameron et al. 1992; Weintraub 1990b). However, unlike Canada, because of its developing country status and deep balance of payments difficulties, Mexico has been particularly anxious to attract inward FDI to trigger its long-promised 'great leap forward' into the status of a middle-income country (Helleiner 1990).

Formal negotiations on NAFTA began in June 1991. Although all three participants anticipated a rapid and successful conclusion to the talks, progress has been slow. There are no real precedents for negotiating a free-trade agreement between developed market economies and one frequently described as a newly industrialising economy (NIE). Domestic US politics, including elections in 1992, and the 1991 recession have dampened expectations that a NAFTA accord can be negotiated quickly[9]; the subjects proving most intractable are agriculture, textiles, energy, automobiles, investment, and a dispute settlement mechanism (*Globe and Mail* 1992, p. B3). A successful conclusion of the Uruguay Round would facilitate completion of the NAFTA talks, since agreements at the multilateral GATT level could be used as a benchmark or floor for negotiations in NAFTA. The difficulties notwithstanding, all three participants remain committed to the establishment of NAFTA.

MNE responses to a North American trading bloc

The impact of regional trading blocs on MNE choices of location is clear. Firms recognise the advantages of proximity to markets, and are aware of the importance of a site within a bloc; many MNEs have moved into Europe in anticipation of 1992, for example. Multinational enterprises in North America resemble their European counterparts, which pressed for the removal of tariff and other barriers in Europe.

There is generally a clear relationship between the degree of firm multinationalisation and its support for freer trade (Milner 1988). Much of the corporate support in both the United States and Canada for first the FTA and now NAFTA comes from firms whose overall operations would be facilitated by the successful negotiation of a regional trading area (Eden & Molot 1991, 1992; Doern & Tomlin 1991). Proximity to markets permits product manufacture for specific tastes as well as innovations in the organisation of production which reduce inventory costs.[10] Another

---

[9] See for example a report in the *Financial Post* (Morton 1991, p. 5) which quotes two key members of Congress who are sceptical that a NAFTA pact would either be presented to or passed by Congress in 1992.

[10] The restructuring or reorganisation of production to reduce inventory—known as 'just-in-time' production—has been pioneered by Japanese corporations. In North America its most common expression is in the automobile industry. Other components of this approach to production include zero-defect policies

reason for relocation by some companies in some industries is non-tariff barriers, for example voluntary export restraints (VERs) or other quota arrangements which reduce market access through trade. The location of Japanese automobile producers in the United States can be partly explained by the imposition of VERs in the automobile sector.

The changing nature of technology

The investment activities of large multinational corporations and innovations in the organisation of production generated by technological change are critical components of the global economy. Although the recession has slowed MNE investment activity in the last two years, the late 1980s witnessed a surge of multinational investment as MNEs prepared themselves for the competitive environment of the next decade. According to Sylvia Ostry, 'the value of aggregate OECD investment flows ha[s] more than tripled [since the mid 1980s], vastly outstripping trade growth of less than 5 per cent a year in the same period' (Ostry 1990b, p. 14).

Worldwide sourcing by multinationals

The reasons for the globalisation of production hardly require reiteration here. Suffice it to note that the migration to cheaper labour sites in East Asia and Latin America, which began in the 1960s, continues by MNEs producing consumer goods which were (and remain) labour intensive (Fröbel et al. 1978; Hoffman & Kaplinsky 1988). By 1987, foreign components, frequently from offshore plants, were being used by close to 90 per cent of US manufacturers (Pastor & Castaneda 1989, p. 210).

Many Third World states offer location incentives to multinationals, among them export processing zones (EPZs) into which components can be imported duty-free for purposes of assembly and then export. Mexico's maquiladoras, a form of export processing zone, were established by the Mexican Government in 1966 to encourage diversification of exports away from staple products.[11] Mexico, together with some of the East Asian newly industrialising countries (NICs), was on the leading edge of the trend to international sourcing. It is the availability of cheap labour in

---

and greater worker responsibility. For a discussion of this approach to production as well as its introduction in North America see Hoffman and Kaplinsky (1988, pp. 121–38, 253–65).

[11] By the second half of the 1980s the composition of Mexico's exports had changed from a majority based on primary commodities (primarily oil) to a majority comprised of manufactured goods. By 1987, 78 per cent of Mexico's exports of manufactures went to the United States (Schott 1989b, p. 10; Weintraub 1988, pp. 15–16).

the maquila factories that so worries labour unions in the United States and Canada, and is at the root of their opposition to NAFTA.

The internationalisation of production has also altered the basis on which international trade occurs; a growing proportion of trade is no longer arm's length, but is accounted for by the movement of goods among related companies. Trade between affiliated companies, whether intra-firm or other forms of non-arm's length transactions accounts for a significant part of both US–Mexican and US–Canadian trade. Approximately 35 to 40 per cent of Canada–US trade is intra-firm and up to 70 per cent is not at arm's length. While figures for Mexico are difficult to find, a significant percentage of Mexico–US trade is also accounted for by the movement of goods between affiliated companies. According to Weintraub 'because of the extensive trade that takes place between affiliates of the same company in Mexico and the United States, imports and exports have become part of the same process'. This explains why intermediate goods have become so important in Mexico's exports of and overall trade in manufactures: exports of intermediate goods rose from 61 per cent of Mexico's manufactured exports in 1980 to 70 per cent in 1986; imports of intermediate goods were 65 per cent in 1986, up from 57 per cent in 1980 (Weintraub 1988, p. 23). Some Canada–Mexico trade is also in intermediate products, primarily automobile parts, but also some consumer electronics.

The shift to lean production methods

Concomitant with worldwide sourcing, and having the opposite impact on MNE location decisions, is the growing significance of knowledge-based production. There are a number of components to the new production style, among them (i) information technologies such as computer-aided design and manufacture, robotics, telecommunications hardware and software (van Tulder & Junne 1988, p. 8); (ii) just-in-time manufacturing, which comprises demand-driven supply of components, zero-defect quality, and minimisation of downtime (Hoffman & Kaplinsky 1988); and (iii) flexible manufacturing systems which combine the two. Called by some authors 'post-Fordism' or 'systemofacture' (Hoffman & Kaplinsky 1988), and by others 'lean production' (Womack et al. 1990), the new factory is located proximate to its suppliers, accepts only defect-free components, utilises mechanised production technology, can rapidly shift production from one product line to another, and employs a highly skilled and flexible workforce.

As a result of these new techniques, the economics of location are changing. The essence of foreign direct investment by MNEs is foreign production and intra-firm trade. As Eden has argued elsewhere (1991), the location selected for an affiliate depends on the affiliate's role in the 'value chain', the range of activities (such as extraction, processing, sales and distribution, technology development) performed by the MNE. Affiliates can be classified according to which of three basic motives for foreign direct investment they fulfil: resource-seeking, cost-reducing or market-driven FDI. Each of these three motives reflects one of the underlying primary activities of the multinational: extraction, processing or sales. A resource-seeking affiliate is set up to extract and process raw materials at the upstream end of the value chain; a cost-reducing affiliate to manufacture parts and make sub- and final assemblies; and a market-driven affiliate to sell at the downstream end.

The choice of affiliate location depends on the motive for FDI, the relative attractiveness of various host locations, and the availability/cost of alternative contractual arrangements. Whereas foreign plants in one location (for example, Mexico) may be established in order to access low-cost labour for subassembly, another affiliate may be located in a high-cost location (for example, Canada) to access the local market. The size and value of intra-firm trade and FDI flows are primarily determined by MNE production strategies, but are also constrained by tariff and taxes (Eden 1991).

As long as labour was a significant factor in overall manufacturing costs, MNEs had an incentive to locate in lower-wage countries. With the introduction of the new production processes, the location calculus is different; as a result some MNEs are relocating parts or all of their assembly activities closer to the final demand for the product. In the North American environment the adoption of the new production style may assuage some of the concerns of labour with respect to the loss of manufacturing jobs to lower-wage Mexican factories. More likely, however, because of their location proximate to the US border, Mexican factories are being integrated into just-in-time delivery systems.

In sum, as we move along in the 1990s the way in which multinational corporations are organising for production is becoming more diverse. At the same time as many firms in a variety of industries continue to establish plants at cheaper production sites, others in some of these same industries are relocating in the developed market economies. Indeed, some corporations, for example the Japanese car manufacturers, are adopting both strategies. This discussion of considerations that influence firm location decisions—the economics of location, as well as MNE responses to the growing importance of regional trading blocs—establishes the parameters for our analysis of the implications of NAFTA for the Asia–Pacific.

Implications of NAFTA for the Asia–Pacific

What are the likely implications of the formation of NAFTA for Pacific Rim countries, in particular, the Asian NICs, Japan, Australia and New Zealand? Given the changing dynamics of technology and trade policy, and how these factors are affecting MNE locational decisions in North

America, what are the implications for intra-firm trade and investment patterns with the Pacific Rim? We address five basic issues in this regard: (1) the potential loss by Asian firms of access to the North American market if NAFTA becomes 'Fortress America'; (2) the increased competition Asian MNEs may face with North American firms in global markets; (3) the impact of a larger and deeper NAFTA on MNE location and trade patterns; (4) the potential weakening of the US commitment to multilateralism; and (5) the potential impact on US–Japan relations.

1. The potential loss of market access

The potential loss of access by Asia–Pacific firms to the North American market depends on the degree of trade diversion generated by NAFTA; that is, the extent to which North American consumers and firms switch from buying products made by Asian firms and transplants to buying them from higher priced domestic firms. This will depend primarily on (i) whether Asian products are close substitutes for North American products; (ii) the relative heights of NAFTA member-country tariff and non-tariff barriers against nonmember-country products; and (iii) the volumes of trade with Asian countries. Table 10.3 provides some data on Asia–Pacific trade with North America in 1989, for Australia, New Zealand, Japan and South Korea.

Of the North American economies, these four Asia–Pacific countries trade most heavily with the United States (with shares of exports and imports in the 11 to 33 per cent range), followed by Canada (shares in the 1 to 4 per cent range) and Mexico (under 2 per cent). South Korea and Japan are the two most involved in trade with the United States; both countries sold about 33 per cent of their exports to, and imported about 24 per cent of their imports from, the United States in 1989. Australia and New Zealand rely almost as much on imports from the United States, but are much less export oriented (about 12 per cent compared to 33 per cent). Thus, any changes in North American trade policies should impact more strongly on Japan and South Korea. If NAFTA raises barriers against non-member-country imports, these barriers are likely to reduce Northeast Asian exports to North America more heavily than the Antipodes.

In terms of developing countries in the Asia–Pacific, a recent study by Kim and Weston (1992) looked at the implications of NAFTA for five East Asian less leveloped countries (LDCs)—China, Indonesia, Malaysia, the Philippines and Thailand, and three East Asian NICs—South Korea, Singapore and Taiwan. Making the assumption that trade diversion was most likely to occur through Mexico as Mexican exports replaced Asian exports, they estimated the amount of lost trade that each Asian country could expect. Using 1986 trade data, they calculated a 'similarity index' for commodities where Mexico faces a 5 per cent or higher US tariff and where Mexican exports currently exceed one million dollars. The highest similarity indices are for Singapore (29.0), followed by Taiwan, Korea and

Table 10.3 Asia–Pacific trade with North America: share of trade with North America, selected countries 1989

	Australia	New Zealand	Japan	South Korea
CANADA				
exports to Canada	$470.03	$149.68	$6 806.93	$1 882.25
imports from Canada ($USm)	$958.50	$172.61	$8 335.83	$1 680.09
Canada export share	1.4%	1.7%	2.5%	3.0%
Canada import share	2.4%	2.0%	4.0%	2.7%
UNITED STATES				
exports to US	$3 712.62	$1 166.59	$93 701.99	$20 694.32
imports from US ($USm)	$9 065.86	$1 472.97	$48 457.44	$15 903.79
US export share	11.2%	13.2%	34.1%	33.2%
US import share	22.7%	16.8%	23.4%	25.9%
MEXICO				
exports to Mexico	$30.06	$124.31	$1 907.68	$461.83
imports from Mexico ($USm)	$75.63	$20.80	$1 729.88	$163.36
Mexico export share	0.1%	1.4%	0.7%	0.7%
Mexico import share	0.2%	0.2%	0.8%	0.3%
WORLD				
exports to World	$33 204.87	$8 830.52	$275 039.71	$62 283.35
imports from World ($USm)	$39 869.09	$8 756.59	$207 356.18	$61 347.46

Note: Country X Export Share is the percentage of total exports from Asia–Pacific country Y that is exported to North American country X; Country X Import Share is the percentage of total imports by Asia–Pacific country Y that is imported from North American country X.

Source: Authors' calculations based on data from the *1989 United Nations International Trade Statistics Yearbook* (1991).

Malaysia (all about 20.0), with the remaining indices being lower. Next the authors calculated a 'trade diversion risk index' which measures the share of each country's exports to the United States in these overlapping categories. China, South Korea and Taiwan all have trade diversion risk indices of around 25 per cent. Multiplying these two indices produces an 'impact coverage index' which estimates the portion of each country's exports to the United States that could be captured by Mexican exporters; this ranges from a low of 0.4 for Indonesia to a high of 5.3 to 5.8 for South Korea[12] and Taiwan. The authors concluded that trade diversion may be larger for the East Asian tigers than for the 'cubs'. It should be noted that using 1986 data may underestimate the trade diversionary effects if Asian export patterns since 1986 have grown more similar to Mexican ones.

However, access to the North American market is not only via exports from the Asia–Pacific, but also through production by Asian transplants in North America. As we have argued above, Asian multinationals have set up plants in all three countries, primarily designed to access the US market. The establishment of Japanese and Korean automotive assembly plants in Canada is the most obvious example of this strategy. Through the FTA, Asian plants in Canada have had substantially tariff-free access to the US market since 1989. In addition, the duty-drawback system in place in Canada allowed automotive transplants to import parts from their Asian parents duty-free. (This latter programme is, however, being phased out under the FTA.) Similarly, through the Mexican maquiladoras programme (which also has a duty-drawback system), and the 806/807 and GSP US tariff laws, Asian transplants in Mexico have had ready access to the US market.

Trade diversion as a result of a NAFTA would depend on the tightness of the domestic content legislation—the rules of origin—and how the Mexican maquiladora duty-drawback programme is treated. Signs suggest that both the US and Canada want to limit the potential for Mexico to be used as a back door for Asian firms to enter their markets; hence, the content rules of a NAFTA are likely to be stringent unless the Asia–Pacific countries are able to lobby successfully to prevent this (*Far Eastern Economic Review* 11 July 1991, pp. 42–6; Kim & Weston 1992, pp. 8–11; *JEI Report* 1991).

2. NAFTA and the Asia–Pacific as competitors

The second issue that arises for the Pacific Rim in connection with NAFTA is the extent to which NAFTA could act as a competitor with the Asia–Pacific in terms of trade and investment flows. It is clear that policy-makers and firms in all three countries do see NAFTA as the way to increase their global competitiveness through reaping the economies of scale from a larger, more integrated market, and from shifting low-skilled labour production to Mexico, thus intensifying the co-production role Mexico plays for multinationals in North America (Weintraub 1990a, 1990b; Morici 1991). All three countries are international debtors and see trade, both internally and externally, as a way to reduce their debt burdens.

---

[12] For another argument on the trade diversion impact on South Korea of additional free-trade areas involving the United States, see Park and Yoo (1989).

Thus, NAFTA reinforces the existing locational attractions to multinationals of a continental production strategy linking low-cost labour sites in Mexico with the research and development stage in the United States, and final assembly in the United States and Canada. Once again, the automotive industry is the prime example. Investment rationales for NAFTA thus dominate trade motivations for US multinationals. Substantial rationalisation of production on a continental basis, however, raises fears of job losses and runaway plants in the minds of the Canadian and United States publics, fears that politicians in an election year in the United States are apt to exploit.

To the extent that North American MNEs become stronger competitors, this affects Asia–Pacific trade in three ways: first by reducing Asia–Pacific exports to North America; second by increasing the competitiveness of North American exports to the Asia–Pacific; and third in terms of increased North American competition in third-country markets. The competition is not just in terms of trade, however; competition for investment increases because North America, and particularly Mexico, would become a more attractive investment location if the content rules are not too stringent.

3. Deepening and expanding NAFTA

The third implication for the Pacific Rim is the potential effects of NAFTA subsequently growing and deepening. It is not clear whether NAFTA will include an accession clause, but already several Latin American countries (for example, Chile) have announced their interest in becoming NAFTA members. The United States has a clear, long-run interest in the extension of a regional trading bloc to Latin America, as a way of fostering its economic and political hegemony in the region.

Accession through additional bilateral agreements with the United States versus joining a trilateral NAFTA pact has differing implications for new members, the US hub, and for nonmembers such as the Asia–Pacific countries (Wonnacott 1990). Whether new members would be able to influence the terms of their entry remains to be seen; although Mexico is clearly redefining and opening the Canada–US free-trade agreement, it is not clear that a fourth country would be allowed this flexibility, unless it negotiated a bilateral treaty with the United States alone. Whether Asia–Pacific countries, in particular Australia and New Zealand, should approach the United States for admission to NAFTA, and whether they would be admitted, are difficult issues. The United States is unlikely to be willing to allow the entry of the Asian NICs to NAFTA, since they are already seen as aggressive users of non-tariff barriers and are being pressured to graduate from the generalised system of tariff preferences the United States offers developing countries.[13]

---

13 Korea and Taiwan, in fact, were graduated from the US GSP in 1988.

The issue of the deepening of NAFTA over time is also of consequence for Pacific Rim countries. Since the agreement will be more than a simple free-trade area that eliminates intra-regional tariff barriers, the question is whether such a pact sets forces in motion that will lead to deeper economic and political cooperation among the three countries, for example, to pressures for a customs union with a common external tariff, improved exchange rate coordination with the Canadian dollar and peso pegged to the US dollar, harmonisation of social policies and environmental standards. If NAFTA deepens, this 'ups the ante' in terms of new members joining later in the game, imposing more stringent terms and more adjustment costs on newer partners.

4. NAFTA and multilateralism

A fourth potential impact of NAFTA concerns the commitment by the three countries to multilateralism. Even if success in the Uruguay Round is deemed to have been achieved (and the signatories are likely to argue that it has), the gains are likely to be small. Does a weak outcome in this GATT round mean that the trend to regional blocs will be strengthened? As John Ruggie (this volume) argues, the 'either/or' view of multilateralism versus regionalism is a false dichotomy; regionalism can complement multilateralism. Some authors fear that the NAFTA pact will be the last nail in the GATT's coffin; others like Ruggie and Weintraub (1990b) see possible ways that regional blocs can complement and reinforce the trend to multilateralism. The rules and the wording embedded in the NAFTA documents, that is, whether they are fully consistent with GATT Article xxiv on preferential trading areas, are crucial determinants of whether regionalism and multilateralism are complementary or competitive policy options.

For Canada and Mexico, however, Helleiner (1990) and Wilkinson (1991) argue that small countries are better off under a multilateral approach because multilateralism offers a way to constrain the behaviour of large, potentially opportunistic players like the United States. In a bilateral or trilateral situation, these authors fear that the United States can exploit, and has already exploited in the FTA negotiations, its bargaining power to extract larger concessions from the smaller players.[14]

---

[14] Helleiner (1990, pp. 15, 17) argues that bilateral bargaining in the FTA did not get Canadian firms protection from US non-tariff measures, nor solve export subsidy issues; the two items most important to Canada. In addition, the United States appears to be interpreting the Canada–US dispute settlement mechanisms very narrowly and opportunistically (witness the recent pork dispute). Overall, he concludes that US concessions have been disappointing. At the same time, he concludes that Canadian concessions, such as more liberalised access for US investors and a services agreement, were required as side payments in order to induce the United States to sign the FTA. Thus, the larger country extracted, on net, higher payments from the smaller country.

There is also a fear that the United States is now less committed to multilateralism. If the Gephardt letter to the US President (Gephardt et al. 1991) is any indication, clearly some members of Congress prefer a 'Fortress North America' approach to unrestricted international trade and investment. Whether the US executive branch can constrain the protectionist thrusts of the Congress in an election year is not clear. Again the content rules built into the NAFTA documents will be crucial components demonstrating the US commitment to multilateralism. Since 28 per cent of NAFTA trade is with Pacific Rim countries, compared to 36 per cent internal NAFTA trade, clearly NAFTA members have an incentive to maintain an open door with their Pacific Rim trading partners (Schott 1991).

5. NAFTA and US–Japanese relations

Lastly is the issue of the impact of NAFTA on US–Japan economic and political relations. Japanese firms, particularly automotive and electronics multinationals, have been heavy investors in Mexico in recent years (Szekely (ed.) 1991; Szekely & Wyman 1988). Intense global competition in automobiles and consumer electronics has prompted the location of Japanese plants in Mexico to take advantage of lower labour costs as well as proximity to the United States. Japan now ranks as Mexico's largest trading partner after the US, and fourth as a source of foreign investment.

Japanese FDI in Mexico, in both the maquiladoras and outside them, totalled close to $1.5 billion in 1989 (Szekely (ed.) 1991, p. 117, Table A-6; Investment Canada 1991, Table 9, p. 37).[15] Thirty-three (of 111) Japanese corporations on the Fortune 500 list have investments in Mexico (Szekely (ed.) 1991, p. vii). Japanese MNEs have located in Mexico to serve what they perceive as the growing Mexican market, but more importantly to use Mexico as an export platform for the United States. Szekely and Wyman argue that 'the United States has replaced the Mexican market as the chief target for Japanese producers expanding their operations in Mexico' (Szekely & Wyman 1988, p. 181). Maquila plants supply components to Japanese industries located in the United States as well as finished goods. Moreover, maquila exports can circumvent US voluntary export restraints on exports from Japan. By 1990 there were more than 70 Japanese maquila firms, up from only eight in 1980 (Szekely (ed.) 1991, p. 121). Many of these Japanese corporations, in the maquiladoras and outside them, began their operations in Mexico during the 1980s, when the Mexican economy was in deep depression. Szekely suggests that Japanese investors found the combination of cheap Mexican labour, an appreciating Japanese yen, and growing US demand 'difficult to ignore' (Szekely (ed.) 1991, p. xi). Although Mexico has thus far pur-

---

[15] For a detailed analysis of the Japanese manufacturing firms in Mexico see Szekely (ed.) (1991).

chased its capital goods and services from the US, more attractive Japanese capital goods and services might well mean a shift in the orientation of Mexican preferences. Morici argues that Japanese MNEs, with their access to skilled labour, capital and technology, may be in a 'better position to exploit new opportunities in Mexico than US and Canadian MNCs' following the conclusion of a NAFTA (Morici 1991, p. 7).

The maquiladoras and Japanese investments in these in-bond factories are contentious issues in the NAFTA negotiations. Already the FTA is being used against Japanese transplants in Canada. The current dispute over whether Honda Civics are North American or Japanese cars demonstrates the United States' willingness to use tighter definitions of domestic content to enforce greater use of local automotive parts production (*JEI Report* 1991, p. 6). The increased vigilance of the Internal Revenue Service in terms of tax payments by Japanese transplants also shows this, as did the recent trip of George Bush to Japan asking for more sales of US-made cars in Japan. The pressure for tighter domestic content legislation is clearly aimed at 'closing the back door'; that is, at preventing Asian manufacturers, particularly from Japan, from using Mexico as an export base. The 50 per cent Canada–US content rule under the FTA is widely expected to be raised to 60 per cent North American content for NAFTA (*Far Eastern Economic Review* 11 July 1991, pp. 42–6).

To the extent that NAFTA is seen by the Japanese as the creation of a fortress designed to keep out its products, it is possible that Japan will respond by intensifying its own trade and investment co-production linkages with the Asian NICs. Schott notes that since 1985 Japanese trade with East Asia has grown twice as fast as that with North America (Schott 1991, p. 12); Japanese investment in East Asia has also increased considerably in recent years. Morici (1991, p. 96) suggests that Japan already has access to East Asian markets through the distribution networks of Japanese *keiretsu* in a way that US and Canadian MNEs cannot replicate in NAFTA.

In the eyes of some, Japanese trade and investment patterns have led to the creation of a *de facto* East Asian trading bloc (Schott 1991, p. 11). The explicit formation of an Asia–Pacific regional economic bloc led by a Japanese regional hegemon is not now on the cards—nor is it part of the plans for Asia Pacific Economic Cooperation—but perceptions of 'Fortress North America' would clearly encourage such a development. A failure of the Uruguay Round and the subsequent protectionist pressures such a failure would likely unleash would also be factors hastening the development of an Asian trade bloc under Japanese leadership.

In summary, given the changing dynamics of technology and trade policies in North America, we argue there are at least five areas that should be of concern to policy-makers in the Asia–Pacific: access to the North American market; increased competition with North America; broadening and deepening of NAFTA; the impact on multilateralism; and

US–Japan relations. Each of these issues poses political and economic problems and opportunities.

The implications of NAFTA for the Pacific Rim, therefore, depend very much on the ability of the Pacific Rim countries to make their views known during the NAFTA negotiation process. In order to avoid the opportunistic view that 'the party without a seat at the table is always wrong', it is essential that the Asia–Pacific countries lobby against high domestic content legislation, for example, and for continued North American support for multilateralism.

Conclusions

The international production activities of large MNEs are a critical factor explaining the direction and size of trade and investment patterns among the North American economies. Their location of foreign plants, either as horizontal competitors or as vertical complementary factories, is the key to understanding MNE pressures for NAFTA, and the likely responses once NAFTA is introduced.

Given the close connections among affiliates of the same MNE family, it is not surprising that FDI and intra-firm trade flows have been silently integrating the three North American economies. Nor is it surprising that American MNEs are generally in favour of NAFTA since there is a clear relationship between the degree of firm multinationalisation and its support for freer trade. Much of the corporate support in both the United States and Canada for first the FTA and now NAFTA comes from MNEs whose overall operations would be enhanced by the successful negotiation of a regional trading arrangement.

Investment decisions by Asian multinationals have been responsive to these same state and market forces. What we see is that corporations have little location commitment and continuously examine location decisions in terms of competitiveness and market access. It is these factors which have determined and will continue to determine MNE location strategies as the largest firms become increasingly global players.

As Canada, the United States and Mexico negotiate to institutionalise the growing integration among their three economies, Pacific Rim policy-makers and multinationals have reason to be cautious about the impact of a NAFTA on their future trade and investment opportunities.

11 Reconstructing Divisions of Labour: Singapore's New Regional Emphasis

GARRY RODAN

Introduction

Singapore's development has entered a qualitatively new stage, one that clearly expresses the inseparability of political and economic relations in the international arena. After having undergone a period of rapid industrialisation on the basis of labour-intensive manufacturing for export, the emphasis is now turning to Singapore's potential to service the industrialisation of other countries in the Asian region now embarking on similar programmes. This is taking creative forms, notably the promotion by the Singapore Government of the concept of borderless economic zones with coherent and integrated divisions of labour that transcend formal national political boundaries.

This attempt to carve out a particular economic niche within the intersection of global and regional divisions of labour carries with it important implications for Singapore's international political relations. New degrees and forms of cooperation between regional governments are involved. So too are questions of sovereignty the management of which demands considerable diplomacy. The political complications of this path are compounded not just by economic nationalism, but by ethnic sensitivities raised by the spread of Southeast Asian Chinese capital with the closer integration of Singapore's economy with others of the region. In political terms, the economic path ahead is a more precarious one, and the same high degree of control that the Singaporean state has been able to exert over the development process in the past will simply not be possible.

The Singapore-promoted 'Growth Triangle' or sub-regional development area is by far the most advanced conceptualisation of a discrete economic zone operating across national borders. However, links consistent with the principles embodied in this notion are a growing phenomenon—the relations between Taiwan and Hong Kong with southern China are examples of other cases involving Asian newly industrialising countries (NICs).

One of the underlying dynamics in this process has been the modification of global strategies by transnational corporations (TNCs). TNCs are coming to view the Asia–Pacific region as an important growth area in its own right which demands more comprehensive and regionally focused operations. This has led to a broader range of manufacturing and non-manufacturing processes being located in the region, and to attempts by the NICs to consolidate privileged spaces in the unfolding divisions of labour. To the extent that the individual NICs retain these spaces in assorted sub-regional economic zones, they limit direct competition between themselves. But this scenario does not guarantee harmonious relations between them and the would-be NICs in the region.

Alongside the greater regional focus of TNCs, the last decade has also witnessed a general increase in the variation of international production roles by the NICs. It is no longer valid to conceptualise global manufacturing production in terms of an emerging and potentially dominant single (new) international division of labour, wherein developing countries engaged in export production differ essentially in the degree rather than the kind of role they play in the world economy.[1] As Gereffi (1989, 1991b) points out, there are important differences in the forms of production that characterise the Latin American and East Asian NICs' global manufacturing programmes. The former involve a range of intermediate goods and industrial components, while the latter have concentrated more on finished consumer goods. Even within these regions there is increasing differentiation unfolding as each NIC establishes a distinctive specialisation or niche within the global economy. This includes specialisation in a particular stage of production within a given industry. This has led Gereffi (1989, p. 100) to argue that 'export networks' rather than nation-states are

---

[1] According to Fröbel et al. (1986), this unfolding structure departed from the traditional dichotomy of advanced capitalist countries essentially monopolising the global production of manufactured goods on the one hand, with the developing countries being locked into the export of raw materials and primary products on the other. Rather, under the new international division of labour (NIDL), manufacturing became a global phenomenon embodying a technological hierarchy within which the advanced capitalist countries continued to retain the most sophisticated, high value-added processes, but a range of other processes were relocated to sites in developing countries offering lower labour costs. The emergence of a sizeable potential industrial labour force in developing countries on the one hand, and the decomposition of the production process as a result of microelectronic technology on the other, rendered the exploitation of lower labour costs the driving force behind this fundamental change.

becoming the appropriate unit of analysis in the study of the global manu-facturing system. In addition, social and political changes in the advanced capitalist countries, including the emergence of sizeable underclasses and the weakening power of trade unions to defend employment conditions, have made low-cost labour widely accessible in many advanced countries. Automation too has contributed to an arresting of the previous pattern of relocating labour-intensive production to developing countries (Soon 1985; Cohen 1991, pp. 123–49).

The net result has been a much more differentiated set of production arrangements within and across nation-states in both developing and developed economies, without any necessary setback for the internation-alisation of production. The emergence within TNCs of greater regional consciousness—whether it be in the Asia–Pacific region, Europe or North America—is indeed part of the process of increased specialisation within the global economy.

The timing of this shift towards more complete regional divisions of labour is quite fortuitous for the NICs. With the labour-intensive phases of industrial development largely behind them, the NICs have been under pressure to identify areas of more advanced technology in which they can still exploit lower labour costs as a basis of international competitiveness. The diminishing proportion of labour to total production costs, as a coun-try moves up the technological hierarchy associated with global export production, has made it more difficult to sustain high levels of industrial growth, and raised questions about the longer term viability of the existing economic strategies.

However, Singapore's problems of dependence on external markets and TNCs are more acute than for the other NICs. It lacks a sizeable domestic market for manufactured goods as a counterbalance to reliance on markets in the advanced industrial economies for a limited range of exports. This is compounded by the exceptional dominance of foreign-based TNCs within Singapore's manufacturing sector. Moreover, the natu-ral limitations to the city-state's land and labour resources have added urgency to the problem. These limitations have accelerated production cost increases and threatened to undercut Singapore's full industrial potential, including that of formative indigenous manufacturing capital focused in labour-intensive production.

The attraction of the Growth Triangle, in particular, is that it offers the possibility of organically linking the industrial expansion of neighbouring states to the Singapore economy, thereby facilitating Singapore's sectoral diversification and reduced dependence. Ironically, this is achieved by encouraging neighbouring states to follow Singapore's earlier path. The Growth Triangle simultaneously offers a chance for capital currently based in Singapore's labour-intensive aspects of manufacturing to remain internationally competitive, and ensures that this manufacturing produc-tion is harnessed to Singapore's aim of greater sectoral diversification. In effect, the idea is to geographically expand the Singapore economy itself.

Singapore's full economic potential simply cannot be realised within its limited borders.

While the new economic direction charted by Singapore's policy-makers is based on a reading of international and regional trends in investment, as with the previous development phase, at the same time it incorporates a central economic role for the state. There are two discernible emphases to the state's contemporary economic role. One is to actively foster favourable investment conditions, particularly physical and social infrastructure, in neighbouring countries for labour-intensive industrial investment. Here the Singaporean state is trying to reproduce the investment climate that prevailed during the city-state's initial experience with export-oriented industrialisation. The other is to instigate new linkages with the international economy through the 'internationalisation' of government-linked companies (GLCs). So despite the rhetoric of economic liberalisation and privatisation in which Singapore's policy-makers have couched recent reforms, it makes more sense to describe the state's economic role as redefined or rationalised, but not reduced in significance.

The content of this chapter thus touches on several theoretical debates. It relates to disputes over: the underlying dynamics of international divisions of labour and the associated strategies of TNCs; the relative importance of markets and states in the development of the NICs; and a quite separate debate over the significance of economic restructuring for the broader constitution of international relations between nation-states.

Singapore's dilemma: structural limitations of the EOI programme

Against the background of the collapse of political merger with Malaysia in 1965 and the dwindling prospect of a common market for Singapore's manufactured goods in the new federation, Singapore's policy-makers instigated a swift and comprehensive shift in industrial strategy from import-substitution to export-orientation (Rodan 1989; Mizra 1986; Deyo 1981; Lee 1973, 1977). A host of measures were adopted to facilitate Singapore's exploitation as a low labour-cost production site for manufactured goods destined for the consumer markets of the advanced capitalist countries. The ability to effect this sudden redirection in economic strategy lay in an unusually high degree of relative political autonomy from both capital and labour enjoyed by the state. Such a circumstance was the consequence of complex historical and socio-political factors.[2]

---

2 First, as a legacy of the class structure emanating from the colonial economy, the domestic bourgeoisie was still based in the trading, banking and services sectors. It was yet to establish a firm base in import substitution industrialisation (ISI) which might have generated sufficient will or capacity to threaten this change in strategy. In any case, the domestic bourgeoisie's failure to com-

The export-orientated industrialisation (EOI) programme met with almost instant success. International investment poured in from the late 1960s, leaping from a cumulative total of $S157 million in 1965 to $S995 million in 1970. By 1978, this sum had climbed to $S5242 million. Manufactured exports, which represented just $S349 million in 1965, amounted to $S1523 million in 1970 and $S12 633 million in 1978 (*Economic Development Board* (hereafter *EDB*) *Annual Report 1983/84*, pp. 8, 10). The contribution of manufacturing to gross domestic product also rose from 15.3 per cent in 1965 to 20.5 per cent by 1970, and 22.6 per cent by 1978 (Department of Statistics 1983, pp. 57–9). The electrical/electronics industry was crucial in this development. It was here that the decomposition of the production process through mechanisation and automation to take advantage of unskilled, lower-cost labour had widest application.

Ironically, Singapore's industrial programme, which had been inspired in large part by the need to generate employment, was by the late 1970s experiencing serious bottlenecks due to labour shortages (*Asian Wall Street Journal* (hereafter *AWSJ*) 31 October 1978, pp. 1, 12). This was beginning to threaten planned technological upgradings in the electrical/ electronics industry and was generally pushing wage costs up and reducing the competitiveness of the most labour-intensive production. However, for political reasons the PAP was averse to the idea of expanding Singapore's already large supply of guest labour to address the problem. Instead, the government embarked on a concerted effort to secure a rapid technological transformation, a 'second industrial revolution', which was expected to reduce the demand for labour. This not only meant greater mechanisation and automation in existing production, but the attraction of new investments in higher value-added production. In the latter case, the aim was to move into areas of middle to high technologies involving reasonably skilled work forces. Here Singapore was expected to retain a cost advantage over manufacturers in the advanced industrial countries at the same time as moving out of competition with unskilled but lower-cost labour in developing countries. During the course of the second industrial revolution, it was envisaged that the manufacturing sector would play an increasingly pivotal role in the overall economy (Goh Chok Tong 1981). The policies of the second industrial revolution involved discouragement of unskilled, low value-added production on the one hand, and

---

prehend the strength of the anti-colonial movement in the lead-up to self-government left it without links to the People's Action Party (PAP) which had grafted itself onto this movement and held office since 1959. For a fuller discussion of these factors see Rodan (1989, chs 2, 3). Second, while the PAP came to office with the support of the trade union movement, the party's internal power struggle in the the early 1960s resulted in the ascendancy of Lee Kuan Yew's faction and the virtual elimination of labour as an effective independent political force. The power base of Lee's left-wing opponents had, of course, been in the trade union movement.

encouragement for manufacturers trying to upgrade on the other. The most controversial of these policies was the 'corrective' wage policy operating between 1979 and 1981, under which wage cost increases of between 54 and 56 per cent were imposed through the National Wages Council (NWC) to apply pressure on employers; supposedly 'corrective' in the sense of bringing wage costs into line with the market. At the same time, though, generous fiscal and tax incentives were provided for investments and production in preferred areas of higher value-added production, including interest free loans and generous tax holidays. Social and physical infrastructures were also substantially improved and expanded, including specialised industrial estates and training centres, and employers' training costs in preferred areas of industry were heavily subsidised. Additionally, the government engaged in direct investments to stimulate higher value-added production, especially in the aerospace and petrochemical industries (Rodan 1985, pp. 142–6).

The period of the second industrial revolution witnessed some important developments. Foreign investments rose substantially from $S6349 million in 1979 to $S12 717 in 1985 (EDB Yearbook 1986/1987, p. 16), during which time value added per worker increased from $S23 992 to $S42 436 (Yearbook of Statistics Singapore 1986, p. 113). In the electronics industry, Singapore became a world leader in the export of computer disk drives, and attracted the first investment in semiconductor wafer diffusion outside the advanced industrial centres. In other industries, such as machinery, chemicals and aerospace, Singapore also managed to attract investments significantly raising the technological sophistication of operations. This seemed to suggest that there was still space in the global economy for Singapore as a lower labour-cost production site, in spite of the corrective wage policy. In the aerospace industry, for example, the cost of Singapore's relatively skilled labour was still approximately half that of Europe or North America (Asian Business November 1984, p. 68). Meanwhile, unskilled, labour-intensive investments waned, and, in many cases, were relocated outside Singapore.

Nevertheless, the strategy did encounter difficulties. First, instead of the manufacturing sector assuming greater strategic importance, it failed to keep pace with the growth in the rest of the economy. Manufacturing's share of gross domestic product fell from 29.15 per cent in 1980 to 24.63 per cent in 1984 (Yearbook of Statistics Singapore 1990, p. 87). Although there were some niches which Singapore could slot into as it lost competitiveness in the most unskilled, labour-intensive aspects of manufacturing, the volume of such investments appeared an insufficient substitute if manufacturing was to serve as the motor of economic growth. Meanwhile, the services sector was making sustained progress, with transport and communications increasing its share of gross domestic product from 11.96 per cent in 1980 to 17.03 per cent in 1984, and financial and business services increasing from 20.53 per cent to 23.86 per cent (Yearbook of Statistics Singapore 1990, p. 87). Although it had been envisaged that the continued development and upgrading of the services sector would be an important complement to Singapore's manufacturing transformation, it now appeared that greater reliance might need to be placed upon it.

Second, much of the increased value added per worker was achieved by introducing higher value-added products, as in the case of the celebrated disk drive industry, without necessarily making a decisive shift away from the assembly process towards the more conceptual stages of production. Continued difficulty was experienced at this stage in attracting engineering and design processes. One constraint here was internal: the lack of a sufficient pool of scientists and engineers to induce such investment. Another constraint was external: the fact that TNCs had to weigh up the attraction of such production in Singapore against existing investments elsewhere that were closer to established markets. In the latter case, however, there was the prospect that the considerable expansion of markets in East Asia would turn the situation around.

Third, in the early 1980s Japanese investors showed a particular lack of interest in Singapore as a site for investments in higher value-added production. At this time, they were not so much motivated by the search for low-cost production sites as the need to secure access to markets in Europe and the United States. This demonstrated that there was no universal logic uniformly adhered to by international capital that would enable Singapore's policy-makers to induce a general response. Rather, the variables influencing investment considerations by international capital proved complex and peculiar. Low-cost labour was but one factor in the calculations of international capital, and not one that carried equal weight among capital of different national origins.

Finally, the fundamental political goal of the strategy, to reduce the need for guest labour, was also proving elusive. In 1985, Singapore had in excess of 150 000 guest workers (*Business Times* 18 October 1991, p. 11). There seemed, over the longer term, a real contradiction between a labour-scarce city-state and the pursuit of an industrial strategy reliant upon the attraction of lower labour costs for expansion. Technological upgrading might limit but not eliminate this contradiction. Interestingly, both South Korea and Taiwan have also recently begun to experience serious labour shortages (*Straits Times* 19 October 1991).

The Singapore experience in the first half of the 1980s also raised the question of whether there was an inherent paradox to EOI success. The further up the international technological hierarchy a country graduated on the basis of labour-cost competitiveness, the less a proportion of overall production costs labour became. In this context, the state's indirect subsidisations of production and various other factors not immediately related to labour cost became more important to investors, since finer judgements had to be made about the comparative advantage of transferring higher value-added production to Singapore. But even with the state playing this role of helping to shape comparative advantage, the longer term viability of the programme was problematic owing to uncertain trade opportunities, and to the possibility of innovations extending automation to an increasing number of semi-skilled processes involving middle-level technologies (*AWSJ* 20 August 1986). This would further shrink the number of industries and processes under pressure to be located outside the advanced capitalist centres.

Given the above points about the uncertain long-term feasibility of the EOI programme, a particularly interesting development in the period of the second industrial revolution was the increasing consideration given by international capital to projected regional markets. This was a major factor behind the establishment of a semiconductor wafer diffusion plant, and of importance in various other investments by computer hardware manufacturers (Rodan 1985). The general expansion and maturity of regional economies and markets was beginning to add a new dimension to the motivation behind production in Singapore by international companies and, indeed, to the pattern of investment by TNCs in the region more generally. Growing regional markets had started to assume more importance, so that production was no longer exclusively for traditional markets and was occurring at the expense of production in the developing countries. To some extent this compensated for the relative exhaustion of growth opportunities for Singapore under the established EOI structure, and even concealed the degree to which this exhaustion was happening.

The inbuilt limitations of an industrial strategy based on lower labour costs have to be faced by all NICs. However, in Singapore's case the situation was more urgent owing to the restricted domestic market. Moreover, Singapore's industrial investment was dominated by foreign-based TNCs attracted exclusively for EOI. As a result, the failure of the second industrial revolution substantively to project Singapore into the upper echelons of the global technological hierarchy carried particularly serious implications for Singapore's economic strategy.

New directions for economy and state

The stimulus for a major revision of Singapore's economic strategy was finally precipitated by the dramatic economic downturn in 1985, when Singapore's economy declined in real terms by 1.8 per cent, followed by a modest growth in 1986 of 1.9 per cent (*Yearbook of Statistics Singapore 1986*, p. 3). A sharp fall in demand due to global recession underlay Singapore's immediate difficulties, but the policies of the second industrial revolution compounded this with high cost structures which not only intentionally reduced the competitiveness of certain traditional activities in manufacturing, but unintentionally undermined competitiveness elsewhere in the economy. The vulnerability arising from extreme dependence upon external demand for manufactured goods, especially electronic goods, was also underlined by the 1985–86 recession. These circumstances brought the larger structural question to the fore and led to a concerted move by

Singapore's policy-makers to reduce reliance upon manufacturing production geared for developed-country markets.

In 1985, the Minister for Trade and Industry, Lee Hsien Loong, headed a top-level review of Singapore's economic strategy (Ministry of Trade and Industry 1986). Most importantly, the Economic Committee, as it was known, called into question the strategic role of the manufacturing sector, criticised the preferential treatment given to it and urged a shift in emphasis towards the services sector, notably to the banking and finance, transport and communications, and intellectual service industries. In keeping with its belief that Singapore's future was as a 'total business centre', it also called for the introduction of incentives for companies extending their commercial and manufacturing roles to include financial, technical, marketing and other corporate services to their networks of related companies in the region or worldwide, companies that used Singapore as their operational headquarters (OHQs).

The Committee's report also thematically and explicitly rejected the interventionist policies of previous decades. Such policies, of course, had deliberately favoured particular forms of manufacturing production. Furthermore, it was argued that the expansive public sector had 'crowded out' the local private sector. Unlike in the past, the report continued, the local private sector was now bigger and capable of playing a more decisive economic role, and towards this end privatisation was recommended. This observation took place in a climate of increased disquiet from the domestic bourgeoisie who had viewed the policies of the second industrial revolution as discriminatory. Being predominantly based outside the manufacturing sector, or within the low-skilled, labour-intensive aspects of that sector, locally based companies were more the recipients of the sticks than the carrots associated with that strategy.

The Economic Committee's inquiry into the Singapore economy was characterised by widespread consultation with the local private sector. The Committee not only comprised representatives from the Singapore Manufacturers' Association, the Singapore Federation of Chambers of Commerce and Industry, and leading local entrepreneurs, it also sought the views of the local business community through various subcommittees and forums. This degree of consultation was unprecedented. However, it would be misleading to portray it as the arrival of the domestic bourgeoisie as an effective political force. The PAP had chosen to adopt this approach for a number of reasons, none of which amounts to serious concern about the political muscle of local entrepreneurs.

For one thing, the new second- and third-generation leaders, Goh Chok Tong, Lee Hsien Loong and others, did not harbour the deep suspicion of the domestic bourgeoisie that Lee Kuan Yew and his first-generation colleagues developed in the 1960s. The consultations also afforded an opportunity to provide substance to the PAP's claim that it was moving away from an authoritarian and paternalistic style of government—characteristics which appeared at the time to be a contributing factor in the

PAP's electoral decline in the 1980s. But there were also structural economic reasons. The capacities and orientations of the domestic bourgeoisie fitted more comfortably into official plans now that greater recognition was being given to the potential for promoting the services sector. For instance, locally based capital was comparatively well represented in the banking and finance industries. It was also connected to networks of overseas Chinese capital throughout Southeast Asia which might have a part to play in the regional economic integration championed in the Economic Committee's report. However, international finance capital had also shown a special interest in the 1980s in the services sector and the 'sales pitch' of the Economic Committee was in no small measure directed at this and other fractions of international capital whose investments in Singapore were part of broader regional strategies.

In the immediate wake of the government's implementing the Economic Committee's recommendations[3], Singapore was to enjoy a rapid turnaround in economic fortunes. Gross domestic product grew by an annual average of 9.5 per cent from 1987 to 1990. Growth in the manufacturing sector was particularly strong. After experiencing negative growth of 6.9 per cent and 3.4 per cent in 1985 and 1986 respectively, manufacturing output grew by 23.6 per cent, 22.8 per cent and 11.2 per cent in subsequent years, with direct exports of manufactured goods rising from $S24 476.9 million in 1986 to $S47 520.3 million in 1990. Steady improvements in the value added per worker in the manufacturing sector also occurred, with the 1985 figure of $S42 436 increasing to $S60 488 by 1990 (*Yearbook of Statistics Singapore 1990*, pp. 3, 110–11).

---

3 The government was quick to put in place recommendations stemming from the Economic Committee's report. First, employer contributions to the Central Provident Fund (CPF) were reduced from 25 per cent to 10 per cent and contributions by employers to the compulsory Skills Development Fund (SDF) halved to 1 per cent. Second, a two-year wage freeze was introduced, and moves were made to break down the heavy reliance upon the central direction of the National Wages Council (NWC) and to promote greater flexibility within the wages structure. Third, a host of government charges on utilities, transport and communications were reduced, as were rents and interest rates affecting business. The corporate tax rate was also lowered from 40 per cent to 33 per cent. Furthermore, as part of the government's attempt to promote Singapore as a base for the servicing of business operations in the Asia–Pacific region, a concessional tax rate of 10 per cent was offered to firms establishing their regional headquarters in Singapore. To complement this, a Services Promotion Division was also created within the Economic Development Board (EDB). In other reforms, the government brought the Development Bank of Singapore (DBS) into line with other banks so that it too would be unable to make investments exceeding 40 per cent of capital funds, and deregulated land development and freight forwarding. Collectively, these policies signalled the government's greater sensitivity to the needs of business in general and the commitment to a more diversified economic structure.

Table 11.1 Growth rates in key economic indicators 1985–90

Year	GDP per cent	Man. output ($S million)	Man. exports per worker ($S million)	Man. value added ($S million)
1985	-1.6	38 818	24 390	42 436
1986	1.8	37 503	24 477	48 352
1987	9.4	46 338	30 501	52 483
1988	11.1	56 805	37 999	55 302
1989	9.2	63 924	42 546	58 413
1990 *	8.3	70 993	47 520	60 488

* Preliminary

Source: Yearbook of Statistics Singapore 1990.

However, this quick turnaround did not obviate the need for a structural transformation of the economy. Rather, it simply provided breathing space within which this might occur. For one thing, the recovery of the manufacturing sector owed much to the strong demand from the US market for electronic products and components, especially in the computer industry. While this was to be welcomed in one sense, it also consolidated the structural dependence, hence susceptibility, of the manufacturing sector. Indeed, it was pointed out as a matter of concern in the *Strategic Economic Plan*, the work of the tripartite Economic Planning Committee released in October 1991, that around 35 per cent of all non-oil domestic exports go to the United States, of which electronic items comprise more than half (*Straits Times* 18 October 1991, p. 48). Furthermore, nearly 90 per cent of the top ten exports are electronics items (*Straits Times* 14 October 1991, p. 36). So this recovery did nothing to alleviate the vulnerability of the manufacturing sector.

A second factor in the recovery was the changing attitude of Japanese investors to Singapore. The rapidly appreciating yen had by this time begun to threaten the competitiveness of export production from Japan, forcing a substantial transfer of production facilities abroad. Threats of trade sanctions against the Japanese because of their substantial trade surpluses was another factor. Export production from sites abroad was one way of attempting to reduce this tension. Certainly Singapore's reduced cost structures aided the republic in luring Japanese investment commitments, which stood at $S244.1 million in 1985 but by 1988 had reached $S691.3 million before falling back slightly to $S541.2 million in 1989. From 1986 Japanese commitments exceeded those by the United States to become the leading source of commitments (*EDB Yearbook 1988/89*, p. 18). Singapore was actually benefiting from a global expansion in Japanese investments, one that was giving the republic an extended if not guaranteed life as a base for global EOI production.

But in spite of Singapore's extended life as an EOI base, fortuitous circumstances now present an opportunity for Singapore's economic transformation, as they did in the mid-1960s when the collapse of political merger with Malaysia coincided with favourable international investment trends. This time, however, two important recent developments in the region open up opportunities for Singapore to move towards greater economic diversification.

The first of these developments is a change in global corporate strategy by many TNCs, leading to the widespread adoption of the concept of 'regional focus' (Ng & Sudo 1991). Increasingly TNCs are decentralising operations in recognition of the need for rapid and locally informed decisions about technologies and markets. To a significant extent, this decentralisation is guided by the notion that the world economy can best be serviced by treating the three dominant economic regions of North America, Europe and the Asia–Pacific region as relatively discrete. The aim is still to operate business globally, but the means for achieving that have been modified and led to more complete and integrated production and management systems within definable regions. In particular, the Asia–Pacific region is no longer viewed exclusively as a centre for low-cost production of goods to be transported back to the markets of Europe and America. Rather, it is now seen to constitute a sizeable market in its own right, and one that is projected to expand considerably.

We saw above that some of the more significant gains in value-added investments in manufacturing by TNCs in the period of the second industrial revolution were influenced by the growth of the Asia–Pacific market. Understandably this nascent trend was given a fillip by the new corporate approach to global business. So TNCs manufacturing in Singapore have been encouraged by head office to explore regional markets more seriously and, what is more, there is now more preparedness to move upstream technologically if regional markets, existing or anticipated, are likely to be better serviced that way. Consequently, investments in production engineering, product development and higher value-added processes across a range of industries are now more forthcoming.[4] This does not necessarily mean there are no limits to the sorts of production that will now be undertaken in the region. So long as there is a global head office at all, it will continue to make sense for the highest level research and devel-

---

4   For some examples of TNCs that have expanding interests in the Asia–Pacific markets investing in these higher value-added areas see 'Du Pont to invest $300m in polymer sector', *Singapore Investment News* February 1989, p. 1; 'SGS-Thomson sets up its third diffusion module', *Singapore Investment News* May 1989, p. 3; 'Glaxo gears up for more Asia–Pacific business', *Singapore Investment News* October/November 1990, p. 3; 'Becton Dickson sets up $130 million plant', *Singapore Investment News* February 1989, p. 3; 'Rosemount setting up new Asia–Pacific support centre', *Singapore Investment News* February 1989, p. 5.

opment (R&D) to be located there. But clearly the possibilities have changed greatly from when the almost-exclusive logic for manufacturing investment in Singapore was the servicing of markets in the United States and Europe.

A logical corollary of this 'regional focus' is the establishment of 'regional centres' which assume many of the functions traditionally undertaken by operational headquarters (OHQs) in the advanced capitalist countries. These regional OHQs have the capacity and authority not only to control subsidiaries but also affiliated and associated companies within the region. As 'total business centres', OHQs serve as more than manufacturing and market bases, they supply R&D, designing, fund-raising, and the distribution process.[5] Singapore's authorities have given priority to pursuing this particular niche, with generous incentive packages for TNCs using Singapore as their OHQ. Special importance seems to be attached to fund management when Singapore's authorities are determining OHQ incentives eligibility (Shunsuke Bando 1990, p. 29). By the end of 1990, 37 TNCs had qualified for the package (Ministry of Trade and Industry 1991, p. 76). Matsushita's headquarters, the third outside Japan, is the largest of such OHQs in Singapore, and will function as the base for 22 of the group's factories and seven sales agencies in Southeast Asia (*Straits Times Weekly* Overseas Edition 2 December 1989, p. 15).

A second and not unrelated development, which enhances the potential for greater economic integration with the region and a consequent accelerated sectoral diversification, is rather ironic. It is the broader and more effective adoption of EOI programmes. As Singapore has been encountering difficulties in transforming its industrial structure through such a strategy, the prospective NICs of Malaysia and Thailand, and to a lesser extent Indonesia, have been making considerable headway with their industrialisation.[6]

Much of this development is being fuelled by rapid increases in manufactured exports to the United States and Europe, as Malaysia, Indonesia and Thailand embark on labour-intensive, export-orientated production, following the earlier path of Singapore. The more abundant labour forces of these countries suggest substantial scope yet for industrial expansion. In Malaysia, for instance, demographic patterns combine with the advantages of a reservoir of rural labour to project an expansion of the work force in

---

5 The actual extent of autonomy of these regional centres from TNC headquarters in the home country obviously varies from case to case, depending amongst other things on local factor endowments and the nature of the technology involved.

6 During the period 1980–88, Singapore's average annual growth in GDP of 5.7 per cent compared with 4.6 per cent for Malaysia and 6.0 per cent for Thailand. For the period 1989–91 though, Singapore's 7.9 per cent expected annual growth in GDP compares with 9.0 per cent for Malaysia and 9.8 per cent for Thailand. See *Far Eastern Economic Review* (hereafter *FEER*) 28 February 1991, p. 72.

the 1990s of 2.9 per cent per annum, five times faster than in Singapore (*FEER* 28 February 1991, p. 72). But in some instances, progress in these would-be NICs has been rapid enough to involve already direct competition with Singapore in relatively skilled areas, such as disk drive manufacture (*Straits Times Weekly* Overseas Edition 22 September 1990, p. 13; 29 September 1990, pp.13–14).

Over time, the relative attractiveness of these emerging NICs (*vis-à-vis* Singapore) as export manufacturing production sites is likely to be greatly enhanced, as infrastructure improves and Singapore's limited labour supply continues to hold back production and raise costs.[7] The increasing exploitation of these sites by other Asian NICs as a means of containing trade surpluses with the United States, and more generally as an avenue for accumulation by emerging TNCs from these countries, is giving this process added impetus.

Thus, Singapore's position as a global manufacturing production site will necessarily become even more narrowly focused on higher value-added products and processes, thereby further compressing the scope for industrial expansion. However, in light of the trend towards strategic management involving 'regional centres', this development is not so much the threat it would otherwise be. On the contrary, to the extent that this creates the opportunity for broader regional divisions of labour which integrate manufacturing with other sectors, it has the potential to be most functional for Singapore's economic transformation.

The borderless economic zone: the Singapore–Johor–Batam Growth Triangle

Certainly the most imaginative initiative from the Singapore Government, which expresses the desire to more fully integrate Singapore's economy with those of the region, has been its championing of the so-called Growth Triangle. This was first outlined by Deputy Prime Minister Goh Chok Tong in December 1989 and further elaborated throughout 1990. The idea is for Singapore, the state of Johor in Malaysia, and Batam and the rest of the Riau Islands of nearby Indonesia, to be jointly developed to form a complementary division of labour. According to Goh, Batam and Johor could provide land, gas, water and labour for industrial development in these states while Singapore could provide the management expertise. The hierarchy of the relationship would have Batam concentrating on labour-intensive industries, Johor on intermediate-level industries and Singapore on capital- and knowledge-intensive industries and services. Goh also envisages the promotion of the triangle as a 'Caribbean tourist play-

---

7 The labour problem's continuing severity is underlined by the increase in foreign workers from around 150 000 in 1985 to 317 000 in 1990. See *Business Times* 29 June 1991, p. 1.

ground', with Johor and the Riau Islands providing the resorts and Singapore the shopping facilities. The Growth Triangle, then, is conceived as a single investment zone transcending formal political boundaries. Instead of separate states competing for capital, under this arrangement there is cooperation to attract capital for the collective benefit.

Clearly, as a concept, the Growth Triangle explicitly rejects the idea of the nation-state as a natural economic division. More importantly, it envisions only rational specialisations as the basis of a division of labour, with questions of economic nationalism relegated. This conception, of course, contrasts sharply with the practical past experience of the Association of Southeast Asian Nations (ASEAN) as a mechanism for regional economic cooperation. Economic competition and political suspicion have previously prevented any serious attempts by member nations to implement or endorse so-called rational divisions of labour within the region. Not least of the concerns here has been the fear that such a formalised division would, owing to Singapore's relatively advanced economic position, simply consolidate that country's economic supremacy. The requirement that all ASEAN activities must result in equal benefit has mitigated against the formation of divisions of labour based strictly along the lines of comparative advantage. By contrast, the Growth Triangle concept forecasts mutual but not equal benefits. Moreover, the intention is to have organic linkages across national borders rather than just complementarities in the respective structures of national economies. The concept is about forming growth regions or zones, not just integrating national economies.

The idea of growth areas operating in 'defiance' of political boundaries has some precedent. The relationship between Hong Kong and Guangdong is in principle similar to that prescribed in Goh's vision. Following the introduction of China's 'open door' policy, Hong Kong companies established manufacturing bases in Guangdong to exploit lower labour costs; the attraction for Guangdong was employment generation and foreign currency from the export production. Importantly, there were historic trade and family ties between Hong Kong and southern China that pre-dated 1949, as there were between Singapore and Johor before independence in 1965. Of course, the triangle concept is a deal more ambitious. Nevertheless, following Goh's statement, speculation surfaced in various quarters about the wider application of such arrangements. One possibility mooted is the formation of a 'Northern Triangle' involving southern Thailand, northern Malaysia and northern Sumatra; another would link Manado in Sulawesi, Davao in Mindanao, and Sandakan in Sabah. Again, these groupings also have historical links that were restricted by imposed political (colonial) divisions. However, there are emerging investment, capital and trade flows underlying the arguments for their contemporary recreation (*Straits Times* 13 November 1990, p. 28).

In the case of Goh's creative concept, there was some sort of basis for it in concrete developments in the region. As we have already seen, TNCs have begun to reorganise their operations in the region to better exploit the range of factor endowments and market opportunities. Malaysia in general, and the state of Johor in particular, were certainly caught up in these developments, and the relationship between Singapore and Johor was evolving accordingly. However, at the time Goh first referred to the Growth Triangle, Singapore's economic relations, and for that matter Johor's, with Batam and the other Riau Islands were minimal. Let us look at the two relationships in turn.

The growth in foreign investment in Malaysia has been quite spectacular since the mid-1980s. Total approved foreign investment in Malaysia has risen from $M5687 million in 1985 to $M12 215 million in 1989 and $M28 168 million in 1990. Important to these gains have been substantial increases from East Asian-based capitals as a response to appreciating currencies and rising domestic labour costs. In 1990, Taiwan-based capital accounted for 36 per cent of approved foreign investment and Japan-based capital 24 per cent.[8] Investments in Johor have increased considerably in that time, from $M827 million in 1985 to $M2736 million in 1989, before dropping slightly to $M2090 in 1990. Johor's share of total foreign investment in Malaysia thus jumped from 14.6 per cent in 1985 to 22.3 per cent in 1989, before dropping to 7.4 per cent in 1990 (Kamil et al. 1991, pp. 57–9). Infrastructure bottlenecks, notably the delay in the completion of a second causeway to Singapore, labour shortages and the emergence of Batam as an alternative site for foreign investors are factors in this relative slowdown. Textiles, chemical, and food manufacturing industries have proven the most attractive to date in Johor, in contrast with the two other major industrial centres in Malaysia (Selangor and Penang), where the electrical and electronics industries are most prominent.

The relationship between Johor's industrial surge and Singapore's economic development has two aspects. First, in absolute terms Singaporean investment increased substantially in this period, from $M184 million in 1986 to $M915 million in 1989 and $M895 million in 1990. The textile, basic metal, and electrical/electronic industries have been the major recipients of this investment. A significant component of this growth is comprised of relocations due to rising costs in Singapore. But second, even before talk of a Growth Triangle, hundreds of TNCs had been operating in Johor while incorporated in Singapore, taking advantage of the republic's liberal trading regime and superior infrastructure, but at the same time exploiting the cheaper labour of Johor (Ng & Wong 1991, pp. 139–40). Production may have taken place in Johor but often payments for export goods were made in Singapore (*Straits Times* 24 July 1990, p. 27).

Substantial foreign-investment increases in Indonesia have been much more recent than in Malaysia. Cumulative (approved) foreign investment

---

8 The rise of Taiwan-based capital has been dramatic. In 1986 it accounted for just 0.64 of total approved foreign investment. See Ministry of Finance, Malaysia 1991.

in manufacturing stood at $US10.6 million in 1985, but then jumped from $US11.4 million in 1988 to $US17.3 million in 1990. Up until the last two years, investment in Batam has been limited and primarily related to the oil industry, so that in 1988 Batam's share of Indonesia's total cumulative foreign investment was just $US2.88 billion or 2.53 per cent (Pangestu 1991, p. 89). Trade and investment links between Indonesia and Singapore, and Indonesia and Malaysia may have been advancing[9], but at the time of Goh's statement there was not yet much interest in the Riau Islands.

The inclusion of Batam in the triangle concept reflects two considerations. First, for security reasons the Singapore government was keen to diversify its source of water supply[10], something which Indonesia could assist with if infrastructure in Batam were improved. Second, the general commitment of the Indonesian Government to the diversification of its own economy, away from a heavy reliance on oil and gas, held out the potential for greater manufacturing investment, which could be serviced in various ways from capital based in or operating from Singapore.

Goh's Growth Triangle concept is therefore more than a recognition of emerging investment patterns. It also embodies political considerations and, what is more, the strategy being pursued to promote the triangle's realisation involves a significant role for the Singapore state. The most conspicuous form of this is direct investment.

Two government-owned companies, Singapore Technologies Industrial Corporation (STIC) and Jurong Environmental Engineering (JEE), have combined with two Indonesian conglomerates, the Salim Group controlled by Liem Sioe Liong, and the Bimantara Citra Group, which is headed by President Suharto's second son, Bambang Trihatmodjo, to establish a $S400 million, 500 hectare industrial park in Batam (*AWSJ* 3 December 1990, pp. 1, 26). STIC has a 30 per cent and JEE a 10 per cent stake in PT Batamindo Investment Corporation (BIC), which is the holding company and developer of the park (*Business Times* 23 May 1990, p. 13). STIC is also forming a joint venture with the Salim Group to develop and manage an even more costly 4000 hectare industrial estate on the adjoining Bintan Island. The first stage of this estate will cost an estimated $S200 million (*Straits Times Weekly* Overseas Edition 28 September 1991, p. 20). Another STIC venture involves joining up with the Singapore company, Wah Chang, and the Salim Group to develop a multi-million-dollar resort in Bintan comprising the development of 19 000

---

9 Whereas between 1979 and 1986 the republic's investment in Indonesia amounted to $US244.8 million, in the subsequent three years the figure rose by nearly $US500 million (Chee 1990, p. 18). This included a four-fold increase in Singapore's investments in Indonesia in 1988, from $US58 million to $US255 million, mainly due to investments by banks in response to deregulations within the Indonesian finance sector (*Straits Times* 13 July 1989).

10 Singapore has been totally dependent upon Johor for its water supplies.

hectares of land (Soh & Chuang 1990, p. 44). The infrastructural and other investments are guided by the notion that Batam will essentially concentrate on the electronics industry and Bintan on light industry and tourism.

The Singapore Government is also the largest shareholder in the Sembawang group of companies, which plans to develop another member of the Riau Islands, Karimun, into a heavy industrial centre. It proposes to do this on a joint-venture basis with Bangun Cipta and members of the Salim Group. One estimate is that the cost of the phased ten-year developments would amount to $S1 billion (*FEER* 27 February 1992, p. 60).

In other measures to foster the Growth Triangle, the government has: streamlined customs procedures to facilitate traffic between Riau and Singapore (*Straits Times* 30 May 1990, p. 40); made Skills Development Fund (SDF) grants available to Singapore-based companies operating in Batam or Johor but training workers in Singapore; rendered income earned by companies in Batam but remitted to Singapore tax free (*Straits Times Weekly* Overseas Edition 12 January 1991, p. 4); provided expertise for a training institute in Johor (*Straits Times* 24 November 1990); and linked Singapore's telecommunications system directly to Batam's to avoid having to be routed via Jakarta (*Straits Times* 30 May 1990, p. 40). Lee Kuan Yew was also instrumental in persuading President Suharto to liberalise investment regulations in Riau.[11]

In its various initiatives then, the Singapore state is playing two complementary roles. First, it is playing a direct part in creating the fundamental physical and social infrastructural conditions in and for its 'neighbourhood' that were so important to Singapore's own earlier industrialisation. Second, it is actively promoting and cultivating the use of Singapore's advanced infrastructural, managerial and other systems in these industrial programmes. At another level, the heavy involvement of the Singapore Government in Batam has engendered a degree of investor confidence because of the record Singapore has built up for efficient and corruption-free investment processing. This factor was made quite explicit by the managing director of the first operation established in the Batam estate, a $S30 million project by a subsidiary of the Japanese giant Sumitomo to manufacture wire harnesses.[12]

Incidentally, the strategic use of direct investments abroad by the Singapore Government is not peculiar to the promotion of the Growth Triangle. Many government-owned companies are now pursuing 'internationalisation' as a logical and even necessary step in their capital accu-

---

[11] This resulted in Indonesia declaring that foreigner investors in Batam could, for the first five years, retain 100 per cent ownership if their investment in manufacturing was completely export-oriented. For the rest of Indonesia, the maximum initial foreign ownership is 95 per cent or less. See *AWSJ* 5 December 1990, p. 10.

[12] See *Asia Magazine* 8–10 February 1991, p. 10.

mulation process.[13] But a number of recent investments by Singapore Technologies Holdings (STH), housing 52 government companies with an annual turnover in excess of $S1 billion, have involved alliances that are either intended to bring relatively advanced technologies to Singapore or secure an interest in the application of such technologies elsewhere.[14] These and other initiatives in direct investment by GLCs and statutory boards like the Economic Development Board (EDB) have been occurring simultaneously with a steady divestment of government shares in various public companies. What is taking place then, is the modification and refinement of the state's investment role and not its diminution.[15]

Though it is certainly premature to talk about a triangle as such, the special attention to developing the Indonesian component has met with a favourable response from investors. Total cumulative foreign investment

---

[13] Gearing up for global expansion began in 1989 with the restructuring of Sheng-Li Holding, which was formed in 1974 by the Ministry of Defence to bring a range of government companies under one management. The 48 companies under Sheng-Li's wing were regrouped to form four main companies: Singapore Technologies Industrial Corporation, Chartered Industries of Singapore, Singapore Aerospace and Singapore Shipbuilding, respectively covering the four areas of industrial, ordnance, aerospace and marine business. Subsequently in 1990, Sheng-Li Holding changed its name to Singapore Technologies Holdings (STH), thereby housing 52 companies under a single banner with an annual turnover in excess of $S1 billion. This was expected to raise the collective profiles of the different companies and effect rationalisations of the group's operations. The government also announced the floating of four STH companies on the stock exchange. In each case, however, the government would retain at least a 50 per cent share and hence control of the company. According to the Minister for Trade and Industry, Lee Hsien Loong, listing the companies is intended to impose greater market discipline and flexibility, resulting in a more effective exploitation of joint venture and other relationships with overseas high technology companies. While there were obvious general economic benefits to be had from this, greater access to advanced technology would also ensure a more profitable deployment of STH's vast cash holdings and this was never far from policy-makers' minds. The partial opening up to the private sector should, therefore, be seen as a means to an end rather than an end in itself. See Economist Intelligence Unit (1989, pp. 9–10).

[14] These include: the establishment with Sierra Semiconductor of the United States of Chartered Semiconductor to build a $S100 million wafer fabrication plant in Singapore; a 50–50 joint venture with Gemplus Card International of France to sell smart cards in the Asia–Pacific region; the establishment of Advanced Computer Systems with IBM to provide various computing services; a joint venture with Grumman World Enterprises Corporation in supercomputers and computer-integrated manufacturing services; joint production with Aerospatiale of 600 Airbus passenger jets; and a $S130 million interest in Pratt and Whitney's programme to manufacture turbofan engine parts. See Chuang 1990.

[15] For a fuller account of the divestment process and the implications for the government's role as an investor see Asher 1989 and Ng 1989.

in Batam Industrial Park by the end of 1990 amounted to $US685.9 million and involved 48 projects. Singapore was the largest investor with $US344 million, followed by the United States with $US165 million and Hong Kong $US111 million (BIDA in Ng & Wong 1991, p. 142). The most common focus of investments has been in labour-intensive electronics and electrical production, including private and government-owned Singapore companies such as NatSteel Electronics, Singatronics and UIC Electronics (Soh & Chuang 1990). However, to date greater interest by Singapore's domestic bourgeoisie has been shown in tourism and property. The list of project commitments in these areas is already extensive.[16] Singaporeans have also dominated the purchase of residential properties in Batam, raising fears of speculation and prompting the Indonesian Government to consider imposing a quota on the number of non-resident foreigners allowed to invest in residential properties in Batam (*Straits Times* 24 March 1990, p. 3; *Straits Times Weekly* Overseas Edition 30 June 1990, p. 20). The Singapore Government's expectation is that this profile will become more diversified as the inflow of TNCs and industrialisation gather pace in Batam and draw directly on the infrastructure of the republic.

The political challenges of the new development phase

Significantly, no detailed trilateral agreement has yet been worked out or even determined necessary to formalise the Growth Triangle concept. Cooperation to date has been largely on a bilateral basis.[17] Indeed, despite public statements of support for the concept, both the Malaysians and Indonesians harbour some reservations, and there are a number of inherent political problems associated with this idea of an 'economic state'.

---

16 This includes: the construction of a $S17.5 million four-star hotel and five blocks of commercial buildings by Farmhill Investment Corporation; the partnership of Haw Par Brothers International with the Indonesian Igata Harapan Group in a proposed $S85 million golf course; the $S30 million investment by Koh Brothers Building and Civil Engineering in a commercial and residential project; the involvement of several Singaporean companies, including Island Club Investment, in partnership with Indonesia's PT Marina City Development Group and various Japanese companies in a $S1 billion 'Waterfront City' project; the Keppel Group's partnership in a $S30 million tourist complex; National Iron and Steel's proposal to build 100 chalets on Batam; and Guthrie GTS's plans to join with Indonesian partners in the development of a multi-million-dollar recreation and tourism project. See Soh and Chuang 1990; Liew 1991, p. 15; *Business Times* 29 March 1990, p. 1.

17 So far, the only formal agreements are embodied in the Singapore–Riau Accord to develop tourism, water supply and industries in the Riau Islands, which resulted in the Memorandum of Understanding (MOU) in 1990.

For one thing, there are understandable Malaysian suspicions that such a division of labour will disproportionately benefit Singapore, and consolidate its economic supremacy over Malaysia (*Straits Times* 24 July 1990, p. 27; 1 September 1990, p. 35; 20 October 1990, p. 23). This is not so urgent a question for Indonesia given the economic gulf between it and Singapore. However, the industrial potential of Malaysia is not reliant upon the Singapore connection for its realisation. Rather, it would appear to have the prospect of a more integrated and sophisticated manufacturing sector in the longer run than is possible within the city-state.

Yet another concern is that the land, labour and natural-resource endowments of Johor and Riau are similar, even if these two states are at different stages of development. It is thus unclear whether deep linkages can be developed and sustained between these states. The obvious complementarities are between Singapore and Batam, and between Singapore and Johor. This raises speculation that the triangle is a marketing device to sell Singapore's special interests in closer bilateral economic integration.[18] Moreover, Johor's attraction of investments in intermediate-level technology is not representative of all states of Malaysia. Hence, the other Malaysian states at a more labour-intensive stage of industrialisation come into competition with Batam for capital investment.

More broadly, there is the multifaceted set of problems around the issues of equality and distribution between states which both Malaysian and Indonesian central governments have to address, but their counterparts are not troubled by in the sovereign city-state. For one thing, the rapid industrialisation of those Malaysian and Indonesian states within the triangle must demonstrably benefit citizens in other states and provinces in those nations. Conspicuously better standards of living in these states, especially where central governments have fostered the Growth Triangle, would be unsustainable politically. Similarly, it would be difficult for Malaysia's central government to grant duty-free status to the state of Johor, to bring it into line with Singapore and Batam, without appearing to discriminate against other Malaysian states. Extending the provision of free-trade zones within Johor may be the best approximation possible in the circumstances.

Another political complication with the Growth Triangle centres around ethnicity. Understandably, there is no official encouragement of a public debate about this issue, but nevertheless there are real concerns in Malaysia and Indonesia that the Growth Triangle may simply consolidate the pre-eminence of Southeast Asian Chinese business groups. Already, of course, there are strong economic ties between the Southeast Asian Chinese of Singapore and Johor for obvious historical reasons. However, one consequence of the Growth Triangle and general development of Johor has been an increasing penetration by Singaporean Chinese

---

18 As Kamil et al. (1991, p. 68) state, 'many are of the opinion that the Growth Triangle is nothing but a corridor to be managed by Singapore'.

investors into residential markets for speculative purposes (*Straits Times* 10 September 1990, p. 29), a trend as we have seen above even more conspicuous in Batam. The ethnicity factor can, of course, easily be exploited for political reasons. In Malaysia, Tengku Razaleigh Hamzah, the president of the nationalist opposition party Semangat '46 or 'Spirit of '46'[19], aroused community concern recently with a claim that the Growth Triangle concept was a scheme to bring Hong Kong Chinese to Johor following the takeover of the colony in 1997 by China (*Straits Times* 4 June 1991, p. 19). There have also been public expressions of concern from within the Indonesian military about the prospect of an enclave of Indonesian Chinese capital forming within the Growth Triangle; the basis of this concern is probably the centrality of the Salim Group in developments in both Batam and Bintan. Riau's Governor, Soeripto, has also had to defend charges contained in two Indonesian newspapers, *Media Indonesia* and *Suara Karya*, that the province is being 'sold off' to Singapore (*Business Times* 27 September 1991, p. 1).

An unavoidable political problem for the Malaysian and Indonesian states, which again poses no problems for Singapore, is reconciling the Growth Triangle with national sovereignty. Neither central government is keen to surrender real powers, nor to be seen to be compromising national interests. The frequency of unilateral relations between Singapore and Johor in the discussions of the Growth Triangle concept already appear to have raised some concern in Kuala Lumpur: either that Singapore, and to a lesser extent Indonesia, may be trying to by-pass the federal government in negotiations, and/or that Johor is acting more autonomously than is appropriate (*FEER* 17 October 1991, p. 39). Given that the first approaches over the Growth Triangle were made to the state rather than federal government, the attitude in Kuala Lumpur is understandable.

However, if in spite of the obvious problems cited above there is to be real progress towards a single investment zone, then some quite specific forms of political cooperation will be required. In particular, there would appear to be a need for a single authority to administer uniform regulations and incentives covering investments within the Growth Triangle. Negotiating such an arrangement will be complicated and cannot, in any case, guarantee uniform efficiency. For instance, even though the Batam industrial estate is a joint Singapore–Indonesia exercise, there are disproportionate bureaucratic delays in investment approvals. There are limits to how far Singapore authorities will be able to institutionalise their model of public administration. Another logical requirement is the free flow of

---

[19] Semangat '46 was formed out of the split within the ruling United Malay National Organization (UMNO) in 1988. UMNO was dissolved, resulting in Prime Minister Mahathir leading the reconstituted UMNO Baru and Razaleigh the Semangat '46. The latter has been particularly concerned about what it views as the watering down of measures to bolster the position of Bumiputras, or indigenous Malays, and the consequent inroads of foreign investors.

labour between the three states. Here the Singaporeans have proposed ways of simplifying the passage of non-Indonesians to Batam and modifications to their own regulations to enable workers from Johor and Batam to be trained in Singapore. But this falls short of a free-labour market, something which would pose a potential threat to Singapore's desire for tight control over the social and ethnic complexion of the population.

Three points emerge from the above. First, Singapore's greater enthusiasm for the Growth Triangle in part reflects the city-state's absence of separate provinces or states and the associated political complications. But second, it also reflects the greater economic reliance of Singapore upon economic integration with neighbouring and regional economies due to the need for structural diversification. Finally, while the implementation of the Growth Triangle concept will involve extensions of the geographic influence of the Singapore state, this influence will be highly conditional and may even come at a cost to domestic state control in certain areas, should a free-labour market eventuate.

There is, however, the danger of over-emphasising the importance of the Growth Triangle as a particular form of economic cooperation. What is most crucial for Singapore is a broader regional application of the principle of comparative advantage, ideally one which is no longer wedded to the concept of the nation-state. At the very least, Prime Minister Goh wishes to see the emergence of a spirit of 'competitive co-operation' between states in the region.[20] But selling this idea is a delicate matter. Hence, in the attempt to persuade the broader regional community of the virtues of the Growth Triangle, Goh has drawn on wider developments in the international economy. He has argued that the formation of cooperative economic groupings in Europe, where there will be a single market from 1992, and North America, which involves Canada, the United States and Mexico in a free-trade zone, threatens the ability of ASEAN countries to attract investment from TNCs. According to Goh:

> On its own, each Asean country does not offer a full range of advantages which Europe and North America can. Asean countries are not yet ready to offer a borderless market to investors. But we can combine resources to make ourselves more competitive. This is the philosophy driving the Growth Triangle. Here we are combining resources to compete for investments as a region (*Newpaper* 24 April 1991, p. 8).

This is a clever way of presenting the case because on the surface it would appear that the emergence of an assortment of sub-regional growth triangles would threaten ASEAN's status as a regional economic forum.

---

[20] According to Goh, 'competitive co-operation' means 'working together to attract generic investments into the region and competing, through the market mechanism, to have particular investments located in your country' (Goh Chok Tong 1991, p. 6).

There is no doubt that the developments cited by Goh are of concern to ASEAN members, and account in large part for the recent surge of regional meetings about and proposals on economic cooperation within Asia. It is in this climate, at the fourth ASEAN Heads of Government Summit in Singapore in January 1992, that significant new ground was broken towards regional economic cooperation. Three important agreements were reached. One was the Framework Agreement on Enhancing ASEAN Economic Cooperation which identifies areas of potential cooperation such as trade, industry, finance and banking, and transport and communications. Moreover, it explicitly recognises the development of sub-regional growth areas, either within ASEAN or involving ASEAN and non-ASEAN states. The agreement thus endorses the Growth Triangle concept, despite the problems outlined above.

Even more significantly, another agreement contained in the Singapore Declaration commits member states to the establishment of an ASEAN Free Trade Area (AFTA) by the year 2008. The proposal actually came from the then Thai Prime Minister Anund Panyarachun, with general acknowledgement of Goh's point that developments in Europe and North America were 'defining the new operating environment for Asean' (Goh in *FEER* 6 February 1992, p. 10), making competition for international investment much fiercer. The prospect of a single ASEAN market comprising about 300 million people and a combined gross national product of $US300 billion is intended to serve as a powerful counter-attraction for investors. To date intra-ASEAN trade has been modest, amounting to just $US25.3 billion in 1991. By contrast, the group's trade with the rest of the world in 1991 was valued at $US268 billion (*Australian Financial Review* 29 January 1992, p. 12).

However, recognising the need to move in this direction and implementing such a vision are different matters. When the idea for AFTA was first mooted, the timetable for change was ten not fifteen years. Indonesian authorities in particular have reservations about the timing of the transition. Understandably they do not want their relatively underdeveloped economic status to be consolidated through a disadvantageous regional division of labour. They would appreciate more time to build up competitiveness in a range of industries. The Agreement on Common Effective Preferential Tariffs (ACEPT) which is designed to phase AFTA in, thus involves the accelerated reduction of tariffs on fifteen product groups, covering manufactured, processed agricultural, and capital goods over the fifteen years. What is not clear, however, is how extensive the list of exemptions to this will be. The possibility of exemptions is built into the agreement and, of course, too extensive a list will undermine the concept of AFTA.

Regardless of the inevitable and unsolved problems of implementing the AFTA, clearly the moves to date are a measure of the concern within ASEAN that the changing global political economy demands a new level of regional economic cooperation. This has worked in favour of gaining acceptance for the Growth Triangle concept. However, since the services sector is as yet covered by a less specific agreement negotiated at the January meeting than is manufacturing, the Singaporeans have some way to go yet before achieving the institutionalisation of the preconditions for a regional division of labour that fully reflects their economic aspirations. The prospects here would be enhanced, of course, should the Growth Triangle demonstrate that Singapore's superiority in this sector can serve to bolster neighbouring economies.

Conclusion

After a period of rapid economic growth following the adoption of an EOI programme, Singapore's policy-makers came to question the wisdom of increased reliance upon this strategy. By the mid-1980s, the scope for sustained industrial expansion began to look problematic. In any case, as the mid-1980s recession underlined, such a strategy brought with it acute vulnerability to changing demand in a handful of industries. Fortuitously, more complex patterns of international capital investment involving regional divisions of labour have presented opportunities for a lessening of direct dependence upon the markets of the advanced capitalist countries, notably that of the United States.

In the subsequent revision of economic strategy, imaginative initiatives have been taken to foster Singapore's economic integration with regional economies, with special attention to the exploitation of Singapore's competitive advantages in the services sector. In the process, we have seen the Singaporean state attempt to shape the investment climates in neighbouring states in an endeavour to harness investment trends to a sub-regional division of labour based on rational specialisations. In this new phase of development, the Singapore state thus continues its active dialectical engagement with international capital. Certainly the Growth Triangle concept and supporting policies are a stark example of the reluctance to passively accept market forces. However, the state is also forced to play a more adventurous role and one in which its political and social control over the now-extended physical environment within which investments are made is reduced. Moreover, development prospects will increasingly depend upon the extent to which Singapore's neighbours come to share a similar vision of 'competitive co-operation'.

The collective political will of states is required not only to ensure that economic integration is possible, but also to address social and political challenges associated with this. Indeed, one of the paradoxes of the Growth Triangle is that while it may transcend the organisational logic of the nation-state, and even threaten to reduce the political power of any individual nation-state, the initiatives and cooperation of states are nonetheless critical to its viability. Sub-regional economies would appear to exert pressure for a reformulation of the state's international relations, but not an abandonment of its function of assisting capital accumulation. But even more importantly, social and political problems stemming from labour migration, increased income inequalities within states, and other possible outcomes of sub-regional economic arrangements will need to be effectively managed. This necessitates new levels and forms of political cooperation between states.

The recent promotion of the Growth Triangle, and the more general attachment to greater regional economic integration by Singapore's policy-makers, also reflects a major shift in the global strategies of TNCs. Previously, TNC investment in export production in the Asia–Pacific region has tended to be primarily motivated by the desire to exploit low-cost labour. Production has been geared largely to consumer markets in the advanced countries outside the region. That strategy has had serious implications for the forms and range of production undertaken in the Asia–Pacific area by TNCs. Now, however, in an endeavour to more fully exploit rapidly expanding markets in the area, we are witnessing changes to manufacturing production located in the region and greater interest in a variety of non-manufacturing activities. The maturity and internationalisation of NIC-based capital—the emergence of regional TNCs—adds another dimension to this process. Such developments are simultaneously a force for more comprehensive economic activity in the region, yet also for increased specialisation. The extent of that specialisation will be as much a political determination as anything else, but as we have seen above, the mood in ASEAN is becoming more accommodative of specialisation in view of larger global economic trends, which have necessitated a more serious pursuit of intra-ASEAN trade.

ASEAN's new preparedness to commit itself to economic cooperation comes at a time when its *raison d'être* has been questioned. In the past, it has been regional security questions, and in the immediate past the question of Cambodia, that have given purpose to the forum. This led to speculation that, in the event of a solution to Cambodia's political problems, the future of ASEAN would be problematic. But while it appears that the changing global political economy has given new life to ASEAN, is this sustainable? In particular, what are the implications of sub-regional economies like the Growth Triangle for ASEAN? Most certainly ASEAN offers a convenient and appropriate forum through which such initiatives can obtain political support. To that extent ASEAN is an important and even necessary facilitator of sub-regional economies. But, once in place, a series of flourishing sub-regional economies would logically demand a modified and more decentralised forum to sort out the various, quite specific cross-state problems of economic integration. The relevance of collective decision-making by all ASEAN members would presumably diminish. At the very least, ASEAN would need to reorient itself to meet such new circumstances. The implications for any broader regional economic grouping would be similar.

Given the complications and challenges associated with sub-regional economies like the Growth Triangle, the success or otherwise of this particular case will have significant ramifications. If the experience is one of substantially accelerated economic development in a politically manageable way, then the Growth Triangle is not only likely to assume the status of a model within policy circles in the region and beyond, it will also be drawn on to support the theoretical and ideological cases against economic nationalism.

12 Indonesia, Thailand and the Northeast Asian Connection

ANDREW J. MacINTYRE

The economic achievements of the four East Asian newly industrialising countries (NICs)—South Korea, Taiwan, Hong Kong and Singapore— have been celebrated and subject to intensive analysis for well over a decade now. More recently the rapid growth of the resource-based economies in Southeast Asia has begun to attract increasing attention as well. Indonesia and Thailand are two countries in this category which are now coming to command greater interest as academics, policy-makers and private investors ponder apparent parallels with the experiences of the Northeast Asian NICs. As they have come to adopt increasingly outward-looking economic policies, Indonesia and Thailand have developed closer linkages with other parts of the Asia–Pacific region and have been forced to redefine their international priorities.

It is clear that there are remarkable economic developments taking place in these two countries. In 1990, GDP grew by 7.0 per cent in Indonesia and 10.0 per cent in Thailand. Over the near quarter of a century from 1965 to 1989, GNP per capita grew at an average annual rate of 4.4 per cent in Indonesia and 4.2 per cent in Thailand. While this does not match the staggering 7.0 per cent in South Korea (or the other East Asian NICs), it is unquestionably an extraordinary achievement, and one not exceeded by many other countries in the world (World Bank 1991c, pp. 204–5). In addition to notching up sustained high levels of GNP per-capita growth, Indonesia and Thailand have had great success in boosting manufactured exports. In 1965 manufactured goods accounted for a mere 4 per cent of total merchandise exports in Indonesia, and 3 per cent in Thailand. Manufactured exports began to surge in the early 1980s in Thailand and the mid-1980s in Indonesia, and by 1989 accounted for 54 per cent of merchandise exports in the former and 32 per cent in the latter (World Bank 1991c, pp. 234–5).

In many ways the comparisons between Thailand and Indonesia and the four East Asian NICs are revealing, for Thailand and Indonesia do indeed appear to be following the export-oriented rapid growth trajectories set by the NICs and Japan before them.

The aim of this chapter is to examine critically such comparisons and to consider the place of Indonesia and Thailand in the wider regional economy. This chapter is divided into three parts. Part 1 explores the comparison between Thai and Indonesian experiences on the one hand, and those of the high-growth Northeast Asian economies on the other. In simple terms, the argument to be advanced is that while Indonesia and Thailand are indeed making extraordinary progress, they display important differences from the so-called Northeast Asian model and, moreover, also differ from each other in significant ways. Part 2 of the paper looks at the nature of Thailand and Indonesia's economic linkages with the broader Asia–Pacific region, and Part 3 looks to the future and considers both what lies ahead for these countries as well as the directions in which analytical inquiry will need to move.

1. Comparisons with Northeast Asia

The experiences of Indonesia and Thailand during the 1980s bear a number of important parallels with those of South Korea and Taiwan in the 1960s. In terms of policy settings and economic outcomes the similarities are striking. At a general level, as in Taiwan and South Korea, Indonesia and Thailand have experienced a long-term structural shift with the agricultural sector being overtaken by industry. More pointedly, in both Indonesia and Thailand there has been a marked shift from reliance on import substitution to greater emphasis on export promotion which, as we have already seen, has resulted in the rapid growth of manufactured exports.

In both Thailand and Indonesia, external shocks played an important role in the shift towards an emphasis on manufactured exports. Both economies suffered heavily from the downturn in the global economy in the early 1980s and the decline in the price of many primary commodities. External pressure for economic reform came sooner in Thailand than in Indonesia, as the Thai economy was battered by the second oil shock of the early 1980s. Conversely Indonesia—an oil-rich country—was buffeted by the collapse in oil prices in the mid-1980s. In both countries, however, we saw a series of currency devaluations, followed by a raft of trade and industry policy reforms paving the way for the rapid growth of manufactured exports during the 1980s.[1] In 1985 manufactured exports exceeded agricultural exports for the first time in Thailand. In Indonesia the change emerged a few years later when manufactured exports began to catch up with oil and gas exports: in 1984 oil and gas exports accounted for 71 per cent of merchandise exports and manufactured goods a mere 7 per cent; by 1989 the gap had been nearly closed, and the figures were 36 per cent and 32 per cent respectively.[2]

But while there are, indeed, some remarkable parallels between the experiences of the successful Northeast Asian economies on the one hand and Indonesia and Thailand on the other, these should not be overdrawn, for there are also fundamental differences. One obvious example is the fact that notwithstanding the rapid expansion of industry in Thailand and Indonesia, primary production has been crucial. The strong growth of the 1970s primarily reflected agricultural expansion in Thailand and the oil boom in Indonesia. Moreover, natural-resource endowments mean that primary commodities are likely to remain important for Thailand and Indonesia for much longer than has been the case in the NICs. Important though differences of this sort are, in terms of theoretical debates about the dynamics of rapid economic growth, the more interesting contrast concerns the role played by the state.

There is now a large and varied literature devoted to the task of explaining the economic achievements of the Northeast Asian NICs and, somewhat earlier, Japan. Intense scholarly debates in this area centre on the causal significance to be attached to various aspects of their experience. Among neo-classical economists there is a general consensus that the key to the remarkable success of these countries was the adoption of outward-looking trade policies, which reduced biases against exporters, together with the maintenance of a stable macroeconomic environment in which prices, if not exactly right, were at least not too far wrong. Neo-classical economists have seen the Northeast experience as an affirmation of the virtues of market forces. They have generally de-emphasised state intervention in the allocation of resources, arguing that efforts to promote the development of particular sectors or industries were either harmful or of little overall positive significance (Balassa 1981; Hughes (ed.) 1988; James et al. 1989; World Bank 1987).

Political scientists (and other dissenters) have tended to regard the neo-classical account of the Northeast Asian experience as too simplistic, and

---

1 Among the reforms introduced were changes to the taxation structure, relaxation of tariff and non-tariff barriers, encouragement of foreign investment in export industries and moves to reduce administrative and infrastructural bottlenecks. See James et al. (1989) for an extensive discussion of the broad similarities in the policies pursued by Indonesia and Thailand in the 1980s, and those of South Korea and Taiwan somewhat earlier.

2 The oil and gas share of exports rose again in 1990 as result of the increase in oil prices resulting from the Gulf War.

have instead given much more emphasis to the role of the state in the rapid economic transformation of these countries. The focus of the 'statist' literature (as it is sometimes called) has been on the political underpinnings of the shift in economic policy from an emphasis on import-substitution towards a more outward orientation, and the significance of state efforts to intervene selectively in the allocation of resources with a view to stimulating industrial development (Wade 1990; Haggard et al. 1991; Haggard 1990; Gereffi & Wyman (eds) 1990; White (ed.) 1988; Deyo (ed.) 1987; Jones & Sakong 1980). Although the manner in which the state has intervened in the allocation of resources has varied[3], scholars working within this 'statist' stream see assorted industry policy initiatives as playing a pivotal role in the rapid expansion of export industries. Neo-classical economists, of course, reject these arguments, and insist that these countries have prospered in spite of rather than because of interventionist policies. The debate between these two schools of thought continues unabated, with little ground being conceded by either side. I am not directly concerned with this dispute here. For the comparative purposes of this chapter, the important point is that while there is, indeed, disagreement about the significance of state intervention, it is generally acknowledged that governments in these countries have not simply adopted a *laissez-faire* approach or dealt with firms on an arms-length basis; intervention has been extensive and in some respects quite elaborate.

In order to highlight the contrast with Indonesia and Thailand, attention will be focused on two key aspects of the experiences of the successful Northeast Asian economies. These are, first, the nature of state intervention in the economy, and second, what might be called the capabilities of the state. This second term refers both to the calibre of the bureaucracy as well as the extent to which policy-makers are constrained by societal interests. Plainly there are a number of other important aspects of the Northeast Asian experience which also require attention. Chalmers Johnson (1987), for example, has highlighted a range of institutional arrangements which characterise these 'developmental states'.[4] Among

---

3 In South Korea, for example, the state has intervened forcefully with an array of incentives and sanctions to induce the private sector to bring corporate investment and production decisions into line with the priorities of government economic planners. In Taiwan, on the other hand, rather than attempting to shape private-sector behaviour, greater emphasis has been placed on using state-owned enterprises as direct instruments for government industrialisation plans.

4 Common to the experiences of Japan, South Korea and Taiwan, Johnson says, are state control of the allocation of bank finance; the weakness and political exclusion of the labour movement; the insulation of the economic bureaucracy from the short-term calculations of politicians; the broader operational autonomy of the state from major economic interests—especially business; administrative or bureaucratic guidance of corporate behaviour; a highly centralised

the variables which we would need to consider in a more substantial comparative study are, for instance, the extent of investment in education, the degree of corporate concentration, the level of direct foreign investment, and more broadly the impact of historical and geographical circumstances. It needs to be emphasised, therefore, that this is only a preliminary exploration of the subject and that the scope is correspondingly modest.

Market intervention

As already seen, there is general agreement that—rightly or wrongly—governments in South Korea, Taiwan and earlier in Japan, did not simply sit passively on the sidelines of the economic playing field and invite firms to go forth and compete. Particularly in South Korea and Japan, the state was actively involved in guiding the process of industrial development by channelling resources to particular sectors, protecting infant industries and providing export incentives. Alice Amsden (1990) has taken the notion of administrative guidance (Johnson 1982) a step further, arguing that in South Korea, in return for generous subsidies and assistance of various types made available to leading firms, the state demanded and secured high economic results. Performance indicators—typically based on export results—were used to determine whether or not firms would continue to be eligible for assistance. In short Amsden argues the state was able to 'discipline' the private sector, and thereby ensure that subsidies were not simply unproductive rents which were consumed by favoured firms (as one would normally expect), but were instead judicious investments of public money which yielded real economic returns in the form of accelerated industrialisation.

If South Korea, Taiwan and Japan can be thought of as capitalist developmental states, in which a rigorous and disciplined form of administrative guidance took place, then the Indonesian experience could perhaps be characterised as undisciplined interventionism, and while certainly not a story of *laissez-faire*, the Thai experience has been much less *dirigiste* than most other industrialising countries.

In Indonesia the state has been very actively and extensively involved in the process of fostering industrialisation, both through regulation and direct investment. Indonesia has a sizeable state-owned enterprise (SOE) sector. SOEs dominate key industries, including oil and gas processing, fertiliser, cement, steel and aircraft production, as well as sugar processing and finance (Hill 1989, p. 5). Prior to the deregulatory reform push in the mid-1980s, Indonesia also had a highly protectionist trade regime, which featured a vast array of non-tariff barriers. However, it should be noted that effective protection levels varied enormously, with SOEs and

industrial structure featuring a small number of large conglomerates; and a limited role for direct foreign investment.

upstream import-substituting industries dominated by politically favoured individuals receiving very extensive protection while others, such as downstream labour-intensive industries (with considerable export potential) received low levels of protection (Hill 1989, p. 16).

By contrast, when compared with Indonesia and the successful Northeast Asian economies, the level of state intervention in the Thai economy has been quite moderate. Thailand does not have a large SOE sector; it has been relatively receptive to direct foreign investment; and its trade regime has been comparatively open (Pasuk 1992, 1980). While effective protection levels have been lower in Hong Kong, Singapore and Malaysia, Thailand has certainly adopted less interventionist trade and industry policies than countries such as South Korea or Indonesia.

The argument that the nature and levels of state intervention in the economies of Indonesia and Thailand differ markedly from Northeast Asian experience can be conveniently illustrated by focusing briefly on one distinctive variable: state intervention in financial markets and, in particular, in the allocation of credit. Governments in virtually all developing countries intervene in credit allocation to some extent. In many instances the net benefits of credit allocation programmes are questionable (World Bank 1989). However, Japan's post-war experience, and particularly that of South Korea since the 1960s, have generated much discussion.[5] One of the most remarked upon aspects of the rapid growth of the successful Northeast Asian economies has been the way in which governments have attempted to allocate credit to officially determined priority industries, often at greatly subsidised rates. Preferential lending was particularly prominent in South Korea, where the government made very extensive use of its control of all the major commercial banks to channel cheap credit to the industrial sector. By the late 1970s, preferential lending in South Korea accounted for up to 50 per cent of outstanding bank credit. The share of credit received by the industrial sector grew from 44 per cent in 1965 to 69 per cent in 1986 (World Bank 1989, p. 57). Again, however, the issue here is not whether selective credit played a *decisive* role in promoting accelerated industrial development, but rather to establish as a point of comparative reference that selective credit *was* used extensively and in a coordinated way to channel resources to deliberately targeted industries in the manufacturing sector.

How have Indonesia and Thailand compared? At first glance, the Indonesian experience bears some remarkable similarities to that of South

---

[5] There has been an interesting recent twist in the literature on this subject with some economists now challenging orthodox assumptions about financial repression. Adapting Oliver Williamson's arguments about internal organisations, Chung Lee and Seiji Naya have suggested that close links between big business and the state in the Northeast Asian NICs constitute a quasi internal organisation and therefore a more efficient allocational mechanism than the market (see Lee & Naya 1988; Lee, forthcoming).

Korea: although there have been recent moves towards financial deregulation, it is quite clear that the state has loomed large in financial markets and had great impact upon the allocation of credit. Until very recently the banking sector has been overwhelmingly dominated by state-owned banks. Private- and foreign-owned banks have played only a small role, with the state banks accounting for 80 to 90 per cent of all loans extended. Using a number of different mechanisms the government (via the central bank) has long maintained an extensive programme of subsidised lending. Between 1968 and 1990, central bank subsidies for preferential credit programmes have amounted to an average 48 per cent of all commercial bank lending. Each year the government has prepared a detailed list ranking priority sectors of the economy which would be eligible for preferential borrowing.

Like South Korea then, there has been very extensive state intervention in Indonesian credit markets. But here the similarities end, for rather than a coherent attempt to channel preferential finance to boost manufacturing, no clear pattern emerges in the allocation of subsidised credit in Indonesia. Certainly the manufacturing sector has not been a big winner; moreover, much of the preferential credit which was earmarked for the manufacturing sector has tended to take the form of financial first-aid (to bail out ailing SOEs) rather than industrial seed money. Preferential credits for exporters only became a significant category in very recent years (and were then terminated in 1989). To the extent that official statistics point to any single sector as deriving a persistently significant gain from preferential lending, it is the agricultural sector (especially rice farmers). Not only has the manufacturing sector not been a big winner, there has been absolutely no sign of the state attempting to 'discipline' large firms favoured with preferential credit on the basis of performance indicators along the lines Alice Amsden has described in South Korea.

There has been a high degree of state intervention in credit allocation in Indonesia, but this intervention has typically been quite undisciplined and of uncertain impact. Notwithstanding the elaborately tailored plans of central bank officials, which nominally governed the allocation of preferential credit, in reality the whole system of preferential credit in Indonesia was subject to serious problems. First, it is widely recognised that there was very significant 'leakage', with politically well-connected non-priority borrowers gaining access to subsidised credit. Prior to recent moves to liberalise the banking industry, it was an open secret in Indonesia that would-be borrowers could gain access to credit programmes supposedly earmarked for priority categories by agreeing to share the interest differential with the bank loans-officer. In short, the effectiveness of many preferential credit programmes was undermined by corruption. Second, the success of many of the preferential credit programmes was further undermined by the associated high risks and transaction costs. And third, given that Indonesia has maintained an open capital account since 1971, the whole notion of channelling credit away from some borrowers in favour of others was dubious, as large firms could readily borrow offshore in Singapore (MacIntyre 1991a).

The Thai experience in this area has also differed markedly from those of the successful Northeast Asian economies. State intervention in the Thai financial sector has been modest (Doner & Unger 1991; Muscat 1991). Although the second largest commercial bank is state-owned, the banking industry as a whole is dominated by private banks. More importantly for present purposes, credit allocation has not been a key policy instrument employed to accelerate economic development. To be sure there have been preferential credit arrangements to channel subsidised loans to various sectors of the economy, but these have never amounted to a significant share of total bank lending. To the extent that there has been a focus for preferential lending in Thailand, it is agriculture which has received the largest single slice of subsidised credit. There has been cheap finance available for the industrial sector and for exporters, but again, in terms of volume, the amounts involved have not been significant. Moreover, of the preferential credit which was extended to support manufacturing, typically this did not take the form of inducements to commence investment and production in new areas of industry.

The degree and nature of state intervention in credit markets in Indonesia and Thailand is in many ways symptomatic of broader differences between these two countries and the successful Northeast Asian economies. While the Indonesian state has intervened extensively, it has done so in a much less coordinated and disciplined fashion than the South Korean or Japanese states, and has often produced little more than a smorgasbord of rent-taking opportunities for the politically well-connected. In Thailand the contrast has been even starker, as the whole economic orientation of the state has been markedly less *dirigiste*. Moreover, in neither Indonesia nor Thailand has state intervention so closely focused on promoting manufactured exports.

A survey of over 100 Korean firms in 1976 found that almost 75 per cent of respondents believed that the most significant benefit to their firm of a strong export performance was continued access to selective government benefits. Moreover 55 per cent of firms surveyed believed that the rigour of taxation audits depended on their export performance (Biggs & Levy 1991, p. 374). It is inconceivable that such a survey in Indonesia or Thailand would generate findings of this sort.

State capabilities

A second major dimension of the Northeast Asian experience which differs significantly from those of Indonesia and Thailand is what in shorthand might be referred to as the political capabilities of the state. There are two key elements here: the calibre of the bureaucracy and the extent to which decision-makers are constrained in the formulation and implementation of policy by societal interests. The fact that the bureaucracies in

South Korea, Taiwan and Japan have generally been staffed by highly educated and disciplined officials, together with the insulation of the principal economic agencies within the bureaucracy from the pressures of rent-hungry societal groups (particularly big business) are seen as key ingredients in their ability to achieve sustained rapid economic growth. As Chalmers Johnson (1987, p. 158) put it:

> ... the political independence of the 'economic general staff' is not easily achieved but ... without it, the setting of long-term economic goals and industry policy is unlikely to produce the results envisaged by theorists of public policy. If, of course, the politicians and their economic bureaucrats are themselves hopelessly corrupt (viz., innumerable African states) then no amount of foreign aid or independent funding will free them from their business sector: the money will simply be siphoned off or otherwise misspent.

Indonesia and Thailand differ from the Northeast Asian pattern in terms of both dimensions of state capability. Although they have indeed adopted more export-oriented economic policies and thus apparently cleared the political hurdles associated with moving away from dependence upon import-substitution, their bureaucracies appear less impressive and in both cases the state seems to enjoy considerably less operational autonomy than in South Korea or Taiwan.

It is difficult to make firm statements about the relative quality of bureaucratic agencies in these various countries, for there are no detailed comparative studies upon which we can draw. Nonetheless, it is safe to say that observers of Indonesia and Thailand are unlikely to disagree with the assertion that in general terms the national bureaucracies of these countries are less well trained, less meritocratic in character and less disciplined than most accounts suggest has been the case in the high-growth Northeast Asian economies. There are pockets of high technocratic competence in the Indonesian and Thai bureaucracies, but these are few in number and, moreover, are located in a sea of administrative corruption and patrimonial rent-taking. In Indonesia, for example, it is virtually impossible for civil servants to survive on their salaries alone. This, of course, only reinforces the tendency towards what Peter Evans (1989) has termed 'klepto-patrimonial' behaviour among government officials.

The extent to which the state has been constrained by societal interests in Thailand and Indonesia also differs significantly from most accounts of the Northeast Asian experience. During the crucial early period of economic reorientation in South Korea and Taiwan (the 1960s and early 1970s), the coercive capabilities of highly authoritarian regimes made it possible to limit and contain demand-making, and in particular to suppress organised labour. To this extent, there are broad parallels in Indonesia and Thailand. The major area of difference lies in the nature of relations between business and the state. In South Korea and Taiwan the state also enjoyed considerable authority and leverage over business (by virtue of the dependence of corporate leaders on continued access to selective subsidies) which made it much easier for policy-makers to resist sectional demands from business groups. Peak-level business associations were certainly consulted on a regular basis by policy-makers, but particularly during the early years, such consultation centred on business cooperation in the implementation rather than the design of economic policy. As one recent review of the literature on the successful Northeast Asian economies put it:

> The significant element of compulsion exercised by the bureaucrats in securing public-private cooperation constitutes a central characteristic of the developmental state.
>
> ...in Japan, and perhaps even more so in Korea and Taiwan, the state has possessed considerable leverage over private business in terms of securing compliance with its strategic choices. The state elites have unambiguously been the senior partner in their relations with business groups (Onis 1991, pp. 116, 119).

By contrast, in Indonesia and Thailand during the 1980s (the period of key economic reforms) the state élite enjoyed neither the same degree of authority and leverage, nor insulation from sectional business demands. The differences are most marked in the case of Thailand. During the 1980s, the tight grip of the military on Thai politics eased, and a semi-authoritarian regime developed under General Prem Tinsulanond, which saw political parties and interest organisations become significant players in the policy process. While key economic agencies were shielded from countervailing populist pressures during the crucial years of economic adjustment, industry groups were closely involved and played an important role in pushing the policy reform process along (Pasuk 1992; Anek 1992a). This took place both through political parties and an inclusionary corporatist structure which enabled peak business groups to push collective demands in top-level decision-making forums (Anek 1988; Doner 1988, 1991). Direct business pressure was thus a very important ingredient in shaping economic policy in Thailand during the 1980s, so much so that it has been suggested that Thailand is becoming a 'bourgeois polity' (Ramsay 1986) with 'liberal corporatist' institutions (Anek 1992b). The point here is that in contrast to the picture contained in most accounts of the reorientation of economic policy in the Northeast Asian NICs, in Thailand business has been not only less beholden and subservient to the state, it appears to have been actively involved in initiating and sustaining policy reform (Anek 1992b, pp. 163–70).

Although the contrast is not as striking in the Indonesian case, the state nonetheless appears to have been considerably more constrained by business interests than in Northeast Asia. While Indonesia has a long established, military-based authoritarian regime that has developed an elaborate corporatist architecture, which effectively limits political participation by societal groups (a system which would certainly earn the respect of Park

Chung Hee or Chiang Kai-shek), the state has lacked the degree of autonomy apparently displayed in South Korea and Taiwan during the 1960s and 1970s. In battles over economic policy in Indonesia during the 1980s one can readily identify the impact of the demands of patrimonially privileged business people along with newly assertive industry associations. While down-stream producers and nascent exporter groups have not been driving the reorientation of economic policy in Indonesia to the same extent as their Thai counterparts, they have played an important coalitional role in supporting the reform-oriented state agencies in the political struggles with those sections of the bureaucracy and their private-sector allies seeking to preserve the status quo (Robison 1988; MacIntyre 1992, 1991b). By comparison with the experience of the Northeast Asian NICs, economic policy in Indonesia frequently appears to be more directly tied to private interests. The pockets of technocratic competence within the Indonesian bureaucracy have considerably less freedom of movement than appears to have been the case in South Korea and Taiwan during the 1960s and 1970s.

The conclusion to emerge from the discussion thus far, is that while Indonesia and Thailand appear to be following a roughly similar developmental trajectory to that mapped out by the successful Northeast Asian economies, they are doing so on the basis of a different political formula. Both in terms of state intervention in the marketplace and the state's political capabilities, Indonesia and Thailand have differed from Northeast Asia in their experience. Peter Evans (1989) has proposed a continuum of state structures ranging from the developmental states of Northeast Asia through to predatory and klepto-patrimonial states, such as that of Mobutu's Zaire. The Thai and Indonesian states are neither as economically efficient as the developmental states, nor as hopelessly corrupt as predatory states, and are thus perhaps best thought of as intermediate cases. Unproductive rent-taking by politicians, bureaucrats and their private-sector cronies are larger problems in Indonesia and Thailand than in the developmental states of Northeast Asia. And yet, nonetheless, moves during the 1980s to reform the economic policy environment in Thailand and Indonesia succeeded in producing strong results.

The implications of the argument here point in a somewhat different direction from the now well-established statist literature on Northeast Asia. It would appear that the links between political structure and economic performance are less clear than indicated by this literature. The Thai and Indonesian cases suggest that strong economic performances can be achieved in the absence of a highly meritocratic, disciplined and insulated state structure if at least the basic elements of the standard liberal economic refrain—macroeconomic stability, the removal of biases against exporters, etc.—are observed. (The improving economic fortunes of a number of Latin American countries in the late 1980s may provide support for this argument.)

Clearly no firm conclusions can be reached on the basis of the brief and partial comparisons presented here. It would appear, however, that Indonesia and Thailand can be seen as providing grist for the neo-classical mill. And yet *a priori* the proposition that political institutions are a significant variable affecting economic performance seems a powerful one— even the World Bank (1991c, pp. 128–36) now happily acknowledges this. Frustratingly for students of comparative political economy, the goal of generating statements about institutional arrangements conducive to rapid economic growth which are not country- or region-specific remains elusive.

2. Regional economic linkages

While Indonesia and Thailand may well differ from the successful Northeast Asian countries in their institutional make-up, there is little doubt that their economies have been profoundly influenced by Japan and the four NICs. The more outward orientation of the Indonesian and Thai economies since the mid-1980s has meant that they are becoming increasingly integrated into international trade and investment structures. Both countries have benefited enormously from their location in the midst of the world's most economically dynamic region. Indeed, this has been a vital contributing factor to their recent growth surges, with much of the new direct foreign investment (FDI) flowing into export industries.

Table 12.1 Foreign direct investment 1983–90

	1983	1984	1985	1986	1987	1988	1989	1990
	(millions of $US)							
Indonesia	292	222	310	258	385	576	682	964
Thailand	348	400	162	261	182	1082	1650	1700
Malaysia	1261	791	695	489	423	719	1846	2958
Philippines	105	9	12	127	307	936	563	530
	(as a percentage of GDP)							
Indonesia	0.4	0.3	0.4	0.4	0.5	0.7	0.7	1.0
Thailand	0.9	1.1	0.4	0.6	0.4	1.8	2.4	2.1
Malaysia	4.2	2.4	2.2	1.8	1.3	2.1	4.9	7.2
Philippines	0.3	0.03	0.04	0.4	0.9	2.4	1.4	1.4

Source: IMF, *International Financial Statistics*, various issues.

Table 12.1 shows the growth of FDI flows into Indonesia and Thailand from 1983 to 1990. Data for Malaysia and the Philippines provide a comparative reference. In the case of Thailand, the size of the investment boom in the late 1980s is quite apparent, with total FDI reaching 2.4 per cent of GDP. Notwithstanding its history of economic nationalism,

Indonesia has also seen FDI pick up markedly in the last few years. Indeed, the two countries are now competitors, vying to attract foreign investment. While the level of FDI in Indonesia and Thailand has reached new peaks, it is important to bear in mind that by comparison with other Southeast Asian countries neither country is heavily reliant upon foreign equity. Malaysia, for instance, far outstrips both countries, and is in turn itself outstripped by Singapore. On the other hand, by comparison with the ailing Philippine economy, Indonesia and Thailand have attracted quite considerable foreign investment.

Table 12.2 Foreign direct investment by country of origin 1989 (percentage of approvals)

From \ To	Indonesia	Thailand	Malaysia	Philippines
Japan	17	44	31	20
NICs	25	25	42	40
Hong Kong	9	7	4	17
South Korea	10	2	2	2
Singapore	4	5	11	3
Taiwan	3	11	25	19
Japan + NICs	42	69	73	60

Source: ADB, Asian Development Outlook, 1991.

Overwhelmingly this surge in FDI has come from within the East Asian region, with Japan being the single largest investor. However, the distribution of the inflow has not been uniform. For example, for the period 1986–89, two-thirds of all Japanese investment into Southeast Asia went to Thailand, while Indonesia (which in cumulative terms has been the largest recipient of Japanese FDI) received only 16 per cent. Conversely, during the same period Thailand received around 27 per cent of Korean investment in Southeast Asia, whereas Indonesia soaked up 63 per cent (Asian Development Bank 1991, p. 46). Table 12.2 provides a profile of the FDI flows into Southeast Asia by country of origin. The share of foreign investment to Indonesia from Japan and the NICs is somewhat lower than for the others, as Indonesia's large oil and gas sector is very much dominated by US firms. The US share of FDI to Indonesia is roughly the same as Japan's, although if the oil and gas sector is discounted, the US share becomes very much smaller. In Thailand, about 10 per cent of total FDI comes from the United States.

The reasons for the recent surge of FDI into Thailand and Indonesia (as well as Malaysia) are not hard to find. Lower labour costs have plainly been an important factor; in Japan and particularly the NICs, rising wage costs have forced labour-intensive manufacturing to relocate. Thailand and Indonesia have not only been able to offer cheaper labour, they have also been actively wooing Japanese and NIC investors with attractive reforms to the policy environment. However, the labour-cost differential between the ASEAN-4 on one hand, and the NICs and Japan on the other, is nothing new. The crucial factor stimulating the recent wave of FDI was the Plaza Agreement in 1985, and the subsequent sharp appreciation of the yen, the won and the new Taiwan dollar. Relocating to another country was the simplest way for Northeast Asian exporters to avoid the heavy blow to their international competitiveness resulting from currency realignments. A further incentive for relocation has been the signs of a rising tide of protectionism in both the United States and Europe.

The investment linkages tying Indonesia and Thailand into the economies of Japan and the NICs are reinforced by trade flows. In 1990, 48 per cent of Indonesia's total trade and 41 per cent of Thailand's total trade was with Japan and the NICs. The United States and Europe figure more prominently in trade than investment figures for Thailand and Indonesia, in large part because they are the crucial markets for key components in the rapidly expanding manufactured-export sector (such as textiles and garments). Trade links between Indonesia and Thailand, and the NICs and Japan are being strengthened as a result of the large FDI flows from the latter to the former. Because Indonesia and Thailand have lacked strong capital goods industries, foreign investors setting up new plants have had to import most of their parts and machinery requirements. This has contributed to increased imports by Indonesia and Thailand from Japan and the NICs. On the other hand, it is likely that as the production of simple consumer goods becomes increasingly uncompetitive in Northeast Asia, countries such as Thailand and Indonesia will be able to take up the role and supply these Northeast Asian markets (Asian Development Bank 1990, pp. 42–3). (This assumes both that Japanese firms vacate these industries rather than preserve their competitiveness through further automation and that Japanese markets are, indeed, accessible to foreign producers.) Tables 12.3 and 12.4 set out direction-of-trade data for Indonesia and Thailand.

Indonesia and Thailand are becoming steadily more integrated into the wider East Asian economy. It is important to note, however, that with the conspicuous exception of Singapore (which is counted here as a NIC rather than as a member of the Association of Southeast Asian Nations (ASEAN)), very little of Indonesia's or Thailand's trade is with other Southeast Asian countries. Overwhelmingly the trade and investment links are with Japan and the NICs. Notwithstanding preferential trade agreements, trade among the resource-rich ASEAN countries is still very modest. While the decision in January 1992 by ASEAN leaders to increase intra-ASEAN economic cooperation and establish an ASEAN Free Trade Area (AFTA) within fifteen years will promote closer economic ties within Southeast Asia, it is unlikely to have a major impact.

Table 12.3 Indonesia: Direction of trade (percentage share)

	1985	1986	1987	1988	1989	1990
			EXPORTS			
Japan	46	45	43	42	42	42
NICs[a]	16	15	18	18	17	18
ASEAN-4[b]	2	2	1	2	3	3
United States	22	20	19	16	16	13
Australia	1	1	2	1	2	2
EC	6	9	9	11	11	12
Rest of the world	7	8	8	9	8	10
			IMPORTS			
Japan	26	29	28	25	23	25
NICs[a]	13	15	17	15	17	18
ASEAN-4[b]	1	1	2	3	4	2
United States	17	14	11	13	13	11
Australia	4	4	4	4	6	5
EC	17	17	18	19	16	19
Rest of the world	21	19	20	19	21	19

[a] South Korea, Taiwan, Hong Kong, Singapore
[b] Thailand, Malaysia, the Philippines, Brunei

Source: International Economic Data Bank, ANU, 1991.

Table 12.4 Thailand: Direction of trade (percentage share)

	1985	1986	1987	1988	1989	1990
			EXPORTS			
Japan	13	14	15	16	17	17
NICs[a]	15	17	16	16	14	15
ASEAN-4[b]	7	5	5	4	4	4
United States	20	18	19	20	22	23
Australia	2	2	2	2	2	2
EC	19	21	22	21	19	21
Rest of the world	24	22	21	21	22	18
			IMPORTS			
Japan	26	26	26	28	30	31
NICs[a]	14	14	15	16	17	17
ASEAN-4[b]	11	8	8	5	5	5
United States	11	14	12	14	11	11
Australia	2	2	2	2	2	2
EC	15	15	15	16	14	15
Rest of the world	21	21	21	20	21	21

[a] South Korea, Taiwan, Hong Kong, Singapore
[b] Indonesia, Malaysia, the Philippines, Brunei

Source: International Economic Data Bank, ANU, 1991.

Ultimately this is because their economies continue to be more competitive than complementary—a fact reflected in the decision of ASEAN leaders to allow a range of as yet to be determined products to be excluded from tariff reductions.

Recognition of this economic reality underlies the recent willingness of Indonesia and Thailand to consider (and then support) some wider forum for regional economic cooperation which embraces Northeast Asia and particularly Japan. Thus, we have seen Indonesia and Thailand support the establishment of the Asia Pacific Economic Co-operation (APEC) meetings. This is despite the fact that the development of wider regional cooperation may well in the longer term erode the importance of their own regional association, ASEAN—an institution which has long been the centrepiece of their foreign-policy frameworks. This is a watershed development in Thai and Indonesian foreign policy. The long-term economic logic of greater integration with the economies of Northeast Asia has led them—very reluctantly—to begin thinking seriously about economic diplomacy and not simply geopolitical issues in Southeast Asia.

In the wake of the establishment of APEC, in December 1990 the Malaysian Prime Minister, Dr Mahathir, put forward a rival proposal for the creation of an East Asian Economic Group (EAEG). Like APEC, the EAEG proposal would have promoted links between ASEAN and the dynamic Northeast Asian economies. Unlike APEC, however, the Mahathir initiative would have excluded the United States, Canada and Australia, and for this reason failed to win sufficient support within the region.

Notwithstanding this surge of interest in regional economic co-operation and integration, the pace of change should not be overstated. Certainly fears about a resurgence of protectionism, with the signing of the North American Free Trade Agreement, and the approach of 1992 and a single European market, have stimulated increasing interest in the development of some form of Pacific economic community. However, much of the recent discussion about an Asia–Pacific economic bloc centring around Japan is, at least from a Southeast Asian perspective, exaggerated.

For Indonesia and Thailand (as for most other countries in the region) Japan is the dominant source of investment, trade and aid. Notwithstanding the analysis of people such as former British Prime Minister, Margaret Thatcher, the prospect of some form of yen-based economic bloc emerging is, from a Southeast Asian perspective, at best many years off. Although the role of the yen is growing (Frankel 1991), it is simply not yet used as extensively as Japan's dominant trading and financial position might suggest (Holloway & Rowley 1991, pp. 187, 195–7). Roughly 80 per cent of intra-Asian trade is still denominated in dollars. Although Japan consumed nearly half of Indonesia's exports in 1989, less than 5 per cent of this total trade was denominated in yen. And neither Indonesia nor

Thailand is yet showing any great enthusiasm to link their currencies more closely to the yen. In spite of the fact that 30 per cent of Thailand's external debt is denominated in yen, Bangkok has resisted giving the yen significantly greater weight in the basket of currencies against which it manages the baht. Similarly, although an increasing chunk of Indonesia's external debt is denominated in yen, it too has refrained from linking the rupiah more closely to the yen. During the latter part of the 1980s, Indonesia was caught between the pincers of exports denominated in a declining US dollar and much of its debt denominated in the rising yen. Rather than easing the repayment burden by 'tying' the rupiah more closely to the yen, Jakarta simply asked Tokyo to relax the terms of repayment. (Reportedly Jakarta even proposed that Japan provide loans to Indonesia denominated in dollars rather than yen.) (*Far Eastern Economic Review* 11 October 1990, pp. 72–8.)

Table 12.5 Selected indicators of yen usage 1989

	Indonesia	Thailand
% of exports ¥ denominated	<5	3
% of imports ¥ denominated	<9	11
% of official reserves ¥ denominated	12	13
% of external liabilities ¥ denominated	35–40	30
% of external liabilities $US denominated	32–42	57

Source: Far Eastern Economic Review 11 October 1990, pp.72–8.

In the longer run, Indonesia and Thailand may well become more enthusiastic about using and holding the yen.[6] Certainly investment, trade and aid flows suggest a trend towards greater economic integration with Japan and Northeast Asia. In the short term, however, Southeast Asian governments remain wary—if not suspicious—of Japan and the possibility of a reassertion of some form of pin-striped Greater East Asia Co-Prosperity Sphere. Southeast Asian memories of World War II remain vivid and painful. At the same time as drawing pride from the Japanese-led ascendence of East Asia, they remain keen to keep the United States as a counterweight to Japan. This does not arise from any great affection for the United States in these countries, but rather a general belief that their interests will be better served if Japan and the United States counterbalance each other. In addition to political concerns about Japan, it remains the case that the United States is a major source of investment and, in particular, the crucial market for manufactured exports. These various con-

---

6 Frankel (1991, p. 3) argues that to the extent the role of the yen is increasing, it is due to the efforts of Washington rather than Tokyo. Where the Japanese Government has been hesitant about the yen becoming further internationalised, US authorities have been keen to see it used more extensively.

cerns about the future regional roles of Japan and the United States appear to have been a significant factor behind Indonesia's opposition to the earlier-mentioned proposal of the Malaysian Prime Minister, Dr Mahathir, for the creation of the EAEG which would not have included the United States (or Canada and Australia). In sum, while there is a long-term logic pointing towards increasing integration in the East Asian region, there are also countervailing political and economic concerns.

3. Thinking about the future

Indonesia and Thailand are becoming wealthier very rapidly. Moreover, the economic prospects for both countries (particularly Thailand) appear relatively encouraging at the start of the 1990s. They do, of course, face a range of economic problems: Indonesia is carrying a high debt-service ratio, while in Thailand infrastructural constraints are becoming acute. More generally, containing inflationary pressures will be a problem for both, as will the fact that private-capital inflows are likely to be squeezed as a result of tight international financial conditions (stemming from Germany's preoccupation with reunification, and Japan's financial shake-out). Nevertheless, in economic terms, many developing countries would be glad to have the problems Thailand and Indonesia face.

And yet it is important to keep this in perspective; although Indonesia and Thailand are following an increasingly export-led high-growth strategy, it will be many years before they achieve the 'upper-middle income country' status enjoyed by South Korea, Taiwan or Singapore today. Even on the basis of rudimentary calculations, it is evident that it will be quite some time before Indonesia or Thailand achieve the per-capita income that South Korea has now. Figure 12.1 provides a simple extrapolation based on the assumption that both countries achieve average annual GDP growth of 7 per cent (which roughly translates to 5 per cent GNP per-capita growth once population increase is included). Seven per cent GDP growth is probably an optimistic figure for Indonesia and a conservative figure for Thailand. On the basis of these assumptions, using 1989 as a base year, Thailand will reach South Korea's *current* position in 27 years, and Indonesia in 45 years.

The most contentious problems these countries will face over the next five to ten years fall squarely within the domain of politics. Setting aside regime-change issues, the fundamental political challenge confronting both Thailand and Indonesia in the 1990s will be managing the emergence of new and assertive groups in society. Predictably business interests will be the most prominent, but labour relations are also certain to become more intensely contested. These developments are the logical outcome of the structural changes arising from a quarter of a century of rapid growth and have important implications for both domestic and foreign economic policy.

Figure 12.1 Income per-capita projections (in 1989 $US)

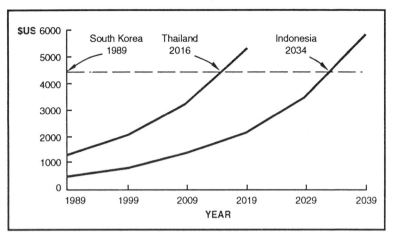

Note: Assuming average annual GDP growth of 7 per cent: 7% GDP growth = 5% GNP per
           capita; 500 = 4,400(1+r)n, where r=GNP per-capita growth and n=number of years to
           catch up.

If Indonesia and Thailand are to have another quarter of a century of
rapid economic expansion, then institutional arrangements must be found
for managing distributional coalitions. In Thailand and to a lesser degree
Indonesia, some emerging business groups have been happy to enter into
de facto alliances with bureaucrats and politicians in order to promote
economic-adjustment measures. But this has been a fortuitous coincidence
of interests and there is no obvious reason why such alliances should
endure and continue to prevail. But as argued earlier, there are challenges
for scholars here as much as for policy-makers. Students of comparative
political economy need to produce accounts of the dynamics of economic
growth which can accommodate significant variation in the national
political framework. A possible way forward for further research in this
area is suggested by Biggs and Levy (1991), who discuss different strategies for industrial development and argue for a tailoring of economic
policy to match domestic political conditions. Adopting Myrdal's (1968)
distinction between 'hard' and 'soft' states, they argue hard states are in a
position to contemplate economic policy paths involving a greater role for
government (because they are less prone to rent-seeking activities by
bureaucratic and private interests), but that such strategies are unlikely to
succeed in soft states. The success of industrial reform efforts lies, they
argue, in '...the goodness of fit between the chosen strategy of industrialization and the institutional environment in which the strategy is to be
implemented' (p. 366). Biggs and Levy go on to present a detailed
discussion of economic policy options appropriate for hard and soft states.
Although more sophisticated typologies may well be possible, this is an
encouraging line of research.

It was argued earlier that in important ways Indonesia and Thailand did not fit the statist models deriving from Northeast Asia. However, understanding the politics of economic policy in Indonesia and Thailand is a prerequisite if we are going to make sense of how they fit into the wider regional political economy. International economic relations are not simply shaped by transnational bargaining. At least insofar as the behaviour of governments is concerned, domestic coalitions are crucial variables shaping preferred international bargaining positions. The analysis of trade diplomacy is inevitably predicated upon conceptions of domestic political economy. While we have relatively sophisticated models on offer for thinking about the dynamics of Japanese, US or Australian political economy, we are less well armed when it comes to the NICs, and particularly the rapidly industrialising countries of Southeast Asia. The first wave of the comparative political economy literature on the NICs was both impressive and encouraging: statist models seemed to be a powerful tool for explaining the political economy of the NICs (Johnson 1987; Haggard 1990; Chu 1989). However, not only is this approach now being critically re-evaluated in its application to Northeast Asian countries (Moon 1988, 1990; Samuels 1987; Rosenbluth 1989), it is unclear that it has ever been terribly useful for explaining the politics of economic policy in Southeast Asia.[7]

Until headway is made in the understanding of the politics of economic policy in these countries, generalisations about their foreign economic policies and their interaction with other countries in the Asia–Pacific region will remain problematic. As an illustration of this point, in January 1992 Thailand, Indonesia and the four other ASEAN countries resolved to establish an ASEAN Free Trade Area within fifteen years. This is a move which appears consistent with their public demands for further trade liberalisation and a successful resolution to the Uruguay Round of GATT through their activities in APEC and the Cairns Group. (Indonesia, Thailand, Malaysia and the Philippines are members of the latter.) And yet in spite of this, it has apparently been agreed that agriculture and services will be exempted from the proposal. Beyond the superficial, we know very little about the interests that are being protected by this move, and more importantly what the coalitional links are which see these interests so effectively defended.[8]

---

[7] Mackie (1988) has explored the application of statist models to Southeast Asia. Subsequent studies have been more squarely in the emerging 'post-statist' literature. See for example, Doner (1988, 1991), Anek (1992a, b), and MacIntyre (1991a, 1992). Parallel to this 'post-statist' literature is a separate and strong structuralist literature on Southeast Asian political economy (Robison 1986; Rodan 1989; Robison et al. 1987).

[8] Encouragingly, Thai scholars are beginning to make headway in the study of the political economy of trade policy (Surin 1991).

An analysis of the pronouncements of trade diplomats such as at the Kuala Lumpur meeting which produced this decision is of little value unless it is grounded in an understanding of the domestic political economy variables which underpin the agreement. To date, however, the political economy of these countries' foreign economic policies has remained largely unexplored.

13 Economic Cooperation and Institution Building in the Asia–Pacific Region

STUART HARRIS

Introduction

What determines whether nations live together in a state of anarchy or of cooperation is of continuing interest to those concerned with international relations. Political scientists tend to ask why nations cooperate rather than continue in conflict, responding to perceptions of rival national interests. Many look to institutions as a prerequisite to such cooperation, although to some observers, collective international action has generally reflected greater concern with the probability of conflict than with the possibility of cooperation (Inis Claude cited by Mitrany 1975, p. 253). Economists, on the other hand, tend to ask what are the barriers to the cooperation that they assume would otherwise naturally occur. Among the barriers, however, are often those provided by the institutional framework existing within nations.

Conflicts between internationalist and nationalist conceptions of world order, in which political and economic aspects have been counterposed have been long standing (see Neff 1990). The nineteenth-century Physiocrats or Cobdenites, like the twentieth-century followers of Woodrow Wilson or functionalists such as Mitrany, saw economic cooperation surmounting national borders and leading to an integrated or cosmopolitan global community.

The benefits of economic cooperation are obviously greater if cooperation is interpreted widely rather than narrowly. Those seeking increased economic cooperation in the Asia–Pacific region would certainly argue against a narrow interpretation. Gains are being sought by them from regional economic cooperation, however, without expectations of advancing human prosperity through an idealised mutually cooperating international society. Nor is there thought of a pure form of liberal trading regime, with a dismantling of all barriers, the eventual erosion of national sovereignty and the ultimate removal of national borders. Moves towards economic cooperation in the region are seen as a means of achieving greater gains from international trade and economic exchanges, despite the clear desire for continued national expressions of sovereignty.

The geographic dimension and the complementary nature of the Asia–Pacific economies determine the broad coverage of that grouping. It is useful for present purposes, however, to divide those economies into two subgroups, principally according to the nature of existing barriers to economic cooperation. Those called here, for convenience, the core economies and consisting basically of those in Southeast and Northeast Asia, have considerable elements of underdevelopment in their market processes. The second, more peripheral subgroup, comprises the United States, Canada, Australia and New Zealand. Japan falls somewhere in between, but is closer to the peripheral subgroup.

Economists within the region have been encouraged by progress over the last decade or so in Asian–Pacific economic cooperation. Political scientists, particularly those from outside the core countries, on the other hand, have seen a lack of institutional development as indicating limited progress at best in regional economic cooperation (see Kahler 1988, p. 329; Segal 1990).

This may be partly because the forms of regional economic cooperation with which most commentators have been familiar, notably the European Community (EC), have been based upon formal rules, international treaties and implementing or enforcing organisations. Yet less formal methods of collective action, based on conventions and collective understandings of the rules of conduct, may be workable as guides to international cooperation (Krasner 1982, pp. 185–206; see also Higgott et al. 1991). Even the General Agreement on Tariffs and Trade (GATT), although a formal contractual arrangement, depends upon such informal understandings and guidelines.

Some economic cooperation arrangements within the region, such as the Association of Southeast Asian Nations (ASEAN) or the Australia–New Zealand Closer Economic Relations Trade Agreement (ANZCERTA, more commonly known as CER), are based on formal contractual agreements. Others such as the Pacific Economic Cooperation Conference (PECC) and the ministerial meetings on Asia Pacific Economic Co-operation (APEC) are not. The emphasis overall in the region has been upon informal means by which existing barriers to economic cooperation can be reduced and cooperation facilitated.

This chapter considers in turn what is meant by the terms 'economic cooperation' and 'institutions', why a particular process is needed at a regional level to advance economic cooperation, and what kind of institutional need that might imply. At the same time, it notes that what constitutes appropriate means for advancing economic cooperation depends upon a variety of factors, including the historical, social and political contexts in which economic-cooperation opportunities and obstacles exist. Those means will also reflect what the objectives of cooperation are perceived to be. These are often dynamic rather than static, and political rather than economic.

Definitional issues

The term 'economic cooperation' implies collaboration for mutual advantage. That collaboration, however, occurs at various levels within a community. Two, in particular, are important here. One involves governmental policy cooperation over a range of activities, from consultation about a specific economic issue (usually to avoid conflict) and collusion in non-competitive or discriminatory market behaviour, to forms of market integration or even policy coordination. This is normally at the national or national-agency level.

The other is linked to the actions of individuals or individual trading units rather than to nations or national agencies. Although national governments influence the institutional framework of laws, regulations, and taxes within which markets work, operators in the market are commonly individuals or individual enterprises. International cooperative activities in these markets may consist of relatively simple processes of exchange, or involve functional links, such as alliances in productive enterprises involving nationals of two or more countries, or perhaps involving collaborative aid projects.

When we speak of economic cooperation between nations, we commonly start from a concept of economic exchange or trading, normally in goods and services, in a competitive market between willing buyers and willing sellers. Not all trade has these characteristics. That may be due to monopolistic features of a trade relationship, or because nations utilise trade, financial or other restrictions which reduce cooperative trade and imbalance the gains from trade.

Although such economic cooperation relates primarily to trade in goods and services, it also covers economic exchanges of factors of production, such as capital (including aid), labour and technology. Nevertheless, if markets are reasonably competitive, reflecting a lack of market impediments and a free flow of information, economic cooperation as defined here will normally occur of its own volition within limits set by transport costs. Economic cooperation in this sense has become a growing feature of the region.

There is a tendency to see such increased cooperation as leading to increased 'integration' of the trading partners, or even a growing 'interdependence'. Both terms are related to economic cooperation but are also loosely used (Cooper 1972). Generally the term 'economic integration' can be taken to imply that effective market limits for factors of production as well as products extend beyond national boundaries and normally operate within inter-governmental legal and institutional arrangements. Such extensions of market boundaries may, of course, have been facilitated by past economic-cooperation processes which reduced market impediments or extended operative legal and institutional arrangements. 'Interdependence', however, is more concerned with the sensitivity at the margin of trading relationships between countries to economic developments within those countries; 'interdependence' implying a two-way sensitivity.[1] That is, it is usually, but not always, a characteristic of a high degree of economic cooperation or integration.

The term 'institutions' tends to mean a variety of things. On the one hand, it relates to the rules of the game in a society, or 'the humanly devised constraints that shape human interaction' (North 1990, p. 3). As such, institutions provide economic, social or political influences on incentives or disincentives to economic exchanges. As already suggested, these rules or regularised patterns of human interaction may be formal or informal.

On the other hand, another sense of the term is as organisations. The various organisational arrangements which shape human interaction in economic exchange include not just governments, government agencies and political parties, but enterprises, unions, industry organisations, educational bodies and the like. For many purposes, there would be advantage in keeping these two concepts of 'institutions' separate. Not only is the dividing line frequently difficult to draw, however, but given the widespread use of the term to mean international organisations as well, in the present context it will cover both, with the distinction being made between the two meanings when necessary.

Why an interest in regional economic cooperation?

Economists argue, from experience as well as from their theory, that economic cooperation within a country tends to emerge naturally from the market's operation. They argue that trade flows to where the demands of the community can best be met according to the gains from the division of labour and specialisation; and production responds to relative factor prices. This also applies to cooperation across national boundaries. If there is such an economic basis for market linkage internationally, cooperation will follow unless barriers exist to prevent it.

Consequently, efforts to increase economic cooperation across national boundaries are essentially responding to a view that such barriers exist, and require removal, not just with respect to trade, but to travel, capital movements and payments, and to other movements of factors of production. Such barriers are of two kinds.

---

1   The following section draws on Harris (1991).

First, barriers exist and, as Coase has pointed out, the need for institutions arises because of transaction costs (Coase 1960). In international exchanges, such costs are likely to be high because of language problems, lack of information about property rights, market imperfections and the like, in addition to transport costs. Second, barriers come from the deliberate or inadvertent actions of governments, such as tariffs, quotas, investment and financial transfer controls and regulations, standards, and other market impediments, as well as differences in legal and institutional frameworks governing economic activities.

The understanding that the economic actors within a country have of the legal and institutional framework governing economic transactions will commonly not exist for economic transactions between countries. This is particularly so if political and social as well as economic interchange has been limited in the past, or where important cultural, social, historical and language differences exist and individual interactions are limited.

In such circumstances, a lack of understanding will exist about each actors' motivations and perceptions of self-interest, not just because of the limited information feedback, but because the mental constructs through which economic actors process that information remain imperfect. Yet for actors in one country to cooperate effectively with those in other countries on economic matters, they need to know that the economic responses to their initiatives will be responsive and predictable. This will only be so if market barriers are not prohibitive, are transparent and relatively stable, there is adequate information about them, and the subjective mental models each participant has of others are not too distorted and can be improved through continuing interaction.

Since market barriers limit the gains from trade and economic specialisation, there are obvious grounds for efforts to minimise them. Consultations leading to cooperative efforts to reduce information gaps may be more effective than unilateral actions. Consultations might also reduce government-induced barriers, especially if the barriers are incidental consequences of actions taken for other purposes. Removing market or legal and institutional barriers is an important objective, therefore, of economic cooperation.

Gains from cooperative action are not restricted, however, to removing such market barriers. Creating a framework or environment of rules of the game and understandings about the conduct of economic interchange is also important. It is widely accepted that cooperative international action is warranted in the positive case of the provision of public goods, such as an international trading regime. Other objectives that can best be pursued collectively to mutual benefit include such things as gains from economies of scale in the provision of information, the use of transport facilities, the control of drug trafficking, or in negotiating copyright practices.

Economic cooperation is both a process and an end result. Part of the end result of the processes of economic cooperation developed in the

region to date is that trading ps have expanded substantially.
Trade among PECC countries, le, on 1988 figures accounted for
almost 66 per cent of all trade, with a little under 59 per cent for
intra-EC trade. Both groups ac or similar percentages of world
trade (around 40 per cent) (PEC

Given the growing intra-reg e and investment links, the need
for further stimulation of close ic cooperation may seem redundant. Yet because countries in the region are becoming economically integrated in production as well as trade, policies being developed nationally for each economy in the region increasingly impinge upon other economies in the region. Activities in one regional country are, therefore, becoming more sensitive to developments elsewhere in the region.

This increased sensitivity to the policies of other regional states makes regional cooperation on the policy environment more necessary rather than less. Moreover, the more interventionist the governments involved, the more that cooperation at governmental level on economic and related policies becomes important. This is especially relevant in the Asia–Pacific region where governments play a greater role in economic management than in Europe or North America. Globally much of the underpinning of economic interaction, and the channels of communication which provide and diffuse the information flows on which market transactions depend, reflect extensive networks of business, professional and scientific contacts. In the Asia–Pacific region, as elsewhere, professional, business or scientific bodies with regional-wide groups or subgroups, such as lawyers, accountants, bankers or geologists, contribute to greater understanding among the countries of the region, or help expand information flows. Networks of academic economists and of policy advisers have been important in the regular Pacific Trade and Development (PAFTAD) meetings. Business cooperation groups at the regional level, such as the Pacific Basin Economic Council (PBEC), as well as bilateral business cooperation groups, chambers of commerce and the like have also been important.

Compared, however, with the extensive regional institutional ties in Europe and North America (governmental and non-governmental), those in Asia and the Pacific remain small in number. Until recently the consequential lack of personnel and communication networks greatly limited economic cooperation among the countries of the region. The situation has improved considerably. The need remains, however, to strengthen the informal links and networks among business leaders and economic officials in the region as well as to expand the information base for mutual cooperation in order to gain from the richer information exchanges they provide and the improvements in subjective mental attitudes they offer. This is necessary to reduce risk and uncertainty, and in general to lower the transaction costs of doing business among regional economies.

Enhanced information flows, and the cooperative economic activities that these contacts lead to, influence the behaviour of governments.

Economists accept that government intervention in markets internationally as well as nationally may be warranted where there is monopoly, where information is imperfect, where externalities are present, or in the provision of public goods, and it is useful to consider each in turn.

First, 175 countries (and presumably more to come) do not necessarily represent a competitive market (Cooper 1986, p. 315); given that several of them have substantial market power, often they do not constitute even a contestable one. Second, information gaps, as has already been argued, were large in the region and remain substantial. Third, national actions commonly have spillover effects; while many will be positive, negative externalities regionally are potentially widespread especially in the context of post-colonial underdevelopment. And fourth, a single country can often gain from imposing a trade restriction, but in doing so inflict a greater loss on the rest of the world as a whole; if a number of countries pursue this approach, the global loss can be large. This is, of course, the underlying logic of the GATT world trading regime.

Historically, as well as the need to reduce market transaction costs (through improved information, networking and consultation) and constraints provided by the institutional and governmental framework, limits to enhanced economic cooperation were caused by the problems of underdevelopment. Specific solutions to these problems, including particularly a lack of capital, inevitably involved governments.

Regional bodies or organisations exist at the inter-government level to help in many fields of economic endeavour. The major one, the United Nations Economic and Social Commission for Asia and the Pacific (ESCAP), like its predecessor, the Economic Commission for Asia and the Far East, has been generally limited in its contribution, for a number of reasons, including its wide spread of membership and its bureaucratic style (Crawford 1981, p. 39).

Those regional economies that had emerged only recently from colonial status accepted cautiously new and indeterminate entanglements, or were hesitant about anything which might compromise their non-aligned status. The start in 1980 of the PECC process provided a way for regional governments to be involved indirectly while avoiding a formal commitment to an economic cooperation process. Direct governmental region-wide links emerged later with the development of APEC in 1989. Acceptance of such direct links arose from an enhanced appreciation of the needs and potential gains from cooperation, as well as from the reassurance gained by ASEAN members through participation in PECC that ASEAN unity would not be undermined.

The search for economic development, particularly in the early postwar decades in the Asia–Pacific region, was a cohesive factor in the region in thinking about economic cooperation. The Colombo Plan, proposed by Australia and established in 1950, emphasised technical programmes, including mutual technical assistance among the developing countries within its membership. The underlying motivation for this included encouraging regional cooperation.

Subsequent moves towards greater economic cooperation within the region included the Association of Southeast Asia (ASA) formed in 1961 by the governments of Malaysia, the Philippines and Thailand, a less than successful forerunner of ASEAN, which was formed in 1967. The Asian Development Bank created in 1966 was also seen as a cooperative mechanism for funding economic development in the region.

The mix of developed and developing countries in the Asia–Pacific region posed problems of diversity of objectives and needs, particularly at the height of the New International Economic Order (NIEO) debate in the 1970s. It also offered opportunities, however, for a less politically charged discussion across the developed/developing divide which has characterised PECC and will most likely be reflected in APEC. In particular, later moves to economic cooperation acknowledged a mutuality of interests and of collective gains from cooperation that were not simply linked to the developing-country status of many of the countries involved.

Should the economic cooperation process be regional?

We have seen that the gains from reducing the various barriers to economic cooperation, particularly those of high transaction costs, and those coming from an incomplete and unpredictable environmental framework for cooperative economic activity, applied and apply especially to the countries in the Asia–Pacific region. We have also observed that given the growing integration of regional markets, the need for cooperation at the policy level to avoid the adverse effects of negative spillovers was also large and growing. These various factors warrant sustained regional effort to improve cooperation processes that will realise the considerable potential gains from enhanced economic exchange.

European and North American commentators have often assumed that regionalism in the Asia–Pacific area was motivated by the desire for the eventual establishment of free-trade areas or preferential trading regimes. The counter argument is then put that collective international action is best achieved at the global level (Lincoln 1990b).

In general terms, there are three broad areas where global frameworks have a clear logic. First, economic policy cooperation for establishing such public goods as internationally agreed rules for civil aviation or for a postal system is appropriately global rather than regional. Such measures are linked to markets which are ultimately optimal at the global level.

Collective action is also necessary to establish and modify many of the basic understandings and principles of international economic exchange which, provided they are commonly adhered to, establish the framework within which cooperative economic relations can be developed. Frequently, such collective action is also better undertaken in global arrangements and organisations rather than in regional ones. The range of such policy cooperation arrangements is extensive, from international agreements setting rules for radio transmissions and international telecommunications, to shipping and civil aviation, as well as many arrangements concerned with international trade law and finance.

Similarly, the advancement of developing countries was for a considerable period seen as requiring global rather than regional attention in the United Nations and related bodies such as UNCTAD. This was in part a political reaction stemming from the emergence of what appeared to be the bargaining strength of the 'Group of Seventy-seven', although global access to capital, technology and preferential trading arrangements was also a factor.

A third reason for a global approach reflects the particular nature of public goods where cooperation is in the interest of all countries, but where there is an incentive for an individual country to free ride. In this context, the conclusions of the political scientist and the economist come close together. Both tend to accept the need for some collective or organised pressure to discourage potential free riders.

As noted earlier, this form of international cooperation underlies significantly the GATT rules for international trade. It is also relevant for some forms of international environmental cooperation, such as that of the Montreal Protocol dealing with the ozone layer, and will most probably be relevant for the eventual global climate change convention. It differs, however, from collaborative action for mutual gain where free riding is not at issue. In such cases, as with international air safety conventions, once cooperation has been established, a strong incentive exists to continue to cooperate. The organisational needs are consequently different.

Whether mutual gain is itself adequate as an incentive has been questioned by some writers who see the inequitable sharing of the gains as a barrier to cooperative action. A state, which in Grieco's terms is a 'defensive positionalist', for example, '...will decline to join...or will sharply limit its commitment to a cooperative arrangement if it believes that gaps in otherwise mutually positive gains favour partners' (Grieco 1990, p. 10). That this is not always true is illustrated by the experience of the 1987 review of CER. The Australian position assumed that, since the smaller country usually has most potential benefit (as well as most potential adjustment cost), New Zealand would expect to gain more than Australia, but Australia would also gain and therefore cooperation was worthwhile.

More generally, even though these three issues are substantially global, regional consultations on their substance frequently have considerable value. Many existing international arrangements were framed by and for Western European and North American countries and reflected their particular problems at the time they were developed and how economic influence and political power was then distributed. It remains largely assumed that other countries' interests are automatically satisfied if they adopt those arrangements. While that assumption is often valid it is not always so; as in the case of international arrangements ranging as widely as economic exchange, telecommunications, the environment and international migration. This is particularly true for the Asia–Pacific region, which has been undergoing a massive economic transformation.

Moreover, the global rules of the game often need detailed elaboration in practice. Again the characteristics of the countries in the region differ substantially from those for which the rules were drafted. Global organisations now also reflect too diverse a range of economic problems among their members to be completely effective or participatory on their own for many matters of regional interest, and some decentralisation of consultation and discussion, if not of formal decision-making, is desirable. In addition, many matters, such as capital movements and investment flows, remain outside internationally agreed rules and accepted practices. For such reasons, regional consultations are warranted to discuss the interests of the region as they are affected by existing or proposed global arrangements.

For example, although in the early post-colonial period, support among the countries of the Asia–Pacific region for existing international institutions such as the GATT was variable and often limited, increased support for such arrangements has been associated with the build up of PECC and APEC. Of the three major economic areas, the American hemisphere, Europe and Asia, only in Asia is trade protection being reduced. Regional consultations have also given strong support to a positive outcome from the Uruguay Round of trade negotiations, as in the declaration made at the November 1991 APEC meeting in Seoul (APEC 1991).

An alternative to regional cooperation is bilateral cooperation. Much economic cooperation in practice between traders and investors will be bilateral. In particular, it may be rational to pursue improved cooperation in achieving what Wolfers termed 'possession' goals in contrast to 'milieu' goals bilaterally (Wolfers 1962, pp. 73–5).

'Possession' goals, in Wolfers terms, aim at enhancing or preserving one or more of the things that a country particularly values. Such values may be in a limited or fixed supply, such as a share of a market. Pursuit of such goals is more likely to be through bilateral rather than regional negotiation. Moreover, bilateral contacts will often provide much of the basis for information transfer. The overlap of interests within the region, however, is too great for an increasing number of issues to be treated bilaterally (Drysdale & Patrick 1979).

'Milieu' goals relate specifically to a nation's aim to shape the conditions beyond the national boundaries within which it exists. They arise from a view, as Nitze has argued, that a country '...can no longer look merely to its narrow competitive interests within whatever structure happens, from time to time, to exist as a result of the policy and will of others or as a result of chance operations of impersonal forces...' (cited in Wolfers 1962, p. 74). While stemming from the interest of individual countries, such shaping of the international policy environment, provided it is achieved cooperatively, has the capacity to be in the national interest of all participants. It would be difficult to achieve bilaterally and, in many cases, would need to be pursued consistently with global principles. Nevertheless, as already indicated, given the large number of global players and the regional interests involved, regional as well as global approaches are necessary.

Broader objectives of economic cooperation?

Although the immediate objective of economic cooperation is to coordinate action for mutual gain, not surprisingly much of the impetus for regional economic cooperation stems from broader, more dynamic and usually political objectives. After all, many major players pursuing a post-World War II international trading regime, or European economic integration, had broader political and not just economic objectives in mind.

Elsewhere in the world, economic cooperation became a path towards economic integration, involving close structural linkages and with separate markets in products and factors of production moving towards a single market. Such structural integration normally requires a high degree of government coordination of the rules and organisations governing economic exchanges and activity.

Discriminatory treatment favouring those cooperating under free trade arrangements or more closely integrated common market or customs union arrangements has often been a feature of such regional cooperation processes, as with the EC. Within the Asia–Pacific region as a whole, there has been limited and probably diminishing interest in this objective (S. Harris 1989). ASEAN has sought to encourage structural integration among its members through tariff preferences. Such measures, however, have not contributed much in the way of market integration among ASEAN-member countries, nor been significant in regional production integration. The stimulus to increased economic growth rates in ASEAN countries seems, for example, to have come predominantly from outside ASEAN.

Nevertheless, with the wider adoption by ASEAN countries of outward-oriented trade policies and less reliance on domestic protection, ASEAN members are now moving specifically towards a genuine free-trade area. The Australia–New Zealand free-trade area is encouraging further economic integration in these two countries, but it is associated with overall substantially falling trade protection levels. And Malaysian Prime Minister Mahathir's proposal for a new East Asian Economic Group, now termed the East Asia Economic Caucus (EAEC), has been explained as aimed at boosting adherence to the open multilateral trading system rather than seeking any form of preferential trading (Noordin 1990).

Economic integration is itself often seen as a means to more than one end. Despite varied motives for European economic integration, many protagonists saw it as important in achieving political integration. Others, supporting economic integration of Europe for economic reasons, argued that regional integration was an effective first step to extending economic integration globally.

In the Asia–Pacific region, economic cooperation has been discussed predominantly as an economic process. This, however, has not been completely the case. Latter-day followers of Cobden and Bright seek to encourage a stable and more cohesive political environment by increasing economic interaction. They do this on the often, but not always, accurate presumption that political conflict will be less among countries with close economic relations. More specifically, security concerns have tended to be linked strongly, if often obliquely, to economic cooperation in the region in two senses.

Given the unresolved border and ethnic disputes among member countries, ASEAN was in one sense a way to 'diffuse the sources of tension' among its members themselves (Acharya 1991). In addition, much of the security concern of Southeast Asia in the early post-World War II decades, before the anxieties about Indochina became dominant, was of threats of communist-inspired internal subversion. For Southeast Asia, in particular, the answer to those threats was seen as economic development and regional solidarity. Regional economic cooperation was one path to both ends, as reflected in the emergence referred to earlier of first, ASA and then ASEAN.

ASEAN, in particular, sought to offset the influence of the major economic powers, the United States and Japan, and to a degree, Australia. Both the United States and the regional countries see cooperation as a means of encouraging changed policies to resolve structural trade imbalances. They have different changes in mind, however (cf. Koo 1990; Nanto 1990). For the smaller regional countries this has contributed, in the past, to caution in approaching economic cooperation organisationally, for fear of strengthening the position of the major powers. On the other hand, regional economic cooperation has also been regarded as a means of diluting such dominance.

Sub-regional cooperation

ASEAN was an early approach to sub-regional economic cooperation. Both the North American and Australia–New Zealand free-trade arrangements illustrate further sub-regional developments. The impetus to sub-regional cooperation is that the smaller the number of those needing to cooperate involved, the easier it should be to reach agreement. At the same time the gains from cooperation are also likely to be smaller. Experience suggests that smaller groups are likely to have more success in achieving formal arrangements, but participants, nevertheless, see benefit in pursuing the wider, less formal, forms of cooperation.

In addition, increased economic cooperation is emerging in various sub-regional contexts of Northeast and Southeast Asia. The Nomura Research Institute listed seven economic cooperation zones already in place or being actively pursued (cited in Noordin 1990). Three such cooperation zones, in Northeast Asia, the Yellow Sea and Southern China, link various of the Northeast Asian economies of Japan, Korea, China, Hong Kong, Taiwan and the former Soviet Far East. Two, the Tonkin–Mekong and the Southern Indochina zones, integrate Indochina with China and Southeast Asian countries. One zone, the Northern Triangle, brings Malaysia, Indonesia and Thailand together, while what is termed the Growth Triangle brings together the geographically close parts of Singapore, Malaysia and Indonesia.

These arrangements are essentially production rather than marketing cooperation arrangements, commonly involving joint ventures or other strategic investment and production alliances. Infrastructure provision is often the basis for inter-governmental cooperation, together with rules for investment and the operation of joint ventures. Whether these arrangements will remain nondiscriminatory will be an important question for the future in the wider regional cooperation context.

What have we learned about regional institutions?

Regionalism in its many shapes is widespread throughout the world with various organisational forms. Some lessons, however, suggest themselves in the Asia–Pacific region. One is that it is important to assess actual or proposed cooperative institutional arrangements in terms of their historical context. Development of an Asia–Pacific regional identity had to accommodate a history of sustained antagonisms, ethnic and other conflicts, or border disputes. Not only did this shape the nature of economic cooperation but mechanisms for such cooperation had to respond to the emergence of many countries from their colonial legacies to an economic framework that reflected their specific needs and capabilities, and the gradual emergence of indigenous preferences.

Achieving a sense of regional community was itself a major need. Not surprisingly, therefore, much of the early discussion was in terms of achieving a Pacific Community, although with a much looser sense of common interest than implied in the European context. This objective reflected the limited contact among many of the countries of the region, a consequence for the core countries in particular of both colonialism and underdevelopment. As a result of their colonial inheritance, their commercial and trading links were commonly with the metropolitan capitals rather than having a regional focus. Despite the large potentialities for regional economic cooperation, most countries in the region consulted more easily with London, Rome or New York than with each other and their officials, and often their businessmen, met mostly in those capitals.

The linguistic, ethnic, cultural and historical differences within the region make it important to see cooperative developments in the context of the existing cultural and social frameworks. In the West, cultural differentiation is much less. Moreover, centuries of experience have helped in understanding or accommodating such differentiation. In the Asia–Pacific region, differences in values, in rule and rules systems, in social understandings and in national aspirations, warn us not to think about cooperative processes or institutions in traditional Western terms. Such differences do not prevent cooperation. Indeed, they point to the need to improve communication and information flows as an important component of economic cooperation as well as an essential prerequisite to its substantial deepening.

Cultural differentiation also reflects the way countries in the region organise themselves politically, economically and socially. The role of governments, in particular, is different in the region, with governments assuming a responsibility for mobilising capital, labour and technology in a manner not paralleled in Western economies.

Because in the Asia–Pacific region there are wide differences in political systems, institutions and economic systems, there remains a limited region-wide congruence of economic objectives or understanding. Nevertheless, as with trade policy, experience has indicated that over time some convergence of expectations and understandings can be achieved to facilitate common interpretations of actions and, increasingly, their future coordination. Considerable time will be required, however, before the common acceptance of objectives and practices experienced in Europe or North America is achieved.

A further difference is that in the West a relatively clear line separates government, the private sector and, indeed, the academic world. Such a dividing line is not evident in the Asia–Pacific region. Government systems operate differently. This was one reason why the tripartite pattern of PECC, involving business, government and the academy, was appropriate in the Asia–Pacific region. It also reflected the region's need to concentrate, not on macroeconomic questions, but on structural and microeconomic questions. Liaison with business, increasingly recognised as necessary by the Organisation for Economic Cooperation and Development (OECD) as it has been broadening its agenda, was built into PECC from the start and is now something that APEC is also encouraging.

The first major proposal for regional economic cooperation in Asia was a Japanese proposal for a Pacific Free Trade Area among the five major developed countries including Japan. Although subsequent suggestions for preferential trading arrangements in the region generated little support, proposals to replicate an institution such as the OECD in the Pacific have been given more attention. In a sense, this was the objective of the Organisation for Pacific Trade, Aid and Development (OPTAD) proposal recognising that effective improvements in economic cooperation in the region needed systematic information, an analytical capacity for regional policy issues, and a consultative forum (see Drysdale & Patrick 1979; see also Drysdale 1988). Moreover, unlike Europe no effective alternative existed for these purposes.

Nevertheless, OPTAD suggested a much less formalised institutional arrangement, and subsequent debate indicated a preference for a decentralised institutional form rather than a centralised OECD-style one (Drysdale 1988). The different regional characteristics reflected in that debate led to the particular formulation of the PECC process with individual task forces and no central secretariat.

Comparisons with the OECD frequently overlook two things. First, for its whole existence, as the Organisation of European Economic Cooperation (OEEC) and then as the OECD, the OECD membership has had some commonality of stated objectives as well as of its basic assumptions about methods based on a relatively liberal market-oriented economic system. By contrast, despite a growing acceptance of a community of interests, the situation in the Asia–Pacific region differs substantially. Second, the OECD was concerned primarily until quite recently with macroeconomic problems rather than with the structural problems important in regional economic cooperation in Asia and the Pacific (Henderson 1988).

Assessments of institutional developments need to consider who gains and loses by the existence of an institution as well as its function. The major economic players cannot help but dominate in any institutional arrangement, and a formal mechanism institutionalises and facilitates that dominance. The history of existing organisations, global as well as regional, indicates that the major players determine the main office holders, often at the expense of quality. In addition, implicit if not explicit quotas for staff give them a grip on much of the analytical process. Moreover, any institution tends to develop its own agenda if only to get its director-general re-elected, and other aspects of importance to members such as the knowledge and information base developed, may be substantially determined by, and respond to the interests of, the major players.

The lack of a formalised institutionalised mechanism has been seen as an advantage of existing organisational arrangements for PECC and, initially at least, APEC. PECC has accepted that some permanent staff are necessary for administrative continuity, but that a less formal, less bureaucratic framework with subject-matter centres in several different locations in the region is preferable and feasible.

APEC has depended upon a formula analogous to that of the Economic Summit (Group of Seven or G-7). PECC and a number of other sources have provided its analytical backup in the way that the G-7 rely on the OECD, GATT and other institutions, with officials of the host country of the day providing the secretariat for APEC analogously to those for G-7 meetings. There is now pressure from the major powers for a permanent APEC secretariat, and ministers in their joint communiqué from the 1991

APEC meeting in Seoul indicated their intention to consider such an institutional arrangement.

Given the gaps in the analytical and policy-support capacity in the region, compared with the much more substantial support the G-7 'sherpas' can draw on, there is some argument for trying to fill that gap through a dedicated secretariat. Irrespective of the problem of how to fill the analytical gap, however, the predictable pull of bureaucratic tidiness and of organisational structures that are familiar is likely to ensure that there will be little resistance from the smaller countries to the establishment of a permanent APEC secretariat, despite the potential disadvantages to them.

The dynamics of regional economic cooperation

Interest in, as distinct from action about, regional economic cooperation in the Asia–Pacific region was often a response to what was happening elsewhere. In particular, interest in such cooperation has risen as concerns emerged about developments elsewhere, notably the Treaty of Rome in the middle to late 1950s, the EEC's common external tariff in the 1960s and then the move to 'Europe 1992', associated with the North American free-trade area. Nevertheless, the logic of the real underlying needs has remained central to the cooperative arrangements that have developed.

Yet in practice, not only has international discussion of economic co-operation been concerned predominantly with organisational questions, there has also been a tendency to judge developments in the Asia–Pacific region against the timetable of developments in European integration. It is easy to argue with Miles Kahler that '...very little has been accomplished in constructing an intergovernmental organisation at the regional level' (Kahler 1988, p. 329). Yet such conclusions fail to recognise not only the centuries-long process of cooperation, successful as well as unsuccessful, in Europe, but also the political pressures for economic integration provided in Europe by two world wars. By contrast, the Asia–Pacific region emerged only recently from colonialism and even more recently from a post-colonial uncertainty, mistrust and lack of self-confidence. Such conclusions also underestimate the specific needs of the region.

The membership question will remain critical to the dynamics of future cooperative institutions. Part of the membership dynamic comes from interpretations brought to the process in the past. Thus, while some saw the value of the process to facilitate interchange between market and non-market economies in the region, others saw membership as a reward for those who passed the market economy test. In practice, many membership problems could be avoided in the PECC, at least temporarily, through its task-force mechanisms, full participation in the work of PECC being possible without full PECC membership. The former USSR availed itself of this facility when its membership was blocked by the United States and

Japan. The non-formal nature of the process enabled China and Taiwan both to participate as full members, with Hong Kong becoming a full member in 1990. APEC has taken that formula forwards to enable the three Chinas to join APEC. Countries now seeking APEC membership include Mexico, Papua New Guinea and some Latin American countries (Woolcott 1991). India also appears to be interested and Vietnam is an obvious future candidate. There are arguments favouring open membership, but as Cooper has suggested, economic cooperation '...must derive from the need for cooperation, not from geography alone' (Cooper 1968, p. 11). APEC ministers have for the present taken a reasonably cautious approach seeking to consolidate existing arrangements before widening membership further. An expanding membership which changed the existing agenda or focus significantly would strengthen the case for a smaller, more specialised consultative group, such as Prime Minister Mahathir's East Asian Economic Caucus.

What institutional development can we expect?

Institutional arrangements and developments in economic cooperation in the region will obviously be closely interrelated. Continued development of cooperation at the broad regional level will involve coalition-building, either to defend the region's interests, including its interest in maintaining the multilateral trading system, and reducing the discriminatory targeting of the region by the United States and EC, or to press a regional view and increase the region's influence in multilateral forums. It will involve in due course growing policy cooperation and implicit, if not explicit, forms of microeconomic policy coordination. This will come about through increased exchanges of information, and discussion of how policies in various regional economies do or might impinge on others. For example, the region as a whole has a significant stake in the US–Japan dispute and will want its views considered by those parties.

Stability and predictability of the institutional framework for economic cooperation in the region will encourage increased regional integration, and help the economies in the region to improve their performance mainly through microeconomic or structural change. This can be sought through closer cooperation and coordination in trade and industrial development, in transport, communications, media, financial and other service sectors, in government procurement, capital supply and aid delivery, in environmental control, and perhaps in measures for food or energy security.

Reduction of trade barriers affecting each other's exports is an area which is being discussed in the APEC as well as PECC context. The basis for such negotiations is that they would be on a most-favoured-nation basis, that is, consistent with the GATT's non-discrimination principles (Drysdale 1991). Although there is a long way to go before agreement is likely on such negotiations, APEC ministers at Seoul endorsed a work programme on the subject.

Increasingly, however, barriers to trade are measures other than tariffs or non-tariff barriers at the border. Standards and regulatory processes, together with government procurement, are among the targets for new or improved rule-making in the Uruguay Round. Nevertheless, there remains considerable scope for harmonising measures which often originate from objectives held in common, such as health and safety. Removal of such disparities, which has been judged in Europe to offer perhaps the greatest gain from 'Europe 1992', may be more important in the Asia–Pacific region. Considerable mutual gain is likely, therefore, from increased harmonising of industrial standards, product definition, testing, certification and other regulatory procedures among the countries of the region.

The current lack of harmonisation is also important in many service fields such as information transfer and electronics, particularly in the rapidly growing field of electronic data interchange, telecommunications, transport and financial systems, and in facilitating technology transfer. Efforts to address these problems in multilateral forums tend to concentrate on US and EC interests. An Asian input into these 'global' discussions would improve the region's competitive position.

Conclusion

Institutionally APEC is clearly a major region-wide development, and has taken further important steps in what has been termed 'the process of institutionalisation' (Higgott et al. 1991, p. 15). The Seoul meeting was seen as a major step forward in APEC's maturity, and it has already surmounted some significant hurdles including membership of the three Chinas. The pressures for additional membership will offer important challenges but of a different kind. Decisions made on membership will need to fit the logic of Cooper's 'need for cooperation' rather than diplomatic politics, whether US hemispheric politics or Asian or other regional politics. Other challenges will include the handling of the continuing US–Japan trade dispute to ensure that regional interests are considered without the dispute dominating or souring the forum.

Equally critical will be treading the line between staying with the important political issues for the region and getting too involved in the detail of the microeconomic structural cooperation which will be the area of important development in regional cooperation in the future. As a political body, APEC needs to avoid becoming bogged down in bureaucratic detail. Yet the tendency will be to move away from a G-7 mode to that of a ministerial meeting of the OECD. Some such development may be necessary in the longer term, starting with a specialist trade ministers' meeting supplementary to the main APEC meetings after the Uruguay Round. The development of an inter-governmental institutional framework within which economic exchange can take place, however, is a political process. The value of the APEC meetings, therefore, depends substantially upon the continued participation of foreign ministers.

It is difficult to assess precisely the achievements of economic cooperation in the region or, indeed, elsewhere. Certainly ASEAN, PECC and now APEC have facilitated communication; the information and analysis flow among the countries of the region has increased considerably, and transaction costs have been reduced. Economic interlinkages within the region have also grown rapidly, and functional cooperation in various forms has expanded substantially.

No study has been made, however, of the relative contribution of different causal factors. Moreover, early problems of economic, social, cultural and institutional differences have become more ambiguous. Although the shape of cooperative mechanisms will remain substantially influenced by differences in preferences, close cooperation itself builds ties and leads to more homogeneous preferences, as the growth in the region's support for the GATT might suggest.

In the face of the growing internationalisation of economies and the diminished autonomy of national governments over their economic policies, governments have three options. By way of protective measures they can resist the change, a response likely to be self-defeating in the long run; they can adjust totally to those changes; or they can accept the need to adjust but seek to ameliorate the adjustment process as it affects them by international collaboration. The process of adjusting will be less costly and more acceptable to the extent that the negative spillover effects of others' actions are reduced by international consultation about and coordination of policies. Given the increased interlinking of regional economies, these spillover effects will increasingly become more important and lend themselves to international cooperation.

To gain substantial benefits of this kind, however, regional economic cooperation will need to move in the long term beyond a constitutive process to accepting the need for collaborative action involving mutual commitments, for example, on investment protection and ultimately perhaps to some elements of macroeconomic policy. That may be a long way off but change does seem to occur quickly these days. To achieve this among other things, the political impetus that has been so important for APEC so far will need to be maintained.

To understand the development of economic cooperation in the Asia–Pacific region, it is necessary to recognise the influence of historical, social and political factors, and the broader dynamic political as well as economic objectives it has reflected. At the same time, the development of cooperation will continue to reflect the logic of the particular economic-cooperation needs of a rapidly growing and integrating region.

14 Competing Theoretical Approaches to International Cooperation: Implications for the Asia–Pacific

RICHARD HIGGOTT

Introduction

The Asia–Pacific has been the most dynamic region of the global economy over the last two decades (USNCPECC 1991). Not surprisingly, therefore, it is in this region that new trends in the global economy have been visible, and where the inevitable tensions that have accompanied these trends have been most obvious. In this context, the Asia Pacific Economic Co-operation (APEC) initiative represents an interesting attempt at both economic cooperation and conflict management. It is an important example of the constraints and opportunities for closer economic cooperation and coordination of economic policy by regional states.

Consequently, the region also becomes an important context in which to consider recent theorising on international economic cooperation. There has been much scholarly concern about how to promote cooperation in an era of eroding US economic hegemony. Yet these issues have received little consideration in non-western and non-northern hemispheric contexts. This chapter attempts to rectify this omission. It poses some questions about our contemporary *theoretical* understanding of cooperation and its *practical* utility for informing our understanding of the Asia–Pacific region.

The central aim is to move beyond a structural realist/neoliberal institutionalist impasse that besets mainstream theorising about cooperation in the international political economy. At the core of this impasse has been a concern with the primacy *states* place on relative gains in a perceived relative gains/absolute gains stand-off. Consequently, the chapter has five broad and very basic working assumptions:

(i) Management of the global economy is predicated on a recognition that explaining the behaviour of states is not exclusively a structural exercise. Agency—meaning here the behaviour of states—is important. And while the agency of major players might be more important than that of smaller players, the growing pluralist international order offers the opportunity for smaller players to be influential in strategic interactions.

(ii) In order to make assumption (i) the chapter rejects the primacy of relative gains in the relative gains/absolute gains dichotomy.

(iii) Interdependence and globalisation has determined the nature of recent theorising in international relations, and in doing so has complicated the earlier, realist derived definitions of 'national interest' by acknowledging the salience of the economic welfare function in international politics.

(iv) The major structural shifts—the rise of the European Community (EC) and Japan in economic status *vis-à-vis* the United States, the increasing salience of the financial and monetary sectors, and the manner in which they have speeded up the processes of globalisation—require the reordering of institutional goals. Incremental adaptation is not sufficient.

(v) There will always be a discrepancy between the theory and practice of cooperation. None of the discussion in this chapter should be taken to imply a new golden dawn for cooperation in international relations. Yet while it is correct to be sceptical about its prospects, this does not negate the possibility of, and the importance of working for, greater cooperation in the longer term.

The chapter examines the non-structural bases of power in international economic cooperation. In this regard the growing importance of technical, entrepreneurial and learned ethical dimensions of economic cooperation offer a way to refine brute rational actor formulations. There is a growing body of theoretical literature on these issues in international cooperation.[1] Yet there has been little attempt to assess its utility in the development of economic cooperation in the Asia–Pacific.

This makes historical sense. The very notion of a 'Pacific' is contested and has been subject to distortion and exaggeration. While the Pacific is much more than an ocean, it is not a coherent region deserving of the hyperbole associated with the oft-heralded arrival of the Pacific Century. Further, there is no formal framework of cooperative institutions comparable to those developed in Europe over the last 30 years. An Asian Community comparable to the European Community is beyond the purview of discussion here. Notwithstanding such cautionary remarks, institutions do matter in international relations, and this has been well illustrated in the Asia–Pacific in the 1980s and 1990s. Formal cooperation and the level of

---

[1] On technical and entrepreneurial forms of leadership see Young (1989, 1991). On the importance of learning in international cooperation see Haas (1980, 1990) and Crawford (1991).

institutionalisation is low, but this does not correlate with the importance of institutional contact for the development of economic relations in the region. The structure of the chapter is fourfold. Part 1 outlines the realist/ liberal theoretical debate about cooperation-building in international relations. Parts 2 and 3 attempt to move beyond the theoretical impasse between these schools of thought by focusing on the prospect of 'learning' cooperation in international relations, and the distinction between power and leadership. Part 4 considers these theoretical questions in an Asia– Pacific context.

1. The realist/liberal impasse in the theory of international cooperation

Theorising about international economic cooperation has gone through a number of phases in the post-World War II era. In the 1960s, integration theory was given impetus by the establishment of the European Economic Community (EEC) and a variety of short-lived, post-colonial organisations. In the mid-1970s it was pronounced obsolete by one of its founding fathers (Haas 1975). The second half of the 1970s saw the development of interdependence theory (Keohane & Nye 1977). By the latter part of the 1980s the study of 'cooperation under anarchy' had generated a broad synthesis of thought in which cooperation (as the counter-factual of conflict) was recognised as central to the contemporary debate between neo-liberal institutionalist and structural realist theories of international relations.[2]

Two issues are crucial to this debate: (i) the role of institutions, and (ii) the degree to which states will pursue relative gains at the expense of cooperation-induced absolute gains. The inevitable pursuit of relative gains by states, it is suggested in the realist literature, establishes the superiority of a realist assertion of the difficulty of cooperation over the liberal institutionalist belief in the possibility of cooperation via the pursuit of absolute gains. Realist arguments about the greater significance of relative gains over absolute gains assert that international competition—doing better than one's competitors—is more important than improving one's welfare. Consequently, this desire for relative success rather than absolute

---

2 The principal institutionalist texts are Keohane (1984a), and his collected essays (1989). See also Oye (ed.) (1986). Nowhere is the impasse better illustrated than in Joseph Grieco's attempts to undermine the neoliberal formulations of Robert Keohane and other liberal institutionalists (see Grieco 1988, 1990). Grieco is not, of course, the only scholar to suggest that cooperation is inhibited by the search for relative gains. See the exemplar structural-realist text of Kenneth Waltz (1979); but see also Gowa (1986), Lake (1984) and Lipson (1984).

success is held up to be a significant inhibitor of cooperation. While fundamentally a security related observation (Waltz 1959, p. 198; 1979, p. 1015) it is a hypothesis that has been extended to the international economic domain (Grieco 1988, 1990).

On the other hand, neoliberal institutionalists assume that states are indifferent to the gains that others might make so long as they engage in welfare maximisation by that transaction. But this dichotomy is misleading. States, contrary to the working assumptions of structural realism, are not simply unitary rational actors exercising clearly defined preferences. Therefore, the debate between realists and neoliberal institutionalists should not be about the possibility or otherwise of cooperation determined by state preferences, but rather the circumstances and constraints under which cooperation may or may not emerge (Powell 1991).

Relative gains arguments may be analytically robust in a two-person game, and in the context of security where the use of force is at issue. But they are flawed when extended to cooperative processes involving more than two actors, where states are interested in both relative gains and absolute gains, and in which relative losses which accompany absolute gains are not 'turned against the state' (Powell 1991, p. 1320). In these circumstances, as Duncan Snidal recently demonstrated, 'the institutionalist case for cooperation remains strong' (1991, p. 701).

The analytic critique of relative gains arguments is also reinforced by wider empirical observation. For example, even in the General Agreement on Tariffs and Trade (GATT)—the quintessential multi-actor context— and even if we only included the major actors (the United States, the EC, Japan), it is still very difficult to judge their preferred pay-off matrix—and the addition of even a few minor actors changes the scoring process considerably. Yet there are other players in GATT who are not minor—in the sense of having zero influence over outcomes. Either separately, in the case of states such as Canada, Australia, India, Brazil and South Korea, or in coalitions such as the Cairns Group, these smaller players can have considerable influence over the negotiation process. Trade talks are quite simply much more comprehensive and complex than two-party negotiations, and the multilateral system remains the frame of reference even for bilateral trade negotiations (Hamilton & Whalley 1989; Sjöstedt 1991; Cooper & Higgott 1992).

Protagonists of relative gains as an inhibitor of cooperation often present a deficient understanding of 'cooperation under anarchy'. Liberal institutionalist scholars make no assumptions about the inevitability of cooperation. On the contrary, Keohane notes the search for relative gains by states even in the context of cooperation. The 'specter of conflict' may be a spur to cooperation, but problems of compliance and enforcement in international relations under anarchy (the absence of higher forms of government) are *the focus of inquiry* not the starting point of analysis. Institutionalist scholars are keen to understand 'the conditions under which cooperation is *likely* [my emphasis] to occur' (Keohane 1984a, p. 54; Axelrod & Keohane 1986, pp. 226–54).

Greater consideration has to be given to factors other than the search for relative gains. Preoccupation with relative position in international relations clearly disadvantages states failing to maximise their absolute gains. Economic policy-makers in the former Soviet Union and the United States must now rue the Cold War conflict when they look at the way in which the Western Europeans, the Japanese and the Asia–Pacific newly industrialising countries (NICs), have been engaged in maximising their absolute economic wellbeing—increasing their relative position *vis-à-vis* the United States.

The emphasis on relative gains that drives realist theorising about cooperation is also time specific. It pays little attention to longer term considerations. It is not an appropriate form of analysis for understanding cooperation in international economic relations where considerations of long term economic wellbeing can be equally as important as short-term political gains. Further, given that even in negative trade games all a state's eggs are not in the same basket, the prospect of short term sacrifice for longer term gain can be sold to members of a multilateral regime.

Relative gains arguments also ignore another longer term goal—the desire to have good, or at least working, relationships with partners and competitors alike. For example, it is in no one's interests to have the Uruguay Round collapse and the existing instruments of multilateralism further eroded. More importantly, none of the major players would wish to be held responsible for the collapse of the negotiations. Negative reputational outcomes are not without flow-on effects to other areas of the international agenda. Linkage can be implicitly significant, it does not have to be explicitly stated. Concessions from actors—for example, the Europeans in the closing stages of the Uruguay Round—can be had from the fear of a reputation for intransigence and unreasonableness. Thus, while the pursuit of relative gains can be a major consideration in the understanding of the nature of cooperation, it is not incommensurable with attempts to enhance cooperation in a manner outlined by neoliberal institutionalism.

Further, as Stein notes, 'states choose strategies, not outcomes' (1990, p. 16). Thus, both circumstance and choice are important. International relations are neither inevitably conflictual nor destined for smooth cooperation. Yet realist treatments of cooperation and conflict, seen as a duality and driven by a desire for methodological parsimony and robustness, sacrifice complexity and nuance. Understanding the constraints and opportunities in the management of the international economy in the 1990s requires a sensitivity to existing rivalries and to the possibilities of institutional cooperation, which are missed if liberalism and realism are seen as mutually exclusive or competing paradigms.

Most international policy-makers recognise that open liberalism maximises *absolute* global welfare but that by processes of selected defection or cheating it is possible to enhance *relative* national welfare. This is the core of a relative gains argument. By extension it is argued that the desire to secure relative gains overrides state commitments to the support of absolute gains. Yet if it were the case that structure was always determinant, there would be little point in non-hegemonic states attempting to enhance economic cooperation at the international level, or indeed having foreign policies.

Even admitting a role for smaller players in international relations is a recognition of the constructive role of thinking in international relations. In the absence of leadership and insight from the major players, 'delusional will can be efficacious and, therefore, rational' (Stein 1990, p. 209). At the margins of any attempt to secure a given outcome, in this case agreement on the shape of international economic cooperation in a given area, the role of smaller players and 'will' can make an important difference.

The relative gains argument also denies the manner in which the institutionalisation of regimes and the development of collaboration and coordination might encourage nations to recognise the interests of others. It is in this regard that attempts by smaller players to engage in constructive coalition building, the creation of information, trust, transparency and confidence building (as with the Cairns Group in the Uruguay Round and the development of APEC) is an important exercise in learning and support for institutionalisation of cooperation. Realism may, in some circumstances, generate cooperation more effectively than liberalism. Realist 'defensive positionalism' is not axiomatically at odds with regime-building. Indeed, an interest based theory of regime formation would expect states, if the return were sufficient, to forgo autonomous decision-making for collaborative decision-making (Stein 1990, p. 45). It is in this context that institutions, and the ability to guarantee trust and transparency, become important.

Further, the realist emphasis on the primacy of relative gains does not take seriously the potential effect of institutional change over time—or at least not in the way that Keohane would exhort us to do (Keohane 1989, p. 14). But an assumption of this chapter, explicated in the next section, is that 'actor learning' in international cooperation is possible. To give but one more example from the current Uruguay Round of multilateral trade negotiations, the very existence of the Cairns Group in the Uruguay Round, let alone its behaviour, represents a quantum leap in learning by smaller players from the Tokyo Round.

While the group would appear to have largely accepted the practices set by the GATT, it has not chosen to accept all the managerial baggage that has accompanied the GATT's existence under US hegemonic leadership. While recognising the role of the United States (and to a lesser extent the EC) as the major players in the international trading regime, without whom meaningful agreement cannot be achieved, the group has actively engaged in the reformulation of the regime's practices in what I would like to call a *non-hegemonic* manner (see Higgott 1991a, pp. 115–25). In similar vein a move from the multilateral arena to the Asia–Pacific region also shows the degree to which understanding the limits and prospects for cooperation must take account not only of existing rivalries but also the prospects for learning cooperation, and in particular the recognition of gains to be derived from *joint* maximising as opposed to *self* maximising activities.

This is not dewy-eyed idealism but rational, egoistic activity in which cooperation is engendered by the spectre of conflict and 'the shadow of the future' (Axelrod & Keohane 1986, pp. 232–4). International trade relations in the Asia–Pacific are not driven by narcissistic concerns with who did best. More dynamic processes are at work. Relative gains do affect the pattern of cooperation but they do not represent a debilitating critique of liberal theories of cooperation. The realist/liberal dichotomy in the study of cooperation needs to be transcended. In the two sections that follow I attempt to sketch several areas of inquiry which can reinforce the liberal institutionalist theory of cooperation against its realist detractors.

2. Progress and learning in international cooperation

Evidence from the post-World War II era suggests that habits of cooperation can be learned. This is not to overstate the speed or even breadth of this process—nor to suggest that reversals are not possible—but to point to its significance over time. Inherent in this analysis is a positive conception of 'progress' in international relations (see Adler et al. 1991).[3] Interdependence requires a heightened learning function in international relations if the pursuit of self-interest is not to mitigate cooperative behaviour. Interdependence requires, and at the same time provides the opportunity for, the learning of shared values amongst international policy-making élites.

Notwithstanding defections, the post-World War II period has seen a variety of norms universalised, at the rhetorical level at least, and largely embedded in various regimes. If the cooperative endeavour is to continue to develop in the 1990s, the consolidation of shared meaning must also continue apace.

There is always going to be the problem of the asymmetries of power in the international system. But interdependence may have a mitigating effect on the abuse of power by major actors. This may be achieved in a number of ways, such as by the moral and reputational concerns of the most powerful, and through the calculation of constraints inherent in interdependence. The logic of cooperation in an era of interdependence is

---

[3] There is a substantial body of literature in international relations on the question of learning, especially associated with the work of Haas (1990).

underwritten by a recognition that, in the words of Crawford (1991, p. 449):

> ...states can no longer 'help' themselves in important areas of public policy—areas ranging from the choice of macroeconomic instruments to environmental policy. Unilateral policies are no longer as useful as they might have been, even for powerful states. Interests are increasingly 'shared' and common goals are hammered out in multilateral fora.

Or so the theory goes. But other explanations are important. Ideas and knowledge in international economic thought, and the role of socialisation in the development of nascent intellectual and policy-making élites are also important.[4] To give but one example, the first generation of post-World War II policy-making élites in the Asia–Pacific derived their ideas about the international economy from the socialisation experiences largely determined in the United States. Today, notwithstanding the 'triumph of neoclassical economics in the developing world' (Biersteker 1992), the Asia–Pacific regional economy does not resonate with these ideas in a pure form. Contemporary ideas about growth, development and competition are much more influenced by the 'success' of Japan and the other Northeast Asian NICs (see *inter alia* Deyo (ed.) 1987; Gourevitch (ed.) 1989; Haggard & Moon (eds) 1989; Haggard 1990; Wade 1990). The dominant ideas-system may be recognised as 'capitalist', but the practice and implementation of economic policy indicates the degree to which Asia–Pacific models are considerably different from archetypical free enterprise conceptions of production and exchange.

There is no sufficiently defined, trans-Pacific intellectual and policy network that might be called an epistemic community.[5] There would appear, however, to be an emerging group conscious of a shared, consensual understanding of the need for economic cooperation in the region. The point is not to overstate the case, but rather to examine the reasons for the developing commitment to regime building, in a variety of different guises among a core group of tripartite (government, business, academic) actors bent on fostering greater dialogue, policy coordination and cooperation through a variety of more or less successful institutional vehicles, notably the Pacific Economic Cooperation Conference (PECC), the Pacific Basin Economic Council (PBEC) and a variety of lesser organisations with membership ranging region wide.[6]

---

[4] The importance of socialisation in international relations is recognised across the intellectual-cum-ideological spectrum. See for example the Gramscian work of Gill (1990a and b), and the more orthodox views of Ikenberry and Kupchan (1990).

[5] Interest in epistemic communities is in its infancy (see Haas (ed.) 1992).

[6] Very little of an empirical nature has been written on the Asia–Pacific economic networks to date. For some exploratory insights see Woods (1991a and b).

It is difficult to know yet whether the research on epistemic communities represents simply another fad in international relations or whether their identification represents an important analytical insight in understanding the prospects for greater policy coordination in the 1990s. Members of epistemic communities (scholars, diplomats, scientific and technical specialists in international organisations, relevant members of the international corporate sector having a commonality of professional interests, experiences and practices shared internationally) are a potentially very strong force for cooperation. On the basis of their shared consensual knowledge they can seek, in a transnational manner, to influence policy-makers. However, their success is dependent on the ability to resist alternative claims to expertise and alternative forms of knowledge— which of itself can represent a form of intellectual closure.

Haas has shown how a shared understanding of a given task by an epistemic community can have considerable influence on the development of government policy towards international economic cooperation and regime building (Haas 1989). This is a two-way process. Influence is from regime to governing élite and vice versa. Haas' formulation is located in the context of international environmental change. It does seem, however, that some of the questions he asks about the development of common state policies towards the questions of international cooperation and policy coordination would be worthy of consideration in the context of international economic cooperation at the regional level in the Asia–Pacific.

Again, I do not wish to overstate the case, rather to suggest that transnational policy élites represent a set of actors in the development of international cooperation that should not be ignored. In the international trade regime or in APEC, they operate with a common set of understandings of a free-trade driven consensual knowledge. A problem is that members of epistemic communities tend to be 'true believers', and as such they are often oblivious to some of the contrasting positions that exist to their own. Specifically, there is little comprehension of the manner in which the doctrine of free trade might be challenged. In GATT, or in APEC, the desire of the true believers is simply to extend the 'free-trade' doctrine to new issue areas such as services and intellectual property without a recognition of the difficulties that such extension implies. A failure to recognise that their given truth is not a universal, but rather a community-accepted truth, leads them to misunderstand the degree to which they themselves contribute to misunderstanding and conflict. 'Fair trade' and 'free trade' are not synonymous, and for many the former has become more important than the latter in an era of increasing economic nationalism.

The role of 'new knowledge' in international cooperation is extremely important. Accepted wisdoms change over time. Nowhere can this be better seen than in the current Uruguay Round of trade negotiations where perhaps one of the major international agenda items of the 1990s— the environment and its relationship to international trade—has not been part of the Round agenda. Similarly, the role of extra actors and the emergence of new actors can also have an important effect on the cooperation process. New participants in the agenda setting roles of regimes can be important factors for change in the nature of power and leadership.

3. Power, leadership, regimes and cooperation

Much of the discussion about the nature of international economic cooperation in the international order in general, and the Asia–Pacific in particular, focuses on the questions of power and leadership. The dominant form of analysis has emphasised the importance of a hegemon to provide the public good of order. In a period of declining US leadership, attention has turned to the question of securing 'cooperation after hegemony' via the quest for alternative sources of leadership in the international political economy. Hegemonic stability theory is properly open to a range of criticisms (see Snidal 1985; Grunberg 1990; Rapkin (ed.) 1990). Principal among them is that it over-emphasises structurally determined understandings of cooperation and change in the Asia–Pacific. Such an analysis allows little or no room for the political voluntarism and influence of agents in an agent/structure relationship (Wendt 1987).

The literature to date sees no alternative to US leadership. The Japanese, it is claimed, practise a reactive foreign economic policy and fail to provide the intellectual and practical leadership that their structural power dictates they should use in the international economy (Nau (ed.) 1989; Calder 1988). In the absence of new arrangements for a post-hegemonic era, such as a *Pax Nipponica, Bigemony*, or a *Pax Consortis*, the United States—in the words of Joseph Nye's (1990b) populist work in the 'renewalist' genre of US foreign policy literature—is *Bound to Lead*. Not only is this a misreading of the issues of leadership and 'followership' in recent US policy overall (see Cooper et al. 1991), it is also an inadequate reflection of the recent history of economic cooperation in the Asia–Pacific.

Neoliberal institutionalist cooperation, in the absence of hegemony, might be difficult but it is surely not impossible. To find it, especially in the Asia–Pacific, it is necessary to look to alternative forms of leadership and the provision of innovative coalition building and agenda setting on the part of other regional state and non-state actors. In the absence of structural leadership from the major regional actor (Japan) and extra-regional actors (such as the United States), smaller power initiative and statecraft have an importance not commonly understood in European and North American analyses of the region. At the risk of stating the obvious, power is important, but it is not all: process matters, technical and entrepreneurial skills matter, commitment matters, vision matters, optimism matters. These assets are not just the preserve of the larger players.

A theory of power and leadership that is structurally driven is too determinist. It leaves little room for policy intervention derived from technical innovation, political creativity and choice. While power-derived leadership in general, and United States structural power in particular, will continue to remain central, other sources of power and leadership will play a greater role in promoting cooperation in the international political economy in the foreseeable future. Lest this argument be misunderstood, post-World War II changes in the United States' relational power *vis-à-vis* the other major players is not seen as having been accompanied by a commensurate decline in its structural power, although its influence is more complex and diffuse in the 1980s and 1990s than it was in the heyday of the so-called Liberal International Economic Order. Rather, the 1980s have been something of an 'interregnum' in which an old order is passing away, but in which a new one has yet to be defined.

Second, it is not suggested that good intentions of smaller players are sufficient to guarantee enhanced cooperation. Political, economic and intellectual influences emanating from other centres of power, especially in Europe and Japan, will evidently have a mitigating influence on the role of the United States, and—as much of the literature on Japanese political influence implies—can be expected to strengthen. Less evident, however, is the assumption that smaller states, individually or collectively, may be sources of leadership and innovation. Constraint and opportunity in the international political economy of the 1990s may not be as politically voluntarist as some scholars of the avowedly neoclassical persuasion might have us believe, but neither will it be as determinist as those of the more structuralist persuasion would suggest.

Awaiting the return of US leadership in the global economic order is not an optimum strategy. Indeed, attempts to secure a return to what was, after all, an idealised state may well inhibit other approaches to problem-solving, coordination and cooperation in the global economic order. While the economic strength of the United States, Japan and the EC may lead to mutual restraint that would minimise the prospect of all-out trade wars in the 1990s, it does not preclude these actors, as recent history tells us, from engaging in bouts of supposedly cooperation inducing, tit-for-tat retaliatory trade strategies that have adverse effects on third parties to these conflicts.

The rules of a post-hegemonic, multi-polar system of economic management are yet to be established. While structural constraints such as size, power and geostrategic location will obviously condition the nature and scope of the role that smaller states may play in the process, the way is open for innovation and initiative in a time that is long on problems and short on solutions. Indeed, the very notion of leadership should be treated in the 1990s in a much wider sense than in the past. As with the concept of hegemonic stability, leadership and other historically located concepts do not emerge from the pure world of ideas but from a combination of the 'mythical', the philosophical and the political (Grunberg 1990). To hang on to such concepts in their presently unrefined forms as key elements in any renewed process of management for the global economy for the 1990s would be inadvisable indeed.

Thus, a principal characteristic of the practice of international economic relations in the 1990s will be the emergence of a more complex understanding of what we might mean by the term 'leadership'. This will have to take on innovative forms. In addition to structural leadership, two other categories—technical and entrepreneurial—might be identified. In the analysis of regime formation, for example, leadership is not simply a function of hegemony. It also requires '…a combination of imagination in inventing institutional options and skill in brokering the interests of numerous actors to line up support for such options' (Young 1989, p. 355). Leadership in the international system under hegemony was conceived of in fairly singular terms. Its strength was primarily of a structural nature, in which power was used to diminish collective action problems inhibiting agreement on the essentials of multilateral agreement. It is this type of leadership that the United States used to establish the post-World War II Bretton Woods and GATT systems.

At the very least, the problematic of regime formation that prevailed under hegemony needs to be reformulated to take account of the changing configurations of power in the 1990s. Some of the more robust realist assertions about the contemporary international trade regime can only be sustained in the most specifically defined contexts. North American discussions of regime theory often ignore the problems of representation for smaller players in any process of regime formation—at both the level of recognition and acceptance. Regime theory is invariably underwritten by assumptions of both benevolence and voluntarism. For smaller participants, these assumptions can, *and at times may*, hold good. That they will, under all circumstances, hold good should not be assumed. Even the most liberal of regime theory can be '…a form of special pleading by and for the powerful and the satisfied' (Keeley 1990, p. 94).

While regime theory recognises the asymmetrical nature of power between individual members, it has, nonetheless, tended to take the asymmetries for granted in assuming how and where leadership in regime change will come about. Further, regime theory assumes that membership in a given regime is 'voluntary' and thus smaller players—by their accession—are granting consent to its principles, norms and rules. The 1990s should assume no such consent. Rather, we should analyse the degree to which major actor preferences are accepted by, or forced upon, smaller players, and the manner in which smaller players might respond.

The important general point to note is that choice in regime theory is not simply between hegemon driven regimes on the one hand, or the abandonment of 'community' to the mercies of realism in international relations on the other. There is an alternative—indeed, there may be several—that emanate from competing perspectives, ideas and contests. To the extent that smaller players occupy a significant role in this process, then they represent important modifications to a realist explanation of cooperation in international trade reform. Regime formation in the 1990s is about more than leadership and followership, it is about voluntary and positive participation.

For example, the *existence* and *activity* of the Cairns Group as a coalition of small states exercising a degree of influence in a round of GATT negotiations is historically unprecedented (see Higgott & Cooper 1990; Cooper & Higgott 1992). Yet the group has been engaged in an exercise in leadership that has accentuated intellectual and entrepreneurial, as opposed to structural, attributes. A knowledge of the group's activity, that cannot be detailed here, does not suggest that it is uninterested in the use of leverage and reciprocity—the traditional stuff of GATT negotiations and economic cooperation in general—that aggregate market position might give it. Bargaining (power and skill) and reciprocity are still at the heart of all trade negotiations. Rather, the group recognises that other avenues of persuasion may prove more fruitful and traditional avenues of brute strength disadvantageous. In short, the activities of the group represent a classic case of strategic interaction in international relations where, as Stein notes:

> Systemic forces structure but do not necessarily determine national choices. They delineate the context in which states interact. They may shape the options and payoffs that states confront. Yet states transform those payoffs into utilities using different decision criteria. The international system sets a framework for interaction but only rarely dictates specific strategies in specific circumstances (Stein 1990, p. 184).

In a period of enhanced systemic indeterminacy, the strategic intervention of smaller players can prove crucial in a way that might not have been the case in the past when the international system was more firmly defined by Cold War factors and the dominant role of one state in the international economy. In the changed environment of the 1990s, leadership should not be seen as the traditional leadership/followership variety that became the norm under hegemony.

Structural leadership from the major actors has to be nurtured and induced by technical and entrepreneurial leadership from other quarters. This is not to imply that major players can be forced to be multilateral in their policies and behaviour if they chose to be otherwise. Rather, it is to suggest that inducements can be two way. Technical, educational, moral and entrepreneurial arguments emanating from third parties can make a difference. What has often been understood by smaller players is now better understood in some of the less structurally determined analyses coming out of the United States. For example, as David Abshire recently noted, as US relative power declines, 'persuasion, coalition-building, and the art of the indirect approach becomes increasingly important' (Abshire 1990, p. 175).

The analysis offered here does not ignore power. Power helps explain state preferences, but other factors count too. At the very least, the behaviour of the Cairns Group in the Uruguay Round offers an illustration of changing appreciations of US leadership in the 1990s. As a coalition of smaller states—with a vested interest in regime change but not prepared to accept their assigned role as free-riders awaiting the hegemon-driven provision of whatever public good might be at stake in a given circumstance —the group has attempted to set and steer the reform agenda in a given area of the negotiations (agriculture). It thus illustrates the development of non-hegemonic approaches to cooperation possible within a neo-liberal formulation. The arguments developed here and in the preceding sections can be extended to inform our understanding of some of the cooperative endeavour at work in the Asia–Pacific region.

4. Economic institution building in the Asia–Pacific

Narrative accounts of the evolution of APEC now abound in the secondary literature and it is not intended that they be reiterated here.[7] Rather, I will suggest that the process of institutionalisation in train in the region represents, for all its limitations, a conceptual framework for cooperation in a post-hegemonic era that differs from many of the conventional assumptions concerning regime creation and regime maintenance outlined and questioned above.

In his threefold definition of institutions, Keohane (1989, p. 4) urges us not to limit our understanding just to formal organisations and regimes, but also to remember the importance of conventions. While they do not specify rules of behaviour, conventions provide the essence of understanding and form the basis of a shared recognition of the utility of cooperation. We may not be able to talk about the existence of explicit rules— the hallmark of a regime—in APEC. It is possible, however, to see the evolution of a process of understanding and, much more central to the APEC agenda (in its work programme for example), a considerable interest in usable information about the individual preferences, policies and performances of APEC members. If, as Keohane argues, 'one of the major functions of institutions is to retain and transmit information' (1989, p. 12), then APEC is engaged in the early stages of institution building for cooperation. The absence of readily digestible, quality information, especially concerning the domestic economic policies and strategies of regional states is a source of uncertainty and misunderstanding in the region, a potential source of future aggravation, and importantly, one that is not beyond resolution. If the commitments expressed at the inaugural

---

7 See *inter alia*, Crawford and Seow (eds) (1981), Soesastro and Han (eds) (1983), Drysdale (1988, 1991), Higgott et al. (1990), Elek (1991), and Woolcott (1991).

and subsequent APEC meetings, and the nature of the work programmes introduced at the Senior Officials Meetings (SOM) have any meaning, then the provision of better information will be an important first on the road to greater regional cooperation.

We also need to distinguish between information and understanding. Both, following Keohane's analogy with banking, are important. Just as 'lenders need to know the moral as well as the financial character of borrowers...governments contemplating international cooperation need to *know* their partners, not merely know *about* their partners' (1989, p. 119). Nowhere is this more important than in such a culturally heterogeneous group as is constituted by the current APEC membership. It is also significant for an understanding of the nature of leadership in the Asia–Pacific.

Policy coordination is dependent on information and expectations. The evolving role of PECC throughout the 1980s—especially with its tripartite structure—and the forward looking outcomes of the APEC I–III meetings, are both concerned with the provision of information and the generation, at a minimum, of consistency of regional expectations and, at best, a growing adherence to common regional goals.

The creation of a better regional information base and greater general understanding is a long way from the achievement of transparency—the 'core requirement' of a regime (Kratochwil & Ruggie 1986). It is, however, an essential step in the process of institutionalisation. It is also a step that, in the Asia–Pacific regional context, has taken a lot of energy, initiative and informal diplomacy. PECC, for example, has invested considerable time and intellectual capital in the nurturing of this process. This behaviour, at both an institutional and an individual level, is illustrative of that kind of non-structural leadership identified in the work of Oran Young in earlier sections of this chapter.

Practices are also an important part of the process of cooperation building. Both at the level of first tier multilateral economic diplomacy (APEC), and at the level of what we might call second tier diplomacy through PECC, the states of the region have laid the foundation for continued interchange throughout the 1990s. These notions of second tier or informal diplomacy are an important weapon in the armoury of the technically advanced foreign policy bureaucracies of middle powers committed to cooperation.

Both APEC and PECC provide the opportunity to nurture, rather than induce, closer cooperation building—thus, we may talk of a gradual institutionalisation taking place in the Asia–Pacific region. Yet beyond that we should not, at this stage, proceed. The work programmes of APEC[8] have made slow, albeit unspectacular, progress. Institutionalisation—meaning

---

8   There are, at present, ten regional projects concerning the review of trade and investment data, trade promotion, expansion of investment, technology transfer within the region, human resources development, regional energy cooperation, telecommunications, fisheries, greater transport efficiency and tourism.

the creation of a bureaucracy or a permanent headquarters for APEC—is now an important agenda item in the wake of APEC III in Seoul in November 1991, but the shape and rate of evolution of this bureaucracy is still indeterminate.

Economic summitry is likely to continue as the principal form of institutional arrangement over the short to medium term with the designated host of an APEC meeting taking on the bulk of the responsibilities for that meeting. Acting as a 'shepherd', the host makes all the necessary arrangements and directs consultations on the agenda-setting process. This type of informal approach leaves scope for research and administrative input from organisations such as PECC, PBEC and ASEAN, while at the same time providing a framework within which even the smallest of members may feel that they can have an input into the organisation. Importantly, and recognising that institutional form is a very political and country-specific agenda item, the current approach avoids the issue of formalising the structure of the organisation prior to the emergence of a greater identification of, and consensus on, its role.

The question of future institutional structure is thus very much contingent on successful, appropriate and acceptable leadership in the region in the 1990s. Leadership of a structural nature over the last few years has been spectacularly absent. The United States has not provided the sort of leadership in the Asia–Pacific region of which its structural power would dictate it is capable. Similarly, Japan, despite its dramatic increases in structural power, has not moved to exert the kind of leadership of which its potential would dictate it too is capable. In such circumstances, other forms of leadership of the type discussed in the previous section have played a more significant role. As bystanders to bilateral conflicts, which have grown between the major actors at a rate faster than the system's ability to manage them, smaller players are sensitised to the damaging effect of such conflicts on global welfare overall. Indeed, smaller players are probably more sensitised to such conflicts than the chief parties to actual conflicts themselves, who are concerned principally with their relative positions *vis-à-vis* the other major actors and inured to the effects of their behaviour on third parties. Indeed, one of the chief spurs to the development of APEC among most of the smaller players of the region was to provide a forum in which they might be able to play a mitigating role in the tense relationship between the United States and Japan.

As other chapters of this volume make clear, the role of Japan in the region in the 1990s, and especially the manner in which it manages its relationship with the United States is crucial. Notwithstanding evidence to the contrary, the prevailing belief in the United States is that Japan (along with the EC) is the source of many, if not most, of America's problems. One does not have to give Japan a clean bill of health in its trade policies to see the overreaction in the US position. Again, third parties are invariably a better judge of these conflicts than the specific parties. But the bilateral US–Japan conflict is a major cause of concern for all in the

Asia–Pacific region. It is also, in addition to the residual mistrust left over from World War II, the major constraint on Japan playing a greater role in cooperation building in the region.

Also, and perhaps surprisingly given the aggressive nature of American policy towards it over the last few years, Japan is still hesitant to champion initiatives in the international economic order in advance of a clearly identified US position—although this reticence is becoming less marked. In addition, for many of the smaller players of the Asia–Pacific region, Japan is presently perceived as less of a threat to an open international system than the United States. Even accepting such an interpretation, Japan is still constrained in the kind of leadership role that it might make, in the Pacific in particular or in the international economic order in general.

In the absence of leadership from what we might call more 'traditional' sources, the quality of both the decision-making and the implementation process can be as important as the more structurally determined assets at a state's disposal in shaping policy outcomes. Thus, the activities of APEC contribute to a growing body of evidence of a more complex conception of leadership appropriate for the changing global political and economic environment of the 1990s. In capsule form, four other points about cooperation and the Asia–Pacific region are worthy of note:

(i) Recent developments give little succour to the relative gains arguments discussed earlier. The APEC initiative—although not without individual and group sensitivies, rivalries and even hostilities—has not faltered for reasons that might approximate relative gains arguments. Those states undergoing continued rapid economic growth (for example, Japan and Korea) are too concerned to see this process continue for their own domestic economic and political reasons to worry about any relative success of their competitors. Those states that have stagnated for the last few years (for example, Australia) or which are at lower levels of development (for example, Thailand and Malaysia) are simply keen to participate in fuller fashion in the process of Asia–Pacific economic growth. Perhaps only the United States—in its relationship with Japan—has a relative gains agenda, but even this is part of a mixed motive game.

(ii) It was suggested in Part 2 that research into epistemic communities might be of some use in our understanding of the evolution of cooperation in the Asia–Pacific area. If that is to be the case then the principal vehicle for furthering cooperative ideas—albeit of a quite specific kind—is the Pacific Economic Cooperation Conference. Since its inception, PECC has taken on some of the characteristics of an Organisation for Economic Cooperation and Development (OECD) type of organisation. It has, for example, begun to publish *Pacific Economic Outlook*, not dissimilar to the OECD *Outlook*. It has, however, shunned centralised bureaucratic evolution of the OECD variety and does not have the capacity for the kind of multilateral surveillance that is central to the OECD role. This decision reflects less a weakness on the part of PECC, when contrasted with the

OECD, than a recognition that a trans-Atlantic type of organisation—appropriate for industrialised countries with different decision-making processes and preoccupied, until recently, with the macroeconomic coordination of similarly developed economies—is less appropriate to current Asia–Pacific experience.

The degree of structural differentiation found among the decision-making and opinion forming élites of most OECD members is not replicated at a region wide level in the Asia–Pacific. Even Australia, which most approximates to what we might call a Weberian rationalist pattern of authority and decision-making relationships, has distinctly blurred lines of membership of the decision-making and opinion forming bodies on Asia–Pacific issues. As Stuart Harris (1989, p. 18) noted:

> the relatively clear line that separates government, the private sector and, indeed the academic world in the West is not evident in the region. Government systems here operate differently. Moreover, the reality of economic cooperation is that the business sectors and not governments can supply much of the knowledge needed for analysing economic issues. The tripartite character of PECC—with government, business and academic involvement—worries some who dislike moving from known patterns and models. Those associated with it see it, however, to be an important institutional innovation meeting the special characteristics of the region—and perhaps the times.

A reading of the membership lists of the national PECC committees around the region confirms the type of representation to which Harris alludes. Importantly for the observer of international cooperation, the building of trans-regional networks and linkages is proceeding apace in the Asia–Pacific region and has been given considerable impetus by PECC and other bodies in the 1980s. Further, among enthusiasts of closer economic cooperation, there is considerable antipathy to the initiative being captured by a single international bureaucracy, or the individual bureaucracies of the member states. Such a move, it is argued, may well lead to rigidity and defensive policy-making rather than transparency and flexibility offered by a leaner organisation (Drysdale 1989, p. 19).

(iii) A further significance of APEC is that it demonstrates the capacity for learning in international cooperation. While it is not the aim of this chapter to provide a discussion of Australian foreign economic diplomacy, it should be briefly noted that one of the principal characteristics of the evolution of APEC has been the use of skilful, careful and technical diplomacy, much of which was copied from the activities and perceived success of the Cairns Group in the early stages of the Uruguay Round. Particularly important has been the continuing importance of middle power diplomacy—especially the ability to act as catalyst, facilitator and manager of a given initiative—in international relations (see Cooper & Higgott 1991; Higgott 1991b).

Yet, while states of the region may be engaged in a variety of processes of learning how to cooperate more closely, all the signals to date are that this is *tactical learning* in which the *behaviour* of regional states—in their gradual receptivity to greater economic cooperation in the face of new circumstances—may have changed. There is no real evidence, however, that changes in behaviour have called forth, or been accompanied by, fundamental *value change*. To the extent that we can know these things at a given point in time, regional values and aims—or more specifically the values of the individual regional states towards questions of economic autonomy, sovereignty and economic policy-making—seem to remain largely unaltered. Tactical learning, of its own accord, may not be sufficient for further institution-building in the Asia–Pacific region.

For fundamental transitions in cooperative economic development to occur—of the kind witnessed in Western Europe—the process of tactical learning needs to evolve into what is now referred to as *complex learning*—in which *beliefs* about the way to reach goals also change. In the recent literature on learning, complex learning represents an important jump from the tactical pursuit of policies—as means to ends—to a 'more effective and efficient alignment of ends and means' (Etheridge 1985, p. 143). Complex learning is qualitatively different from tactical learning to the extent that it represents a process of 'cognitive re-evaluation' (Breslauer 1991, p. 688).

To date, initiatives and discussions of closer economic cooperation in the Asia–Pacific region are largely couched in terms of tactical rather than complex learning—they are pursuing behavioural responses, not cognitive ones, to changing circumstance. Even in those quarters most strongly supportive of the APEC initiative—such as the inner reaches of the Asia–Pacific economic policy network in Australia—suggestions for policy options for the region only represent a move up the curve of tactical learning. Cases in point are to be found in the recent Australian proposed suggestions for the development of regular Heads of State meetings, or the exhortations to improve regional market access, reduce physical bottlenecks and increase harmonisation of domestic legislation and rules (see Elek 1992). While all are sensible initiatives they do not, indeed cannot, address the major problems of a structural nature—especially in the relationship between the US and Japan—which, for the time being at least, and as Johnson and Ravenhill have shown us in their contributions to this volume, seem to fall into the 'too hard box'.

Notwithstanding aspirations in some quarters, there is little likelihood at this stage that APEC has sufficient institutional strength to mitigate tension in the economic war of words across the Pacific between the United States and Japan. It is still premature to suggest that APEC might provide 'a convenient regional framework within which Japan can move towards a position of shared policy leadership with the United States' (Drysdale 1991, p. 6). More generally, it is difficult to see the recent attempts at cooperation in the Asia–Pacific representing an exercise in complex as opposed to tactical learning.

In summary then, while the possibility of newer forms of grouping and cooperation cannot be ruled out, to date all the signals are that the development of APEC represents an exercise in tactical learning, in which the behaviour of regional states—in their gradual receptivity to greater economic cooperation in the face of new circumstances—has changed, but where their values, beliefs and aims have remained largely unaltered. This of its own accord may not be sufficient for further institution building in the Asia–Pacific region. For that to occur, the process of tactical learning needs to evolve into complex learning

(iv) The final significance of APEC is that it has attempted to build confidence in the region. As such, the activities of the group are an important contribution to an as yet underdeveloped avenue of investigation in international political economy—the creation of *confidence-building measures* in the resolution of international economic conflict. I use the term here not to mean reform *per se*—be it in arms reductions or market liberalisation. Rather (borrowing from the study of international security), I mean the regulation of the negotiating environment designed to improve communication, understanding and provide reassurance about the intentions of the participants to the negotiations in such a way as to reduce the prospect of conflict. As such, confidence-building measures are intended to generate predictability and monitor deviations from the norm in state behaviour (see Byers et al. 1987). A major problem in the region has stemmed precisely from the lack of confidence of states in the intentions of their partners on the one hand, and their own abilities to compete successfully in the absence of protectionist support mechanisms on the other.

Yet even if formal cooperation and the level of institutionalisation in the Asia–Pacific region are still low there is no necessary correlation between the degree of institutionalisation and its importance. Highly developed formal institutions—such as the UN in the first part of the 1980s—can be of little real importance, while nascent institutions can become more important at a rate faster than their institutional growth would suggest. Depending on how we define institutions, this hypothesis is not beyond the imagination in the Asia–Pacific context in the 1990s. At the very least, it is time that we started thinking about the Asia–Pacific region in the context of institutional analysis, and as a serious object of study for students of cooperation in the 1990s.

Conclusion

It has been a central proposition of this chapter that understanding cooperation in the Asia–Pacific region requires us to move beyond the realist/neoliberal discourse and look at the changing balance in the relationship between states, power and coalitions of interests in contemporary international economic relations. Structure is important, power is important, but so too is process. States might *hope* and *work* for outcomes, but they *choose* strategies in international economic relations. The recent history of international economic cooperation in the Asia–Pacific demonstrates that state policy-makers are acutely aware of the fuzzy nature of circumstance and choice and the growing importance of statecraft.

At the theoretical level, the development and institutionalisation of regimes and the decision to cooperate are determined by actions that are supposed to maximise both relative and absolute gains. But, regardless of the self-maximising urges of actors in international economic relations, it has been suggested, that 'pro-social behaviour' can be learned. That states may want to guard against relative losses *vis-à-vis* competitors, does not mean they are disinterested in cooperation, or that they are unable to cooperate.

At a practical level, pessimistic analysts of the international economy highlight a declining commitment to multilateralism in the global economy and a shift towards hardening regional trade blocs. Optimists stress the virtues of globalisation and the economic potential of the Pacific region. The argument represents the age old dispute between the optimistic and the pessimistic drunk—the former sees the bottle as half full, the latter sees it as half empty. The conclusions to this chapter are not dissimilar. They represent two cheers—or maybe one and a half cheers—for cooperation. Ingenuity in human affairs gave us the notion of collective goods. As Stein notes: 'The history of international trade agreements illuminates the human creation (or social construction) of collective goods' (Stein 1990, p. 208). Time has seen substantial mitigation of the initial private and/or mercantilist and aggressive nature of international trade, and a growing commitment—in theory if not always in practice—to liberal trade as a public good.

Pivotal in the advancement of this public good has been the GATT—with its instruments and codes. Even in a period when the GATT is in poor odour we must not lose sight of these longer term perspectives. GATT rounds may be long, tedious and painstaking exercises, but an historical interpretation sees them as part of the working out of inexorable tensions between conflict and cooperation in international economic relations. Similarly, and notwithstanding the historical, cultural, economic and, in some cases, ideological disparities that remain a major feature of the regional landscape, the question of greater economic cooperation will be an increasingly important item on the policy agenda in the Asia–Pacific region in the years to come. Scholars of the cooperative enterprise must locate recent developments in historical and theoretical contexts. Thus APEC is historically important in the context of the development of the Asia–Pacific region, and theoretically interesting in that it offers theoretical support to neoliberal institutional analysis.

This is not just an uncritical reading of either APEC or liberal institutionalism. APEC is clearly the product of a particular stage in the evolution of a post-hegemonic international economic environment. Similarly, liberal institutionalism is located on the one part of the spectrum of theoretical analysis dealing with the question of cooperation. Neoliberalism is what one of its most adroit critics, Robert Cox, would call 'problem solving' rather than 'critical' theory. It is also positivist and rational-deductive in epistemology. Does this, however, mean Cox is correct in his assertion that liberal institutionalist analysis takes 'the existing order as given, as something to be made to work more smoothly, not as something to be criticised or changed' (Cox 1991, p. 26; see also Cox 1986)? In many instances Cox is correct. But it is not axiomatic that neoliberal institutionalism is status quo-oriented and, indeed, such an assertion is as North American centric as the approaches Cox has done so much to criticise on these same grounds. Liberal institutionalism can be static and reinforcing of existing orders, but when addressed without the baggage of hegemony it can also be a force for change.

As this chapter suggests, there is life for regime theory after hegemony. Relative power (whether of the United States or other actors) is not the only factor to consider in an analysis of the prospects for cooperation. Systemic explanations of how governments respond to trade and investment flows must depend not only on structure—the distribution of power— but also on process. While such a form of analysis may lack the parsimony of neorealism, it offers a more satisfactory explanation of state behaviour for the scholar, along with more useful advice to the practitioner.

The 1990s needs substantial innovation in the techniques of cooperative problem-solving. Intensive consultative processes entailing the exchange of information and the creation of transparency, burden sharing and shared principles of problem-solving need to be enshrined in a more issue specific context. To the extent that Asia Pacific Economic Cooperation, limitations notwithstanding, exhibits such characteristics, it represents an innovative model for the 1990s offering some chance to move beyond the adversarial approaches epitomised by most game theoretic approaches to cooperation.

Problem-solving approaches are, of course, not without their own problems. Lengthy consultations amongst the technical experts, diplomats, bureaucrats and academics from would-be epistemic communities dealing with a specific issue of their competence—and underwritten by their own values and subjectivities—often lack the political will and clout behind them to make necessary breakthroughs. All such processes will ultimately need the decision-taking abilities of senior political figures. But any such approaches still require a mechanism for negotiation. Surely much more so than at any time in the post-Cold War era, the prospects of a minimising of differences between competing system values offers at least the potential for cooperative endeavours. It would seem bizarre that, at a time when we are able to make considerable headway in the process of arms control and arms reductions, we become log jammed on generating cooperation and minimising conflict in the international economy.

15 The Pacific Economic Future: Towards Conventions of Moderation?

RICHARD HIGGOTT, RICHARD LEAVER,
AND JOHN RAVENHILL

The remarkable economic growth in the Pacific over recent decades has been generated by, and has itself fed, significant economic imbalances both within and between Pacific countries. The sustained export-led growth first of Japan, then of the East Asian newly industrialising countries (NICs), and most recently of some ASEAN members has only been possible because the United States has run large deficits on its trade account which, in turn, were the product of the imbalance between investment and domestic savings. This regional experience therefore validates the general belief articulated in most chapters of this volume—that the condition of economic interdependence is, politically speaking, a two-edged sword, generally conducive to strain as much as to cooperation, and that claims for the ultimate primacy of one outcome over the other can be no more than testaments of faith.

That, however, could be small theoretical comfort. If the Japanese economist Takenaka (1991, p. 63) is right in recently saying—as many others have said before him—that this triangular pattern of Pacific trade, where Japan plays 'supplier' to the United States' 'absorber', is ultimately unsustainable, then what we need are insights that can guide the process of adjustment to a more sustainable Pacific economy. Here the two-edged sword is no more useful than the articles of faith for thinking about the scope or content of the necessary correctives, or how the costs of making them should be shared.

Will it, for example, be the willingness of foreign purchasers of US Treasury bills which buckles first? Perhaps the US Government and its people will refuse to continue mortgaging their future by running up an enormous bill for interest payments on domestic and foreign debts? Though each of these more novel concerns has occasionally been at the frontline of the adjustment debate, the issue which continues to generate the most political tension concerns the willingness of the US Government and its citizens to tolerate large trade imbalances. Trade continues to function as the core item on the agenda of Pacific politics, and the issue around which policy debates are, for better or worse, fixed in the first instance. The recent reflation of the Japanese trade surplus to dramatic levels during a United States election year suggests that this order of political visibility is not about to change.

Beneath the surface of this constant attention to the politics of Pacific trade, there has, however, been significant change in the ways that the nature of this tension is composed, explained and (sometimes) explained away. For heuristic purposes, we can think of the trade issue as a composite of three specific problems that meld in different proportions through time.

The first source of tension pertains to the sheer speed with which the export-oriented East Asian economies have entered into world (and especially US) markets. If one country's export-led growth necessarily corresponds to someone else's domestic adjustment problem, then the much-celebrated speed of East Asian growth creates some of its own resistances. Indeed, if there is a single logic lying behind the use of non-tariff barriers by successive US administrations through the last two decades, it is the attempt to moderate what would otherwise be an excessive rate of domestic adjustment prescribed by the rapid penetration of East Asian exports.

The second, and perhaps more important, source of political tensions points to the distinctive morphology of Pacific economic interdependence. As Ruggie has frequently emphasised, the greatest successes of post-war trade liberalisation have occurred in the domain of intra-industry trade, where a portion of the potential gains from trade have been exchanged for a less intense process of domestic adjustment. That, however, is a success story most strongly associated with the growth of the Atlantic rather than the Pacific economy. In the Pacific, trade expansion has predominantly taken on the divergent rather than convergent characteristics of *inter*-industry trade. Although the prospect of trade gains along more strictly Ricardian lines excites many orthodox economists, the very idea that established industrial sectors might have to be 'cleaned out' to make way for more competitive East Asian industries sends shivers down the spines of those raised on the mid-Atlantic convention of commercial damage limitation. It gives rise to an impulse, often seen in the United States, to make Japan conform to the more universal custom.

Political tensions over trade issues can also be traced to a third source which has a 'second order' quality. Previous failures to contain the dimensions of the trade problem fuel a mounting sense of bad faith, which in turn infects future efforts at management. As Leaver's chapter documents, efforts at managing 'the Japan problem' have an episodic quality the history of which extends back more than two decades. Very little that is positive or preventive seems to have been learned over the passage of time;

on the contrary, each new US awakening to the issue appears more rather than less intense than the one which preceded it. The result has been a gradual but seemingly inevitable tendency to escalation.

This escalatory spiral is amply confirmed by the general evolutionary trend in negotiating strategies along both sides of the Pacific. While the front line of US strategy is made up by the Structural Impediments Initiative (SII), it was recently reinforced by the altogether more imposing threat of economic sanctions contained in 'Super 301', actions that were, as Ruggie puts it, tailored with Japan in mind. Yet in the very period in which 'Super 301' was implemented, Japanese governments have attained positions of strength or approximate equality in markets which flank the existing commercial relationship between the world's two largest economies. As a number of analysts have argued (for example, Segal 1990, p. 296), the metaphor that best seems to capture the character of this bilateral stand-off is the contemporary strategist's stock-in-trade—'mutual assured destruction'.

Through time, the relative contributions of these three basic problems to the aggregate mix of trading tensions have changed. In earlier decades, it was commonly argued by those advocating a 'technology gap' model that the Japanese 'economic miracle' would eventually converge around the average rate of growth for advanced capitalist countries, and that as it did so, the adjustment problem presented by rapid export-led growth would quietly fade away. In these simpler times, disparities in levels of intra-industry trade within the Pacific economy were explained primarily in terms of the whims of nature. Nature's bounty in North America, when compared to its paucity in East Asia, seemed to require manufacturing surpluses sufficient to offset inevitable East Asian raw materials deficiencies. Furthermore, insofar as the formula for the post-war reconstruction of Japan was invoked to explain such disparities in regional trading patterns, most analysts accepted that an overriding strategic imperative forced, and unquestionably justified, the dealing of the crooked hand that favoured Japanese national capital, bureaucratic continuity and established modes of industrial organisation.

Viewed from the perspective of the end of the Cold War, it is clear that the mix of factors feeding the trade imbalance, and perceptions of it, have both changed radically. The expected slower trajectory of growth has for some time been manifest in Japan, where exports no longer provide the primary engine of that country's economic expansion. But medium-term growth prospects for the US economy have become disproportionately more depressing in recent years. Consequently, it is still too soon to hope that we have seen the last of that particular cause of trade tension which can be traced back to a substantial real gap in growth rates.

In addition, as Richardson shows in his chapter, radically different factor endowments are no longer automatically accepted as a compelling explanation for the enduring problem of inter-industry trade. Ravenhill's carefully argued chapter strongly suggests that US complaints of continued restrictive trade practices by Japan are well grounded. Finally, many current-day US trade complainants experience resentment rather than inspiration when reminded that it was overwhelmingly the decision of their government to bring down a more accommodating 'reverse course' in occupation policy through the late 1940s, and that the economic costs entailed in that preference for strategic and social stability were, for many years, not regarded as sufficient to question the overall prudence of the policy.

This shift through time in the mix of sentiments about, and explanations for, the character of Pacific trade can be described as a movement from a relatively soft and obliging position to one which is altogether more forbidding. This is precisely the kind of change that sits most uneasily in the company of trade-restricting commercial instruments of a non-tariff kind that themselves seem animated by the strategist's logic of assured destruction.

At this point, it is useful to extend the MAD metaphor. Strategists have gradually come to accept that life in the shadow of assured destruction is not necessarily stable over the very long run. Maintenance of the condition is expensive, but the high cost never purchases peace of mind. Assured destruction is permanently tension-ridden, and highly prone to constructing major incidents out of minor accidents. It also seems to require periodic crises of resolve, and perhaps minor wars, to make credible the more general threat that would otherwise be incredible. The strategic parable inevitably begs the question of whether there is not 'a better way' to begin the post-Cold War commercial relationship between the world's two largest national economies.

Beyond bilateralism?

A number of chapters in this volume have addressed at length important aspects of the prospects for regional and multilateral solutions to the current dilemmas of interdependence, and the extent to which these approaches contradict or complement each other. They reach no common conclusion about probable outcomes. It would be both tedious and tendentious to try to manufacture preferences for NAFTA, APEC or other regional proposals where none exist. If there is common ground, it can be located in two deep-seated convictions: that questions of agency remain as important as questions of structure; and that the possibility of cooperative inter-state solutions is not yet foreclosed. It is not necessary to accept Wendt's admonition that 'anarchy is what states make of it' in order to resist the determinist tendencies of neo-realism (Wendt 1992, p. 395).

Though the authors all manifest an interest in questions of cooperation, the path which leads from their convictions to policy recommendations is neither short nor direct. Anticipations of a long and winding road follow from the appreciation, cautiously noted by Higgott, that regional states may just be engaged in a process of *learning* how to cooperate. To date, as he suggests, the signals suggest that the changed behaviour of regional states which underlies the impetus to cooperate should best be described as tactical learning, where values and aims remain largely unaltered. For fundamental transitions in cooperative economic development to occur—of the kind witnessed in Western Europe—tactical learning needs to evolve into complex learning, where beliefs about the way to reach goals also change. Since current cooperative initiatives seem to place the major structural problems of regional change in the 'too hard' box, it is difficult to see why they should be regarded as exercises in complex rather than tactical learning. Talking around problems may buy time, but for what end? There is no guarantee that borrowed time will in itself lead to the discovery of lasting cooperative solutions.

More pertinently, the literature on cooperation tends to give more attention to where the Pacific economy might be heading rather than where it is coming from. At a time when talk of post-Cold War orders is rife, it is all too easy to imagine that post-war history is now bunk and that the past imposes no constraints. To do so would be unwise.

Though it is common for many international political economy (IPE) scholars to argue that most of the current problems in the world economy are the products of decay from a prior and more perfect age of economic multilateralism and hegemonic leadership, that assumed trajectory does not accurately describe the historical path of evolution of the Pacific economy. In the Pacific, there has been no golden age of multilateralism against which the present represents a fall from grace. There is one important reason for this; the whole design of the post-war Pacific economy closely paralleled the bilateral architecture which informed strategic alliance-building.

The contrast between Pacific bilateralism and European regionalism that is commonly accepted at the strategic level applies equally at the economic. In Europe, regional principles infused both economic and political thinking at an early date, where they were envisaged as the building blocks of a genuinely multilateral order. But in the post-war reconstruction of the Pacific, principles of regionalism were abandoned first by Washington in its administration of the Japanese occupation, and later rejected by both Japanese and regional governments during the drafting of the Peace Treaty. As the chapter by Eden and Molot reminds us, the sequence of bilateral treaties which radiated out from the American 'hub' to the East Asian 'rim' provided the conduits through which economic as well as strategic issues were channelled.

In economic terms, there were two obvious expressions of the primacy of bilateralism: the large share of US bilateral aid programmes committed to the region; and the guaranteed access to the deep and broad US market which East Asian manufactured products once enjoyed in full measure. This bilateral skeleton was overlaid with what was, at first, nothing more than a purely nominal adherence to multilateralist principles that provided a thin veil of respectability. Insofar as 'adherence to multilateralism' meant keeping existing markets open, then it interested East Asian exporters who increasingly had to contend with US manipulation of market access. Insofar as the cant of multilateral principles opened non-Pacific markets to East Asian exports, then it also interested Washington by relieving some of the pressures of adjustment on US shoulders. But insofar as multilateralism meant the comprehensive abolition of import restrictions within the region, it interested neither.

The contemporary imprint of this bilateral inheritance already shapes the on-going process of economic adjustment in the Pacific in a number of ways, most of which are less than helpful. Gilbert Winham's robust criticisms of Washington's Super 301 market-opener—the strongest manifestation of economic bilateralism—highlight one of these costs. As he points out, if Super 301 actions prove able to satisfy the interests of US export industries, then the domestic process by which multilateral tariff bargains are normally struck will fall hostage to the unyielding mercy of import-competing industries. In this respect, Winham shores up Vernon's recent worries that successive iterations of the Japanese–US bilateral game 'will continue to generate interactions of a destructive kind' (Vernon 1990, p. 67).

However, the logic of Winham's argument can be extended to a more general conclusion that complicates Vernon's preferred solution—namely, that the bilateral relationship should be placed on a multilateral basis. When put in a dynamic context, Winham's argument strongly suggests that bilateralism will corrode the social coalitions that are necessary to the sustenance of economic multilateralism. If that is indeed a legitimate extension of his argument, then it is also a good example of one of the neo-realist's parables of politics in an anarchic environment—that necessity is more often the mother of inhibition rather than of invention.

Put simply, wide acceptance that 'a better way' is needed to organise the Pacific economy does not automatically call forth a range of feasible solutions that will satisfy that need. The implication of this for those forward-looking analysts whose normative orientation is towards regional or multilateral solutions to the problems of economic adjustment are profound. The problem which they have yet to confront is how their preferred vision(s) can be fathered from the lineages of bilateral power that have dominated the post-war Pacific.

The politics of patronage

The above argument suggests that the Asia–Pacific region has historically been shaped by an abundance of bilateral 'leadership', but all too little regionalism or multilateralism. Since this pattern of synchronous bilateralism linked the pre-eminent global superpower to a series of unquestionably minor allies, each 'spoke' in the Pacific 'wheel' came to be tempered by the tensions and torsions peculiar to patron–client relationships.

One generic feature of patron–client relationships is most disturbing in the context of our current concerns. Because this form of relationship is not marked by equality, it establishes all too clear understandings about the rights of patrons and the obligations of clients which continue to guide their behaviour in the face of uncertainty. Insofar as these understandings come to be internalised, then patron–client relationships tend to reproduce behaviour even in new circumstances where the forces of change have shifted the initial degree of inequality. Put simply, a relationship built around presumptions of patronage is highly resistant to the impact of contextual change.

The unyielding character of relationships of patronage and clientelism is not just an academic point of interest only to those preoccupied with the taxonomy of political forms. If the end of the Cold War does indeed reopen for negotiation a range of social and economic policies conceived under the influence of superpower rule, then the prevalence of clientelism in the Pacific will tend to suppress dialogue precisely at the point in time when it is most needed.

As an example, consider the current debate about a post-Cold War security policy for the Pacific region. In response to some preliminary stirrings for a conceptually and geographically broader Pacific security dialogue, the Bush administration enunciated the vision that it should function as the 'hub' in a 'spoked wheel' of diverse bilateral relationships. Since the genealogy of this image can already be traced all the way back to Dulles, and since that is precisely how the international politics of the Pacific has been structured since his time, the very idea that something so old can be made to appear new again expresses rather pithily the ability of patronage to inoculate against change.

Much the same point holds for the pressing problem of who should make the first sacrifice in the name of a more balanced Pacific trade outcome. Though no one questions the causal relationship between the US domestic savings deficit and the trade deficit, United States political leaders—as evidenced by their continued inaction on the budget deficit, and their preference for seeking scapegoats—still fail to give sufficient recognition to that linkage. Meanwhile, some altogether more contentious arguments about the import-restricting nature of Japanese industrial organisation and society that properly remain matters for further investigation have nonetheless gradually moved Japanese governments towards an acceptance of *de facto* management of their exports to the United States.

The contrasting and somewhat counter-intuitive presumptions of guilt and innocence that prevail in both of these policy domains are testimony to the lingering and pervasive qualities of the politics of patronage. They demonstrate that 'the playing field' on which forward-looking questions about regionalism and multilateralism are currently being addressed is itself not politically level. There is no neutral ground. This context of political patronage also needs to be brought into juxta-position with the question of 'international leadership'. Through the last decade, concerns about this question have overshadowed the study of international political economy in both senses of the word; they have both dominated and obscured it. Nowhere is the obsessive preoccupation with leadership more apparent than in that segment of the IPE sub-field con-cerned with the US–Japan relationship (well documented by, and reflected in, Rosecrance & Taw 1990). The obscurity comes by courtesy of the almost total fixation of that concern upon, in general, the economic attributes of 'international leadership' and, in particular, the 'public goods' which leaders are commonly thought to supply (see Kindleberger 1981).

An appreciation of the importance of the politics of leadership is only now beginning to make a long-overdue impact upon the constellation of established debate, with Cowhey (1991) making a particularly important contribution on the issue. By highlighting how the substantial strength of an economically dominant state gives its governing élite the ability to defect from the rules of any multilateral system, he recaptures the theme of private benefit made long ago in neo-Marxist discussions of hegemony that was lost in the rush to 'public goods' interpretations of leadership (see Block 1977 for an extended argument about the privileges that came to Washington through its violation of the Bretton Woods rules). His argu-ment also underscores the importance both of the consent offered by smaller players for the maintenance of the system, and of the domestically based signals of commitment that a leader must send to those smaller players in order to evoke that consent. While Cowhey's attention falls upon the structural characteristics of the domestic political system in a hegemonic state that are conducive to, or suppress, such commitments, the overall argument could be cast more broadly across the whole domestic domain without blurring the overall focus upon the origins of international consent.

If Cowhey's basic point is right, and there is no one-to-one correspon-dence between the economic prerequisites for leadership and the political performance of the role, then a series of important questions needs to be explored. For instance, the paradox in Japanese behaviour which Rix calls 'leading from behind' is likely to be an important site in further develop-ment and deepening of this argument. In the past, questions posed by this apparent incongruity would probably have been shelved and promptly for-gotten under the old-fashioned realist heading of 'the will to power'. If, however, there is a 'market' separate from that dealing with the economic attributes of hegemonic leadership where the demand for, and supply of, perceptions of consent are transacted—a kind of 'forward market' in leadership—then the prevalence of relatively unyielding patterns of patronage within the Pacific should lead us to suspect that it would not function smoothly.

The corollary is that some of the hopes which have recently been invested in greater economic transparency as a means to maintaining an open Pacific economy may well be disappointed. As both Harris and Higgott show, this aspiration is at the core of the Pacific economic cooperation movement, and while both find the idea normatively appealing, they are more cautious about asserting its probability than some of the leading proponents of Pacific cooperation (see Drysdale 1988, Elek 1992). In an environment where clientelism is the norm within both the domestic and international levels, the chances that calls for transparency will be honoured seem remote.

The politics of assimilation

A third legacy of the Pacific's bilateral architecture and the associated presumptions of patronage lies in the importance it confers upon the theme of assimilation. The combination of patronage and bilateralism is conducive to 'solving' issues of social difference through the promotion of similarity.

Assimilationist ideas have historically had a strong presence in the Asia–Pacific region. In the pre-war period, the dominant strand in US thinking about Asia amounted to an extended exercise of self-projection onto societies which were presumed to be infinitely malleable. After the war, the task of assimilation was pursued with a vengeance during the Occupation of Japan. That banner was carried forward with marginally less urgency under the guise of the metaphor of convergence that, as Chalmers Johnson noted in this volume, occupied the 'official position' on the spectrum of Western interpretations of post-Occupation Japan. Today, as Japan's trading pattern continually fails to conform to the intra-industry norm anticipated under the embedded liberalism of the post-war trade regime, the current thrust of US policy is to shift the balance between the requirements of multilateralism on the one hand and domestic autonomy on the other in a way that inevitably involves greater intrusion into domestic political, economic, and social domains in pursuit of a literal notion of 'making similar'.

The continuing importance of this broad theme—and its correspondingly narrow conception of adjustment—is demonstrated by its ability to prowl the literature in guises that, at first glance, seem reasonable. For example, notions of assimilation are frequently implicit in the culturalist arguments that attend much of the contemporary analysis of 'international leadership'. The unflattering contrast commonly drawn between a Japan said to be guided by 'inward-looking exceptionalism' (Funabashi 1991–92, p. 60)—and therefore lacking in any conception of manifest destiny—and a United States the ideas and ideals of which are alleged to generate the consent which is the ultimate repository of US power, implicitly draws upon the unquestioned proposition that there is only one (United States) standard for 'international leadership'. No doubt the acceptability of such implicit standards has been buoyed by the arrival of the moment of Cold War victory, which to many will make the Social Darwinist presumption—that the drift of history should flow with the victor—seem quite natural.

But if the question of a single norm for assimilation were considered behind a Rawlsian 'veil of ignorance', then it is by no means clear that arguments favouring Japanese convergence to a US norm would stand. As Leaver's chapter reminds us, the post-war power of the US hegemon was founded on a unique combination of basic resource endowments—large internal market, high degree of self-sufficiency, low external dependence on trade. This combination was so atypical that it hindered diffusion of the US social model; it also sustained the basic credibility of US threats to retreat into economic isolationism. Japan's more asymmetrical mix of geo-economic characteristics places it closer to the pack of other advanced capitalist countries. In addition, and partly like nineteenth-century Britain, it could be argued that Japan's higher level of external trade dependence would give future Japanese governments strong interests in the establishment and maintenance of open trading and financial orders. On the other hand, the deeply ingrained psychology of primary resource insecurity may well lead those governments to skew the terms of trade against primary products to an unparalleled degree. It is simply not clear which, if either, of these forms of capitalist society should be allowed to own the laboratory for genetic engineering.

Pursuant to this point, it is worth recalling that, through recent years, the single most important East Asian entry in the long regional history of assimilationist thinking has been the 'flying geese model', which postulated that the NICs and then ASEAN would follow the path pioneered by Japan (ably reviewed by Awanohara 1987). Indeed, the proposition that the experience of the NICs constitutes the only workable policy model for developing countries made a clean sweep of the field of development studies in the 1980s. Whatever else it showed, this new orthodoxy reflected the high demand that existed for Japanese-style solutions in many countries that, like Japan and then the NICs, had no option but to cope with an unbalanced package of initial resource endowments.

However, the 'flying geese' model now looks far too simplistic. The second and third flights of geese are proving even more vulnerable than mother goose to the general growth of protectionism. For South Korea and Taiwan, export-oriented growth has recently meant restraining their exports to the US while liberalising their domestic markets (which appears, ironically, to have worked primarily to the benefit of Japan). Rising domestic labour costs and US protectionism have combined to force their firms into offshore investment in the lower labour-cost countries of the region, particularly China, Indonesia, Malaysia and Thailand.

Korea and Taiwan currently face a difficult decade as they attempt to cope with demands for democratisation while seeking new export markets and moving to more technology-intensive exports. Given this context, claims that their export-oriented growth path has permanently 'solved' the dilemmas of development must remain open to serious question for some time to come.

At the same time, as the chapters by MacIntyre and Rodan demonstrate, the recent experiences of the ASEAN countries simply do not conform to models made either in Japan or the NICs. Foreign investment is a more important engine of growth; access to markets in North America is heavy; linkage between the export-oriented manufacturing and the local economies is minimal (on this, see Bernard & Ravenhill 1992); and it remains to be seen whether the weaker state apparatuses of the ASEAN countries will be able to drive effective bargains with foreign investors. Many ASEAN countries will be hard-pressed to provide the stability of political and economic environments needed to sustain the high rates of economic growth enjoyed in the second half of the 1980s.

In the context of our current concerns, the emphasis must be on increasing regional diversity and complexity—themes that run in all directions across the singular course of assimilationist thinking. Furthermore, since the goal of assimilation is unlikely to be remotely feasible unless it is pursued from a position of strength, attempts to engineer convergence are likely to require force. If, however, the strategist's MAD metaphor accurately captures the disposition of the Pacific economy, then would-be economic adjusters will have to quickly learn the parable that took twenty years to percolate through the ranks of strategists: that weapons-systems committed to assured destruction cannot also be conscripted into strategies for war-fighting.

If, therefore, economic adjustment is to be understood as something other than a narrowing process where convergence around some (or other) national prototype is contrived, then in what directions should economic adjustors look for their analogues of arms control thinking?

Adjustment without assimilation?

Answers to this question require, first of all, an appreciation of the complete range of strategic choices for Pacific economic adjustment. These all derive from the symbiotic relationship between international regime and domestic structure which formed the foundation of the Bretton Woods system, and which Ruggie called 'embedded liberalism'. Insofar as Japan's mode of industrial organisation and its resultant trade patterns have come to be regarded as systematic violations of the core presumptions behind that definition of the domestic–international relationship, the current policy thrust of the United States and its allies is to change the balance between the requirements of multilateralism on the one hand, and domestic autonomy on the other. In effect, this route to adjustment seeks to extend the field of competence of formal international norms so that East Asian domestic structures will come to more closely resemble the OECD standard.

This encroachment of 'the international' upon 'the domestic', it is important to remember, is not sanctioned by the current rules of the GATT. As Saxonhouse (1988, p. 248) points out, GATT's Article III acknowledges that internal taxes, charges, laws and regulations affecting the sale, purchase, distribution and transportation of goods will vary across countries; the Article only requires that imported goods be treated in the same manner as locally produced goods for purposes of taxation and other charges. Nonetheless, the effort to bring some of these 'domestic exclusions' back into the fold clearly would extend the field of play for other GATT norms, and work towards an international remedy through assimilation.

There is, however, a second strategic route through which this domestic–international tension, most acutely manifest in the politics of the Pacific, could be addressed—namely, through agreement about more permissive international norms that are capable of enveloping a more diverse field of national characteristics. In effect, this route calls for an increase in the international tolerance for provincialism.

At this point, many IPE scholars wedded to one or another of the many versions of international regime theory will undoubtedly say that such proposals for new 'rules of the game' risk sacrificing the real gains assured by the continuing Bretton Woods compact for the very long chance of a better world. Their position is covered by a colloquial refrain heard with increasing frequency in Pacific diplomatic forums: 'if it ain't broke, don't fix it'.

In response to this counsel of caution, the important objection is that the working rules of the game are already no longer those agreed to at Bretton Woods. They have been comprehensively redrafted throughout the last decade within the private confines of Japanese–US relations.

The main lines of that process of redrafting within both the commercial and financial domains has been clearly spelled out by many essays in this volume. Until the United States began to record systemic trade deficits, the working rule of the multilateral system was that the burden of economic adjustment lay with deficit rather than surplus countries. However, the United States' turn to multilateral coordination—a process that reaches its greatest intensity with Japan—has, at least for the singular case of the US economy, succeeded in shifting presumptions about the onus for adjustment away from deficit economies (the US) and towards surplus economies (Germany and particularly Japan).

A similar point can be made about the much-vaunted financial underwriting of the US deficit provided by Japanese capital during recent years. Though some see in this the long-overdue beginnings of a socially necessary process of global financial management, it is surely more pertinent to note—as Calleo and Allin (1990, p. 102) have done—that the private use of the globally scarce resource of capital to finance the deficit of one of the world's richest countries inescapably poses blunt and embarrassing moral questions.

In summary, the working rules behind current international practices express a principle of two classes of citizenship. Multilateral coordination through the G-7 process cushions Washington quite comfortably from the application of the harsh principles of adjustment intrinsic to the multilateral system it fathered nearly half a century ago. Yet the majority of members of the international community—especially in the expanding global periphery—experience those disciplines with peculiar force. Defenders of this status quo have the responsibility to indicate how the systemic goals of growth and stability—let alone morality—can be secured under the influence of what amounts to just another form of separate development.

At this juncture, a concern with those worthwhile systemic goals suggests now—as it did in 1944—-that neither deficit nor surplus economies should be singularly burdened with presumptions about adjustment. Keynes was surely correct to argue that both deficit and surplus economies shared blame for the tendency to disequilibrium which their surpluses and deficits respectively induced, and that they should therefore share the costs of adjustment. Any convention which forces adjustment costs onto deficit countries is no less arbitrary than one which makes surplus countries pay. From the point of view of systemic stability and efficiency, it may be that the most logical and defensible position on Pacific adjustment issues would seek to link the private conditions, which are currently extended to the single case of the US economy, to the normative expansion of the multilateral system as a whole.

A strategic agenda along these lines is, of course, a long way removed from the current log of Pacific economic diplomacy. The region, insofar as it shares any collective diplomatic identity, still labours to raise a meaningful contribution for the defence of the ailing GATT system, and seems to completely lack—where it does not consciously forswear—any higher aim. It may be that current Pacific economic diplomacy is caught in a low-level equilibrium trap. As cultural diversity is universally acknowledged as a primary feature of the region, a strategy which turned diversity into a virtue instead of regarding it as a defect might constitute the most appropriate measure of the political maturity of the Pacific.

Bibliography

Abshire, D. 1990, 'The Nature of American Global Economic Leadership in the 1990s', *The Global Economy: America's Role in the Decade*, eds W. Brock & R. Hormats, W.W. Horton, New York

Acharya, A. 1991, 'The Association of Southeast Asian Nations: "Security Community" or "Defence Community"?', *Pacific Affairs*, vol. 64, no. 2, pp. 159–77

Aderhold, R., Cumming, C. and Harwood, A. 1988, 'International Linkages Among Equities Markets and the October 1987 Market Break', *Quarterly Review*, Federal Reserve Bank of New York, vol. 13, no. 2, pp. 34–46

Adler, E., Crawford, B. and Donnelly, J. 1991, 'Defining Progress in International Relations', *Progress in Post War International Relations*, eds E. Adler & B. Crawford, Columbia University Press, New York

Aera 1991, 16 April pp. 6–9.

Aggarwal, V.K. 1985, *Liberal Protectionism: The International Politics of Organized Textile Trade*, University of California Press, Berkeley and Los Angeles

Aggarwal, V.K., Keohane, R.O. and Yoffie, D.B. 1987, 'The Dynamics of Negotiated Protectionism', *American Political Science Review*, vol. 81, no. 2, pp. 345–66

Aho, C.M. 1989, 'More Bilateral Trade Agreements Would Be a Blunder: What the New President Should Do', *Cornell International Law Journal*, vol. 22, no. 1, pp. 25–38

Aida, Y. 1990, 'Amerika no hōkai' (The Collapse of America), *Voice*, September, pp. 116–34

Aliber, R.Z. 1986, 'Fixed Exchange Rates and the Rate of Inflation', *Alternative Monetary Regimes*, eds C.D. Campbell & W.R. Dougan, Johns Hopkins University Press, Baltimore

Amsden, A. 1990, *Asia's Next Giant: Late Industrialization in Korea*, Oxford University Press, New York

Anderson, K. and Tyers, R. 1987, 'Japan's Agricultural Policy in International Perspective', *Journal of the Japanese and International Economies*, vol. 1, March, pp. 131–46

Anek Laothamats 1988, 'Business and Politics in Thailand: New Patterns of Influence', *Asian Survey*, vol. 28, no. 4, pp. 451–70

——1992a (forthcoming), 'The Politics of Structural Adjustment in Thailand: A Political Explanation of Economic Success', *The Dynamics of Economic Policy Reform in South-east Asia and the South-west Pacific*, eds A. MacIntyre & K. Jayasuriya, Oxford University Press, Kuala Lumpur

——1992b, *Business Associations and the New Political Economy of Thailand*, Westview, Boulder, CO

Arase, D. 1988, *Japanese Objectives in Pacific Economic Cooperation*, Resource Systems Institute, East-West Center, Honolulu

——1991, 'Japan in Post-Cold War Northeast Asia', paper presented to the Workshop on Major Powers and the Security of Southeast Asia: The Post-Cold War International Order, Institute of Southeast Asian Studies, Kuching, Sarawak

Areeda, P. 1992, 'Antitrust Policy in the 1980s', *Policy Change in the 1980s*, ed. M. Feldstein, University of Chicago Press, Chicago

Artis, M. and Ostry, S. 1986, *International Economic Policy Coordination*, Chatham House Papers No. 30, Royal Institute of International Affairs, London

Asahi Shimbun 1991, 'Kibishii shisen: kachikan toi-hajimeta Bei' (Strict Gaze: America Begins to Question Our Value System), 6 January

Asai, M. 1991, 'The World's Credit Card Policeman', Asia Foundation, Translation Service Center, *Articles from the Japanese Press*, no. 1458, 6 May

Asher, M. 1989, 'An Economic Perspective', *Privatisation: Singapore's Experience in Perspective*, eds I. Thynne & M. Ariff, Longman, Singapore

Asian Development Bank 1990, *Asian Development Outlook 1990*, Asian Development Bank, Manila

——1991, *Asian Development Outlook 1991*, Asian Development Bank, Manila

Asia-Pacific Economic Cooperation (APEC) 1991, *APEC Declaration on the Uruguay Round*, 14 November

Australian 1990, 'Tax Low on World Scale', 20 September

——1991, 'Politics Spook Wall Street—4 pc Drop', 18 November

Australian Financial Review 1990, 'Tokyo Heads World Sell-Off of US Bonds', 13 September

Axelrod, R. 1984, *The Evolution of Cooperation*, Basic Books, New York

Axelrod, R. and Keohane, R.O. 1986, 'Achieving Cooperation Under Anarchy: Strategies and Institutions', *Cooperation Under Anarchy*, ed. K. Oye, Princeton University Press, Princeton

Awanohara, S. 1987, '"Look East"—The Japan Model', *Asian–Pacific Economic Literature*, vol. 1, no. 1, pp. 75–89.

Balassa, B. 1965, 'Trade Liberalisation and "Revealed" Comparative Advantage', *The Manchester School of Economic and Social Studies*, vol. 33, no. 2, pp. 99–123

——1966, 'Tariff Reductions and Trade in Manufactures Among the Industrial Countries', *American Economic Review*, vol. 56, no. 3, pp. 466–72

——1986, 'Intra-Industry Specialization: A Cross-Country Analysis', *European Economic Review*, vol. 30, no. 1, pp. 27–42

Balassa, B. ed. 1981, *The Newly Industrializing Countries in the World Economy*, Pergamon, New York

Balassa, B. and Noland, M. 1988, *Japan in the World Economy*, Institute for International Economics, Washington, DC

Baldwin, R.E. 1988, 'Hysteresis in Import Prices: The Beachhead Effect', *American Economic Review*, vol. 78, no. 4, pp. 773–85

——1991 (forthcoming), 'Are Economists' Traditional Trade Policy Views Still Valid?', *Journal of Economic Literature*

Baldwin, R.E. ed. 1991, *Empirical Studies of Commercial Policy*, University of Chicago Press, Chicago

Barnds, W.J. 1991, 'The United States and Japan: A Time of Troubles', *CAPA Report* No. 2, The Asia Foundation, Center for Asia Pacific Affairs, June, 4pp

Bartelsman, E.J., Caballero, R.J. and Lyons, R.K. 1991, 'Short and Long Run Externalities', National Bureau of Economic Research Working Paper No. 3810, Cambridge, MA

Barton, J.H. 1990, 'Toward an International Antitrust Code', monograph, Stanford University Law School, July

Batam Industrial Development Authority (BIDA) 1990, *Development Data*

Baucus, M. 1989, 'A New Trade Strategy: The Case for Bilateral Agreements', *Cornell International Law Journal*, vol. 22, no. 1, pp. 1–24

Bennett, P. and Kelleher, J. 1988, 'The International Transmission of Stock Price Disruption in October 1987', *Quarterly Review*, Federal Reserve Bank of New York, vol. 13, no. 2, pp. 17–33

Berg, T.G. 1987, 'Trade in Services', *Harvard International Law Journal*, vol. 28, no. 1, pp. 1–30

Bergsten, C.F. 1972, 'The New Economics and US Foreign Policy', *Foreign Affairs*, vol. 50, no. 2, pp. 199–222

——1987, 'Economic Imbalances and World Politics', *Foreign Affairs*, vol. 65, no. 4, pp. 770–94

——1990, 'The World Economy After the Cold War', *Foreign Affairs*, vol. 69, no. 3, pp. 96–112

Bergsten, C.F. and Graham, E.M. 1991, *Global Corporations and National Governments: Are Changes Needed in the International Economic and Political Order in Light of the Globalization of Business?*, Institute for International Economics, Washington, DC

Bernard, M. and Ravenhill, J. 1992, *New Hierarchies in East Asia: The Post-Plaza Division of Labour*, Working Paper, Department of International Relations, Research School of Pacific Studies, Australian National University, Canberra

Bhagwati, J. 1978, *The Anatomy and Consequences of Exchange Control Regimes*, Ballinger, Cambridge, MA

——1987, 'Trade in Services and the Multilateral Trade Negotiations', *The World Bank Economic Review*, vol. 1, no. 4, pp. 539–47

——1988, *Protectionism*, MIT Press, Cambridge, MA

——1989a, 'Super 301's Big Bite Flouts the Rules', *New York Times*, 4 June

——1989b, 'Is Free Trade Passé After All?', *Weltwirtschaftliches Archiv*, vol. 125, no. 1, pp. 17–44

——1989c, 'United States Trade Policy at the Crossroads', *The World Economy*, vol. 12, no. 4, pp. 439–79

——1990, 'Aggressive Unilateralism: An Overview', *Aggressive Unilateralism: America's 301 Trade Policy and the World Trading System*, eds J. Bhagwati & H.T. Patrick, University of Michigan Press, Ann Arbor

——1991a, *The World Trading System at Risk*, Princeton University Press, Princeton

——1991b, 'Jumpstarting GATT', *Foreign Policy*, no. 83, Summer, pp. 105–18

Bhagwati, J. and Patrick, H.T. eds 1990, *Aggressive Unilateralism: America's 301 Trade Policy and the World Trading System*, University of Michigan Press, Ann Arbor

Biersteker, T.J. 1992, 'The Triumph of Neo-classical Economics in the Developing World: Policy Convergence and the Basis of Governance in the International Economic Order', *Governance Without Government: Order and Change in World Politics*, eds J.N. Rosenau & O.E. Czempiel, Cambridge University Press, Cambridge

Biggs, T. and Levy, B. 1991, 'Strategic Interventions and the Political Economy of Industrial Policy in Developing Countries', *Reforming Economic Systems in Developing Countries*, eds D. Perkins & M. Roemer, Harvard Institute for International Development, Cambridge, MA

Blackhurst, R., Marian, N. and Tumlir, J. 1977, 'Trade Liberalization, Protectionism and Interdependence', *GATT Studies in International Trade*, vol. 5, pp. 1–79

Blais, A. 1986, 'The Political Economy of Public Subsidies', *Comparative Political Studies*, vol. 19, no. 2, pp. 201–16

Bliss, J.C. 1987, 'GATT Dispute Settlement Reform in the Uruguay Round: Problems and Prospects', *Stanford Journal of International Law*, vol. 23, no. 1, pp. 31–55

Block, F.L. 1977, *The Origins of International Economic Disorder: A Study of United States International Monetary Policy from World War II to the Present*, University of California Press, Berkeley

Bonanno, G. and Brandolini, D. 1990, *Industrial Structure in the New Industrial Economics*, Clarendon Press, Oxford

Boner, R.A. and Krueger, R. 1991, *The Basics of Antitrust Policy: A Review of Ten Nations and the European Communities*, World Bank Technical Paper No. 160, November

Brander, J.A. 1987, 'Shaping Comparative Advantage: Trade Policy, Industrial Policy, and Economic Performance', *Shaping Comparative Advantage*, eds R.G. Lipsey & W. Dobson, C.D. Howe Institute, Toronto

Breslauer, G.W. 1991, 'What Have We Learned About Learning?', *Learning in US and Soviet Foreign Policy*, eds G.W. Breslauer & P.E. Tetlock, Westview Press, Boulder, CO

Bresnahan, T.F. and Reiss, P.C. 1991, 'Entry and Competition in Concentrated Markets', *Journal of Political Economy*, vol. 99, no. 5, pp. 977–1009

Brittan, L. 1992, 'A Framework for International Competition', text of an Address to the World Economic Forum, Davos, Switzerland, 3 February

Brittan, S. 1991, 'Defects in the Policy Model', *Partners in Prosperity*, Report of the Twentieth Century Fund Task Force on the International Coordination of National Economic Policies, Priority Press, New York

Brooms, J. 1990, 'Recent Developments in Trans-Tasman Business Law', manuscript, 17th International Trade Law Conference, September

Brown, D. and Garman, D.M. 1990, 'Human Resource Management and International Trade', *Industrial Relations*, vol. 29, Spring, pp. 189–213

Bueno, G.M. 1988, 'A Mexican View', *Bilateralism, Multilateralism and Canada in US Trade Policy*, ed. W.J. Diebold, Ballinger Publishing Company, Cambridge, MA

Buzan, B. 1988, 'Japan's Future: Old History Versus New Roles', *International Affairs*, vol. 64, no. 4, pp. 557–83

Byers, R.A., Larrabee, S.F. and Lynch, A. eds 1987, *Confidence Building Measures and International Security*, East West Center for Security Studies, New York

Caballero, R.J. and Lyons, R.K. 1989, 'The Role of Externalities in US Manufacturing', Discussion Paper No. 431, Department of Economics, Columbia University, September

——1990, 'Internal Versus External Economies in European Industry', *European Economic Review*, vol. 34, no. 4, pp. 805–28

Calder, K.E. 1988, 'Japanese Foreign Economic Policy Formation: Explaining the Reactive State', *World Politics*, vol. 40, no. 4, pp. 517–41

Calleo, D. 1982, *The Imperious Economy*, Harvard University Press, Cambridge, MA

Calleo, D. and Allin, D.H. 1990, 'Geostrategic Trends in the World Economy', *Australia and the World: Prologue and Prospects*, ed. D. Ball, Strategic and Defence Studies Centre, Research School of Pacific Studies, Australian National University, Canberra

Camdessus, M. 1990, 'The Prescription: Sound Economics', *International Herald Tribune*, 25 September

Cameron, D.R. 1978, 'The Expansion of the Public Economy: A Comparative Analysis', *American Political Science Review*, vol. 72, no. 4, pp. 1243–61

Cameron, M., Eden, L. and Molot, M.A. 1992, 'North American Free Trade: Cooperation and Conflict in Canada–Mexico Relations', *A New World Order: Canada Among Nations 1991–92*, eds C. Maule & F. Hampson, Carleton University Press, Ottawa

Camps, M. and Diebold, W.J. 1986, *The New Multilateralism: Can the World Trading System Be Saved?*, Council on Foreign Relations, New York

Canzoneri, M. and Gray, J. 1985, 'Monetary Policy Games and the Consequences of Non-Cooperative Behavior', *International Economic Review*, vol. 26, no. 3, pp. 547–64

Carbaugh Jr, J.E. and Kase, H. eds 1991, *Teki to shite no Nihon: Amerika wa nani o ikatte iru no ka* (Japan as the Enemy: What Makes America Angry?), Kōbunsha, Tokyo

Carter, C.A., McCall, A.F. and Sharples, J.A. 1990, *Imperfect Competition and Political Economy*, Westview, Boulder, CO

Caves, R.E. 1985, 'International Trade and Industrial Organization: Problems, Solved and Unsolved', *European Economic Review*, vol. 28, no. 3, pp. 377–95

——1988, 'Trade Exposure and Changing Structures of US Manufacturing Industries', *International Competitiveness*, eds A. Michael Spence & H.A. Hazard, The MIT Press, Cambridge, MA

Caves, R. and Barton, D. 1990, *Efficiency in US Manufacturing Industries*, The MIT Press, Cambridge, MA

Chang, I. 1991, 'HDTV: The Latest High-Tech, High-Stakes Battleground', *Harvard International Review*, vol. 13, no. 4, pp. 50–3, 64

Chee, L. 1990, 'The Lure of the Archipelago', *Singapore Business*, vol. 14, no. 5, pp. 16–21

Chenery, H.B. 1960, 'Patterns of Industrial Growth', *American Economic Review*, vol. 50, no. 4, pp. 624–54

Christelow, D. 1985–86, 'Japan's Intangible Barriers to Trade in Manufactures', *Quarterly Review*, Federal Reserve Bank of New York, vol. 10, Winter, pp. 11–18

Chu, Y. 1989, 'State Structure and Economic Adjustment of the East Asian Newly Industrializing Countries', *International Organization*, vol. 43, no. 4, pp. 647–72

Chuang, P.M. 1990, 'Defence Group Takes the Offensive', *Singapore Business*, vol. 14, no. 7, pp. 27–36

Coase, R. 1960, 'The Problem of Social Cost', *Journal of Law and Economics*, vol. 3, October, pp. 1–44

Coate, M.B. and Kleit, A.N. 1990, *Exclusion, Collusion, and Confusion: The Limits of Raising Rivals Costs*, Working Paper No. 179, Bureau of Economics, US Federal Trade Commission, October

Cohen, B.J. 1965, 'Capital Controls and the US Balance of Payments: Comment', *American Economic Review*, vol. 55, no. 1, pp. 172–6

——1974, 'The Revolution in Atlantic Relations: A Bargain Comes Unstuck', *The United States and Western Europe*, ed. W. Hanrieder, Winthrop, Cambridge

——1977, *Organizing the World's Money: The Political Economy of International Monetary Relations*, Basic Books, New York

——1990, 'The Political Economy of International Trade', *International Organization*, vol. 44, no. 2, pp. 261–81

Cohen, R. 1991, *Contested Domains: Debates in International Labour Studies*, Zed Books, London

Cohen, S.S. and Zysman, J. 1987, *Manufacturing Matters: The Myth of the Post-Industrial Economy*, Basic Books, New York

Comanor, W.S., George, K., Jacquemin, F. and Katzenbach, J.A. 1990, *Competition Policy in Europe and North America: Economic Issues and Institutions*, Harwood Academic Publishers, Chur, Switzerland

Committee for Economic Development 1990, 'Foreign Investment in the United States: What Does it Signal', a statement by the Program Committee, Washington, DC, September

Condliffe, J. 1950, *The Commerce of Nations*, W.W. Norton, New York

Cooper, A.F. and Higgott, R. 1991, *Middle Power Leadership in the International Order: A Reformulated Theory for the 1990s*, Centre for International Trade and Investment Policy Studies, Discussion Paper No. 6, Norman Paterson School of International Affairs, Carleton University, Ottawa

——1992, 'The Cairns Group and the Uruguay Round: The Politics of Two Level Games', *World Agriculture and the GATT: International Political Economy Yearbook*, eds W. Avery & D. Rapkin, Lynne Rienner, Boulder, CO

Cooper, A.F., Higgott, R. and Nossal, K.R. 1991, 'Bound to Follow? Leadership and Followership in the Gulf Conflict', *Political Science Quarterly*, vol. 106, no. 3, pp. 391–410

Cooper, R.N. 1968, *The Economics of Interdependence: Economic Policy in the Atlantic Community*, McGraw-Hill, New York

——1972, 'Economic Interdependence and Foreign Policy in the Seventies', *World Politics*, vol. 24, no. 2, pp. 159–61

——1980, *The Economics of Interdependence*, 2nd ed., Columbia University Press, New York

——1985, 'Economic Interdependence and Coordination of Economic Policies', *Handbook of International Economics*, eds R.W. Jones & P.B. Kenen, North-Holland, Amsterdam and New York

——1986, 'Economic Interdependence and Coordination of Economic Policies', *Economic Policy in an Interdependent World: Essays in World Economics*, ed. R.N. Cooper, MIT Press, Cambridge, MA

——1987, 'Industrial Policy and Trade Distortion', *The New Protectionist Threat to World Welfare*, ed. D. Salvatore, North-Holland, New York

Cooper, W.H. 1991, 'Japan–US Trade: The Structural Impediments Initiative', *Current Politics and Economics of Japan*, vol. 1, pp. 73–81

Corden, W.M. 1990, *Strategic Trade Policy. How New? How Sensible?*, WPS 396, World Bank Working Paper, April

Corker, R. 1990, *The Changing Structure of Japanese Trade Flows*, IMF Working Paper 90/107, International Monetary Fund, Washington, DC

Corrigan, E.G. 1987, 'A Perspective on the Globalization of Financial Markets and Institutions', *Quarterly Review*, Federal Reserve Bank of New York, vol. 12, Spring, pp. 1–9

Cowhey, P.F. 1991, 'Elect Locally—Order Globally: Domestic Politics and Multilateral Cooperation', American Political Science Association, Washington, DC, September, mimeo

Cox, R. 1986, 'Social Forces, States and World Orders: Beyond International Relations Theory', *Neo-realism and its Critics*, ed. R.O. Keohane, Columbia University Press, New York

——1989, 'Middlepowermanship, Japan, and Future World Order', *International Journal*, vol. 44, no. 4, pp. 823–62

——1991, *Perspectives on Multilateralism*, Programme on Multilateralism and the United Nations System, United Nations University, Tokyo

Crane, G.T. and Amawi, A. eds 1991, *The Theoretical Evolution of International Political Economy: A Reader*, Oxford University Press, New York

Crawford, B. 1991, 'Towards a Theory of Progress in International Relations', *Progress in Postwar International Relations*, eds E. Adler & B. Crawford, Columbia University Press, New York

Crawford, J. 1981, 'The Pacific Basin Co-operative Concept', *Pacific Economic Cooperation: Suggestions for Action*, eds J. Crawford & G. Seow, Heinemann, Selangor, Malaysia

Crawford, J. and Seow, G. eds 1981, *Pacific Economic Cooperation: Suggestions for Action*, Heinemann, Selangor, Malaysia

Cumings, B. 1988, 'Power and Plenty in Northeast Asia: The Sources of US Policy and Contemporary Conflict', *Security and Arms Control in the North Pacific*, eds A. Mack & P. Keal, Allen and Unwin, Sydney

Currie, D.A., Holtham, G. and Hughes Hallett, A. 1989, 'The Theory and Practice of International Policy Coordination: Does Coordination Pay?', *Macroeconomic Policies in an Interdependent World*, eds R.C. Bryant, et al., International Monetary Fund, Washington, DC

Davidow, J. 1991, 'The Relationship Between Anti-Trust Laws and Trade Laws in the United States', *The World Economy*, vol. 14, no. 1, pp. 37–52 de Ghellinick, E., Geroski, P.A. and Jacquemin, A. 1988, 'Inter-Industry Variations in the Effect of Trade on Industry Performance', *Journal of Industrial Economics*, vol. 37, pp. 1–19

Deardorff, A.V. 1989, 'Economic Perspectives on Antidumping Law', *Antidumping Law and Practice: A Comparative Study*, eds J.H. Jackson & E.A. Vermulst, University of Michigan Press, Ann Arbor

——1990, 'Should Patent Protection Be Extended To All Developing Countries?', *The World Economy*, vol. 13, no. 4, pp. 497–507

Department of Foreign Affairs and Trade (DFAT) 1990, *Recent Developments in Asia Pacific Direct Investment*, Research and Policy Discussion Papers No. 7, Department of Foreign Affairs and Trade, Canberra

Department of Statistics 1983, *Economic & Social Statistics, Singapore 1960–1982*, Singapore National Printers, Singapore

Destler, I.M. 1991, 'The United States and Japan: What is New?', paper presented to the 32nd Annual Convention of the International Studies Association, 21 March, Vancouver

Destler, I.M. and Henning, C.R. 1989, *Dollar Politics: Exchange Rate Policymaking in the United States*, Institute for International Economics, Washington, DC

Deyo, F. 1981, *Dependent Development and Industrial Order: An Asian Case Study*, Praeger, New York

Deyo, F. ed. 1987, *The Political Economy of the New Asian Industrialism*, Cornell University Press, Ithaca

Dick, A.R. 1991a, 'The Competitive Consequences of Japan's Export Cartel Associations', unpublished

——1991b, 'Are Export Cartels Efficiency-Enhancing or Monopoly-Producing?', unpublished

Dickens, W. and Lang, K. 1988, 'Why It Matters What We Trade', *The Dynamics of Trade and Employment*, eds L. D'Andrea Tyson, W.T. Dickens & J. Zysman, Ballinger, Cambridge, MA

Dixit, A. 1984, 'International Trade Policy for Oligopolistic Industries', *Economic Journal*, vol. 94, Supplement, pp. 1–16

Dobson, W. 1991, *Economic Policy Coordination: Requiem or Prologue?*, Policy Analyses in International Economics No. 30, Institute for International Economics, Washington, DC

Doern, G.B. and Tomlin, B.W. 1991, *Faith and Fear: The Free Trade Story*, Stoddart, Toronto

Doner, R. 1988, 'Weak State–Strong Country?: The Thai Automobile Case', *Third World Quarterly*, vol. 10, no. 4, pp. 1542–64

——1991, *Driving a Bargain: Automotive Industrialization and Japanese Firms in Southeast Asia*, University of California Press, Berkeley

Doner, R. and Unger, D. 1991, 'The Politics of Finance in Thai Economic Development', paper presented at the Second Workshop on Government, Financial Systems and Economic Development: A Comparative Study of Selected Asian and Latin American Countries, East-West Center, Honolulu

Dornbusch, R. 1988, 'The Adjustment Mechanism: Theory and Problems', *International Payments Imbalances in the 1980s*, ed. N.S. Fieleke, Federal Reserve Bank of Boston, Boston

Draft Final Act Embodying the Results of the Uruguay Round of Multilateral Trade Negotiations 1991, doc. MTN. TNC/W/FA, GATT, 20 December

Drucker, P. 1986, 'Japan and Adversarial Trade', *Wall Street Journal*, 1 April

——1987, 'Japan's Choices', *Foreign Affairs*, vol. 65, no. 5, pp. 923–41

Drysdale, P. 1988, *International Economic Pluralism: Economic Policy in East Asia and the Pacific*, Allen and Unwin, Sydney

——1989, 'Growing Pains: New Group Could Calm US–Asian Friction', *Far Eastern Economic Review*, 16 November

——1991, 'Open Regionalism: A Key to East Asia's Economic Future', *Pacific Economic Papers*, vol. 197, July

Drysdale, P. and Garnaut, R. 1989, 'A Pacific Free Trade Area?', *Free Trade Areas and U.S. Trade Policy*, Institute for International Economics, Washington, DC

Drysdale, P. and Patrick, H. 1979, *An Asian-Pacific Regional Economic Organization: An Exploratory Concept Paper*, Washington Library of Congress, Congressional Research Service, Washington, DC

Dulforce, W. and Gardner, D. 1991, 'Bush Makes Concession to Unblock Trade Talks', *Financial Times*, 11 November

Economic Planning Committee 1991, *The Strategic Economic Plan*, Ministry of Trade and Industry, Singapore

Economist, The 1985, 'A Gatt for Services', 12 October

——1988, 'Blocking Out a Yen Block', 17 September

——1990a, 'GATT Brief: Centre Stage for Services?', 5 May

——1990b, 'A Question of Definition: A Survey of International Banking', 7 April

——1990c, 'Netting the Future: A Survey of Telecommunications', 10 March

——1990d, 'Japan: Asia's Emerging Standard-Bearer', 21 July

——1990e, 'Who Dares Wins...and Loses', 1 September

——1991a, 'Too Much Good Living', 20 April

——1991b, 'GATT and Services: Second Best', 3 August

Economist Intelligence Unit 1989, *Singapore Country Report*, The Economist Intelligence Unit, London

Eden, L. 1991, 'Multinational Responses to Trade and Technology Changes: Implications for Canada', *Foreign Investment, Technology and Growth*, ed. D. McFetridge, Investment Canada, Ottawa

Eden, L. and Molot, M.A. 1991, 'From Silent Integration to Strategic Alliance: The Political Economy of North American Free Trade', *Occasional Papers in Trade Law and Policy*, Centre for Trade Policy and Law, Carleton University, Ottawa

——1992, 'The View from the Spokes', *North America Without Borders? Integrating Canada, the United States, and Mexico*, ed. S.J. Randall with H.W. Konrad and S. Silverman, University of Calgary Press, Calgary

Elek, A. 1991, 'Asia Pacific Economic Co-operation', *Southeast Asian Affairs 1991*, Institute of Southeast Asian Studies, Singapore, pp. 33–48

——1992, 'Pacific Economic Cooperation: Policy Choices for the 1990s', *Asia Pacific Economic Literature*, vol. 6, no. 1, pp. 1–15

Encarnation, D.J. 1992, *Rivals Beyond Trade: America versus Japan in Global Competition*, Cornell University Press, Ithaca

Encarnation, D.J. and Mason, M. 1990, 'Neither MITI nor America: The Political Economy of Capital Liberalization in Japan', *International Organization*, vol. 44, no. 1, pp. 25–54

Ennis, P. 1990, 'Separating the Revisionists', *Tokyo Business Today*, vol. 58, no. 1, January, pp. 30–1

Epstein, G. 1985, 'The Triple Debt Crisis', *World Policy Journal*, vol. 2, no. 4, pp. 625–57

Etheridge, L. 1985, *Can Governments Learn*, Pergamon Press, New York

Etō, J. and Homma, N. 1991, 'Nihonjin wa naze Amerika ga kirai ka' (Why Japanese Dislike the United States), *Bungei shunjū*, June, pp. 94–109

Etō, J. and Nakanishi, T. 1991, '"Nichi-Bei dōmei" no yomei' (The Last Days of the 'Japanese–American Alliance'), *Voice*, July

European Communities, Commission of 1989, *EEC Competition Policy in the Single Market*, Luxembourg

——1991, *XXth Report on Competition Policy*, Luxembourg

Evans, P. 1989, 'Predatory, Developmental, and Other Apparatuses: A Comparative Political Economy Perspective on the Third World', *Sociological Forum*, vol. 4, no. 4, pp. 561–87

External Affairs, Department of 1991, *North American Free Trade: Securing Canada's Growth Through Trade*, Supply and Service, Ottawa

Fagan, D. 1990, 'Ottawa Hopes Mexicans' Visit Will Expand Trade Opportunities', *Globe and Mail*, Toronto, 22 January

——1992, 'Canada's Trade Deficit With Mexico Soars', *Globe and Mail*, Toronto, 24 January

Fallows, J. 1989, 'Containing Japan', *The Atlantic Monthly*, May, pp. 40–54

Fallows, J., Johnson, C., Prestowitz, C. and van Wolferen, K. 1990, 'Beyond Japan-Bashing: The "Gang of Four" Defends the Revisionist Line', *U.S. News & World Report*, 7 May, pp. 54–5

Feis, H. 1947, 'The Conflict Over Trade Ideologies', *Foreign Affairs*, vol. 25, no. 2, pp. 217–28

Feketekuty, G. 1990, 'U.S. Policy on 301 and Super 301', *Aggressive Unilateralism: America's 301 Trade Policy and the World Trading System*, eds J. Bhagwati & H.T. Patrick, University of Michigan Press, Ann Arbor

——1991, 'Changes in the World Economy and Implications for the World Trading System', unpublished

Feldstein, M. 1988, 'International Economic Cooperation: Introduction', *International Economic Cooperation*, ed. M. Feldstein, University of Chicago Press, Chicago

Feldstein, M. ed. 1992, *Policy Change in the 1980s*, University of Chicago Press, Chicago

Feltham, I.R., Salen, S.A., Mathieson, R.F. and Wonnacott, R. 1991, *Competition (Antitrust) and Antidumping Laws in the Context of the Canada–US Free Trade Agreement*, Canadian Chamber of Commerce and the United States Chamber of Commerce, The Committee on Canada–United States Relations, Ottawa

Finger, J.M. 1981, 'The Industry–Country Incidence of "Less than Fair Value" Cases in US Import Trade', *Quarterly Review of Economics and Business*, vol. 21, no. 2, pp. 260–79

——1991, 'That Old GATT Magic No More Casts Its Spell (How the Uruguay Round Failed)', *Journal of World Trade*, vol. 25, no. 2, pp. 19–22

Finger, J.M. and Dhar, S. 1991, 'Do Rules Control Power? GATT Articles and Arrangements in the Uruguay Round', unpublished

Finger, J.M., Hall, H.K. and Nelson, D.R. 1982, 'The Political Economy of Administered Protection', *American Economic Review*, vol. 72, no. 3, pp. 452–66

Foreign Policy Institute 1991, 'The Future of US–Japan Relations', School of Advanced International Studies, Johns Hopkins University, August, 9pp

Frankel, J.A. 1988, 'International Nominal Targeting: A Proposal for Policy Coordination', *International Payments Imbalances in the 1980s*, ed. N.S. Fieleke, Federal Reserve Bank of Boston, Boston

——1991, 'Is a Yen Bloc Forming in Pacific Asia?', *AmEx Bank Review*, November

Frankel, J.A. and Rockett, K.E. 1988, 'International Macroeconomic Policy Coordination When Policymakers Do Not Agree on the True Model', *American Economic Review*, vol. 78, no. 3, pp. 318–40

Friedman, G. and LeBard, M. 1991, *The Coming War With Japan*, St. Martin's Press, New York

Friedman, M. 1989, 'Internationalization of the US Economy', *Fraser Forum*, February, pp. 7–15

Frischtak, C., Zachau, U. and Hadjimichael, B. 1989, *Competition Policy for Industrializing Countries*, The World Bank, Washington, DC

Fröbel, F., Heinrichs, J. and Kreye, O. 1978, 'The World Market for Labor and the World Market for Industrial Sites', *Journal of Economic Issues*, vol. 12, no. 4, pp. 843–58

Fröbel, F., Jürgen, H. and Kreye, O. 1980, *The New International Division of Labour*, Studies in Modern Capitalism, Cambridge University Press, Cambridge

Fukuyama, F. 1989, 'The End of History?', *The National Interest*, vol. 16, Summer, pp. 3–18

Funabashi, Y. 1988, *Managing the Dollar: From the Plaza to the Louvre*, Institute for International Economics, Washington, DC

——1990, *Asahi Evening News*, 5 October

——1991a, *Reisengo (After the Cold War)*, Iwanami Shinsho, Tokyo

——1991b, 'Don't Circle the Wagons: East Asian Economic Bloc Wrong Answer to Western Regionalism', *Asahi Evening News*, 15 March

——1991–92, 'Japan and the New World Order', *Foreign Affairs*, vol. 70, no. 5, pp. 58–74

Fung, K.C. 1991, 'Characteristics of Japanese Industrial Groups and Their Potential Impact on US–Japan Trade', *Empirical Studies of Commercial Policy*, ed. R.E. Baldwin, University of Chicago Press, Chicago

Gaimushō 1989, *Gaikō seisho: waga gaikō no kinkyō* (Foreign Relations Blue Book: Recent Developments in Japan's Foreign Relations), Ministry of Foreign Affairs, Tokyo

——1990, *Wagakuni no seifu kaihatsu enjo* (Japan's Official Development Assistance), Ministry of Foreign Affairs, Tokyo

——1991, *Wagakuni no seifu kaihatsu enjo* (Japan's Official Development Assistance), Ministry of Foreign Affairs, Tokyo

Gardner, R.N. 1980, *Sterling–Dollar Diplomacy in Current Perspective*, Columbia University Press, New York

Gelber, H.G. 1991, 'National Power, Security and Economic Uncertainty', Institute for the Study of Conflict, Ideology & Power, Boston University, April

General Agreement on Tariffs and Trade (GATT) 1988, *Review of Developments in the Trading System*, General Agreement on Tariffs and Trade, Geneva

——1989, *Review of Developments in the Trading System*, General Agreement on Tariffs and Trade, Geneva

George, A. 1991, 'Japan's America Problem: The Japanese Response to U.S. Pressure', *The Washington Quarterly*, vol. 14, no. 3, pp. 5–19

Gephardt, R., et al. 1991, Letter to the Honourable Carla Hills United States Trade Representative, 23 October

Gereffi, G. 1989, 'Development Strategies and the Global Factory', *The Annals of the American Academy of Political and Social Science*, vol. 505, September, pp. 92–104

——1991a, 'Mexico's "Old" and "New" Maquiladora Industries: Contrasting Approaches to North American Integration', paper presented at Conference, Facing North/Facing South, University of Calgary, May

——1991b, 'International Subcontracting and Global Capitalism: Reshaping the Pacific Rim', Political Economy of the World System Conference on Pacific–Asia and the Future of the World-System, University of Hawaii at Manoa, March 28–30

Gereffi, G. and Wyman, D. eds 1990, *Manufacturing Miracles: Paths of Industrialization in Latin America and East Asia*, Princeton University Press, Princeton

Gerlach, M. 1989, '*Keiretsu* Organization in the Japanese Economy: Analysis and Trade Implications', *Politics and Productivity: The Real Story of Why Japan Works*, eds C. Johnson, L. D'A. Tyson & J. Zysman, Ballinger, Cambridge, MA

——1992, 'Twilight of the *Keiretsu*? A Critical Assessment', *Journal of Japanese Studies*, vol. 18, no. 1, pp. 79–117

Geroski, P. 1987, '"Comment" on Brander', *Shaping Comparative Advantage*, eds R.G. Lipsey & W. Dobson, C.D. Howe Institute, Toronto

Gewirtz, C. 1991, 'Dollar's Inability to Reach New Highs Confounds Analysts', *International Herald Tribune*, 1 July

Ghosh, A.R. and Masson, P.R. 1988, 'International Policy Coordination in a World with Model Uncertainty', *IMF Staff Papers*, vol. 35, no. 2, pp. 230–58

Giarini, O. ed. 1987, *The Emerging Service Economy*, Pergamon Press, London

Gill, S. 1990a, *American Hegemony and the Trilateral Commission*, Cambridge University Press, Cambridge

——1990b, *Trilateralism*, Cambridge University Press, Cambridge

——1991, 'Group of Seven (G7) Macroeconomic Cooperation and International Finance', paper presented at the Annual Convention of the International Studies Association, Vancouver, March

Gilpin, R. 1975, *U.S. Power and the Multinational Corporation*, Basic Books, New York

——1987, *The Political Economy of International Relations*, Princeton University Press, Princeton, NJ

——1989a, 'Where Does Japan Fit In?', *Millennium*, vol. 18, no. 3, pp. 329–42

——1989b, 'The Global Context', *The United States and Japan in the Postwar World*, eds A. Iriye & W.I. Cohen, The University Press of Kentucky, Lexington

Ginsburg, T.B. 1991, 'A Colder Peace? Issues in the US–Japan Security Alliance', *CAPA Report* No. 1, The Asia Foundation, April, Center for Asia Pacific Affairs, pp. 17–22

Gleysteen Jr, W.H. 1991, 'Comment', *Yen for Development: Japanese Foreign Aid and the Politics of Burden-Sharing*, ed. S. Islam, Council on Foreign Relations Press, New York

Globe and Mail 1991, 'Pulp and Paper Woes Mount', Toronto, 4 September

——1992, 'Free-trade Discord Apparent', Toronto, 23 March

Globerman, S. 1988, 'The Impacts of Trade Liberalization on Imperfectly Competitive Industries: A Review of Theory and Evidence', Economic Council of Canada Discussion Paper No. 341

Godfrey, J. 1992, 'Mexico or Canada: Which is Developed?', *Financial Post*, 31 January

Goh, C.T. 1981, 'Towards Higher Achievement', Budget Speech, *Singapore Government Press Release*, Ministry of Culture, 6 March

——1991, 'Strategy for ASEAN Competitiveness in the World Economy—A Singapore Perspective', keynote address at the CSIS–Asia Society Conference, Bali, 4 March, *Singapore Government Press Release*, Ministry of Information & The Arts

Goldberg, L. and Ordover, J. 1991, 'Nontariff Barriers to Trade and Competition: Theory and Evidence', unpublished

Goldstein, J. 1986, 'The Political Economy of Trade: Institutions of Protection', *American Political Science Review*, vol. 80, no. 1, pp. 161–84

——1988, 'Ideas, Institutions, and American Trade Policy', *The State and American Foreign Policy*, eds G.J. Ikenberry, D.A. Lake & M. Mastanduno, Cornell University Press, Ithaca

Gordon, B.K. 1988, *Politics and Protectionism in the Pacific*, Adelphi Paper, No. 228, International Institute for Strategic Studies, London

——1991, 'The Vanishing Trade Deficit', *Asian Wall Street Journal*, 28 May

Gourevitch, P. ed. 1989, 'The Pacific Region: Challenges to Policy and Theory', *The Annals of the American Academy of Political and Social Science*, vol. 505, September

Government of Canada, Bureau of Competition Policy, Consumer and Corporate Affairs Canada 1991, 'OECD Committee on Competition Law and Policy: Canadian Follow-up to March 25–26 Discussions on Policy Convergence and Linkages', unpublished

Gowa, J. 1986, 'Anarchy, Egoism and Third Images', *International Organization*, vol. 40, no. 1, pp. 167–86

Graham, E.M. and Ebert, M.E. 1991, 'Foreign Direct Investment and National Security: Fixing the Exon-Florio Process', unpublished, Washington, DC

Graham, E.M. and Richardson, J.D. 1991, 'Global Competition Policies', Institute for International Economics, unpublished

Grieco, J. 1988, 'Anarchy and the Limits of Cooperation: A Realist Critique of the Newest Liberal Institutionalism', *International Organization*, vol. 42, no. 3, pp. 485–508

——1990, *Cooperation Among Nations: Europe, America and Non-Tariff Barriers to Trade*, Cornell University Press, Ithaca

Grossman, G.M. 1990, 'Promoting New Industrial Activities: A Survey of Recent Arguments and Evidence', *OECD Economic Studies*, vol. 14, Spring, pp. 87–125

Grossman, G.M. and Helpman, E. 1991, *Innovation and Growth in the Global Economy*, The MIT Press, Cambridge, MA

Grossman, G.M. and Richardson, J.D. 1985, 'Strategic US Trade Policy: A Survey of Issues and Early Analysis', *Special Papers in International Economics*, No. 15, Princeton University, April

Grubel, H.G. and Lloyd, P.J. 1975, *Intra-Industry Trade: The Theory and Measurement of International Trade in Differentiated Products*, Macmillan, London

Grunberg, I. 1990, 'Exploring the Myth of Hegemonic Stability', *International Organization*, vol. 44, no. 4, pp. 431–77

Grunwald, J. and Flamm, K. 1985, *The Global Factory: Foreign Assembly in International Trade*, The Brookings Institution, Washington, DC

Haas, E. 1975, *The Obsolescence of Regional Integration Theory*, Institute of International Studies, University of California, Berkeley

——1980, 'Why Collaborate? Issue-Linkage and International Regimes', *World Politics*, vol. 32, no. 3, pp. 357–405

——1990, *When Knowledge is Power: Three Models of Change in International Organizations*, University of California Press, Berkeley

Haas, P. 1989, 'Do Regimes Matter? Epistemic Communities and Mediterranean Pollution Control', *International Organization*, vol. 43, no. 3, pp. 377–404

Haas, P. ed. 1992, 'Knowledge, Power and International Policy Coordination', *International Organization*, Special Issue, vol. 46, no. 1

Haberler, G. 1990, 'Strategic Trade Policy and the New International Economics: A Critical Analysis', *The Political Economy of International Trade*, eds R.W. Jones & A.O. Krueger, Basil Blackwell, Oxford

Hadley, E.M. 1982, 'Is the U.S.–Japan Trade Imbalance a Problem? Economists Answer "No", Politicians "Yes" ', *Journal of Northeast Asian Studies*, vol. 1, no. 1, pp. 35–56

Hagelstam, J. 1991, 'Mercantilism Still Influences Practical Trade Policy at the End of the Twentieth Century', *Journal of World Trade*, vol. 25, no. 2, pp. 95–105

Haggard, S. 1990, *Pathways from the Periphery: The Politics of Growth in the Newly Industrializing Countries*, Cornell University Press, Ithaca

Haggard, S., Byung-kook, K. and Moon, C. 1991, 'The Transition to Export-led Growth in South Korea: 1954–1966', *Journal of Asian Studies*, vol. 50, no. 4, pp. 850–73

Haggard, S. and Moon, C. eds 1989, *Pacific Dynamics: The International Politics of Industrial Change*, Westview Press, Boulder, CO

Hamilton, C. and Whalley, J. 1989, 'Coalitions in the Uruguay Round', *Weltwirtschaftliches Archiv*, vol. 125, no. 3, pp. 547–62

Harris, R.G. 1989, 'Trade and Industrial Policy for a "Declining?" Industry: the Case of the US Steel Industry', Queen's University Institute for Economic Research Discussion Paper No. 766

Harris, S. 1989, 'Regional Economic Cooperation, Trading Blocs and Australian Interests', *Australian Journal of International Affairs*, vol. 43, no. 2, pp. 16–24

——1991, 'Varieties of Pacific Economic Cooperation', *The Pacific Review*, vol. 4, no. 4, pp. 301–11

Hart, M. 1989, 'A Practitioner Looks at the Canada–U.S. Free Trade Agreement and Its Implications for Mexico', paper prepared for an international symposium on Region North America: Canada, the United States and Mexico, Baylor University, Waco, Texas, 11–13 October

——1990, *A North American Free Trade Agreement: The Strategic Implications for Canada*, Institute for Research on Public Policy, Halifax

Hartshorn, J.E. 1982, 'Two Crises Compared: OPEC Pricing in 1973–1975 and 1978–1980', *OPEC: Twenty Years and Beyond*, ed. R. El Mallakh, Westview Press, Boulder, CO

Hasegawa, H. 1991, 'Yomigaeru "kichiku Bei-Ei" to "hai-Nichi" no shinshō' (The Resurrection of the Mental Images of 'Brutal America and England' and 'Anti-Japanese'), *Aera*, vol. 4, no. 23, pp. 9–39

Hayden, B. 1988, 'Leadership in the Asia–Pacific Region', *Australian Foreign Affairs Record*, vol. 59, no. 6, pp. 237–42

Hayes, T.C. 1989, 'Japan Grip Still Seen On Patents', *New York Times*, 24 November

Hazledine, T. 1989, 'Why the Free-trade Gain Numbers Differ So Much: Analysis of An Encompassing General Equilibrium Model', Department of Agricultural Economics, University of British Columbia, unpublished

——(forthcoming), 'Industrial Organization Foundations of Trade Policy: Modeling the Case of Canada–US Free Trade', *Australian Journal of Agricultural Economics*

Helleiner, G.K. 1981, *Intra-Firm Trade and Developing Countries*, Macmillan, London

——1989, 'Introduction', *Trade Policy, Industrialization and Development: New Perspectives*, ed. G.K. Helleiner, Oxford University Press, New York

——1990, 'Considering a US–Mexican Free Trade Area', prepared for a conference on Mexico's Trade Options in the Changing International Economy, Universidad Tecnologica de Mexico, Mexico City, 11–15 June

Helpman, E. 1984, 'Increasing Returns, Imperfect Markets, and Trade Theory', *Handbook of International Economics*, eds R.W. Jones & P.B. Kenen, North Holland, Amsterdam

——1989a, *Monopolistic Competition in Trade Theory*, Princeton University International Finance Section, Special Paper No. 16

——1989b, 'The Noncompetitive Theory of International Trade and Trade Policy', *Proceedings of the World Bank Annual Conference on Development Economics 1989*, supplement to the *World Bank Economic Review* and *The World Bank Research Observer*, pp. 193–216

Helpman, E. and Krugman, P.R. 1985, *Market Structure and Foreign Trade: Increasing Returns, Imperfect Competition, and the International Economy*, The MIT Press, Cambridge, MA

——1989, *Trade Policy and Market Structure*, The MIT Press, Cambridge, MA

Henderson, D. 1988, 'The State of International Economic Cooperation', *World Today*, vol. 44, no. 12, pp. 213–15

Henning, C.R. 1991, 'The G-7 Dilemma: Agreeing on Cost Sharing', *Economic Insights*, vol. 2, no. 3, pp. 2–5

Higgott, R. 1991a, 'Towards a Non Hegemonic IPE: An Antipodean Perspective', *The New International Political Economy*, eds C.N. Murphy & R. Tooze, Lynne Rienner, Boulder, CO

——1991b, 'The Politics of Australia's International Economic Relations: Adjustment and Two Level Games', *Australian Journal of Political Science*, vol. 26, no. 1, pp. 2–28

Higgott, R. and Cooper, A.F. 1990, 'Middle Power Leadership and Coalition Building: The Cairns Group and the Uruguay Round of Trade Negotiations', *International Organization*, vol. 44, no. 4, pp. 589–632

Higgott, R., Cooper, A.F. and Bonnor, J. 1990, 'Asia–Pacific Economic Cooperation: An Evolving Case-Study in Leadership and Co-operation Building', *International Journal*, vol. 45, no. 4, pp. 823–66

——1991, 'Cooperation in the Asia–Pacific Region: APEC and the New Institutionalism', *Pacific Economic Papers*, vol. 199, September

Hill, H. 1989, *Indonesia: Export Promotion in the Post-OPEC Era*, Working Papers in Trade and Development, Research School of Pacific Studies, Australian National University, Canberra

Hindley, B. 1980, 'Voluntary Export Restraints and the GATT's Main Escape Clause', *The World Economy*, vol. 3, no. 3, pp. 313–41

Hirschman, A.O. 1981, *Essays in Trespassing: Economics to Politics and Beyond*, Cambridge University Press, New York

Hoffman, K. and Kaplinsky, R. 1988, *Driving Force*, Westview Press, Boulder, CO

Holloway, N. and Rowley, A. 1991, 'Towards a Yen Bloc', *Japan in Asia*, ed. N. Holloway, Review Publishing Company, Hong Kong

Holmes, P. 1991, *Trade and Competition Policy: The Consumer Interest*, National Consumer Council, Working Paper No. 5, London

Holtham, G. and Hughes Hallett, A. 1987, 'International Policy Cooperation and Model Uncertainty', *Global Macroeconomics: Policy Conflict and Cooperation*, eds R. Bryant & R. Portes, Macmillan, London

Homma, N. 1989, 'America in the Mind of the Japanese', *The United States and Japan in the Postwar World*, eds A. Iriye & W.I. Cohen, The University Press of Kentucky, Lexington

Horstmann, I.J. and Markusen, J.R. 1986, 'Up the Average Cost Curve: Inefficient Entry and the New Protectionism', *Journal of International Economics*, vol. 20, pp. 225–47

Hudec, R.E. 1975, 'Retaliation Against "Unreasonable" Foreign Trade Practices: The New Section 301 and GATT Nullification and Impairment', *Minnesota Law Review*, vol. 59, no. 3, pp. 461–539

——1990, 'Thinking About the New Section 301: Beyond Good and Evil', *Aggressive Unilateralism: America's 301 Trade Policy and the World Trading System*, eds J. Bhagwati & H.T. Patrick, University of Michigan Press, Ann Arbor

Hufbauer, G.C. and Chilas, J.G. 1974, 'Specialization by Industrial Countries: Extent and Consequences', *The International Division of Labour: Problems and Perspectives*, ed. H. Giersch, J.C.B. Mohr, Tübingen

Hughes, H. ed. 1988, *Achieving Industrialization in East Asia*, Cambridge University Press, Melbourne

Hunter, L., Markusen, J.R. and Rutherford, T.F. 1991, 'Trade Liberalization in a Multinational-Dominated Industry: A Theoretical and Applied General Equilibrium Analysis', unpublished

Hyun, J.T. and Whitmore, K. 1989, 'Japanese Direct Foreign Investment: Patterns and Implications for Developing Countries', World Bank, Industry and Energy Department Working Paper, Industry Series Paper No. 1, Washington, DC

Ichikawa, H. 1990, 'A Survey of Japan's Competition Policy and Related Problems', unpublished

Iida, T. 1991, *Nihon Keizai Shimbun*, 6 May

Ikenberry, G.J. 1992, 'A World Economy Restored: Expert Consensus and the Anglo-American Postwar Settlement', *International Organization*, vol. 46, no. 1, pp. 289–322

Ikenberry, G.J. and Kupchan, C.A. 1990, 'Socialization and Hegemonic Powers', *International Organization*, vol. 44, no. 3, pp. 283–315

Inada, J. 1990, 'ODA to nihon gaikō: tai-firipin enjo ni tsuite no jirei kenkyū' (ODA and Japanese foreign policy: a case study of aid to the Philippines), *Nihon no ODA to kokusai chitsujo* (Japan's ODA and the International Order), ed. T. Igarashi, Kokusai mondai kenkyūjo, Tokyo

Industry Commission, Australia 1990, *Strategic Trade Theory: The East Asian Experience*, Information Paper, Canberra, November

Inoguchi, K. 1987, *Posuto-haken shisutemu to Nihon no sentaku* (The post-hegemonic system and Japan's options), Chikuma Shobō, Tokyo

——1991 'Wangango no sekai chitsujo' (World Order After the Gulf), *Nihon Keizai Shimbun*, 19 March, translated in *Economic Eye*, vol. 12, no. 2, pp. 24–6

Inoguchi, T. 1986, 'Japan's Images and Options: Not a Challenger, But a Supporter', *Journal of Japanese Studies*, vol. 12, no. 1, pp. 95–119

——1991, 'Japan's Role in a Multipolar World', *Yen for Development: Japanese Foreign Aid and the Politics of Burden-Sharing*, ed. S. Islam, Council on Foreign Relations, New York

Inoguchi, T. and Okimoto, D. eds 1988, *The Political Economy of Japan: Volume 2. The Changing International Context*, Stanford University Press, Stanford

Inside U.S. Trade 1991, 'GATT Tuna Ruling Spawns Environmentalist, Congressional Backlash', 6 September

——1992a, 'PMA Official Criticises Dunkel Text For Being Too Soft on Developing Countries', 10 January

——1992b, 'Business Groups Target Eight Countries for Special 301 Investigation', 28 February

International Herald Tribune 1990, 'Inflation Surges in U.S.', 19 September

——1991, 'Huge Savings in Nuclear Cuts, U.S. Report Says', 29 October

International Monetary Fund 1991, *World Economic Outlook, May 1991*, International Monetary Fund, Washington, DC

International Trade Reporter 1991a, 'U.S.–EC Leaders Head Into Full Week of "Make-or-Break" Meetings on GATT Talks',vol. 8, no. 44, p. 1610

——1991b, 'Commission Analyzes Problems Posed in Post-Uruguay Round Period', vol. 8, no. 38, p. 1405

——1992, 'Customs Rules That Canadian Honda Civics Failed to Meet Content Standards Under FTA', vol. 9, no. 10, p. 384

Investment Canada 1990, *Canada–U.S.–Mexico Free Trade Negotiations: The Rationale and the Investment Dimension*, August

Iriye, A. and Cohen, W.I. 1989, *The United States and Japan in the Postwar World*, The University Press of Kentucky, Lexington

Irwin, D. 1990, 'Mercantilism as Strategic Trade Policy: The Anglo–Dutch Rivalry for the East India Trade', *Journal of Political Economy*, vol. 99, no. 6, pp. 1296–1314

Ishihara, S. 1991, *The Japan That Can Say No*, Simon and Schuster, New York

Ishihara, S., Watanabe, S. and Ogawa, K. 1990, *Sore de mo 'No' to ieru Nihon* (The Japan that Can Still Say 'No'), Kōbunsha, Tokyo

Islam, S. ed. 1991, *Yen for Development: Japanese Foreign Aid and the Politics of Burden-Sharing*, Council on Foreign Relations, New York

Izawa, M. 1990, From *Rekishi kaido*, Asia Foundation, Translation Service Center, *Articles From the Japanese Press*, no. 1305, 2 April

Jacquemin, A. 1982, 'Imperfect Market Structure and International Trade: Some Recent Research', *Kyklos*, vol. 35, no. 1, pp. 75–93

——1987, *The New Industrial Organization: Market Forces and Strategic Behavior*, The MIT Press, Cambridge, MA

James, W., Naya, S. and Meier, G. 1989, *Asian Development: Economic Success and Policy Lessons*, University of Wisconsin Press, Madison

Japan Economic Institute 1991, *Japan and the North American Free Trade Agreement*, Report No. 39A, 18 October

Johnson, C. 1982, *MITI and the Japanese Miracle*, Stanford University Press, Stanford

——1987, 'Political Institutions and Economic Performance', *The Political Economy of the New Asian Industrialism*, ed. F. Deyo, Cornell University Press, Ithaca

——1988a, 'The Japanese Political Economy: A Crisis in Theory', *Ethics and International Affairs*, vol. 2, pp. 79–97

——1988b, 'Understanding the Japanese Economy: Barriers to Increasing Trade', *Economic Development Quarterly*, vol. 2, no. 3, pp. 211–16

——1990a, 'The Future of Japanese–American Relations: Seeking a New Balance', *Analysis* (National Bureau of Asian and Soviet Research), vol. 2, pp. 21–7

——1990b, 'Trade, Revisionism, and the Future of Japanese–American Relations', *Japan's Economic Structure: Should It Change?*, ed. K. Yamamura, Society for Japanese Studies, Seattle

——1991, 'Where Does Mainland China Fit in a World Organized into Pacific, North American, and European Regions?', *Issues and Studies*, vol. 27, no. 8, pp. 1–16

Jones, L. and Sakong, I. 1980, *Government, Business, and Entrepreneurship in Economic Development: The Korean Case*, Harvard University Press, Cambridge, MA

Jorde, T.M. and Teece, D.J. eds 1992, *Antitrust, Innovation, and Competitiveness*, Oxford University Press, New York

Julius, D. 1990, *Global Companies and Public Policy: The Growing Challenge of Foreign Direct Investment*, The Royal Institute of International Affairs, Chatham House Papers, Pinter Publishers, London

——1991, 'Foreign Direct Investment: The Neglected Twin of Trade', Group of Thirty Report No. 31, New York

Kahler, M. 1988, 'Organizing the Pacific', *Pacific–Asian Economic Policies and Regional Independence*, eds R. Scalapino, et al., Institute of East Asian Studies, University of California, Berkeley

Kakabadse, M.A. 1987, *International Trade Services*, Croom Helm, for the Atlantic Institute for International Affairs, London

Kalla, P. 1986, 'The GATT Dispute Settlement Procedure in the 1980s: Where Do We Go From Here?', *Dickinson Journal of International Law*, vol. 5, Fall, pp. 82–101

Kamil, Y., Pangestu, M. and Fredericks, C. 1991, 'A Malaysian Perspective', *Growth Triangle: The Johor–Singapore–Riau Experience*, ed. Lee Tsao Yuan, Institute of Southeast Asian Studies, Singapore

Katz, L.F. and Summers, L.H. 1989, 'Can Inter-Industry Wage Differentials Justify Strategic Trade Policy?', *Exchange Rate and Trade Policies for International Competitiveness*, ed. R.C. Feenstra, University of Chicago Press, Chicago

Kawai, M. 1991, 'Japan's Demand for Foreign Securities in the 1980s', Seminar Paper, Australia–Japan Research Centre, Australian National University, February

Keeley, J. 1990, 'Towards a Foucauldian Analysis of Regimes', *International Organization*, vol. 44, no. 1, pp. 83–105

Kenen, P.B. 1988, *Managing Exchange Rates*, Council on Foreign Relations, New York

——1989, *Exchange Rates and Policy Coordination*, University of Michigan Press, Ann Arbor

——1991, 'Comment', *Partners in Prosperity*, Report of the Twentieth Century Fund Task Force on the International Coordination of National Economic Policies, Priority Press, New York

Kennedy, P. 1988, *The Rise and Fall of the Great Powers: Economic Change and Military Conflict from 1500 to 2000*, Unwin Hyman, London

Keohane, R.O. 1980, 'The Theory of Hegemonic Stability and Changes in International Regimes, 1967–77', *Changes in the International System*, eds O.R. Holsti, R.M. Silverson & A.L. George, Westview, Boulder, CO

———1984a, *After Hegemony: Cooperation and Discord in the World Political Economy*, Princeton University Press, Princeton, NJ

———1984b, 'The World Political Economy and the Crisis of Embedded Liberalism', *Order and Conflict in Contemporary Capitalism*, ed. J. Goldthorpe, Clarendon Press, Oxford

———1989, *International Institutions and State Power*, Westview Press, Boulder, CO

Keohane, R.O. and Hoffmann, S. 1991, 'Institutional Change in Europe in the 1980s', *The New European Community: Decisionmaking and Institutional Change*, eds R.O. Keohane & S. Hoffmann, Westview Press, Boulder, CO

Keohane, R.O. and Nye, J.S. 1977, *Power and Interdependence: World Politics in Transition*, Little Brown, Boston

Kessides, I. 1984, 'Industrial Organization and International Trade: Some Recent Developments', World Bank Country Policy Department, CP Discussion Paper No. 1984–32, June

Kim, H.S. and Weston, A. 1992, *Implications of a North American Free Trade Agreement for East Asian Developing Countries*, North South Institute, Ottawa

Kindleberger, C. 1981, 'Dominance and Leadership in the International Economy: Exploitation, Public Goods, and Free Rides', *International Studies Quarterly*, vol. 25, no. 2, pp. 242–54

Kissinger, H. 1990, Printed text of speech to the Japan Society, New York

Klepper, G. 1990, 'Entry Into The Market for Large Transport Aircraft', *European Economic Review*, vol. 34, June, pp. 775–98

Kojima, K. 1971, *Japan and a Pacific Free Trade Area*, Macmillan, London

———1986, 'Japanese Style Direct Foreign Investment', *Japanese Economic Studies*, vol. 14, no. 3, pp. 52–82

Komiya, R. and Irie, K. 1990, 'The U.S.–Japan Trade Problem: An Economic Analysis from a Japanese Viewpoint', *Japan's Economic Structure: Should It Change?*, ed. K. Yamamura, Society for Japanese Studies, Seattle

Komiya, R. and Itoh, M. 1988, 'Japan's International Trade and Trade Policy, 1955-1984', *The Political Economy of Japan: Volume 2. The Changing International Context*, eds T. Inoguchi & D.I. Okimoto, Stanford University Press, Stanford

Koo, B.H. 1990, 'Korea's Perspectives on Asia-Pacific Economic Cooperation', *Economic Cooperation in the Asia Pacific Region*, eds J. Hardt & Y. Kim, Westview, Boulder, CO

Koyama, K. 1990, 'Prospects on the Petroleum Demand-Supply Balance in the Pan-Pacific Region', *Energy in Japan*, March

Krasner, S. 1982, 'Structural Causes and Regime Consequences: Regimes as Intervening Variables', *International Organization*, vol. 36, no. 2, pp. 185–206

——1987, *Asymmetries in Japanese-American Trade: The Case for Specific Reciprocity*, Institute of International Studies, University of California, Berkeley

Kratochwil, F. and Ruggie, J. 1986, 'International Organization: A State of the Art on an Art of the State', *International Organization*, vol. 40, no. 4, pp. 753–76

Krause, L.B. 1991, 'Regionalism in World Trade: The Limits of Economic Interdependence', *Harvard International Review*, vol. 13, no. 4, pp. 4–6

Kravis, I.B. and Lipsey, R.E. 1989, 'Technological Characteristics of Industries and the Competitiveness of the US and its Multinational Firms', National Bureau of Economic Research Working Paper No. 2933, Cambridge, MA

Kreinin, M.E. 1988, 'How Closed is the Japanese Market? Additional Evidence', *The World Economy*, vol. 11, no. 4, pp. 529–42

Krishna, K. and Thursby, M. 1990, 'Trade Policy with Imperfect Competition: A Selective Survey', *Imperfect Competition and Political Economy*, eds C.A. Carter, A.F. McCalla & J.A. Sharples, Westview, Boulder, CO

Krueger, A.O. 1990, 'Theory and Practice of Commercial Policy: 1945–1990', National Bureau of Economic Research Working Paper No. 3569

Krugman, P.R. 1985, 'Increasing Returns and the Theory of International Trade', *Advances in Economic Theory, Fifth World Congress*, ed. T.F. Bewley, Cambridge University Press, Cambridge

——1987a, 'Is Free Trade Passé?', *Journal of Economic Perspectives*, vol. 1, no. 2, pp. 131–44

——1987b, 'Is the Japan Problem Over?', *Trade Friction and Economic Policy: Problems and Prospects for Japan and the United States*, eds R. Sato & P. Wachtel, Cambridge University Press, Cambridge

——1988, 'The Persistent US Trade Deficit', *Australian Economic Papers*, vol. 27, no. 51, pp. 149–58

——1989, 'Industrial Organization and International Trade', *Handbook of Industrial Organization*, eds R. Schmalensee & R. Willig, North-Holland, Amsterdam

——1990a, 'Japan is Not Our Nemesis', *New Perspectives Quarterly*, vol. 7, Summer, pp. 41–5

——1990b, *Rethinking International Trade*, The MIT Press, Cambridge, MA

——1991, 'Introduction', *Trade With Japan: Has the Door Opened Wider?*, ed. P.R. Krugman, University of Chicago Press, Chicago

Krugman, P.R. ed. 1986, *Strategic Trade Policy and the New International Economics*, The MIT Press, Cambridge, MA

Kudrle, R. 1991, 'Good for the Gander? Foreign Direct Investment in the United States', *International Organization*, vol. 45, no. 3, pp. 397–424

Kurth, J.R. 1989, 'The Pacific Basin Versus the Atlantic Alliance: Two Paradigms of International Relations', *Annals of the American Academy of Political and Social Science*, vol. 505, September, pp. 34–45

LaFeber, W. 1989, 'Decline of Relations During the Vietnam War', *The United States and Japan in the Postwar World*, eds A. Iriye & W.I. Cohen, University Press of Kentucky, Lexington

Lake, D. 1984, 'Beneath the Commerce of Nations: A Theory of International Economic Structures', *International Studies Quarterly*, vol. 28, no. 2, pp. 143–70

Lawrence, R.Z. 1987, 'Imports in Japan: Closed Markets or Minds?', *Brookings Papers on Economic Activity*, vol. 2, pp. 517–48

——1991, 'Efficient or Exclusionist? The Import Behavior of Japanese Corporate Groups', *Brookings Papers on Economic Activity*, vol. 1, pp. 311–41

Layne, C. 1991, 'Why the Gulf War Was Not In The National Interest', *The Atlantic Monthly*, July, pp. 55, 65–81

Leamer, E. 1988, 'Measures of Openness', *Trade Policy and Empirical Analysis*, ed. R.E. Baldwin, University of Chicago Press, Chicago

Leaver, R. 1989, 'Restructuring in the Global Economy: From "Pax Americana" to "Pax Nipponica"?', *Alternatives*, vol. 14, no. 4, pp. 429–62

——1992, 'The Gulf and the New World Order: Economic Dimensions of a Problematic Relationship', *Australian Journal of Political Science*, vol. 27, no. 2, pp. 242–57

Lee, C. and Naya, S. 1988, 'Trade in East Asian Development with Comparative Reference to Southeast Asian Experiences', *Economic Development and Cultural Change*, vol. 36, no. 3, supplement, pp. S123–52

——(forthcoming), 'The Government and Financial System in the Economic Development of South Korea', *World Development*

Lee, S.A. 1973, *The Industrialisation of Singapore*, Longman, Camberwell

——1977, *Singapore Goes Transnational*, Eastern Universities Press, Singapore

Lehner, U.C. and Murray, A. 1990, 'Strained Alliance: "Selling of America" to Japanese Touches Some Very Raw Nerves', *Wall Street Journal*, 19 June

Levinsohn, J. 1991, 'Testing the Imports-As-Market-Discipline Hypothesis', unpublished

Levinson, M. 1988, 'Is Strategic Trade Fair Trade?', *Across the Board*, June, pp. 47–51

Lewis, F. 1991/92, 'The "G-7½" Directorate', *Foreign Policy*, no. 85, Winter, pp. 25–40

Lexenomics, Inc. 1990, 'The Relationship Between Competition Policy and Anti-Dumping Law: The Canadian Experience', unpublished

Liew, S.L. 1991, 'Creating Competitive Advantage Through the Growth Triangle', *Economic Bulletin*, vol. 20, no. 1, pp. 14–17

Lincoln, E.J. 1990a, *Japan's Unequal Trade*, The Brookings Institution, Washington, DC

——1990b, 'Japan's Role in Asia–Pacific Cooperation: Dimensions, Prospects and Problems', *Economic Cooperation in the Asia Pacific Region*, eds J. Hardt & Y. Kim, Westview, Boulder, CO

Lipsey, R.E. 1989, 'The Internationalization of Production', National Bureau of Economic Research Working Paper No. 2923, Cambridge, MA

——1991, 'Foreign Direct Investment in the US and US Trade', National Bureau of Economic Research Working Paper No. 3623, Cambridge, MA

Lipsey, R.E. and Kravis, I.B. 1986, 'The Competitiveness and Comparative Advantage of US Multinationals, 1957–1983', National Bureau of Economic Research Working Paper No. 2051, Cambridge, MA

Lipsey, R.G. and Dobson, W. eds 1987, *Shaping Comparative Advantage*, Policy Study No. 2, C.D. Howe Institute, Toronto

Lipson, C. 1982, 'The Transformation of Trade: The Sources and Effects of Regime Change', *International Organization*, vol. 36, no. 2, pp. 417–55

——1984, 'International Cooperation in Economics and Security', *World Politics*, vol. 37, no. 1, pp. 1–24

List, F. 1856, *National System of Political Economy*, Lippincott, Philadelphia

Little, J.S. 1987, 'Intra-Firm Trade: An Update', *New England Economic Review*, May–June, pp. 46–51

Lobsters From Canada 1990, USA 89-1807-01, Final Report of the Panel, 25 May

Lohr, S. 1988, 'The Growth of the "Global Office" ', *New York Times*, 18 October

Los Angeles Times 1989, 'The Price of Jeans in Japan' (editorial), 12 November

——1990, 'Talks Revealed Much Sympathy for US', 7 April

——1991, 'Apprehension Over Trading Blocs', 30 July

——1992, 'Loose Talk From Japan', 23 January

Lowe, P. 1991, 'Resource Convergence and Intra-Industry Trade', Research Discussion Paper No. 9110, Economic Research Department, Reserve Bank of Australia, Sydney

Lyons, B. 1979, 'International Trade, Industrial Pricing and Profitability: A Survey', presented at the 6th Conference of EARIE, Paris, unpublished

MacIntyre, A. 1991a, 'The Politics of Finance in Indonesia: Controls, Confusion and Competition', paper presented at the Second Workshop on Government, Financial Systems and Economic Development: A Comparative Study of Selected Asian and Latin American Countries, East-West Center, Honolulu

——1991b, *Business and Politics in Indonesia*, Allen and Unwin, Sydney

——1992 (forthcoming), 'Politics and the Reorientation of Economic Policy in Indonesia', *The Dynamics of Economic Policy Reform in South-east Asia and the South-west Pacific*, eds A. MacIntyre & K. Jayasuriya, Oxford University Press, Kuala Lumpur

Mackie, J.A.C. 1988, 'Economic Growth in the ASEAN Region: The Political Underpinnings', *Achieving Industrialization in East Asia*, ed. H. Hughes, Cambridge University Press, Melbourne

Magun, S. 1991, 'The Impact of a United States–Canada–Mexico Free Trade Agreement', paper presented at the Conference, Facing North/Facing South, University of Calgary, Calgary, 2–5 May

Markusen, J.R. 1985, 'Canadian Gains from Trade in the Presence of Scale Economies and Imperfect Competition', *Canada–United States Free Trade*, eds J. Whalley & W.R. Hill, University of Toronto Press, Toronto

Markusen, J.R. and Venables, A.J. 1988, 'Trade Policy with Increasing Returns and Imperfect Competition: Contradictory Results from Competing Assumptions', *Journal of International Economics*, vol. 24, pp. 299–316

Marston, R. 1991, 'Pricing to Market in Japanese Manufacturing', *Trade With Japan: Has the Door Opened Wider?*, ed. P.R. Krugman, University of Chicago Press, Chicago

Martin, M. 1991, 'U.S. Trade Gap Hits 8-Year Low', *International Herald Tribune*, 17–18 August

Maskus, K.E. and Konan, D.E. 1991, 'Trade-related Intellectual Property Rights: Issues and Exploratory Results', unpublished

Matsushita, M. 1988, 'Coordinating International Trade with Competition Policies', *The New GATT Round of Multilateral Trade Negotiations*, eds E. Petersmann & M. Hilf, Kluwer Law and Taxation Publishers, Deventer, Netherlands

McCulloch, R. 1988, 'United States–Japan Economic Relations', *Trade Policy Issues and Empirical Analysis*, ed. R.E. Baldwin, University of Chicago Press, Chicago

Messerlin, P. 1991a, 'The EC Antidumping Enforcement: Procedures', unpublished

——1991b, 'The EC Antidumping Enforcement: Determinants, Impact and Cost', unpublished

Mikesell, R. 1947, 'The Role of the International Monetary Agreements in a World of Planned Economies', *Journal of Political Economy*, vol. 55, no. 6, pp. 497–512

Milner, H.V. 1988, *Resisting Protectionism: Global Industries and the Politics of International Trade*, Princeton University Press, Princeton

——1992, 'International Theories of Cooperation Among Nations: Strengths and Weaknesses', *World Politics*, vol. 44, no. 3, pp. 466–96

Milner, H.V. and Yoffie, D.B. 1989, 'Between Free Trade and Protectionism: Strategic Trade Policy and a Theory of Corporate Demands', *International Organization*, vol. 43, no. 2, pp. 239–72

Ministry of Finance, Malaysia 1991, *Economic Report 1990/91*, Kuala Lumpur

Ministry of Trade and Industry, Singapore, Economic Committee 1986, *The Singapore Economy: Future Directions*, Singapore National Printers, Singapore

——1991, *Economic Survey of Singapore 1990*, Singapore National Printers, Singapore

Mitrany, D. 1975, *The Functional Theory of Politics*, Martin Robertson, London

Miyoshi, M. 1987, 'The Japanese–U.S. Trade Friction: Some Perspectives From the Japanese Business Community', *Trade Friction and Economic Policy*, eds R. Sato & P. Wachtel, Cambridge University Press, Cambridge

Mizra, H. 1986, *Multinationals and the Growth of the Singapore Economy*, Croom Helm, Beckenham

Moffitt, M. 1987, 'Shocks, Deadlocks, and Scorched Earth: Reaganomics and the Decline of U.S. Hegemony', *World Policy Journal*, vol. 4, no. 4, pp. 553–82

Molot, M.A. 1974, 'The Role of Institutions in Canada–United States Relations: The Case of North American Financial Ties', *Continental Community? Independence and Integration in North America*, eds W.A. Axline, et al., McClelland and Stewart, Toronto

——1991, 'What We Need Are More Answers', *Policy Options*, vol. 12, no. 3

Montagnon, P. 1990, *European Competition Policy*, The Royal Institute of International Affairs, Chatham House Papers, Pinter Publishers, London

Moon, C. 1988, 'The Demise of a Developmentalist State? Neoconservative Reforms and Political Consequences in South Korea', *Journal of Developing Societies*, vol. 4, no. 1, pp. 67–84

——1990, 'Beyond Statism: Rethinking the Political Economy of Growth in South Korea', *International Studies Notes*, vol. 15, pp. 24–7

Moore, R.E. 1990, 'A Test of Strategic Trade Policy in the Semiconductor Industry: The Impact of Japanese Policy on US Firms', *International Economic Journal*, vol. 4, Spring, pp. 97–108

Morici, P. 1991, *Trade Talks With Mexico: A Time For Realism*, National Planning Association, Washington, DC

Morici, P. and Megna, L. 1983, *US Economic Policies Affecting Industrial Trade: A Quantitative Assessment*, National Planning Association, Washington, DC

Morita, A. and Ishihara, S. 1989, *'No' to ieru Nihon* (The Japan That Can Say 'No'), Kōbunsha, Tokyo

Morrison, C.J. 1989, 'Markup Behavior in Durable and Nondurable Manufacturing: A Production Theory Approach', National Bureau of Economic Research Working Paper No. 2941, April

Morse, E.L. 1990, 'The Coming Oil Revolution', *Foreign Affairs*, vol. 69, no. 5, pp. 36–56

Morse, R. 1987, 'Japan's Drive to Pre-Eminence', *Foreign Policy*, no. 69, Winter, pp. 3–21

Morton, P. 1991, 'Wilson Upbeat but Trade Doubts Grow', *Financial Post*, 25 November

Mundell, R.A. 1968, *International Economics*, Macmillan, New York

——1973, 'Uncommon Arguments for Common Currencies', *The Economics of Common Currencies*, eds H.G. Johnson & A.K. Swoboda, George Allen and Unwin, London

Murakami, K. 1991, 'Nichi-Bei kankei ga sengo saiaku' (Japan–U.S. Relationship Worst Since World War II), *Zaikai tembō*, July, pp. 128–33

Murata, R. 1991, 'Apprehension Over Trading Blocks', *Los Angeles Times*, 30 July

Muscat, R. 1991, 'Government, Financial Systems and Economic Development: Thailand', paper presented at the Second Workshop on Government, Financial Systems and Economic Development: A Comparative Study of Selected Asian and Latin American Countries, East-West Center, Honolulu

Myrdal, G. 1968, *Asian Drama: An Inquiry Into the Poverty of Nations*, Pantheon, New York

Nakanishi, T. 1991, 'A New Regional Order', *Journal of Japanese Trade and Industry*, May–June, pp. 8–11

Nakasone, Y. 1991a, From the *Yomiuri Shimbun*, Asia Foundation, Translation Service Center, *Articles from the Japanese Press*, no. 1498, 26 August

——1991b, 'Nihon wa samitto de dokuji senryaku o Soren mō ichidan no seiji kaikaku hitsuyō' (Japan Should Adopt Its Own Summit Strategy Requiring Much More Political Reform From the Soviet Union), *Nikkei Business*, 8 July

Nakatani, I. 1991, 'The Nature of "Imbalance" Between the US and Japan', proceedings of the Seventh Biennial Conference of the Japanese Studies Association of Australia, *Japan and the World*, Australian National University, Canberra, July, pp. 33–9

Nakayama, T. 1991, Speech to the 11th Australia–Japan Ministerial Committee Meeting

Nanto, D.K. 1990, 'Asia–Pacific Cooperation and US–Japan Relations', *Economic Cooperation in the Asia Pacific Region*, eds J. Hardt & Y. Kim, Westview, Boulder, CO

Nau, H. ed. 1989, *Domestic Trade Politics and the Uruguay Round*, Columbia University Press, New York

Neff, S. 1990, *Friends But No Allies: Economic Liberalism and the Law of Nations*, Columbia University Press, New York

Nelson, D. 1987, 'The Domestic Political Preconditions of US Trade Policy: Liberal Structure and Protectionist Dynamics', a paper prepared for the World Bank Conference on Political Economy: Theory and Policy Implications, Washington, DC

——1989, 'The Political Economy of Trade Policy', *Economics and Politics*, vol. 1, no. 3, pp. 301–14

Ng, C.Y. 1989, 'Privatisation in Singapore: Divestment with Control', *ASEAN Economic Bulletin*, vol. 5, no. 3, pp. 290–318

Ng, C.Y. and Sudo, S. 1991, *Development Trends in the Asia–Pacific*, Institute of Southeast Asian Studies, Singapore

Ng, C.Y. and Wong, P.K. 1991, 'The Growth Triangle: A Market Driven Response?', *Asia Club Papers No. 2*, Tokyo Club Foundation for Global Studies, Tokyo

Nicoliades, P. 1991a, 'The Competition Effects of Dumping', *Journal of World Trade*, vol. 24, no. 5, pp. 115–31

——1991b, 'EC Anti-dumping Policy', *Tokyo Club Papers*, vol. 4, no. 1, pp. 127–49

Niskanen, W.A. 1989, 'The Bully of World Trade', *Orbis*, vol. 33, no. 4, pp. 531–8

Nivola, P.S. 1991, 'More Like Them? The Political Feasibility of Strategic Trade Policy', *The Brookings Review*, vol. 9, no. 2, pp. 14–21

Noda, M. 1991, 'Nihon kabushiki kaisha-kō "samurai shihon-shugi" no mujun to genkai' (The Contradictions and Limits of Japan, Inc.'s 'Samurai Capitalism'), *Shūkan daiyamondo*, 31 August, pp. 72–7

Noland, M. 1990, *Pacific Basin Developing Countries: Prospects for the Future*, Institute for International Economics, Washington, DC

——1991, 'SII at Nine Months: Notes on the Structural Impediments Initiative', unpublished

Noordin, S. 1990, 'Thrust for Greater Economic Ties', *New Sunday Times*, Malaysia, 18 August

Norman, V.D. 1988, 'Trade Under Imperfect Competition—Theoretical Ambiguities and Empirical Irregularities', presented at the European Economic Association Annual Meeting, Bologna, August

——1989, 'EFTA and the Internal European Market', *Economic Policy*, vol. 9, October, pp. 423–65

——1990, 'Assessing Trade and Welfare Effects of Trade Liberalization: A Comparison of Alternative Approaches to CGE Modelling With Imperfect Competition', *European Economic Review*, vol. 34, June, pp. 725–45

North, D. 1990, *Institutions, Institutional Change and Economic Performance*, Cambridge University Press, Cambridge

Nye Jr, J.S. 1990a, 'Soft Power', *Foreign Policy*, no. 80, Fall, pp. 153–71

——1990b, *Bound to Lead: The Changing Nature of American Power*, Basic Books, New York

Ogura, K. 1991, ' "Rinen no teikoku" to "sōshitsu no min" to no kiretsu' (The Crevice between 'the Empire of Ideas' and the 'Lost People'), *Gaikō Forum*, June, pp. 4–11

Ohmae, K. 1985, *Triad Power: The Coming Shape of Global Competition*, The Free Press, New York

——1990, *A Borderless World*, Harpers, New York

Okamoto, Y. 1991, 'Ningen kankei to shite no Nichi-Bei kankei' (The Japanese-American Relationship as [a Problem of] Human Relations), *Chūō kōron*, July, pp. 142–55

Okimoto, D.I. 1987, 'Outsider Trading: Coping With Japanese Industrial Organization', *Journal of Japanese Studies*, vol. 13, no. 2, pp. 383–414

Ōkita, S. 1990, *Approaching the 21st Century: Japan's Role*, The Japan Times, Tokyo

——1991, 'Japan: Better to Spend These Billions on Aid Than on Arms', *International Herald Tribune*, 17 April

Olson, M. 1965, *The Logic of Collective Action*, Harvard University Press, Cambridge, MA

Onis, Z. 1991, 'The Logic of the Developmental State', *Comparative Politics*, vol. 24, no. 1, pp. 109–26

Ono, Y. 1991, 'Orderly Marketing Arrangement in the Context of the GATT Regime', *Economics & Politics*, vol. 3, no. 2, pp. 151–62

Ordover, J.A. 1990, 'Economic Foundations of Competition Policy', *Competition Policy in Europe and North America: Economic Issues and Institutions*, eds W.S. Comanor, et al., Harwood Academic Publishers, Chur, Switzerland

Organization for Economic Cooperation and Development (OECD) 1984a, *Competition and Trade Policies*, Committee of Experts on Restrictive Business Practices, Paris

——1984b, *Merger Policies and Recent Trends in Mergers*, Paris

——1984c, *Competition and Trade Policies: Their Interaction*, Paris

——1984d, *Competition Law Enforcement: International Cooperation in the Collection of Information*, Paris

——1985, *Competition Policy and the Professions*, Paris

——1987a, *Competition Policy and International Trade*, Paris

——1987b, *Twenty Five Years of Antitrust Policy: Achievements and Challenges*, Paris

——1988a, *Competition Policy in OECD Countries, 1986–87*, Paris

——1988b, *International Mergers and Competition Policy*, Paris

——1989a, *Competition Policy in OECD Countries, 1987–88*, Paris

——1989b, *Predatory Pricing*, Paris

——1989c, *Competition Policy and Intellectual Property Rights*, Paris

——1991a, *Competition and Economic Development*, Paris

——1991b, *Strategic Industries in a Global Economy: Policy Issues for the 1990s*, Paris

Orr, R. 1990, *The Emergence of Japan's Foreign Aid Power*, Columbia University Press, New York

Ostry, S. 1990a, *Governments and Corporations in a Shrinking World*, Council on Foreign Relations, New York

——1990b, 'Trends in the World Trading System: Canadian Policy Response', Address to the Harvard Club of Ottawa, February

Oudiz, G. and Sachs, J. 1984, 'Macroeconomic Policy Coordination Among the Industrial Economies', *Brookings Papers on Economic Activity*, vol. 1, pp. 1–75

Oye, K. ed. 1986, *Cooperation Under Anarchy*, Princeton University Press, Princeton

Paavonen, T. 1983, 'Reformist Programmes in the Planning for Post-War Economic Policy During World War II', *Scandanavian Economic History Review*, vol. 31, no. 3, pp. 178–200

Pacific Economic Cooperation Conference (PECC) 1991, *PECC Newsletter*, vol. 1, no.4

Pangestu, M. 1991, 'An Indonesian Perspective', *Growth Triangle: The Johor–Singapore–Riau Experience*, ed. Lee Tsao Yuan, Institute of Southeast Asian Studies, Singapore

Park, Y.C. and Park, W.A. 1991, 'Changing Japanese Trade Patterns and the East Asian NICs', *Trade With Japan: Has the Door Opened Wider?*, ed. P.R. Krugman, University of Chicago Press, Chicago

Park, Y.C. and Yoo, J.H. 1989, 'More Free Trade Areas: A Korean Perspective', *Free Trade Areas and U.S. Trade Policy*, ed. J. Schott, Institute for International Economics, Washington, DC

Pastor, R.A. and Castaneda, J.G. 1989, *Limits to Friendship: The United States and Mexico*, Vintage Books, New York

Pasuk Phongpaichit 1980, 'The Open Economy and Its Friends: The "Development" of Thailand', *Pacific Affairs*, vol. 53, no. 3, pp. 440–60

——1990, *The New Wave of Japanese Investment in ASEAN*, ASEAN Economic Research Unit, Institute of Southeast Asian Studies, Singapore

——1992 (forthcoming), 'Technocrats, Businessmen and Generals: Democracy and Economic Policy Making in Thailand', *The Dynamics of Economic Policy Reform in South-east Asia and the South-west Pacific*, eds A. MacIntyre & K. Jayasuriya, Oxford University Press, Kuala Lumpur

Pear, R. 1991, 'Balanced Budget: Soon a $362 Billion Mirage', *International Herald Tribune*, 17–18 August

Peltzman, S. 1976, 'Toward a More General Theory of Regulation', *Journal of Law and Economics*, vol. 19, no. 2, pp. 211–40

Petri, P.A. 1984, *Modeling Japanese–American Trade: A Study of Asymmetric Interdependence*, Harvard University Press, Cambridge, MA

——1991a, 'Market Structure, Comparative Advantage, and Japanese Trade Under the Strong Yen', *Trade With Japan: Has the Door Opened Wider?*, ed. P. Krugman, University of Chicago Press, Chicago

——1991b, *One Bloc, Two Blocs or None? Political–Economic Factors in Pacific Trade Policy*, Department of Economics Paper No. 297, Department of Economics, Brandeis University, Waltham, MA

——1991c, *Platforms in the Pacific: The Trade Effects of Direct Investment in Thailand*, Department of Economics Paper No. 298, Department of Economics, Brandeis University, Waltham, MA

Polanyi, K. 1944, *The Great Transformation*, Beacon Press, Boston

Pomfret, R. 1991, 'International Trade Policy with Imperfect Competition', unpublished

Powell, R. 1991, 'Absolute and Relative Gains in International Relations Theory', *American Political Science Review*, vol. 85, no. 4, pp. 1303–20

Prestowitz Jr, C.V. 1988, *Trading Places: How We Allowed Japan to Take the Lead*, Basic Books, New York

Prestowitz Jr, C.V., Tonelson, A. and Jerome, R.W. 1991, 'The Last Gasp of GATTism', *Harvard Business Review*, March–April, pp. 130–8

Putnam, R.D. and Bayne, N. 1987, *Hanging Together: The Seven-Power Summits*, revised ed., Harvard University Press, Cambridge

Pyle, K.B. ed. 1987, *The Trade Crisis: How Will Japan Respond*, Society for Japanese Studies, Seattle

Ramsay, A. 1986, 'Thai Domestic Politics and Foreign Policy', *ASEAN in Regional and Global Context*, eds K. Jackson, S. Paribatra & J.S. Djiwandono, Institute for East Asian Studies, University of California, Berkeley

Rapkin, D.P. 1990, 'Japan and World Leadership?', *World Leadership and Hegemony: International Political Economy Yearbook*, ed. D.P. Rapkin, Lynne Rienner, Boulder, CO

——1991, 'Uncertain World Order Implications of Japan's Rapid Ascent', paper presented at the Seventh Biennial Conference of the Japanese Studies Association of Australia, Canberra, July

Rapkin, D.P. ed. 1990, *World Leadership and Hegemony: International Political Economy Yearbook*, Lynne Rienner, Boulder, CO

Rapp, W.V. 1986, 'Japan's Invisible Barriers to Trade', *Fragile Interdependence: Economic Issues in U.S.–Japanese Trade and Investment*, ed. T.A. Pugel, Lexington Books, Lexington

Rauch, J.E. 1991, 'Balanced and Unbalanced Growth', unpublished

Ravenhill, J. 1992, 'The "Japan Problem" in Pacific Trade', *Economic Relations in the Pacific in the 1990s: Conflict or Cooperation?*, eds R. Higgott, R. Leaver & J. Ravenhill, Allen and Unwin, Sydney

Reich, R.B. 1983, 'Beyond Free Trade', *Foreign Affairs*, vol. 61, no. 4, pp. 773–884

——1991a, *The Work of Nations*, Knopf, New York

—— 1991b, 'Dumpsters', *The New Republic*, 10 June

Report to the U.S. Congress Concerning the President's Request for the Extension of Fast-Track Procedures Implementing Legislation for Trade Agreements 1991, Advisory Committee for Trade Policy Negotiations, Washington, DC

Richardson, J.D. 1987, '"Strategic" Trade Policy: Research and Practice in the United States', *Shaping Comparative Advantage*, eds R.G. Lipsey & W. Dobson, C.D. Howe Institute, Toronto

——1989, 'Empirical Estimates of Gains from Trade Liberalization Under Imperfect Competition: A Survey', *OECD Economic Studies*, vol. 12, Spring, pp. 7–51

——1990a, 'The Political Economy of Strategic Trade Policy', *International Organization*, vol. 44, no. 1, pp. 107–35

——1990b, 'International Trade, National Welfare, and the Workability of Competition: A Survey of Empirical Estimates', *Imperfect Competition and Political Economy*, eds C.A. Carter, A.F. McCalla & J.A. Sharples, Westview, Boulder, CO

——1992, 'US Trade Policy in the 1980s: Turns — and Roads Not Taken', *Policy Change in the 1980s*, ed. M. Feldstein, University of Chicago Press, Chicago

Riddle, D.I. 1986, *Service-Led Growth*, Praeger, New York

Rix, A. 1992, 'Managing Japan's Aid: ASEAN', *Power and Policy in Japanese Foreign Aid*, eds B. Koppel & R. Orr, Westview, Boulder, CO

Roberts, M.J. 1989, 'The Structure of Production in Colombian Manufacturing Industries', The World Bank, unpublished

Roberts, M.J. and Tybout, J.R. 1991, 'Size Rationalization and Trade Exposure in Developing Countries', *Empirical Studies of Commercial Policy*, ed. R.E. Baldwin, University of Chicago Press, Chicago

Robison, R. 1986, *Indonesia: The Rise of Capital*, Allen and Unwin, Sydney

——1988, 'Authoritarian States, Capital-Owning Classes, and the Politics of Newly Industrializing Countries: The Case of Indonesia', *World Politics*, vol. 41, no. 1, pp. 52–74

Robison, R., Hewison, K. and Higgott, R. eds 1987, *Southeast Asia in the 1980s: The Politics of Economic Crisis*, Allen and Unwin, Sydney

Robson, P. 1980, *The Economics of International Integration*, George Allen and Unwin, London

Rodan, G. 1985, *Singapore's 'Second Industrial Revolution': State Intervention and Foreign Investment*, ASEAN–Australia Economic Papers No. 18, ASEAN–Australia Joint Research Programme, Canberra

——1989, *The Political Economy of Singapore's Industrialization: National State and International Capital*, Macmillan, London

Rogoff, K. 1985, 'Can International Monetary Policy Coordination Be Counterproductive?', *Journal of International Economics*, vol. 18, no. 3/4, pp. 199–217

Roosa, R.V. 1982, *Economic Instability and Flexible Exchange Rates*, Institute of Southeast Asian Studies, Singapore

Rosecrance, R. and Taw, J. 1990, 'Japan and the Theory of International Leadership', *World Politics*, vol. 42, no. 2, pp. 184–209

Rosenbluth, F. 1989, *Financial Politics in Contemporary Japan*, Cornell University Press, Ithaca

Rosenthal, D.E. 1990, 'Competition Policy', *Europe 1992: An American Perspective*, ed. G.C. Hufbauer, The Brookings Institution, Washington, DC

Rostow, W.W. 1985, 'Is There Need for Economic Leadership?: Japanese or U.S.?', *American Economic Association Papers and Proceedings*, May, pp. 285–91

Ruggie, J.G. 1982, 'International Regimes, Transactions, and Change: Embedded Liberalism in the Postwar Economic Order', *International Organization*, vol. 36, no. 2, pp. 379–415

——1991a, 'Embedded Liberalism Revisited: Institutions and Progress in International Economic Relations', *Progress in Post-war International Relations*, eds E. Adler & B. Crawford, Columbia University Press, New York

——1991b, 'Unravelling Trade: Global Institutional Change and the Pacific Economy', paper presented to the Fulbright Symposium on Managing International Economic Relations in the Pacific in the 1990s, 16-17 December, Australian National University, Canberra

Ruigrok, W. 1991, 'Paradigm Crisis in International Trade Theory', *Journal of World Trade*, vol. 25, no. 1, pp. 77–89

Russett, B. 1988, 'US Hegemony: Gone or Merely Diminished and How Does It Matter?', *The Political Economy of Japan: Volume 2. The Changing International Context*, eds T. Inoguchi & D. Okimoto, Stanford University Press, Stanford

Sakakibara, E. 1990, *Shihon-shugi koeta Nihon* (The Japan That Has Gone Beyond Capitalism), Tōyō Keizai Shimpōsha, Tokyo

Salinger, M.A. 1984, 'Tobin's *q*, Unionization, and the Concentration-Profits Relationship', *RAND Journal of Economics*, vol. 15, no. 2, pp. 159–70

Samuels, R. 1987, *The Business of the Japanese State: Energy Markets in Comparative Historical Context*, Cornell University Press, Ithaca

Sanger, D.E. 1990a, 'Contrasts on Chips', *New York Times*, 18 January

——1990b, 'Behind the Thai Boom: The Japanese', *New York Times*, 10 May

——1991, 'Fair-Trade Has a Twist: Japanese Charge a US Rival', *New York Times*, 12 August

——1992, 'A Top Japanese Politician Calls U.S. Work Force Lazy', *New York Times*, 21 January

Sasaki, T. 1991, 'Postwar Japanese Politics at a Turning Point', *Japan Foundation Newsletter*, vol. 18, no. 5–6, pp. 1–7

Sassa, A. 1991, 'Posuto Maruta ni okeru Nihon no chii' (Japan's Position After Malta), *Chūō kōron*, March, pp. 48–52

Satō, H. 1991, 'Japan's Role in a Post-Cold War World', *Current History*, vol. 90, April, pp. 145–7, 179

Saxonhouse, G.R. 1983, 'The Micro- and Macro-Economics of Foreign Sales to Japan', *Trade Policies in the 1980s*, ed. W.R. Cline, Institute for International Economics, Washington, DC

——1986, *What's Wrong With Japanese Trade Structure*, Australia–Japan Research Centre Research Paper No. 137, Australia–Japan Research Centre, Australian National University, Canberra

——1988, 'Comparative Advantage, Structural Adaptation, and Japanese Performance', *The Political Economy of Japan: Volume 2. The Changing International Context*, eds T. Inoguchi & D.I. Okimoto, Stanford University Press, Stanford

Saxonhouse, G.R. and Stern, R.M. 1989, 'An Analytical Survey of Formal and Informal Barriers to International Trade and Investment in the United States, Canada, and Japan', *Trade and Investment Relations Among the United States, Canada, and Japan*, ed. R.M. Stern, University of Chicago Press, Chicago

Sazanami, Y. 1981, 'Possibilities of Expanding Intra-Industry Trade in Japan', *Keio Economic Studies*, vol. 18, no. 2, pp. 27–43

SCEAIT 1990, House of Commons, Standing Committee on External Affairs and International Trade, vol. 58, *Hearings on Canada–US–Mexico Trade Negotiations*

Schmalensee, R. and Willig, R. eds 1989, *Handbook of Industrial Organization*, North-Holland, Amsterdam

Schmiegelow, H. and Schmiegelow, M. 1990, 'How Japan Affects the International System', *International Organization*, vol. 44, no. 4, pp. 553–88

Schott, J.J. 1989a, *More Free Trade Areas?*, Institute for International Economics, Washington, DC

——1989b, 'A North American Free Trade Area: Ideal or Viable Policy Option', paper presented to the Symposium on Region North America: Canada, the US and Mexico, Baylor University, Waco, Texas

—— 1991, 'Trading Blocs and the World Trading System', *The World Economy*, vol. 14, no. 1, pp. 1–17

Scotton, G. 1991, 'Canadian Trade With Mexico May Fall in '91', *Financial Post*, 12 September

Segal, G. 1990, *Rethinking the Pacific*, Clarenden Press, Oxford

Sheard, P. 1991, 'The Economics of Japanese Corporate Organization and the "Structural Impediments" Debate: A Critical Review', *Japanese Economic Studies*, vol. 19, no. 4, pp. 30–78

Shelp, R.K. 1986–87, 'Trade in Services', *Foreign Policy*, no. 65, Winter, pp. 64–84

Shiraishi, M. 1990, *Japan's Relations With Vietnam: 1951–1987*, Cornell University, Southeast Asia Program, Ithaca

Shunsuke, B. 1990, 'The Change in Singapore's Economy and Investment Environment', *Pacific Business and Industries*, vol. 1, pp. 28–32

Simon, H.A. 1969, 'The Architecture of Complexity', *The Sciences of the Artificial*, ed. H.A. Simon, The MIT Press, Cambridge, MA

Sjöstedt, G. 1991, 'Trade Talks', *International Negotiations: Analysis, Approaches, Issues*, ed. V.A. Kremenyuk, Jossey Brass Publishers, Oxford

Snidal, D. 1985, 'The Limits of Hegemonic Stability Theory', *International Organization*, vol. 39, no. 4, pp. 579–614

——1991, 'Relative Gains and the Pattern of International Cooperation', *American Political Science Review*, vol. 85, no. 3, pp. 701–26

Soesastro, H. 1991, 'Concepts of the Pacific Basin in the Western Pacific', paper presented to the Seminar on the Pacific Basin, Mexico City, 12–14 February

Soesastro, H.J. and Han, S.J. eds 1983, *Pacific Economic Cooperation: The Next Phase*, Centre for Strategic and International Studies, Jakarta

Soh, S. and Chuang, P.M. 1990, 'Investing in Riau — Promises and Perils', *Singapore Business*, vol. 14, no. 12, pp. 30–53

Solomon, R. 1991, 'Background Paper', *Partners in Prosperity*, Report of the Twentieth Century Fund Task Force on the International Coordination of National Economic Policies, Priority Press, New York

Soon, K.C. 1985, 'The Labour Process and Capital Mobility: The Limits of the New International Division of Labour', *Politics and Society*, vol. 14, no. 2, pp. 185–222

Spero, J.E. 1988–89, 'Guiding Global Finance', *Foreign Policy*, no. 73, Winter, pp. 114–34

Stein, A. 1990, *Why Nations Cooperate: Circumstance and Choice in International Relations*, Cornell University Press, Ithaca

Stern, P. 1990, 'Commentary', *Aggressive Unilateralism: America's 301 Trade Policy and the World Trading System*, eds J. Bhagwati & H.T. Patrick, University of Michigan Press, Ann Arbor

Stern, R.M. ed. 1989, *Trade and Investment Relations Among the United States, Canada, and Japan*, University of Chicago Press, Chicago

Sterngold, J. 1990a, 'Japan's Pride is Wounded', *New York Times*, 26 March

—— 1990b, 'Japan Begins to Hear the Market's Message', *New York Times*, 15 April

——1990c, 'Japan Builds East Asia Links, Gaining Labor and Markets', *New York Times*, 8 May

Stigler, G.J. 1971, 'The Theory of Economic Regulation', *Bell Journal of Economics*, vol. 2, no. 1, pp. 3–21

Stockwin, J.A. 1982, *Japan: Divided Politics in a Growth Economy*, Weidenfeld and Nicolson, London

Stockwin, J.A. ed. 1988, *Dynamic and Immobilist Politics in Japan*, Macmillan, London

Stokes, B. 1990a, 'Little Hope for Stalled GATT Talks', *National Journal*, 15 December

——1990b, *The Inevitability of Managed Trade: The Future Strategic Trade Policy Debate*, The Japan Society, New York

Strange, S. 1986, *Casino Capitalism*, Basil Blackwell, Oxford

Sudo, S. 1988a, 'The Road to Becoming a Regional Leader: Japanese Attempts in Southeast Asia, 1975–1980', *Pacific Affairs*, vol. 61, no. 1, pp. 27–50

——1988b, 'Japan–ASEAN Relations: New Dimensions in Japanese Foreign Policy', *Asian Survey*, vol. 28, no. 5, pp. 509–25

Surin Maisrikrod 1991, 'Understanding Thai–US Trade Disputes', PhD dissertation, Department of Political Science, University of Hawaii, Manoa

Suzuki, Y. 1990, 'Autonomy and Coordination of Monetary Policy in a Global Economic Order', *Cato Journal*, vol. 10, no. 2, pp. 565–71

Szekely, G. ed. 1991, *Manufacturing Across Borders and Oceans*, Center for U.S.–Mexican Studies, University of California, San Diego

Szekely, G. and Wyman, D. 1988, 'Japan's Ascendance in US Economic Relations with Mexico', *SAIS Review*, vol. 8, no. 1, pp. 171–81

Takaoka, H. and Satake, T. 1991, 'Reports on Results of FY1990 Foreign Direct Investment Survey', *EXIM Review*, vol. 11, no. 1, pp. 1–25

Takenaka, H. 1991, 'The Japanese Economy and Pacific Development', *The Pacific Economy: Growth and External Stability*, ed. M. Arif, Allen and Unwin, Sydney

Takeuchi, K. 1989, 'Does Japan Import Less Than It Should? A Review of the Econometric Literature', *Asian Economic Journal*, vol. 3, no. 2, pp. 138–70

——1990a, 'Problems in Expanding Japan's Imports of Manufactures From Developing Economies: A Survey', *Asian Economic Journal*, vol. 4, no. 1, pp. 94–142

——1990b, *Does Japanese Direct Foreign Investment Promote Japanese Imports From Developing Countries?*, World Bank Staff Working Papers WPS 458, World Bank, Washington, DC

Thaler, R.H. 1989, 'Anomalies: Interindustry Wage Differentials', *Journal of Economic Perspectives*, vol. 3, no. 2, pp. 181–94

Thomson, G. 1989, 'A Single Market for Goods and Services in the Antipodes', *The World Economy*, vol. 12, no. 2, pp. 207–18

Thomson, G. and Langman, C. 1991, 'The Removal of Trade Remedy Law in Trans-Tasman Commerce', *Canada–United States Law Journal*, vol. 17, no. 1, pp. 203–7

Thurow, L. 1985a, 'America, Europe and Japan: A Time to Dismantle the World Economy', *Economist*, 9 November

——1985b, *The Zero-Sum Solution: Building a World-Class American Economy*, Simon and Schuster, New York

——1990, 'GATT is Dead', *Journal of Accountancy*, vol. 170, no. 3, pp. 36–9

Tirole, J. 1989, *The Theory of Industrial Organization*, The MIT Press, Cambridge, MA

Tobin, J. 1982, *Essays in Economics: Theory and Policy*, The MIT Press, Cambridge, MA

Toichi, T. 1990, 'International Oil Marketing Entering New Phase', *Energy in Japan*, February

Tonelson, A. 1991, 'What is the National Interest?', *The Atlantic Monthly*, July, pp. 35–52

Tranholm-Mikkelsen, J. 1991, 'Neo-Functionalism: Obstinate or Obsolete? A Reappraisal in the Light of the New Dynamism of the EC', *Millennium: Journal of International Studies*, vol. 20, no. 1, pp. 1–22

Tybout, J. 1989, 'Entry Exit, Competition and Productivity in the Chilean Industrial Sector', The World Bank, unpublished

Tyson, L.D. 1991, *Who's Bashing Whom: Trade Conflicts in High-Technology Industries*, Institute for International Economics, Washington, DC

United Nations Conference on Trade and Development (UNCTAD) 1989, *Trade and Development Report*, United Nations, New York

United States National Committee of the Pacific Economic Cooperation Conference (USNCPECC) 1991, *Pacific Economic Outlook 1991–92*, Washington, DC

UPI 1992, 'Former Japanese Foreign Minister Says U.S. Business System Is Not the Best', Tokyo, 11 March

van Tulder, R. and Junne, G. 1988, *European Multinationals in Core Technologies*, John Wiley, New York

van Wolferen, K.G. 1986–87, 'The Japan Problem', *Foreign Affairs*, vol. 65, no. 2, pp. 288–303

——1991, 'Japan: No Compass, No Brakes', *The National Interest*, vol. 25, Fall, pp. 26–35

Venables, A. 1990, 'The Economic Integration of Oligopolistic Markets', *European Economic Review*, vol. 34, June, pp. 753–69

Vernon, R. 1990, 'The Japan–U.S. Bilateral Relationship: Its Role in the Global Economy', *The Washington Quarterly*, vol. 13, no. 3, pp. 57–68

Vietor, R.H.K. 1984, *Energy Policy in America Since 1945*, Cambridge, London

Viner, J. 1947, 'Conflict of Principle in Drafting a Trade Charter', *Foreign Affairs*, vol. 25, no. 4, pp. 612–28

Viscusi, W.K., Vernon, J.M. and Harrington Jr., J.E. 1992, *Economics of Regulation and Antitrust*, D.C. Heath, Lexington, MA

Vogel, E. 1986, 'Pax Nipponica?', *Foreign Affairs*, vol. 64, no. 4, pp. 751–67

Voice 1991, 'Zento tanan no Amerika keizai' (The Many Future Difficulties of the American Economy), May, pp. 100–25

Vollrath, T. 1985, *Dynamics of Comparative Advantage and the Resistance to Free Trade*, Foreign Agricultural Report No. 214, US Department of Agriculture, International Economics Division, Washington, DC

Vousden, N. 1990, *The Economics of Trade Protection*, Cambridge University Press, Cambridge

Wade, R. 1990, *Governing the Market: Economic Theory and the Role of Government in East Asian Industrialization*, Princeton University Press, Princeton

Wallerstein, I. 1991, 'Japan and the Future Trajectory of the World-System: Lessons From History', *Geopolitics and Geoculture*, ed. I. Wallerstein, Cambridge University Press, Cambridge

Waltz, K.N. 1959, *Man, the State and War: A Theoretical Analysis*, Columbia University Press, New York

——1970, 'The Myth of National Interdependence', *The International Corporation*, ed. C.P. Kindleberger, The MIT Press, Cambridge, MA

——1979, *Theory of International Politics*, Addison Wesley, Reading, MA

Watts, W. 1991a, 'Initiatives for Improving Japan–U.S. Communication', *IHJ Bulletin*, vol. 11, no. 2

——1991b, 'The United States and Japan: Communications Disconnect', *The Daily Japan Digest*, vol. 2, no. 169, 24 September, pp. 4–5

Wayne, L. 1989, 'The Realities of "Friday the 13th" ', *New York Times*, 22 October

Webb, M.C. 1991, 'International Economic Structures, Government Interests, and International Coordination of Macroeconomic Adjustment Policies', *International Organization*, vol. 45, no. 3, pp. 309–42

Weintraub, S. 1988, *Mexican Trade Policy and the North American Community*, Center for International and Strategic Studies, Washington, DC

——1990a, 'The Impact of the Agreement on Mexico', *Making Free Trade Work*, ed. P. Morici, Council on Foreign Relations, New York

——1990b, 'The North American Free Trade Debate', *Washington Quarterly*, vol. 13, no. 4, pp. 119–30

——1990c, *A Marriage of Convenience: Relations Between Mexico and the United States*, Oxford University Press, New York

Welfield, J. 1988, *An Empire in Eclipse: Japan in the Postwar American Alliance System*, The Athlone Press, London

Wendt, A. 1987, 'The Agent Structure Problem in International Relations', *International Organization*, vol. 41, no. 3, pp. 335–70

——1992, 'Anarchy is What States Make of It', *International Organization*, vol. 46, no. 2, pp. 391–425

Whalley, J. and Hill, W.R. 1985, *Canada–United States Free Trade*, volume II in the research program of the Royal Commission on the Economic Union and Development Prospects for Canada (the 'Macdonald Commission'), University of Toronto Press, Toronto

White, G. ed. 1988, *Developmental States in East Asia*, Macmillan, London

Wickes, R. 1992, 'Japan's Manufactured Imports', Department of Foreign Affairs and Trade (mimeo), Canberra

Wilkinson, B.W. 1991, 'Regional Trading Blocs: Fortress Europe Versus Fortress North America', *The New Era of Global Competition: State Policy and Market Power*, eds D. Drache & M. Gertler, McGill-Queen's University Press, Montreal and Kingston

Williamson, J. and Miller, M.H. 1987, *Targets and Indicators: A Blueprint for the International Coordination of Economic Policy*, Policy Analyses in International Economics No. 22, Institute for International Economics, Washington, DC

Willig, R. 1983, 'Competition-Related Trade Issues', prepared for OECD, unpublished

Winham, G.R. 1986, *International Trade and the Tokyo Round Negotiation*, Princeton University Press, Princeton, NJ

Wolf, M. 1987, 'The European Community and the Developing Countries in the International Trading System', *Aussenwirtschaft*, vol. 42, Heft 1, pp. 41–64

Wolfers, A. 1962, *Discord and Collaboration: Essays on International Politics*, Johns Hopkins, Baltimore

Wolff, A.W. 1990, 'U.S.–Japan Relations and the Rule of Law: The Nature of the Trade Conflict and the American Response', *Japan's Economic Structure: Should It Change?*, ed. K. Yamamura, Society for Japanese Studies, Seattle

Womack, J.P., Jones, D.T. and Roos, D. 1990, *The Machine That Changed The World*, Rawson Associates, New York

Wonnacott, R.J. 1990, 'U.S. Hub and Spoke Bilaterals and the Multilateral Trading System', C.D. Howe Institute Commentary no. 23, Toronto, October

Woods, L.T. 1991a, 'A House Divided: The Pacific Basin Economic Council', *Australian Outlook: The Australian Journal of International Affairs*, vol. 45, no. 2, pp. 264–79

——1991b, 'Non-Governmental Relations and Pacific Cooperation: Back to the Future?', *The Pacific Review*, vol. 4, no. 4, pp. 312–21

Woolcott, R. 1991, 'APEC: The Regional Economic Wave of the 1990s', *Backgrounder*, vol. 2, no. 21, pp. 3–6

World Bank 1987, *World Development Report 1987*, Oxford University Press, New York

——1989, *World Development Report 1989: Financial Systems and Development*, Oxford University Press, New York

——1991a, 'Press Release No. 16', 15 October

——1991b, *World Tables 1991*, World Bank, Washington, DC

——1991c, *World Bank Development Report 1991*, Oxford University Press, New York

Yamamura, K. 1990, 'Will Japan's Economic Structure Change? Confessions of a Former Optimist', *Japan's Economic Structure: Should It Change?*, ed. K. Yamamura, Society for Japanese Studies, Seattle

Yamamura, K. ed. 1989, *Japanese Investment in the United States: Should We Be Concerned?*, Society for Japanese Studies, Seattle

——1990, *Japan's Economic Structure: Should it Change?*, Society for Japanese Studies, Seattle

Yamamura, K. and Yasuba, Y. eds 1987, *The Political Economy of Japan: Volume 1. The Domestic Transformation*, Stanford University Press, Stanford

Yasutomo, D. 1986, *The Manner of Giving: Strategic Aid and Japanese Foreign Policy*, Lexington Books, Lexington

Yoffie, D. 1983, *Power and Protectionism*, Columbia University Press, New York

Yoffie, D. and Milner, H.V. 1989, 'An Alternative to Free Trade and Protectionism: Why Corporations Seek Strategic Trade Policy', *California Management Review*, vol. 31, no. 4, pp. 111–31

Young, O. 1989, 'The Politics of International Regime Formation: Managing Natural Resources and the Environment', *International Organization*, vol. 43, no. 3, pp. 349–75

——1991, 'Political Leadership and Regime Formation: On the Development of Institutions in International Society', *International Organization*, vol. 45, no. 3, pp. 281–308

Name Index

Subject Index